CEMETERY OF THE MURDERED DAUGHTERS

CEMETERY OF THE MURDERED DAUGHTERS

Feminism, History, and Ingeborg Bachmann

Sara Lennox

UNIVERSITY OF MASSACHUSETTS PRESS
Amherst and Boston

LC 2006008285
ISBN 1-55849-552-5 (PAPER) ISBN 1-55849-551-7 (CLOTH)
Designed by Sally Nichols
Set in Adobe Granjon
Printed and bound by The Maple-Vail Book Manufacturing Group

Library of Congress Cataloging-in-Publication Data

Lennox, Sara.
Cemetery of the murdered daughters : feminism, history, and Ingeborg
Bachmann / Sara Lennox.
p. cm.
Includes bibliographical references and index.
ISBN 1-55849-552-5 (pbk. : alk. paper) — ISBN 1-55849-551-7 (library
cloth : alk. paper) 1. Bachmann, Ingeborg, 1926–1973—Criticism and
interpretation. 2. Feminist criticism. 3. Feminism and literature. I.
Title.
PT2603.A147Z7655 2006
838'.91409—dc22
2006008285

British Library Cataloguing in Publication data are available.

For my father,
and in memory of
Sigi and Susanne

CONTENTS

PREFACE

This book has been a long time in the making, and I've incurred many debts along the way. I would not have started or continued this project without the encouragement of editors (often also good friends) who included my essays on Bachmann in journals and collections: Monika Albrecht, Ute Brandes, Gisela Brinker-Gabler, Jeanette Clausen, Susan Cocalis, Donald Daviau, Elke Fredericksen, the late Marilyn Sibley Fries, Rainer Nägele, the late Henry Schmidt, Inge von Weidenbaum, and Sigrid Weigel. I would also like to thank fellow Bachmann scholars Karen Achberger, Robert Pichl, Karen Remmler, and Leslie Morris for their generosity with information and materials. Hanna Schnedl-Bubenicek and Ursula Kubes-Hofmann offered me hospitality and good company in Vienna. Dr. Heinz Bachmann gave me permission to publish material from the Bachmann archive. Early stages of my research were supported by the Research Council of the University of Massachusetts and the Austrian-American Association of Boston.

Many friends and colleagues accompanied me on the intellectual journey that this book records, and I thank them for their counsel and comradeship along the way. My feminist sisters in Women in German stood behind me through the hard decades during which early feminists in German Studies like me established themselves in the U.S. academy, and I thank them for being there. The long years of friendship with Wiggies like Angelika Bammer, Sara Friedrichsmeyer, and Patricia Herminghouse, along with those mentioned above and many others, have been especially important for me. I thank my colleagues

in the German Studies Association, especially the women historians, for helping me learn to think historically. The support of senior male colleagues Peter
Uwe Hohendahl and Frank Trommler also emboldened me to elaborate sometimes iconoclastic ideas. My colleagues in the former Department of Germanic
Languages and Literatures, now the Program in German and Scandinavian
Studies, especially Barton Byg, have contributed to the transformation of our
field and my own thinking which made this book possible. Over many years
my friend Arlene Avakian and other UMass Women's Studies colleagues have
been central to my learning to think of gender as always complexly inflected by
many other changing social categories, particularly ethnicity and race, and my
friend Sabine Broeck helped me to understand how to think about gender and
race in German-speaking contexts. Though John Bracey often disagreed with
me, his ideas have left a strong imprint on these pages. I thank Julia Demmin
for understanding and encouragement at many crucial moments. In the early
years of this book my son, Jonathan, patiently listened to me talk through my
ideas about Bachmann over many a meal and helped me to weather many crises of confidence; as an adult he kindly saved me from many a computer catastrophe. Finally, for over twenty-five years the staff and students of the Social
Thought and Political Economy Program helped me to acquire the education
in interdiscplinarity that, I hope, informs this book and also to remember what
my real priorities are. They and countless other activist friends and allies again
and again demonstrated their political steadfastness on the occasions I discuss
in Part Two and continue to the present day. I thank them for their principled
solidarity, which keeps hope alive in these hard times.

Somewhat or substantially revised, the chapters of this book first appeared in
the following books and journals: chapter 1 as "Ingeborg Bachmann," *German-
Language Women Writers: A Bio-Critical Sourcebook*, ed. Elke Fredericksen and
Elizabeth Ametsbichler (Westport, CT: Greenwood Publishers, 1998), 56–68;
a much earlier version of chapter 2 as "The Feminist Reception of Ingeborg
Bachmann," *Women in German Yearbook 8*, ed. Jeanette Clausen and Sara
Friedrichsmeyer (Lincoln: University of Nebraska Press, 1993), 73–111; chapter 3
as "In the Cemetery of the Murdered Daughters: Ingeborg Bachmann's
Malina," *Studies in Twentieth Century Literature* 5.1 (Fall 1980), 75–105; chapter
4 as "Christa Wolf and Ingeborg Bachmann: The Difficulties of Writing the
Truth," *Responses to Christa Wolf: Critical Essays*, ed. Marilyn Sibley Fries
(Detroit: Wayne State University Press, 1989), 128–148; chapter 5 as "Geschlecht,
Rasse und Geschichte in 'Der Fall Franza,'" *text + kritik Sonderband Ingeborg*

Bachmann, ed. Sigrid Weigel (München: edition text + kritik, 1984), 156–179; chapter 6 as "Bachmann and Wittgenstein," *Modern Austrian Literature* 18 3/4 (1985), 239–259; chapter 7 as "Bachmann Reading/Reading Bachmann: Wilkie Collins' *The Woman in White* in the *Todesarten*," *German Quarterly* 61.2 (Spring 1988), 183–92; chapter 8 as "Representing Femininity in Ingeborg Bachmann's *Der gute Gott von Manhattan*," *Thalia's Daughters: German Women Dramatists from the Eighteenth Century to the Present*, ed. Susan Cocalis and Ferrel Rose (Tübingen: Francke Verlag, 1996), 191–220; parts of chapter 9 as "White Ladies and Dark Continents in Ingeborg Bachmann's *Todesarten*," *The Imperialist Imagination: German Colonialism and Its Legacy*, ed. Sara Friedrichsmeyer, Sara Lennox, and Susanne Zantop (Ann Arbor: University of Michigan Press, 1998), 247–63; parts of chapter 9 as "The Woman Who Rode Away: Postcoloniality and Gender in 'Three Paths to the Lake,'" *If We Had the Word: Ingeborg Bachmann. Views and* Reviews, ed. Gisela Brinker-Gabler and Markus Zisselsberger (Riverside, CA: Ariadne, 2004), 208–20; and parts of chapter 10 as "Gender, Kalter Krieg und Ingeborg Bachmann," *"Über die Zeit schreiben" 3: Literatur- und kulturwissenschaftliche Essays zum Werk Ingeborg Bachmanns,* ed. Monika Albrecht and Dirk Göttsche (Würzburg: Königshausen & Neumann, 2004), 15–54.

My father, Hayes Sidney King, no longer a patriarch but now a beloved friend, is responsible for my becoming a politically aware and engaged feminist, and I am happy that I can dedicate my book to him. Sigrid Brauner and Susanne Zantop, dear friends whom I have lost, inspired me again and again by their example, and I also dedicate this book to their memory.

ABBREVIATIONS CITING BACHMANN WORKS

Aufnahme   *Die kritische Aufnahme der Existentialphilosophie Martin Heideggers.* 1949. Ed. Robert Pichl. München: Piper, 1985.

Franza   *The Book of Franza and Requiem for Fanny Goldmann.* Trans. Peter Filkins. Evanston, IL: Northwestern UP, 1999.

"GG"   "The Good God of Manhattan." Trans. Valerie Tekavec. *Ingeborg Bachmann and Christa Wolf: Selected Prose and Drama.* Ed. Patricia A. Herminghouse. New York: Continuum, 1998. 55–97.

GuI   *Wir müssen wahre Sätze finden: Gespräche und Interviews.* Ed. Christine Koschel and Inge von Weidenbaum. München: Piper, 1983.

Malina   *Malina.* Trans. Philip Boehm. New York: Holmes & Meier, 1990.

Paths   *Three Paths to the Lake.* Trans. Mary Fran Gilbert. New York: Holmes & Meier, 1989.

Reportagen   *Römische Reportagen: Eine Wiederentdeckung.* Ed. Jörg-Dieter Kogel. München: Piper, 1998.

"Sightseeing"   "Sightseeing in an Old City." Trans. Margaret McCarthy. *Ingeborg Bachmann and Christa Wolf: Selected Prose and Drama.* Ed. Patricia A. Herminghouse. New York: Continuum, 1998. 3–7.

Songs   *Songs in Flight: The Collected Poems of Ingeborg Bachmann.* Trans. Peter Filkins. New York: Marsilio, 1994.

Storm   *In the Storm of Roses: Selected Poems.* Trans. and ed. Mark Anderson. Princeton: Princeton UP, 1986.

"To Die" "To Die for Berlin." Trans. Lilian Friedberg. *"If We Had the Word"*: *Ingeborg Bachmann. Views and Reviews*. Ed. Gisela Brinker-Gabler and Markus Zisselsberger. Riverside, CA: Ariadne, 2004. 7–17.

TP *"Todesarten"-Projekt*. Ed. Dirk Göttsche and Monika Albrecht. 4 vols. München: Piper, 1995.

TY *The Thirtieth Year*. Trans. Michael Bullock. New York: Alfred A. Knopf, 1964.

W *Werke*. Ed. Christine Koschel, Inge von Weidenbaum, and Clemens Münster. 4 vols. München: Piper, 1978.

CEMETERY OF THE MURDERED DAUGHTERS

INTRODUCTION

$\mathcal{A}$s readers familiar with Ingeborg Bachmann's writing will recognize, the title of this book, *Cemetery of the Murdered Daughters*, is borrowed from an episode that appears both in Bachmann's novel fragment *The Book of Franza* and in her only finished novel, *Malina* (1971)—the "overture," as she termed it, to the novel cycle "Ways of Death," an anatomy of contemporary Austrian society left uncompleted when she died in 1973. In both *Franza* and *Malina*, the "cemetery of the murdered daughters" is an image that occurs in a dream of the protagonist. In *Malina*, it is the first of the many "dreams of this night" recounted in the novel's second chapter:

> A large window opens, larger than all the windows I have seen, however not onto the courtyard of our house in the Ungargasse, but onto a gloomy field of clouds. A lake might lie below the clouds. I have a suspicion as to what lake it could be. But it's no longer frozen over, it's no longer Carnival and the hearty men's glee clubs which once stood on the ice in the middle of the lake have disappeared. And the lake, which cannot be seen, is hemmed by the many cemeteries. There are no crosses, but over every grave the sky is heavily and darkly overcast; the gravestones, the plaques with their inscriptions are scarcely recognizable. My father is standing next to me and takes his hand off my shoulder, since the gravedigger is heading our way. My father looks at the old man commandingly; fearful of my father's gaze, the gravedigger turns to me. He wants to speak, but merely moves his lips for a long time in silence, and I only hear his last sentence:
>
> This is the cemetery of the murdered daughters.
>
> He shouldn't have said that to me, and I weep bitterly. (*Malina* 113–14)

How should this multivalenced image be interpreted? This book's title gestures toward its multiple meanings: it points not just toward Bachmann's texts but also toward the reading strategies that feminists, among others, have elaborated in order to understand those texts and the various factors that enable those strategies. Specifically, it directs attention to some of the various ways I want to address "Feminism, History, and Ingeborg Bachmann," my subtitle.

In a 1953 poem, "Message," Bachmann wrote: "Our godhead, / History, has reserved us a grave / from which there is no resurrection" (*Storm* 55). My title first connects the death and destruction of almost all of Bachmann's female figures to their historical situation and insists upon historical causes for their devastation. Or, as Bachmann put it in a 1971 interview, "It is such a big error to believe that people are only murdered in a war or in a concentration camp—people are murdered in the midst of peace" (*GuI* 89). This is a point I elaborate at length in subsequent chapters. As well, "In the Cemetery of the Murdered Daughters" was the title of my first scholarly tussle with Bachmann's writing in 1980 (an article included here as chapter 3). The title thus also points to this book's concern with the historicity of reading practices and to the use of my own scholarship as an exemplum to demonstrate that historicity. Politically, from the perspective of feminism, "cemetery of the murdered daughters" designates the "woman-as-victim-of-patriarchy" stance that not only informed my own 1980 article on Bachmann but also inflected those of many other feminists, who viewed Bachmann's texts and her life (which they sometimes conflated) as evidence for the legitimacy of their own position.

From a later, rather different, and somewhat more historically specific feminist perspective, the "murdered daughters" can be viewed as a synecdochal representative of *all* victims, either of "the whites" (as *The Book of Franza* seems to suggest) or more particularly of National Socialism. From yet another feminist perspective, the very conception of a "cemetery of the murdered daughters" can become the target of a far-reaching feminist critique of white women who, while denying their own racial privilege, arrogate the status of victims to themselves—or, in the German/Austrian context, targets of a similar critique of white Christian ("Aryan") women who consider women's subordination by the National Socialist regime (which many of them supported) to parallel the treatment of the millions the Nazis murdered. From that standpoint, the title of my book could (and does) represent a repudiation of that feminist posture, banishing to the graveyard of history any notion that the "daughters" *tout court* are always and everywhere victims of the fathers *tout court*.

To come, finally, to the position I would take at the moment (and expand upon below), one might regard the dream image of the cemetery of the murdered daughters as a device to illustrate how fascism and an ostensibly postfascist era could configure the psyches of female figures, a conception at which Bachmann could arrive as a consequence of her encounter with Frankfurt School theory, which showed her how deeply domination is anchored within the psyche. Thus, perhaps only Bachmann's *figures* (and not Bachmann herself) imagine themselves as consigned to the "cemetery of the murdered daughters," like real-life Austrians and Germans after 1945 regarding themselves as entirely victims of a regime which they in fact helped to sustain.

I have begun by invoking these various interpretations of a central image in Bachmann's work not just to justify the book's title, but also to broach some of the themes that account for its subtitle, "Feminism, History, and Ingeborg Bachmann." This volume is not just one of the first English-language book-length examinations of the texts of a twentieth-century woman writer of world stature. I intend it also as a methodological experiment that stresses the varieties of interpretations enabled by a reader's "positionality": that is, her political stance, her social location, and the questions that emerge from the historical moment at which she writes. In its entirety, the study aims not just to illuminate Bachmann's writing but also to read her texts through a *variety* of feminist lenses in order to make at least three points: to show, first, that the questions feminist scholars pose to texts (or to any object of analysis) derive from a specific sociohistorical context and from particular "determinate" (that is, historically specific) political needs; second, that asking different kinds of feminist questions about an object of study can produce different, potentially conflicting, feminist answers; and, third, that the analyses that emerge have different kinds of implications for feminist theory and practice.

This book is thus very deliberately anything but a unified monograph. On the contrary, here I try to present a range of varied, perhaps even contradictory readings of Bachmann which, I argue, are neither right nor wrong but simply *different*. Further, I maintain, each of the readings that follows *and* the methodological experiment in its entirety are enabled by particular historical circumstances. Doubts about the universal applicability of the conclusions at which scholars arrived have emerged in a number of disciplines (such developments themselves a consequence of a changed historical situation), but oddly, to my mind, the concrete consequences for scholarly research of such demands for greater epistemological modesty have rarely been explored, and in practice most Western scholars continue to make truth claims as unabashedly as ever. Moreover, even scholars who call for a recognition of scholarly "situatedness" have frequently failed to conceive of "situatedness" also as an ever changing position within *time*. Indeed, the entire question of the epistemological implications of change over time (in scholarly approaches and elsewhere) seems to have disappeared even as a blip on theorists' radar screens since Marxism's *crise de confiance*, the abandonment of universal history, and the recognition of the rhetoricity of history writing. Scholars seem now rarely to ponder the ways that their own scholarly frameworks may be historically specific (that is, how the questions they ask may ultimately relate to their own historical situations). The methodological experiment of this book is in contrast premised upon the assertion that situatedness in time has epistemological consequences similar to those of situatedness in space. In this introduction I want to elaborate at greater length the theoretical justification for that experiment and end by explaining how I propose to present my analyses of Bachmann's texts as a vehicle for addressing the methodological conundrums the book poses. I hope that the experiment will be seen not as instrumentalizing Bachmann's texts for purposes foreign to them but rather as continuing my long-term project of elaborating feminist readings of Bachmann's texts that address the needs of successive generations of feminist readers.

Why have challenges to universalism and claims for the situatedness of knowledge emerged now? Many scholars now concede that the skepticism toward universalizing paradigms (aka "metanarratives") which began to emerge in the mid-1960s can finally be traced to decolonization movements after 1945 (among many other impulses, of course) and to other efforts that decolonization inspired (including the U.S. civil rights movements and, indirectly, feminism). Such struggles enabled the emergence of political subjects in the non-Western world and in the West for whose subjectivity universalist Western paradigms had not provided. Though the voices of those new subjects were heard in a wide variety of venues—from debates about the content of school textbooks to battles over canon formation to postcolonial cultural production—at the loftiest theoretical levels the relationship between new theoretical permutations and the real-life political changes that may have underwritten them was less often recognized. (It is startling, for instance, that in her extended introduction to Jacques Derrida's *Of Grammatology*, Gayatri Chakravorty Spivak never thematizes how her own intellectual formation as a Western-educated Indian woman might have shaped her understanding of the new French theory.) Robert Young's *White Mythologies: Writing History and the West* (1990) was among the first scholarly investigations to discern that decolonization struggles like those of the Algerian war of independence (1954–1962) produced the intellectual reverberations that led to the rise of French poststructuralism and related developments grouped together under the rubric "postmodernism." Young put it succinctly: "Postmodernism can best be defined as European culture's awareness that it is no longer the unquestioned and dominant center of the world" (19). Despite the transformations that postmodernism has called forth in many areas of the U.S. academy, it remains surprising that at the levels of abstraction at which debates about "incredulity toward [Western] metanarratives" (Lyotard xxiv) have been conducted, scarcely a theorist has ventured to investigate whether alternative models might exist elsewhere or in what ways postmodern theory might pertain to the non-Western world. Enrique Dussel observes, for instance: "Although [postmodern philosophers] theoretically affirm *difference*, they do not reflect on the origins of these systems that are the fruit of a rationalization proper to the management of the European centrality in the world-system, before which they are profoundly uncritical, and, because of this, they do not attempt to contribute valid alternatives (cultural, economic, political, etc.) for the peripheral nations, or the peoples or great majorities who are dominated by the center and/or the periphery" (18). Subsequent thinkers may have to tease out from postmodern theory those elements relevant for understanding post-Eurocentric political, social, and cultural arrangements which postmodern theorists themselves did not consider.

Another group of scholars, however, many of non-Western origin though frequently teaching in departments of history and anthropology at U.S. universities, have more recently probed the relationship between challenges to universalist paradigms and situatedness from another perspective. These scholars argue that recent historical developments in non-Western societies have given the lie to the universalizing postulations of Western theory. Though nineteenth-century European social theorists conceived modernity to be a phenomenon that would assume identical forms everywhere (cf. Marx's proclamation that a triumphant capitalist bourgeoisie would create "a world after its own image" [Tucker 477]), these scholars have shown that the diffusion of capitalism throughout the globe (i.e., the phenomenon now known as globalization) has produced heterogeneous, not homogeneous, political, social, and cultural effects, bringing into being other parts of the world that are just as modern as the West but differently so. In the mid-1980s Arjun Appadurai called the forms of social organization he had observed in contemporary Latin American, India, and East Asia "alternative modernities," and Arif Dirlik argues: "Modernity may no longer be approached as a dialogue internal to Europe or EuroAmerica but as a global discourse in which many participate, producing different formulations of the modern as lived and envisaged within their local social environments" ("Modernity" 17). Such scholars conclude that categories of European theory may be necessary but are not sufficient to grasp such new realities. Dipesh Chakrabarty, for instance, comments on political modernity in India, his own country of origin: "European thought has a contradictory relationship to such an instance of political modernity. It is both indispensable and inadequate in helping us think through the various life practices that constitute the political and the historical in India" (*Provincializing* 6). As he underlines, it is European theory's untenable extrapolations from the experiences of a particular cultural grouping to all of humanity, the blindness of European theorists to their own situatedness, that now calls that theory into question: "The shadow of cultural diversity . . . now falls across all universalistic assumptions about the history of human nature that often underlie propositions of modern political philosophies. Their inherent Eurocentrism is what makes these assumptions suspect in the eyes of practitioners today" ("Universalism" 653). At least some scholars of "alternative modernities" are quite aware of the epistemological consequences of renouncing universalisms, potentially calling into question, warns Dirlik, "the very notion of science, and the claims of the social and cultural sciences to scientificity" ("Globalization" 19). Within the framework of his project of "provincializing Europe," Chakrabarty has been among the most inventive in proposing alternative models. But, as it is far from clear to these scholars how to understand the phenomenon of globalization itself, so the issue of what analytic paradigms will or should succeed European theory is far from resolved. Moreover, though these scholars have determinedly drawn universal frameworks into question, to the best of my knowledge they have less directly thematized in what ways a recognition of the situatedness and partiality of *all* perspectives also demands an acknowledgment of the drastic reduction in the truth claims that their *own* scholarly investigations are entitled to make.

U.S. feminist theorists, on the other hand, arrived at their critique of universalism via a different route, one that from the outset necessitated a recognition of the partiality and provisionality of feminist analysis (although the majority of feminist scholars have still not taken that critique to heart when their own work is in question). Of necessity, feminist thought must assert the masculinist partiality of theories that purport to be universal but denigrate women. In the early 1980s, some feminist theorists tried to elaborate an alternative female/feminist perspective. Adapting Georg Lukács's *History and Class Consciousness* for feminist purposes, they argued that speakers who assumed the standpoint of women (analogous to Lukács's standpoint of the proletariat) would be capable of articulating truths about and for women (cf., for instance, Hartsock). But unfortunately for such "standpoint theorists," at about the same time the vigorous interventions of American women of color, at a series of explosive conferences and in a variety of influential anthologies, were forcing white feminists to recognize how frequently their allegations about "all women" were based in fact on false extrapolations from their own white, middle-class experience. In Donna Haraway's oft-quoted words, "White women . . . discovered (that is, were forced kicking and screaming to notice) the non-innocence of the category 'woman'" (*Simians* 157).

In the wake of these highly charged encounters, various feminist thinkers turned to postmodern theory for tools that could help them understand differences among women. Attempting to adjudicate between cultural feminism and postmodernism, and responding to the demand to identify the social location of the individual or group speaking for feminism, in 1988 Linda Alcoff advanced the term "positionality" to describe the specificity of the position from which any individual feminist (or, by extension, any other person) acts and speaks: "The concept of positionality includes two points: first, . . . that the concept of woman is a relational term identifiable only within a (constantly moving) context; but, second, that the position that women find themselves in can be actively utilized (rather than transcended) as a location for the construction of meaning, a place from where meaning is constructed, rather than simply the place where a meaning can be *discovered*" (434, emphasis in original). Feminist standpoint theory still survives as an important perspective within feminist thought, though now transmuted into "an influential part of a more general paradigmatic shift, in both political and scientific thought, away from universalistic theoretical frameworks that would neither account for the particular location of the social subject, nor would they usually accept that it is relevant to do so," as two feminist commentators observe (Stoelzler/Yuval-Davis 317). Subsequent theorists have refined Alcoff's definition by showing how female identity comes into being at "the intersection of different and often competing cultural formations of race, ethnicity, class, sexuality, religion, and national origin, et cetera, and so forth" (Friedman, *Mappings* 21), and her position is now generally accepted by most academic feminists. Because women are variously situated, many feminists conclude that it is impossible for any observer to assume a "God's-eye view" that would permit her to speak on behalf of all women, let alone to make allegations claiming more general, even universal, validity. This is, for instance, the basis of Iris M. Young's critique of Seyla Benhabib's attempt "to articulate a post-metaphysical defense of moral and political universalism" (Benhabib 174).

Benhabib's model "support[s] a conceptual projection of sameness among people and perspectives at the expense of their differences," Young argues (168). Because feminist theorists have generally been more immediately concerned than other scholars with producing knowledge that can authorize and legitimate praxis, the question of how to ground feminist truth claims has seemed a particularly urgent one. Many feminist thinkers have struggled with the dilemma of how to reconcile an insistence on knowledge's situatedness and partiality with a recognition that some kinds of knowledge seem more "true" (or at least "less false" [Harding 185]) to feminists than others. Susan Hekman observes: "If there are multiple feminist standpoints, then there must be multiple truths and multiple realities. This is a difficult position for those who want to change the world according to a new image" (351). This is an issue that I consider later in this introduction.

How might we factor history into these critiques of universalism? That will, I hope, be the contribution of this book, as I make a plea here for a more emphatically historicized conception of positionality. Though Alcoff invoked the ever changing context within which women are positioned, change over time has received very little attention in recent theorizing. Most theorists of situatedness and positionality have failed to emphasize that knowledge production varies not just synchronically, as a consequence of the social categories that construct the knower or the social location he or she occupies, but also diachronically, because of the changing historical forces that act upon him/her. Though we would surely wish to jettison Marxism's certainty about what direction history is moving, it may nonetheless be salutary to recall Marxism's emphasis on the inevitability of historical change. In the *Communist Manifesto,* Marx and Engels queried rhetorically: "Does it require deep intuition to comprehend that man's ideas, views and conceptions, in one word, man's consciousness, changes with every change in the conditions of his material existence, in his social relations and in his social life?"(Tucker 489). As they emphasize, knowledge produced at any moment by a situated human subject, producer and product of those processes, will necessarily change over time. Bertolt Brecht put it even more pithily: "Da es so ist, bleibt es nicht so" (3: 1233): because it's like that now, it won't stay that way.

Adding such an understanding of history to arguments for situatedness or positionality makes it possible to emphasize that the determinants shaping the situated subject are constantly in the process of change *and* that the knowledge he or she produces will change both in response to changing constellations of determinants and as a consequence of the emergence of new historical problems which his or her knowledge production is intended to address. A focus on the *activity* of meaning-making undertaken by a historically situated subject (that is, meaning as actively produced from the perspective of a particular positionality) may make the concrete implications of this historicizing of positionality easier to grasp. In *Materialist Feminism and the Politics of Discourse*, Rosemary Hennessy uses the term "reading" to denote knowledge production under such conditions, extending the definition "to include all of those meaning-making practices which enable one to act and which shape how one makes her way through the world" (91). For Hennessy (as for many other contemporary feminist scholars), "reading," knowledge production, or meaning-making is never a practice exterior to discourse or ideology (defined in Louis Althusser's sense as "the imaginary relationship of individuals to their real conditions of existence" [162]) but is instead patched together from the interpretive frameworks (i.e., preexisting grids of meaning) ready to hand. Each new reading, and all readings in the conglomerate, are interventions into discourse/ideology which potentially, and to a lesser or greater degree, change all available systems of interpretation. Thus each new reading is produced within a historical context that is potentially at least slightly different from the one that went before. As Marx might have put it, people are simultaneously changed by history and change it. Contesting readings of all sorts can thus be conceived of as historically situated struggles *over time* to determine whose meanings are going to prevail.

One might thus understand this process of reading (in this case, of texts, to bring the issue closer to the specific concerns of this book) as analogous in some ways to Walter Benjamin's conception, in his "Theses on the Philosophy of History," of how the "historical materialist" appropriates the past. For Benjamin, a narrative of the past is not given for all time but is, rather, actively constructed to meet current political needs. He contrasts the position of the historical materialist to that of the historicist, whose ambitions for historiography are encapsulated in the famous phrase of the nineteenth-century historian Leopold von Ranke, history "as it really was": "wie es eigentlich gewesen" (Ranke 7). But since, for Benjamin, any narrative of history is always interpretation from a particular standpoint, there exists no representation of the past that is a perfect reflection of "what really happened" or that would be valid for all time. On the contrary, the story we tell about the past is the story that is important to us in the present: as Benjamin puts it, "To articulate the past historically . . . means to seize hold of a memory as it flashes up at a moment of danger. Historical materialism wishes to retain that image of the past which unexpectedly appears to man singled out by history at a moment of danger." And, as the present constantly changes, so does our version of the past: "As flowers turn toward the sun, by dint of a secret heliotropism the past strives to turn toward that sun which is rising in the sky of history." Our constructions of the past are thus as transient as the present: "The true picture of the past flits by. The past can be seized only as an image which flashes up at the instant when it can be recognized and is never seen again." Moreover, since at any moment constructing the past is a highly politicized undertaking, the project of reading the past also involves a struggle over whose meaning will prevail. As Benjamin puts it, "Only that historian will have the gift of fanning the spark of hope in the past who is firmly convinced that *even the dead* will not be safe from the enemy if he wins. And this enemy has not ceased to be victorious" (255).

Without mentioning Benjamin at all, Elizabeth Grosz has provided a more recent gloss on this position that underlines its relevance for contemporary feminism. In the millennium issue of *Signs*, she writes: "What *counts* as history, what is regarded as constituting the past, is that which is deemed to be of relevance to concerns of the present. . . . [I]t is only the interests of the present that serve to vivify or reinvigorate the past. The past is always propelled, in virtual form, in a state of compression or contraction, to futures beyond the present. . . . The past cannot be exhausted through its transcription in the present because it is also the ongoing possibility (or virtuality) that makes *future* histories, the continuous writing of histories, necessary. History is made an inexhaustible enterprise only because of the ongoing movement of time, the precession of futurity, and the multiplicity of positions from which this writing can and will occur" (1019–1021). What Benjamin and Grosz have alleged to be true of history is true, I would maintain, of all interpretive practices, all reading, which also becomes an inexhaustible enterprise that comprises contending interpretations undertaken from a multiplicity of positions across the ongoing movement of time. Out of the abundance of what is present in the text, we appropriate what is most useful to us "in a moment of danger."

Despite feminists' intense theoretical interest in "readings" in the broader and narrower sense, to the best of my knowledge only Donna Haraway has concretely explored the clash of interpretations that is a consequence of readings undertaken from different feminist positionalities. In a 1988 article, "Reading Buchi Emecheta: Contests for Women's Experience in Women's Studies," Haraway examines readings, this time in the narrower sense, of Nigerian novelist Buchi Emecheta's texts by a Nigerian woman, an African American woman, and herself, a Euro-American woman. Chikwenye Okonjo Ogunyemi, the Nigerian, is critical of Emecheta's works for their failure to affirm the community of African women as powerful, self-sufficient heterosexual women who can be conceptualized as "co-wives with an absent husband." Barbara Christian, an African American lesbian, praises Emecheta's writing for according with her own "agenda of affirming lesbianism within Black feminism and within the model of the inheritance from Africa of the tie between mother and daughter" ("Reading" 118). Haraway herself stresses the aspects of Emecheta's writing in which she perceives "a space for political accountability and for cherishing ambiguities, multiplicities and affinities without freezing identities" ("Reading" 120). Haraway emphasizes that none of these readings can be faulted for its hostility toward women's interests, for "all are part of a contemporary struggle to articulate sensitively-specific and powerfully-collective women's liberatory discourses." These readings are neither right nor wrong but merely different, each undertaken from the perspective of the specific positionality of the reader. "All readings," Haraway avers, "are also mis-readings, re-readings, partial readings, imposed readings, and imagined readings of a text that is originally and finally never simply there. Just as the world is *originally* fallen apart, the text is always already enmeshed in contending practices and hopes" ("Reading" 122–23).

Though Haraway here celebrates the different readings that even differently positioned feminist readers can produce, it is obvious that such partiality and provisionality pose multiple problems for theory and practice. What guarantees that "situated knowledges" (cf. Haraway, "Situated Knowledges") possess any validity at all? On what basis could one knowledge-claim be judged better than another? What criteria could we conceivably use? Or is it perhaps impossible to adjudicate between contending truth-claims at all? Might these varied standpoints make communication impossible even among groups potentially sharing common interests? Dirlik observes, for instance; "To abandon [claims to universal knowledge] is also to resign to the parochialness—and hence the relativity—of all knowledge, which not only abolishes the commonalities born of centuries of global interactions, but also rules out communication across societal boundaries (wherever those may be drawn at any one time and place)" ("Our Ways"). Kathleen Lennon and Margaret Whitford note: "The problem of legitimation remains, so long as the *only* alternative to a discredited value-free objectivity appears to be a postmodern pluralist free-for-all" (4). And such a postmodern free-for-all (cf. Jane Flax: "We set differences to play across boundaries" [91]) does not in any sense guarantee a transformation in feminists' interest. Even should feminist theory, as Nancy Fraser and Linda Nicholson counsel, drastically reduce its claims and its reach, "tailor[ing] its methods and its categories to the specific task at hand, using multiple categories when appropriate and forswearing the metaphysical comfort of a single feminist method or feminist epistemology" (35), how do we know that *this* theory is the most adequate to the "task at hand"? Why does *this* analysis rather than some other best enable feminist action? On what basis could we ever choose among them?

I would like to propose that Marx, with a little help from Georg Lukács, can assist us in finding a solution to these dilemmas. In his second Feuerbach thesis, Marx writes: "The question whether objective truth can be attributed to human thinking is not a question of theory but is a *practical* question. Man must prove the truth, that is, the reality and power, the this-sidedness of his thinking in practice. The dispute over the reality or non-reality of thinking which is isolated from practice is a purely *scholastic* question" (Tucker 144). Lukács, a neo-Kantian before he became a Marxist, continued to ponder the dilemma of how to discern the truth about the external world and in 1922 published *History and Class Consciousness*, regarded as orthodox Marxism's classical solution to the problem. Lukács argued that members of the bourgeoisie, whose consciousness is a product of their social location and interests ("social being determines consciousness"), are incapable of understanding the nature of a social reality whose indwelling tendencies are moving history in a direction that demands the abolition of the bourgeoisie as a class. Indeed, Lukács writes: "From a very early stage the ideological history of the bourgeoisie *was nothing but a desperate resistance to every insight into the true nature of the society it had created and thus to a real understanding of its class situation*" (66, emphasis in original). The proletariat, however, which in Lukács's Hegelian Marxist narrative constitutes the identical subject/ object of history, has the capacity both to understand society correctly and to change it (which is after all the point, as Marx emphasizes). Thus Lukács observes: "As the bourgeoisie has the intellectual, organisational and every other advantage, the superiority of the proletariat must lie exclusively in its ability to see society from the centre, as a coherent whole. This means that it is able to act in such a way as to change reality; in the class consciousness of the proletariat theory and practice coincide and so it can consciously throw the weight of its actions onto the scales of history—and this is the deciding factor" (69). Of course, Lukács recognizes that not every member of the working class possesses an identical or accurate understanding of the processes that inform social reality; fatefully, he attributes true class consciousness only to the most advanced members of the working class, the so-called "conscious vanguard" that in his view would of necessity choose the organizational form of the Communist Party. Given the harmony of theory and practice that is the proletariat's achievement, the continued success or even survival of the Party conversely provides the assurance that the Party's view of reality is true. As Lukács puts it: "The preeminently practical nature of the Communist Party, the fact that it is a fighting party presupposes its possession of a correct theory, for otherwise the consequences of a false theory would soon destroy it" (327). The chorus of the party anthem of the German Democratic Republic (GDR) compressed into a single sentence the philosophical consequences to be drawn from Lukács's argument: "The Party, the Party, the Party is always right."

Fortunately (or not), the Party no longer provides such epistemological reassurance, but that does not mean that what Marx maintains in his second thesis is wrong. What Richard Wolff observes about postmodern Marxist theory might also be true of feminist theory: "The point about theories is not whether they conform to some absolute standard or test of truth; rather it is that they reflect and transform society *differently*. On that difference rests their value and their significance for Marxists. Upon their differences Marxists must base their decisions to support, reject, attack, or transform alternative theories" (182). Positionality describes not just feminists' (or others') "subjective" choice of politics but also their "objective" social location. Those are both postures they share with many others, and postulations of various sorts undertaken from that positionality may be construed not as universally or eternally true but as potentially valid, hence also as a possible foundation for practice, for those so situated at that point in time. The "truth" (now understood of course in a much more limited and restricted sense) for that grouping might be determined by exploring the degree to which the postulation serves the grouping's interests. (For instance, the allegation that men are superior to women could never be "true" for feminists—though it might be "true" for some groups of men!) Action on the basis of a particular postulation—praxis—might then act as a kind of touchstone to determine whether the purported utility of the postulation in fact stands up in practice. "Truth" in this sense would have to be understood as a political, not an epistemological, variable, and the validity of any particular assertion would be a political achievement, not a given. Moreover, in epistemology as in real practical politics, feminists would be compelled to alter their "truths" if what they asserted they believed (e.g., "men can never be relied upon") prevented them from collaborating with other political groupings to accomplish what they needed. In this sense, the quest for feminist (or other) "truth" would be an undertaking something like the process of coalition-building that Bernice Johnson Reagon describes:

> Coalition work is not work done in your home. Coalition work has to be done in the streets. And it is some of the most dangerous work you can do. And you shouldn't look for comfort. Some people will come to a coalition and they rate the

success of the coalition on whether or not they feel good when they get there. They're not looking for a coalition; they're looking for a home! They're looking for a bottle with some milk in it and a nipple, which does not happen in a coalition. You don't get a lot of food in a coalition. You don't get fed a lot in a coalition. In a coalition you have to give, and it is different from your home. You can't stay there all the time. You go to the coalition for a few hours and then you go back and take your bottle wherever it is, and then you go back and coalesce some more. (359)

Truth arrived at via coalition-building—a political, not a philosophical, accomplishment: this could provide the epistemological basis on which we might, as Susan Stanford Friedman suggests, "reinvent a singular feminism that incorporates myriad and often conflicting cultural and political formations in a global context" (*Mappings* 4)

Especially under conditions of globalization, cooperation on the basis of self-interest also furnishes a much more reliable sticking compound for political alliance than moralizing demands for mutual recognition. As Satya Mohanty puts it, "a simple recognition of *differences* across cultures" leads only "to a sentimental charity, for there is nothing in its logic that necessitates our attention to the other" (21). And, should enough participants in such a coalition decide that, politically, certain "truths" or values are in the interest of everyone, we might arrive at something like universalisms after all, as Anthony Giddens proposes: "Humankind in some respects becomes a 'we,' facing problems and opportunities where there are no 'others'" (27). Perhaps that might be a vehicle that could allow us in some nonhomogenizing way or other, via a very roundabout route, to arrive at the utopia evoked by Marx in the *Communist Manifesto*: "In the place of the old bourgeois society, with its classes and class antagonisms, we shall have an association, in which the free development of each is the condition for the free development of all" (Tucker 491), or, similarly, in that stirring line from the "Internationale": "We have been naught, we shall be all!"

What is the relevance of this theoretical excursus for this book? Its applications are, I think, multiple. First, the readings of Bachmann's texts at which I arrive by Part Three address what seems to me a major lacuna in feminist analysis today. To vary the metaphor, I think feminist theorists have, so to speak, painted themselves into a corner. Through its absolutely essential analysis of white women's obliviousness to their own privilege, feminism created in white women an attitude of obligation and guilt, though not particularly of solidarity, toward women of color domestically and internationally. Otherwise, feminism has focused on the one hand upon women's equal rights with men and, on the other, upon the damage inflicted by men on women: rape, battering, sexual harassment, and so on. The practical consequence has been a liberal feminist politics that envisions women's integration into the existing society as soon as men learn (or are compelled) to behave. What is missing in feminist analyses of contemporary society (though very visible in contemporary feminist analyses of other historical periods) is how the present order of globalized capitalism is detrimental, in gender-specific ways, even to privileged women. An analysis of how "we"—Northern, First World, white women—are also profoundly damaged, though much less obviously and visibly than Southern women and Northern women of color, by a social order that is not just patriarchal could motivate and energize feminist practice. The absence of this analysis may explain why feminists are absent, as feminists, from the contemporary antiglobalization movement. In my view (that is, from the perspective of my current reading of Bachmann), it is precisely such an understanding of First World (in this case, Central European) women's situatedness within an analogous social order at a somewhat earlier period of history (though one also dominated by the U.S. promotion of capitalism's global sway) which informs Bachmann's writing. Bachmann's analysis of her period and of the situation of women within it is enabled by her profound appropriation of a Frankfurt School analysis, whose leading theorist, Theodor W. Adorno, declared: "There's no right way to live when the world is wrong" ("Es gibt kein richtiges Leben im falschen" [*Minima Moralia* 42]). Like many other great modernist writers—Kafka's name springs most immediately to mind—Bachmann reveals the deformities, scars, and wounds we might not see without her help. In her Frankfurt lectures of 1959-1960 she maintained: "But change is indeed possible. And the transforming effect of new works educates us to new perception, new feeling, new consciousness" (*W* 4: 195). This is the kind of reading of Bachmann's texts—addressing current political issues, transforming consciousness in order to promote change—that I want to mobilize for feminist readers.

More specifically, I argue that Bachmann quite deliberately writes from the perspective of a "historicized positionality," and that is also how she portrays her characters. In her Frankfurt lectures she declares that twentieth-century writing like that of the European modernists differs from nineteenth-century realism because the great nineteenth-century novelists portrayed figures acting within history, whereas twentieth-century writers displayed "history/story *within* the I/psyche" ("die Geschichte *im* Ich" [*W* 4: 230])—a phrase I often invoke in this volume. Bachmann's great accomplishment in the "Ways of Death," the unfinished novel cycle she left behind, was the representational strategy she devised to portray those historically induced deformations of consciousness. As I detail in subsequent chapters, she chose in the "Ways of Death" to construct female figures who are completely products of the discourses of femininity of their era and then to reveal the consequences for women. Though these female figures are rarely wives, they inhabit a world in which masculinity and femininity, defined by notions of extreme gender polarity, are entirely irreconcilable; they prefer the domestic sphere (or ostentatiously assume the roles of men when they leave it); the cosmetic disciplining of the female body is second nature to them. But though the focus of the "Ways of Death" is on women's realm, the private sphere and intimate relations, Bachmann also insists that women's domestic circumstances are informed by a larger political context, one that did not suddenly disappear from the world in 1945: "The massacres may be over, but the murderers are still among us" (W 3: 341). Or, as she maintained in a 1971 interview, "If, for example, I say nothing in this book *Malina* about the Vietnam War, nothing about so-and-so many catastrophic conditions of our society, then I know how to say it in a different way" (*GuI* 90–91)—another of my favorite quotes.

It is important to emphasize, however, that because these female figures are entirely constructed as merely the point at which discourses of femininity intersect, they have access to no language whatsoever that would allow them to speak either about their own condition or about circumstances outside the purview of women. In *Malina*, the novel that constitutes the "overture" to "Ways of Death," Bachmann instead *displays* the costs of this historical situation, the psychic disintegration of an unnamed protagonist torn between an indifferent lover and a cerebral and passionless housemate, Malina. By the end of that novel the unnamed woman disappears, and only Malina, now revealed as her male doppelgänger and the embodiment of masculine rationality, is left to narrate the later volumes in the cycle, which are presented as apparently realistic accounts of the everyday lives of female figures completely in compliance with dominant discourses on femininity. Only by way of a somber subtext that disrupts the realistic surface does Bachmann ironically reveal her figures' destruction—their "Ways of Death—by their male-dominant society and their particular male lovers. Given her project, it is more than a little ironic that many of her earliest feminist readers (including me!—see chapter 3) identified with Bachmann's figures. But now the reading of their historicized positionality at which this book arrives instead understands the positionality of these entirely socially constructed figures as situated within and inflected by all the other social determinants of the period about which Bachmann wrote.

At the same time, readings derived from this notion of historicized positionality must direct attention to the ways Bachmann also packages her analysis of femininity in historically determinate forms: that is, in the terms that were available to her. That is to say, her critical portrait of the situation of Central European women is itself a historical construct confined within the discourses of her time. In her radio plays and fiction of the 1950s, Bachmann both reproduces and challenges the dominant gender discourses of her period but always within the framework of the gender dichotomies that the decade provided. Certainly her focus on male figures during this period can be understood as an exploration of masculine (or "generically human") identity under siege, destabilized by the anomie of a mass consumer society and its absence of a coherent value system— a common lament of 1950s intellectuals throughout the West. In this regard these texts may be understood as Bachmann's far-reaching critique of the culture of Germany's "economic miracle," while her male figures' frequent attraction to female seductresses can be read as a protest against the 1950s reimposition of domestic order and bourgeois respectability. But by exploring masculine insecurities as they are played out within their relationships to women, by solving men's problems at women's cost, Bachmann also shows herself to be both influenced by and contributing to the reassertion of male control over women at which the decade's gender discourses aimed. Even in the "Ways of Death" she continued to draw upon the analyses of oppression available to her in the decade before the emergence of the second wave of feminism, particularly those of the Frankfurt School, to understand the oppression of women. As a consequence of her reliance on those approaches, themselves not unimplicated in male dominance, her texts display a number of features that feminists now would regard as problematic: on the one hand an elision of masculinity, instrumental rationality, totalitarian control, fascism, European imperialism, and patriarchy; on the other hand, the postulation of a rebellious female otherness that can express itself only in eroticism, hysteria, psychosomatic symptoms, parapraxes, dreams, or madness. The historicized positionality of these texts (and their author) thus also becomes apparent in the incompatibilities between their positions and our own, and readings undertaken from the standpoint of the (feminist) reader's historicized positionality must also reveal the ways in which Bachmann is speaking about and from an era that is no longer (like) our own.

Apart from this new approach to specific Bachmann texts, I hope my book will also be considered valuable for its attentiveness to the newest research in women's history, a reach across disciplinary boundaries far too seldom attempted by feminist literary scholars, and for its attempt to read Bachmann as simultaneously useful for our time and limited by her own. But these are not the reasons

I term the book an experiment in feminist methodology. What makes it experimental is my self-reflexive attention to *myself* as a reader and my effort to explain why it is that I read as I do. Three different developments in feminist methodology led me to undertake this experiment. First, I was dissatisfied with the 1990s methodology of "confessional criticism" in English and American literature as well as the explosion of feminist memoirs in the last decade (see Nancy Miller). Fascinating as I found those texts, I perceived a disjuncture between their authors' emphasis on their own uniqueness and the general feminist agreement that the subject was socially constructed. What was missing was an exploration of how those writers were *like* everyone else who was similarly situated, not how they were different. Second, though Jane Gallop's *Around 1981* was quite useful for formulating my project (see chapter 3), I also considered her critique of the feminist literary theory written in 1981, undertaken from her own later perspective, rather unfair. Of course, her historical hindsight allowed her to discern what she believed those earlier writers had overlooked (especially attention to race and the writing of women of color), but that was a general failing of the white academic feminism of the period, and it is likely that "around 1981" Gallop herself would have done no better. (It also appeared to me that directing such critiques at what I now considered the omissions of my *own* work might be a way of addressing these issues without incurring the charge of trashing other feminists' work that was leveled at Gallop in the volume *Conflicts in Feminism* [Gallop/Hirsch/Miller].) An investigation of how and why feminist literary theory changed seemed to me more useful than self-righteous indignation after the fact about what it had once done wrong. Third, I was very taken by the Haraway analysis of feminist responses to Emecheta's texts (explored above); but Haraway examined feminist readers who were differently positioned in "space," so to speak. Certainly, I too can identify some of the social determinants or discursive axes (shared with many others) of my positionality or the location from which I read and write. I am (in no particular order) U.S.-American, female, white, of North European heritage, heterosexual, of lower-middle-class midwestern origin but now of middle-class income and tastes, a home owner, divorced, mother of a grown son, in my early sixties, raised a Methodist, influenced by the U.S. and German student movement, trained in comparative literature and professionally active in the discipline of German Studies, full professor at an underfunded state university located in a very white, quite genteel small town in New England, director of an interdisciplinary program for undergraduates, "et cetera, and so forth" as Friedman puts it (*Mappings* 21). Though surely those different social and cultural formations "interpellate" me into a range of (frequently contradictory) subject positions (as Althusser would have it), I cannot hope to trace their implications here. My own interest in the neglected category of "history" led me, however, to ponder what the results might be if the *spatial* determinants remained the same and I examined changes over *time*. And these considerations led me to the experiment I undertake in Part II of this book: situating essays on Bachmann that I wrote in the 1980s in the context of the historical factors that acted on me then.

I thus investigate "Feminism, History, and Ingeborg Bachmann" in a variety of ways. The book's three sections undertake somewhat different projects. Part I, "Bachmann and History," consists of two chapters. The first, "Bachmann in History: An Overview," briefly situates Bachmann herself and her writing in the history of her period (my final chapter addresses the historical situatedness of both Bachmann and her texts at much greater length). Chapter 1 is intended as an introduction and general orientation for English-language readers, who may not be completely familiar either with Bachmann's writing or with the Austrian/German context within which she wrote. It provides basic information about her biography and a chronology and brief description of her publications. In effect, this chapter establishes a baseline upon which my subsequent efforts to read Bachmann's texts and readings of Bachmann's texts historically may be understood (or: "read").

Chapter 2, "Bachmann's Feminist Reception," begins the process of historicizing by examining how other feminist scholars and critics have read Bachmann. In the 1950s, she gained her fame as the author of two poetry volumes, but her prose texts of the 1960s and early 1970s were much less favorably received during her lifetime. Her reputation today as one of German literature's outstanding twentieth-century writers is due to her feminist reception from the mid-1970s onward. This chapter explores how the feminist rediscovery of Bachmann was enabled by the particular theoretical assumptions of German (and later U.S.) feminism, itself a product of the cultural climate out of which the women's movement grew, and reads those and subsequent feminist readings of Bachmann against the backdrop of developments in feminist theory *and* the larger historical changes that influenced feminist transformations. From the late 1970s to the mid-1980s, feminist readings of Bachmann were dominated by a radical feminist analysis alleging that all women were victims of all men. Patriarchy had been responsible not only for the oppression of women but also for the repression of femininity, which could "speak" only in venues exterior to male control. It was feminists' task to retrieve elements of women's culture previously "hidden from history" and develop alternatives to patriarchal culture. The theoretical texts of Hélène Cixous, Luce Irigaray, and Julia Kristeva enabled feminist scholars to discover such alternatives in expressions of femininity that disrupted a phallogocentric symbolic order as well as "in our mothers' gardens." Bachmann's texts were read as a contribution to that endeavor, sometimes even as an anticipation of French feminist theory *avant la lettre*. By the mid-1980s this reading had expressed itself in a veritable explosion of feminist Bachmann scholarship, as chapter 2 demonstrates. However, once the radical feminist model was drawn into question (primarily because of critiques of its implicit racism), I identify several years of uncertainty in feminists' readings of Bachmann, as if they were now unsure how to proceed, and a number of well-known feminist scholars examine Bachmann from a perspective in which gender and feminist issues play no role. In Germany, as I show, that approach continues to some degree into the present, though the German editors of the critical edition of the "Ways of Death" have invested a great deal of energy into promoting excellent Bachmann scholarship that is both feminist and historically specific. Meanwhile, once a new, more historically based feminist method influenced by cultural studies became established in U.S. literary studies, U.S.-trained scholars produced quite innovative new readings of Bachmann by viewing her texts through the lens of feminist variants of the new theoretical paradigms (e.g., postcolonial theory, queer theory) that emerged in the course of the 1990s.

Part II, "A History of Reading Bachmann," focuses on my experiment in historicizing positionality. I wrote the five essays included there between 1980 and 1987. All of them, I hope, offer interesting and useful readings of Bachmann's works; several have played quite an influential role within Bachmann research; and each, I think, provides insights into Bachmann's work that no subsequent scholar has drawn into question. For these reasons, I am very happy to make these essays accessible to a broader readership. Each one, however, is also very clearly a product of its time; were I to address the same questions now, I would write a quite different essay. So here is where the experiment comes in. To frame each essay (that is, to historicize the positionality that informed the perspective from which I wrote it) I have composed a brief, perhaps rather idiosyncratic, historical preface that details the context relevant for me at the time the essay was written. (*En passant*, these frames also form an intellectual history of U.S. academic feminism in the context of the larger political developments impacting upon it.) At the conclusion of each essay I have then undertaken a reading (a reading of the reading, so to speak) that explains in what ways my older essay can be understood as a product of and a feminist response to that historical situation. That is, my current reading understands the older reading as stressing those aspects of Bachmann's text that "flash up at a moment of danger," "at an instant when [they] can be recognized and [are] never seen again." My readings of Bachmann from the 1980s are, I would now argue, appropriate for their historical moment—neither worse nor better than the ones I would write today but simply different.

Chapter 3, "In the Cemetery of the Murdered Daughters: *Malina,*" reads the "overture" to Bachmann's "Ways of Death" through the lens of the cultural feminist approach that dominated U.S. and German feminist theory and practice in 1981, when my essay appeared. That approach is responsible for Bachmann's feminist rediscovery and for a shift in scholarly emphasis from her poetry to her prose. My essay is also the first to connect Bachmann, psychoanalysis, and French feminist theory (and can thus also serve as a baseline against which to measure subsequent developments in feminist Bachmann scholarship). In it, I understand *Malina* as an endeavor to explain why women have no authentic voice of their own and in what ways they can "speak" nonetheless. The essay understands Bachmann's interest in Wittgenstein, psychoanalysis and love/eroticism to derive from her attempt to identify forms of speech outside the categories of Western reason (an explanation of Bachmann's intentions I still think is true, though today I would judge it differently). Although the essay concludes that Bachmann herself finds no way to concretize the utopian vision of sensual pleasure and erotic joy that *Malina* also contains, it proposes that what we as feminists learn from this text may allow the "murdered daughters" to turn men's knowledge against them and realize Bachmann's utopia yet.

Chapter 4, "Christa Wolf and Ingeborg Bachmann: Difficulties of Writing the Truth," written in 1983, offers a reading that gives expression to the shifts in feminist emphasis accompanying the early days of the Ronald Reagan and Helmut Kohl regimes. In my reading of Christa Wolf's reading of Bachmann, I continue to emphasize the search for a feminist alternative to male dominance, but patriarchy is now seen to express itself quite concretely in masculinist warmongering, a special concern for peace-loving women. Drawing on a very sensitive but still quite Marxist 1966 essay by Wolf, I also now read Bachmann's texts as a social critique directed specifically at fascism, imperialism, and other destructive elements of twentieth-century society. (In *this* essay, Wittgenstein's thought is evidence of insoluble dilemmas of Western culture.) I also use Wolf's analysis to argue that Bachmann's limitations were rooted in her sociohistorical context. Conversely, I trace Wolf's indebtedness to Bachmann as far as her *Cassandra* lectures (published the same year I wrote the essay), showing how Bachmann's anatomy of the status of subjectivity in *her* society increasingly enabled

Wolf's own examination of alienation within GDR socialism. I finally determine that Bachmann's and Wolf's analyses were converging, as Wolf came to
accept the cultural feminist approach very apparent in her novel *Cassandra* (and
also to propagate a cultural feminist reading of Bachmann) just as U.S. feminists
were moving in other directions. In a year of great anxiety about the stationing
of cruise and Pershing missiles in Europe, I note both Bachmann's and Wolf's
pessimism about the possibility of change but also propose (rather gloomily
myself) that the texts of these writers may nonetheless help us to forestall the
worst.

Chapter 5, "Gender, Race, and History in *The Book of Franza*," appeared in
the landmark 1984 special Bachmann issue of *text + kritik* that proclaimed the
(cultural) feminist discovery of "the other Ingeborg Bachmann." Under the
influence of the new U.S. feminist attentiveness to race, however, and my own
involvement in Jesse Jackson's presidential campaign, my essay, published here
for the first time in English, takes a somewhat different tack. I believe I was the
first Bachmann scholar to propose that her protagonist's imprecations against
"the whites" might in fact be directed at the crimes of European imperialism.
U.S. feminists' attention to differences among women also encouraged me to
insist upon the historical specificity of Bachmann's critique (and, by exploring
via the *New York Times* the historical background of the events to which the
novel alludes, to discover that it takes place at a particular moment of Cold War
tension). In fact, beginning with something of a polemic directed at the sins and
omissions of ahistorical feminist scholarship, my essay reads Bachmann's novel
via the (also rather gloomy) optic of German Critical Theory, maintaining that
Bachmann extends the Frankfurt School analysis to address colonialism as well
as fascism. Though I continue to regard Bachmann's protagonist mainly as an
innocent victim of (white) men, I also stress that as a white woman she belongs
and has acceded to the oppressor culture and thus has no access to a location
exterior to male power (a position that represented something of a sea change in
feminist analysis). In perceiving the only utopian moment of the novel to be one
where white, brown, and black hands dip silently into the same bowl of food, I
also show how strongly I had been influenced by the coalition politics towards
which U.S. feminism increasingly moved in the mid-1980s.

I am sure I could not have written chapter 6, "Bachmann and Wittgenstein,"
without my background in feminist theory, but I remain uncertain about
whether or not it is a feminist essay. Its lack of attention to gender certainly bears
witness to a widespread loss of confidence in feminist theory and practice and
my own dubiousness about the continuing utility of feminist scholarship on

Bachmann. The essay continues my polemic against extracting Bachmann's writing from history and proposes my examination of her indebtedness to Wittgenstein as one way to explore her connections to the Austrian tradition. Though I am far from being a Wittgenstein expert, I think that reading him through Bachmann's eyes also helped me to provide insights into his thought somewhat different from those of professional philosophers. Both my Frankfurt School training and my more recent encounter with poststructuralism (via feminism) allowed me to understand Wittgenstein's thought (and Bachmann's interest in it) as deriving from a critique of totalizing (European) theories. By examining Bachmann's dissertation on Heidegger, I could also demonstrate her ability to connect very abstract philosophical postulations to their concrete political manifestations (e.g., Heidegger's support for National Socialism) and to show why she might have considered Wittgenstein's thought to be an antidote to Heidegger's. Bachmann, my essay argues, is able to grasp the connections between Wittgenstein's *Tractatus* and his later *Philosophical Investigations*, which renounce the quest for a totalizing linguistic paradigm altogether and content themselves with a range of heterogeneous "language games." Wittgenstein, I maintain, also helped Bachmann to understand the relationship of universal truth-claims to the triumphs of Western imperialism, but both, I conclude, were unable to imagine a mediation between their far-reaching critique and a practice that might realize it. And perhaps it is here, after the last sentence of my essay, that feminism might enter after all.

In chapter 7, "Bachmann Reading/Reading Bachmann: *The Woman in White* in the 'Ways of Death,'" a certain corner is turned—in my own work, in Bachmann research, in literary scholarship, in feminist theory and practice. Though I was certainly not aware then how weighted the concept would become in my own thinking, it is nonetheless no coincidence that the term "reading" appears—twice!—in the title. In my own scholarship, the essay signals my feminist appropriation of the new cultural-materialist/new-historicist/materialist-feminist/cultural-studies methodology that had more generally taken hold of U.S. literary scholarship around 1987. The essay also marks a change in my own reading of Bachmann, catalyzed by the discovery that she had borrowed the name of the heroic English captain in *The Book of Franza* from the villain in a novel by the prolific Victorian writer Wilkie Collins. This and other intertextual allusions in Bachmann's writing forced me to recognize that all was not as it seemed in Bachmann's texts. Once I understood that her narrative stance in the "Ways of Death" was almost always ironic, I could grasp how her figures are constrained by (or constructs of) the discursive context to which her writing alludes or from which it borrows. The characters' self-presentation, judgment, and consciousness of themselves is configured by that context, but we readers must see further. In particular, this essay argues that Franza's belief that her beloved captain is freeing her is itself a product of the discourse upon which the Victorian romance also draws, while the apparently innocent whiteness of Wilkie Collins's title is transmuted into the European imperialists against whose power Franza inveighs. Writing this essay taught me to think more complexly about reading itself, showing me how to be more attentive to the politics of literary forms and to recognize the clash of contradictory paradigms within a single text. It also showed me how readings that rather evidently have nothing to do with an author's intentions (the "white" of Wilkie Collins's title as a racial category) can nonetheless be legitimate and useful (especially when they flash up in a moment of danger!). In my work and in feminist literary scholarship as a whole, this essay is representative of the emergence of an entirely new approach—a method that provides the foundation for the essays of this book's third section, "Reading Bachmann Historically."

Written from the perspective of the new historically based theory, the essays of Part Three explore a positionality of a different kind. Through them I want to explode once and for all the claim that there can ever be a *single* correct reading by showing that even a single reader, writing at (approximately) the same point in history but asking different kinds of questions about a text, will still come up with quite different, even potentially contradictory answers. Part Three thus emphasizes the second half of Alcoff's definition of positionality, "the position that women find themselves in . . . actively utilized as a location for the construction of meaning." Here I investigate what happens when the perspective assumed by a particularly positioned reader is deliberately chosen, and the three chapters employ, respectively, methods enabled by theories of sexuality, by postcolonial theory, and by materialist feminism, to ask three quite different kinds of questions about Bachmann texts. Of course, the fact that I am able to utilize different perspectives does not of course mean that my choice of perspectives and methods is not itself historically constrained. Obviously, I did not invent these theoretical approaches (though I believe I am the first to apply them to Bachmann's texts); all three approaches (which, at least as I apply them, could probably all find a home under the more general rubric "cultural studies") gained widespread currency in U.S. literary studies during the 1990s. Moreover, a 1997 *PMLA* forum on "the actual or potential relations between cultural studies and the literary" ("Forum" 257) seems to suggest that the turn to cultural studies is no longer even controversial. Most participants in the forum agree that at a historical point when literature divorced from its cultural context seems increasingly overspecialized, supportive of dominant ideologies, and irrelevant, a cultural studies approach is the appropriate course for departments of literary studies to pursue. As well, occasional caviling aside, the forum seems to attest to a particular U.S. appropriation of cultural studies that marks a shift away from the sociological and mass and popular culture emphases of its earlier British practitioners and now sees little difficulty in applying the techniques of cultural studies to literary texts (and, conversely, literary techniques of close reading to cultural phenomena). As Lutz Koepnick, a forum participant from my own field of German Studies, puts it, "Literary culture is an essential part of the force field of institutions, meanings, and practices that cultural studies takes as its object; there is no reason that the works of, say, Shakespeare or Goethe cannot be examined from a cultural studies perspective" (266). In the same forum, Lily Phillips proposes that the preeminence of cultural studies may derive from a growing acknowledgment of the importance of the positionality for which this introduction has argued: "Cultural studies has emerged forcefully because the awareness of positionality, context, and difference is endemic to this historical period. The need to acknowledge that there are limits to our models of the world and to think paradigmatically is a gauntlet thrown down by our historical situation, not just by cultural studies" (274). For historical reasons that we will doubtless comprehend entirely only after the fact, the project of "reading [an author's texts] historically" seems to have become virtually de rigeur. As Antony Easthope puts it in his book *Literary into Cultural Studies*, "the old paradigm has collapsed, . . . the moment of crisis symptomatically registered in concern with theory is now passing, and . . . a fresh paradigm has emerged, its status as such proven because we can more or less agree on its terms and use them" (5).

Of the final three chapters, chapter eight, "Bachmann and Theories of Gender/Sexuality: Femininity in 'The Good God of Manhattan,'" is most able to borrow its methodology from an established corpus of feminist scholarship. Premised upon the contemporary feminist assumption that both gender and sexuality are cultural constructs rather than biological givens, this essay sets out to discover how Bachmann undertook such constructions in a radio play written in 1957 and in what relationship those constructions might stand to other historical developments of the period. As well, in my approach to this radio play I attempt to explore the postulate that cultural productions are patched together out of heterogeneous materials and discover that a reading emphasizing this text's contradictory representations of femininity and sexuality can be especially illuminating. Specifically, I argue that in this play Bachmann relies on notions of sexuality and femininity like those that Herbert Marcuse advanced in *Eros and Civilization* (which Bachmann probably read shortly after it was published in 1955, possibly during her visit to the United States in summer 1955, which provides the setting for this play). Like Marcuse, Bachmann represents both Eros and women as potent forces hostile to civilization, thus also a powerful source of civilizational critique. At the height of the Cold War in the one-dimensional society of "Manhattan," I maintain, these may have seemed the only sites at which any subversion at all could have been imagined. But as I myself critique, from a Foucauldian perspective, Marcuse's and Bachmann's conception of a form of opposition exterior to a single, totalitarian, and repressive order, I argue that it is also possible to discern a second and somewhat submerged discourse of gender and sexuality in Bachmann's radio play. Within that discourse, femininity and female sexuality are seen to be products of the power that calls them into being. Though Bachmann's earlier feminist readers, I finally conclude, stressed the most obvious reading of her play and similar aspects of later texts, a reading that emphasizes their contradictory elements and understands the historical reasons for them may be of more use to feminists of the present day.

Whereas chapter 8 is informed by a very substantial body of feminist analysis, the feminist postcolonial theory that underwrites chapter 9, "Bachmann and Postcolonial Theory: White Ladies and Dark Continents," has emerged only in very recent years. In fact, it was back in 1984 that I first discovered the episode of the "White Lady" among Bachmann's unpublished papers in the Vienna archive. Though I believe that even then I grasped something of the reading of that fragment that I have elaborated here, I had to wait fifteen years for the theory to be developed that would allow me to explain it to others. This chapter provides the strongest substantiation for my argument that Bachmann's "Ways of Death" cycle constructs the female psyche in terms (often borrowed from other literary texts) that their society makes available. I examine Bachmann's treatment of the representation of femininity, race, and exotic otherness, and I also show how she conveys to careful readers that they should read her texts against the grain. *The Book of Franza* might be read, I suggest, as the story of a typical European tourist's conviction that the exotic and uncontaminated orient can assuage the depredations wrought upon her by Western civilization (though that tourist drinks Coca-Cola all throughout her journey). Countess Kottwitz's sexuality is "awakened" only when she is "raped" by an African student with proverbially prodigious sexual capabilities, and Bachmann tells us how to read this scene when the countess, in the scene immediately preceding the rape, orders a cocktail called a "White Lady." In the long story "Three Paths to the

Lake," Elisabeth, a good liberal who believes she supports justice for all, is taken aback when people formerly subject to the Austro-Hungarian empire and post-colonials now inhabiting Europe act in ways contrary to her sentimental preconceptions of them—an exoticizing perspective quite like that of D. H. Lawrence's story "The Woman Who Rode Away," to which Bachmann's text alludes. I finally ask how feminists should read such very complex anticolonialist texts of the sort that Bachmann has written and whether, in placing postcolonial figures at the service of an exploration of the White Lady's psyche, Bachmann reveals that she has not entirely jettisoned Eurocentrism after all.

My designation for the method employed in chapter 10, "Bachmann and Materialist Feminism," is something of a *Verlegenheitslösung*, as the Germans put it—a solution arrived at for want of anything better—for I'm not sure that the method I employ here has been christened yet. (Since other self-designated materialist feminists are decidedly more orthodoxly Marxist than I, I might also have called my method "cultural materialism" or, even more generically, "cultural studies," a term now almost a catchall for any method whatsoever that connects texts and contexts.) In this chapter I read Bachmann's portrait of women (choosing to be) confined to the private arena during the Cold War era as itself a symptom and reflex of the Cold War. To theorize the importance of gender within Cold War politics, I draw on very recent texts by feminist and other sorts of historians of Germany and Austria. Expanding on my brief historical overview in chapter 1, I also respond to Monika Albrecht's and Dirk Göttsche's injunction to treat Bachmann more historically (Albrecht, "Vorwort" vii) by showing that Bachmann herself was not entirely untainted by Cold War politics. This chapter explores Bachmann's evolving critique of the Cold War era and women's situation within it, but it also shows how she was forced to package her critique in materials available to her. That inevitably meant, as Bachmann herself observed in her Frankfurt lectures, that some of her readers would believe she sanctioned the conditions she was trying to decry. The essay also explores the variety of formal methods she employed to represent the psychic damage wrought by her society and speculates about why those methods were so frequently misunderstood as un- or even antipolitical. The chapter includes an analysis of the almost completed story "Sterben für Berlin" (To die for Berlin) that Bachmann wrote three months after the Berlin Wall went up, and it connects the narrative strategies employed there to those of the "Ways of Death." In its reprise of and expansion on topics broached in chapter 1, my book refuses, like Benjamin's "Theses on the Philosophy of History" (253–264), a linear and progressive historical narrative. In ending with a quite different reading of *Malina* than that of chapter 3—the first study of Bachmann I pub-lished—my book also once more argues for the "historicized positionality" of this Bachmann reader.

In offering readings of my readings of my readings, I feel at times as if I had entered a hall of mirrors or some tunnel of infinite regress. On the other hand, each new self-reflexive move, I think, makes my point even more emphatically. Where the feminist reader stands, in space and in time, determines what she sees. In all likelihood, her readings will hold true (which is to say, given my definition of "truth," be politically useful) only for those of us similarly situated. Of course, what is to count as "we" and as "similarly situated" can also be shaped at least in part not just by our "objective" situation but also by how we con-sciously and deliberately conceive of our political visions and political needs. Whatever the "cemetery of the murdered daughters" means, it is probably not a place to which we wish to be consigned; we too seek intellectual tools that can, in Kafka's words, function as "the axe for the frozen sea inside us" (16), a sea much like the icy lake on which Bachmann's cemetery borders. The various readings of Bachmann's texts in this volume are intended finally to assist femi-nists in understanding why and in what ways the daughters were murdered and how we ourselves might avoid that fate and envision, even realize, a happier one. That is the importance of Bachmann's writing—and feminist readings of it.

To demonstrate finally that "historicized positionality" does not condemn feminist or other readers to hapless political isolation, let me conclude this intro-duction by again invoking Susan Stanford Friedman, a fellow graduate student at the University of Wisconsin at Madison thirty-some years ago, whose recent book *Mappings* I have already cited. In concluding her introduction of *Mappings*, she assumes a political stance so similar to my own (because we are both white U.S. women academics "of a certain age"? because of that formative experience in Madison? because we were then "similarly situated"? because we, as engaged feminist literary scholars, still are?) that it can also serve as my conclusion: "While attempting to respect their rich complexity and unresolved contradic-tions, I have turned to these texts with a frankly instrumentalist intent—for what they have to teach academic feminism, for their potential interventions in the great debates of the day, and for their collective wisdom and pleasure. The stories they tell matter. So do the stories we tell about them" (13).

PART I
Bachmann and History

CHAPTER 1

Bachmann in History
AN OVERVIEW

*Avec ma main brulée, j'écris
sur la nature du feu.*
—Ingeborg Bachmann,
Malina, *quoting Flaubert*

*H*istory left its scars on Ingeborg Bachmann's life and work. She was the product of a turbulent period of Austrian history that included depression, Austro-fascism, National Socialism, defeat and occupation, economic recovery, and political restoration. She hated and condemned the political course that Austria and Germany had taken but, as a member of a generation before the emergence of the student movement and the second wave of feminism, felt powerless to influence the direction of political events. Although she rebelled against her era's conceptions of femininity, she was also entrapped by them; an independent woman who lived by her writing, she suffered through self-destructive love affairs and numbed her pain with alcohol and tranquilizers. Like the female figures of her fiction, Bachmann was often a victim of her inability to resolve her own contradictions.

Born in 1926 in the small city of Klagenfurt in the province of Carinthia, Austria, Bachmann was the eldest daughter of a local high school teacher and a housewife. Her petty bourgeois family experienced firsthand the economic straits that made many Austrians, still mired in the depression, welcome their country's annexation by a more prosperous Germany. Bachmann recalled the entry of Hitler's troops into Klagenfurt in April 1938 as a traumatic moment that shattered her childhood. During her lifetime, however, she never revealed that her own father had joined the Nazi party in 1932, even before Hitler came to power in Germany. Drafted into defense work for the Nazis in the last year of the war, Bachmann swiftly abandoned Klagenfurt after the German defeat in order to begin her university studies. After a semester spent in Innsbruck and in Graz, she continued her study of philosophy at the University of Vienna, receiving her doctorate in 1950 with a dissertation on Heidegger. From 1951 to 1953 she worked first as a secretary, then as a scriptwriter for Rot-Weiss-Rot, the radio station of the American occupation forces. There she coauthored *Die Radiofamilie* (The radio family), a comic radio series designed to ease Austrians' transition to postwar, postfascist society. She published poetry and prose in Vienna, enjoying the mentorship of an older generation of Viennese literary figures, including Jewish émigrés returned from exile, and began her close friendship with the poet Paul Celan. Nevertheless,she found the political and literary atmosphere of Vienna corrupt, stagnant, and stifling. Preferring self-imposed exile, she left Vienna in July 1953 to take up residence in Italy with her gay friend, the composer Hans Werner Henze, and never again lived permanently in Austria.

Bachmann was encouraged in her resistance to Austria's restoration of prewar power structures by her encounter with the Gruppe 47, the influential group of young antifascist authors who dominated West Germany's literary scene (though they failed to affect its politics) until the early 1960s. First invited to the Gruppe 47's semiannual meetings in 1952, she won its first prize for the four poems she read there in 1953. Her first volume of poetry, *Die gestundete Zeit* (Mortgaged time), was published at the end of that year. In August 1954 the news magazine *Der Spiegel* featured Bachmann on its title page, depicting her as a poet whose accomplishment proved that Germany could once more compete on the stage of world literature, and she achieved literary prominence overnight. In spring 1954, Bachmann moved to Rome, which would remain her semi-permanent residence for the rest of her life. Italy left its imprint on many poems in her second lyric volume, *Anrufung des Großen Bären* (Invocation of the great bear; 1956). Under the pseudonym Ruth Keller she also reported on political and cultural events in Italy for Radio Bremen and the *Westdeutsche Allgemeine Zeitung*. Her first radio play, "Ein Geschäft mit Träumen" (A business with dreams; 1952), had been completed in Vienna and originally broadcast by Rot-Weiss-Rot. In a second radio play, "Die Zikaden" (The cicadas; 1954), she drew on her contacts with the artists' colony on the Italian island of Ischia, where she had lived with Henze. In 1955 she attended an international summer school, led by Henry Kissinger at Harvard, for young European artists and intellectuals, and that encounter with the United States laid the foundation for her most successful radio play, "Der gute Gott von Manhattan" (The good God of Manhattan; 1957). During the 1950s, Henze set a number of Bachmann's poems to music, and she produced several opera libretti for him. Their close collaboration ended in 1958 when Bachmann met the Swiss author Max Frisch, and her intense and painful relationship with Frisch lasted until 1962.

In the late 1950s Bachmann turned away from poetry, suspicious of her own easy facility with language. In 1959–1960, holding the first chair for poetics at the University of Frankfurt, she delivered a series of badly received lectures on problems of contemporary literature. In 1961 she published her first volume of short stories, *Das dreißigste Jahr* (The thirtieth year), and her previously enthusiastic critics responded skeptically, terming Bachmann a "fallen poetess" who could no longer meet the standards of her early work. Devastated by negative reviews and her separation from Frisch the next year, Bachmann suffered a physical and psychic collapse from which she never completely recovered. In 1963–1964 she spent a year in Berlin on a Ford Foundation fellowship and, increasingly dependent on tranquilizers, sleeping pills, and painkillers, traveled to Prague, Egypt, and the Sudan in an attempt to regain her health. As a younger generation of Germans and Austrians took politics to the streets, Bachmann withdrew into her art. From the early 1960s onward she worked on a novel cycle she called "Todesarten" (Ways of death). She finished the cycle's "overture," the novel *Malina* (1971) and a volume of short stories drawn from the "Ways of Death" milieu, *Simultan* (Three paths to the lake; 1972) before her death, leaving behind in various stages of completion several novel fragments (including *Requiem für Fanny Goldmann* (Requiem for Fanny Goldmann) and *Das Buch Franza* (The book of Franza; published in 1978). In fall 1973 Bachmann incurred burns over a third of her body when she apparently fell asleep with a burning cigarette. On 17 October 1973 she died in a Roman hospital from her burns and the convulsions brought on by withdrawal from a drug that her doctors could not identify.

In her 1959 "Frankfurt Lectures on Poetics," Bachmann insisted that literature was always a product of its historical conditions: "Probably no one believes any more that writing literature takes place outside of the historical situation—that even a single writer exists whose starting point isn't determined by the conditions of the time." It was the task of the writer to confront historical circumstances and to envision alternatives to them: "In the happiest of cases he can succeed at two things: at representing, representing his time, and at presenting something for which the time has not yet come" (*W* 4: 196). Bachmann's lectures on the problems of contemporary literature may also be read as a statement of her own project: whatever its genre, her writing always attempted to illuminate the problems of the present and to envision utopian realms where those problems would be resolved. Her writing is rooted in history in several ways.

Her success with readers of her poetry in the 1950s and feminist readers of her fiction after her death derived from their perception that her texts captured their own contemporary concerns, though the avant-garde complexity of her texts (itself a historical product) also allowed them to interpret her treatment of social problems in a variety of ways compatible with their own political positions. The limitations of Bachmann's writing were also a consequence of her historical situation: though she could portray alternatives to the social forms that destroy her female figures, in the era before the second wave of feminism she could never imagine any means of moving those figures from here to there.

In its famous 1954 lead story, *Der Spiegel* called Bachmann's poetry a "stenogram of its time." Bachmann's poems, along with those of her friend Paul Celan, signaled a turning point for postwar German literature. Until Bachmann and Celan, only two lyrical avenues seemed open to postwar German poets: either to escape the contemporary situation via a retreat into religion, nature, or aestheticism, or—the route initially chosen by the antifascist authors of the Gruppe 47—to focus on the trials of the postwar period using the plain, unadorned language of everyday life. But by 1953, Germans were ready to put their tribulations behind them. Through their appropriation of an astonishing repertoire of lyric traditions and techniques, Bachmann and Celan reestablished the connections of German poetry to the European tradition and to its own problematic past. Bachmann's poetry seemed clearly located in the context of postwar concerns, acknowledging a German history that included National Socialism and its aftermath, a social order that had restored "yesterday's hangmen" to places of honor. But, as *Der Spiegel* noted, the message of those poems could seem both very concrete and also shadowy and imprecise. Thus some readers could consider poems that treated such themes as loss, isolation, fear, or flight as a response to the historical situation; others could call them existentialist accounts of the condition of man in the modern world; and still others could regard them as beautiful evocations of timeless universal concerns.

The title poem of Bachmann's first collection, *Die gestundete Zeit,* already strikes a new literary note. "Harder days are coming" (*Storm* 43), it warns, urging watchfulness and caution. The poems often give voice to the desire to flee a compromised reality, but they almost always combine the impulse toward flight with a sober recognition of the impossibility of escape. Some of her most political poems speak directly about the cultural atmosphere of the postwar period, as in the poem "Every Day": "War is no longer declared, / only continued" (*Storm* 53). In "Leaving Port," the poem with which the collection opens, a ship embarks on a perilous voyage for an uncertain destination, and the poet counsels steadfastness, even defiance: "Stay calm on deck" (*Storm* 27). And in "Wood Chips" she cautions, "Make sure you stay awake!" (*Storm* 45). Sometimes Bachmann draws upon an alternative utopian imagery derived from nature, love, or art: "But like Orpheus I know of / life on the side of death" (*Storm* 35). Mainly, however, hope is sustained through the will of the poet alone, often through the power of her language to state what is true: "As long as [the bile]'s bitter, I intend / to write the word of the beginning" (*Storm* 45).

Bachmann's unmistakable tone, her ability to find concrete and sensuous expression for abstract concerns, continued into her second volume, *Anrufung des Großen Bären*. This collection is generally considered to be stronger poetically and more regular metrically, employing simpler language and more complex symbolism drawn from a variety of Western traditions. Contrasts between Germanic coldness and Mediterranean light, warmth, and vibrancy often shape the poems. Many are less explicitly political, less obviously defiant. Yet the world of this collection is still an imperiled one, the poet proclaiming apocalyptically, for instance, that "a torrent is coming over the earth. / We shall be witnesses" (*Storm* 123). The collection oscillates between danger and a destructive emptiness on the one hand, and on the other a powerful invocation of utopia, often figured as fairy-tale, love, or an intact natural world. Here, too, the poet's language is often the vehicle for her redemption, and she proclaims; "Yet the song above the dust / one day will rise above us" (*Storm* 153), and "You, my word, deliver me!" (*Storm* 113).

It was parallel to her poems, with which they shared many themes and motifs, that Bachmann produced a series of radio plays (a popular genre in the decade after the war because Germans still owned the radios the Nazis had given them) as well as "radio essays," dramatized discussions of figures whose influence was discernible elsewhere in Bachmann's work: Robert Musil, Ludwig Wittgenstein, Marcel Proust, Simone Weil, the logical positivists of the Vienna Circle. Especially in their emphasis on dream, illusion, irreality, and interiority, Bachmann's radio plays displayed many of the characteristics typical of a literary form also employed by many other German authors of the period. Laurenz, the protagonist of "A Business with Dreams," is a meek and docile office worker who discovers a store that will sell him the secret fantasies for which he's always longed: riches, power, romance. But in the dream store the currency is time, and extravagant dreams may cost a whole lifetime. Laurenz has so thoroughly internalized the norms of his joyless life that even though the time at his disposal is empty, he's unwilling to pay so high a price. When he returns to reality, he is fired, so now he has plenty of time, but "Time for what?" (W 2: 47). In "The Cicadas," six figures have sought asylum from society on a southern island, but Bachmann offers them no opportunity to fulfill their concrete wishes there. She warns that escape from reality, especially into art, can produce people like cicadas, so dried out from their lack of contact with real life that their singing becomes inhuman. In "The Good God of Manhattan," Bachmann turned for the first time to the constellation of themes that would shape her later prose. The Good God represents domination as an all-powerful social principle that refuses to tolerate anything inimical to its rule and is prepared to resort to violence in order to enforce its dictates. In this radio play, Bachmann connects domination to the question of gender relations: the God persecutes a pair of lovers because their passion threatens the quotidian order that is his domain. Bachmann endows her female figure, Jennifer, with a greater capacity for love than her partner but also shows that, for women, love can lead simultaneously to bliss and (self-)destruction. The utopian power of Jennifer's love is not mighty enough to overcome the temptations of everyday life to which her lover Jan succumbs, and the God blows Jennifer to bits while sparing Jan, who has taken a break from ecstasy to catch up on the news in a bar.

It is now easy to recognize that all three radio plays were intended as critiques of the crass and ugly consumer culture of the 1950s and that they advanced their challenge from the vantage point of a utopian alternative to the bad present— though one that could be presented in the plays only as tentative, partial, and finally unachievable. But as in the case of her poems, the form of Bachmann's radio plays, itself a product of the 1950s, could allow her audience to ignore the intensity of her social criticism and instead regard the plays as treatments of Being, myth, or timeless and unchanging human dilemmas.

Although she had always written occasional short stories, in the late 1950s Bachmann began a more total transition from poetry and radio plays to prose. The seven stories of The Thirtieth Year (1961) continue to explore many of the same themes: the consequences of fascism for the postwar period; the conflict between individual happiness and a hostile social order; the search for a utopian alternative to the present order; language as a vehicle of co-optation or redemption; and the connection of gender issues to other forms of social control. The volume's first story, "Youth in an Austrian Town," is a semiautobiographical account that reveals the psychic cost of growing up in the 1930s and 1940s in the Austrian provinces. "Among Murderers and Madmen," set in Vienna ten years after war's end, shows how latent and overt allegiances to fascism continue to shape postwar intellectual life. In the title story, an unnamed thirty-year-old male protagonist negotiates an existential crisis: he rebels against a social reality he suddenly perceives as intolerable; he questions the stability of his own identity, the meaning of the world, and his own ability to grasp it through language; and finally he again reconciles himself to everyday life. Like "The Thirtieth Year," two other stories thematize language's incapacity to convey truth: in "A Wildermuth," a trial judge seeks complete linguistic accuracy and ends in madness, and the father of "Everything" tries to preserve his son from contamination by corrupt everyday language but succeeds only in abandoning him to the imperfect reality that his mother represents.

The two stories most popular with feminists link women's accommodation to gender norms with all other aspects of an oppressive social order. In "A Step towards Gomorrah," Charlotte hopes that her challenge to gender roles in a lesbian relationship with Mara will shatter all other social conventions, including language, and inaugurate a counterorder. But the love affair founders before it begins because she merely reverses the roles she wants to repudiate, assuming the same kind of domination over Mara that men have exercised over her. "Undine Goes" is an even more radical invocation of a utopian arena outside the social reality ruled by men. Unlike Hans Christian Andersen's "Little Mermaid" and other figures in the ondine tradition, this Undine admires the world men have made but refuses to sacrifice her own principles to accommodate herself to their order. She renounces the love of men and, as language fails her, returns to her own watery realm.

Although Bachmann thereafter published almost nothing new until the early 1970s, she had begun to work on the "Ways of Death" novel cycle even before *The Thirtieth Year* appeared. The multivolume cycle she planned was intended as an anatomy of her entire society, a portrait of the twenty years since 1945 from the vantage point of Vienna and Austria, and, like many great European novels of the nineteenth century, it would use a series of female figures to investigate the mores of the time. In previous centuries, such an examination of the situation of individuals within society might have been undertaken via a grand narrative of action in the external world. But now, Bachmann argued, those dramas of suffering and passion must be portrayed as intrapsychic, as "history/story *within* the I/psyche" ("die Geschichte *im* Ich" [*W* 4: 230]), so that in the "Ways of Death" "the real settings" are "interior ones" (*Franza* 4). Premised on an understanding of the constitution of the human psyche with some affinities to the analyses of the Frankfurt School, the "Ways of Death" would show how a single principle of social domination produced human subjects that voluntarily yield to its destructive power. It is probably possible to read the female protagonists as figures for the state of subjectivity in Bachmann's time, as Madame Bovary or Anna Karenina figured subjectivity in the nineteenth century. But feminist scholars have argued that it is more productive to read the "Ways of Death" as an exploration of the damage done to *female* subjectivity in a society founded on the principles of male dominance and female subordination. Despite the contemporary setting of the "Ways of Death," Bachmann's avant-garde techniques sometimes made it difficult even for feminists to recognize that her novels addressed the social construction of femininity of a particular era, and some feminist readings of Bachmann have been as ahistorical as those of her earlier critics.

The first of Bachmann's "Ways of Death" remained a fragment, and her editors named it *Der Fall Franza* (The Franza case) when they published it in 1978 in Bachmann's *Werke* (Works); the editors of the *"Todesarten"-Projekt* now term it *Das Buch Franza* (The book of Franza). The status of the novel is contested in Bachmann criticism: while some scholars have regarded it as the most complex of the "Ways of Death" novels, central to the cycle, others maintain that Bachmann abandoned *Franza* altogether, perhaps considering it too obvious, and integrated most of its material into *Malina*. In a foreword to *Franza*, Bachmann argued that the "virus of crime" (*Franza* 3) had not vanished from the world after 1945 and explained that her book would show that the murderers, still among us, were now wreaking a havoc no longer even termed criminal. In this fragment, one of those murderers is the famous Viennese psychiatrist Leopold Jordan, who has deliberately set about to drive his wife, Franza, mad, and she flees from Vienna to join her beloved brother Martin on a trip to Egypt and the Sudan. Within the logic of the novel, Egypt is a site outside the boundaries of the West and also stands for a stage of psychic development before "the Greeks" (i.e., the oedipus complex, patriarchy) assume control. Jordan is a figure for the reigning principle of white male reason; Franza terms his treatment of her fascist and identifies with other victims of white men, including Jews and people "from a lower race" (*Franza* 79). Franza's childhood relationship to her brother had seemed a utopian alternative to the present gender order, and at war's end in their village of Galicien she had imagined that fascism was forever vanquished. But now Martin has become a white man too and can no longer understand or help his sister. In Egypt, Franza proclaims that she is beyond the power of whites but continues to deteriorate physically and mentally, a "decomposition" (*Franza* 119) that finally allows her to draw the structures of Western thought into question but cannot undo the devastation that Jordan has caused. She discovers in Cairo a German doctor who had carried out medical experiments in concentration camps and begs him to put her out of her misery, but he refuses indignantly, and Franza is surprised to discover that he is afraid of her. Later, as Martin climbs the Great Pyramid, a white exhibitionist rapes Franza. Remembering that she'd also been raped by Jordan, she smashes her head against stones of the pyramid while shouting "No!" in her "other voice" (*Franza* 140, translation modified). She dies the next day. Although Franza resists at the end, she can't move beyond victimhood. The novel builds a monument to her destruction, however, by showing why it happened: the murderers are men (fascists, whites, Enlightenment reason) who refuse to tolerate forms of female subjectivity that challenge the limits they have set. Yet Franza's absence also speaks; she is like the Egyptian queen Hatshepsut, whose successor had tried to eradicate all traces of her from the walls of her Theban temple but forgot that though he had eradicated her, she was still there: "It can still be read, because nothing is there where in fact something should be" (*Franza* 109).

In the late 1960s, Bachmann laid *Franza* aside when she devised a new plan for her novel cycle. The overarching narrator of all the "Ways of Death" was now to be a man, Malina, who would tell the stories of female figures so congruent with the gender norms of their time that they couldn't even recognize the damage that had been done to them. The novel *Malina* would inaugurate her cycle, showing why its unnamed female protagonist narrator (the "I") can't write her own book called "Ways of Death" because she can't remember or tell what's happened to her. She vanishes into the wall at the end of the novel, leaving Malina behind. There is little dramatic exterior action in this novel; history is present in the form of the psychic deformations for which it is responsible. The protagonist's clearest insight into her situation takes place in her dreams, the focus of the novel's second chapter (called "The Third Man," a title borrowed from Orson Welles' film about corruption in postwar Vienna), in which an all-powerful father figure torments and persecutes her, often in scenes that recall concentration camps. By the end of the dream chapter the protagonist can acknowledge: "Here there is always violence. Here there is always struggle. It's the eternal war" (*Malina* 155).

In waking life, the protagonist seems initially to be entangled in a conventional triangle, torn between her lover Ivan and the man who shares her apartment in the Ungargasse, Malina. But although the novel is set in contemporary Vienna amid characters who also recur, in Balzacian fashion, in *Franza* and *Three Paths to the Lake*, its experimental form—a mix of dialogues, musical scores, arias, interviews, letters, literary quotations, and long stream-of-consciousness passages—soon makes clear that the stage for this action is really intrapsychic.

Each man represents one inadequate option for women. In love with sadistic Ivan, the protagonist withdraws entirely into the private realm, embraces her dependence upon him, frantically tries to please, and believes she's happy—as he mistreats, neglects, and finally abandons her. Calm, steady, colorless Malina is, Bachmann acknowledges, the frenetic and anxiety-ridden protagonist's doppelgänger, who can take control of the details of her chaotic daily life only at the cost of the ecstasy and passion that reason can't comprehend and that the protagonist associates with femininity. Says the protagonist: "I have lived in Ivan and die in Malina" (*Malina* 223). A utopian narrative that threads its way through this novel, "The Secrets of the Princess of Kagran," is a fairy-tale of a love affair with a stranger in ancient times. But at the end of this tale the princess dies too, and, even though the fairy-tale narrative proclaims that "a day will come" when conflict is resolved and happiness is achieved, such fulfillment remains in the realm of fantasy. If this protagonist represents another voice for women, it's one that can't as yet explain its own condition or even offer an account of it, except in the distorted and disguised language of dreams, parapraxes, and hysterical symptoms. After the end of *Malina*, the "Ways of Death" will be told from the dispassionate perspective of reasonable, reliable Malina and seem to take the form of realistic narratives, though a somber subtext will always undercut their conventional surface.

The narrative stance of the five stories of *Three Paths to the Lake* is similarly ironic. The protagonists of the middle three stories are so utterly absorbed by the intensely feminine concerns of the private realm that they can't recognize the disastrous consequences for themselves. In "Problems Problems," Beatrix has withdrawn so completely from all external concerns that she's succumbed to narcissism and spends her time either sleeping or at the beauty parlor. Nearsighted Miranda of "Eyes to Wonder" refuses to wear her glasses so she can avoid seeing anything unpleasant (including her lover's unfaithfulness). By dedicating her story to Georg Groddeck, whose *Book of the It* argues that all physical symptoms have psychic causes, Bachmann underlines the pathological costs of Miranda's cheery feminine inability to engage with reality. Franza Jordan reappears in "The Barking," attempting to care for her husband's neglected elderly mother; the two women collude in their refusal to acknowledge Jordan's ruthlessness and brutality. Only when senility overtakes old Mrs. Jordan can she find expression for her rage: she imagines herself surrounded by the barking of innumerable dogs, her revenge for her son's refusal to let her keep a pet because the dog couldn't stand him.

The middle stories are framed by two longer stories about gifted career women whose professional activities in the public arena help to secure Western hegemony over the rest of the world, though in the female realm of reproduction: one a translator, the other a photographer, both function as media through which the activities of others pass. Though each meets every objective criterion for female autonomy and success, both are emotionally distraught and on the verge of psychic breakdown. In "Word for Word," Nadja leaves the international conference where she's been working as a simultaneous translator for an unsuccessful fling with a married bureaucrat. She's finally consoled when, in a Bible in a hotel desk drawer, she finds a sentence she can't translate, a sign she has not been completely subsumed by her function. In "Three Paths to the Lake," a companion piece to "Youth in an Austrian Town," Elisabeth, a fifty-year-old photojournalist, returns to her hometown, a thinly disguised Klagenfurt, and tries to figure out what's gone wrong with her life. Both frame stories thematize language's inability to convey what is really important, and Elizabeth rages, "Hasn't it ever occurred to anyone that you kill people when you deprive them of the power of speech and with it the power to experience and think" (*Paths* 173). Her passionate and destructive love affairs with men have all ended badly, and she concludes, "It would be best if men and women kept their distance and had nothing to do with each other until both had found their way out of the tangle and confusion, the discrepancy inherent in all relationships" (*Paths* 175). At the story's end, she decides helplessly to accept an assignment in Vietnam in the vain hope that something she does can make the world a little better.

When Bachmann died, she left behind several unfinished "Ways of Death" (mostly written before *Malina*), of which *Requiem for Fanny Goldmann*, published in 1978, and *Gier* (Greed), published in 1982, were the most nearly complete. The protagonists of these fragments, realistic texts with an ironic subtext more like *Three Paths to the Lake* than *Malina*, are also represented as products of a male-dominated social order to which they accommodate themselves and which finally destroys them. Some of Bachmann's readers have succumbed to the temptation to conflate Bachmann's unhappy life and her writing, viewing her, like her female figures, as merely a victim of the social system that produced her. Bachmann's own words may provide more guidance to her readers. In 1972 she responded emphatically to an interviewer, "I myself am a person who never resigned herself, never ever resigned herself, who can't even conceive of that" (*GuI* 118). In the last year of her life she could still maintain: "And I don't believe in this materialism, in this consumer society, in this capitalism, in this monstrosity that's taking place here, and people who enrich themselves on us without having any right to do so. I really do believe in something, and I call it 'A Day Will Come.' And one day it will come. Well, probably it won't come, because it's been destroyed for us so many times, for thousands of years it's been destroyed. It won't come, but I believe in it nonetheless. For if I weren't able to believe in it, then I couldn't write any more" (*GuI* 145).

CHAPTER 2

Bachmann's Feminist Reception

> One must in general be able
> to read a book in different
> ways and to read it
> differently today than
> tomorrow.
>
> (*Ingeborg Bachmann,*
> Wir müssen wahre Sätze finden)

> Every reader, when he reads,
> is in reality a reader of
> himself.
>
> —*Ingeborg Bachmann,*
> Werke, *quoting Proust*

*S*ince the late 1970s, the enthusiastic response of feminist readers, critics, and scholars to the writing of Ingeborg Bachmann has produced a radical reassessment of her work. As I explained in chapter 1, she owed her reputation during her lifetime to the two highly accomplished volumes of lyric poetry she published in the 1950s, *Die gestundete Zeit* and *Anrufung des Großen Bären*. Her critics responded more negatively to her subsequent attempts at prose fiction, *The Thirtieth Year* (1961) and the first finished volumes of her "Ways of Death" cycle, *Malina* (1971) and *Three Paths to the Lake* (1972). But after her death in 1973, feminist readers rediscovered her fiction, now focusing their attention on representations of femininity in the "Ways of Death," augmented in 1978 by the posthumous publication of two novel fragments, *The Franza Case* (now called *The Book of Franza*) and *Requiem for Fanny Goldmann*. By the 1980s "the other Ingeborg Bachmann," as Sigrid Weigel termed her ("Andere" 5), had achieved the status of cult figure within German feminism; feminist literary scholars' spirited and subtle reinterpretations of her writing had produced a renaissance in Bachmann scholarship; and Bachmann's texts had become central to the German feminist literary canon.

In a study of Bachmann's reception before 1973, Constance Hotz argues that 1950s journalists constructed an image of her that met the political needs of their era, turning Bachmann into an "exemplum for [Germany's] reconstruction, its reattainment of international standards, its reachievement of recognition in the world" (72). Here I want to advance a similar thesis about Bachmann's reception by German (and some American) feminists. The feminist reading that produced "the other Ingeborg Bachmann" is, I maintain, also a product of its time, emerging from the cultural climate out of which the German feminist movement grew to advance an interpretation of Bachmann consistent with the movement's theoretical assumptions. This chapter is thus intended to illustrate two of my central theses about the historicity of literary production and reception: that readings of a text, as well as the text itself, are responses to the discursive and other pressures of the historical period from which they emerge; and that since different kinds of readings serve different political ends, disagreements about interpretations in fact are very often the consequence of the different political "positionalities" of those who advance them. After sketching out the political landscape that produced German feminism, I trace the steps by which a particular feminist reading of Bachmann, with affinities to American radical feminism and allegiances to its own version of French feminist poststructuralism, came into being. As I demonstrate, by the mid-1980s that feminist approach had produced an outpouring of Bachmann studies and gained an almost hegemonic control over Bachmann scholarship.

By the end of the 1980s, however, some uncertainty had become apparent in approaches to Bachmann's writing, deriving from a more general confusion about what now counted as a feminist perspective. The course henceforth pursued by feminist Bachmann scholars corresponded generally to the different directions taken by feminist literary scholarship in Germany and Austria, on the one hand, and in English-speaking countries, on the other. Especially in German-speaking countries a number of mostly younger, mostly women scholars continued to apply a feminist-poststructuralist method mainly to Bachmann's prose works. But at least an equal number of both younger and more established scholars in Germany and Austria, even those who had previously identified as feminists, now pursued other aspects of Bachmann's works without making gender a central category of their analysis, even in cases where questions about gender might easily have been posed. Particularly in Britain and North America, in contrast, both younger and more established scholars responded to the critiques of early 1980s feminism to advance more differentiated, historically and culturally specific notions of femininity and gender. They elaborated feminist versions of the many new methods (cultural studies, new historicism, minority studies, postcolonial studies, queer theory) now employed in English-speaking German Studies and also advanced new and creative approaches to Bachmann's writing. At the end of this chapter I argue that feminist Bachmann scholars today confront the challenge of continuing to assert the necessity of gender-based approaches to Bachmann's works while also pursuing new feminist approaches that are adequate to the scholarly and political demands of the new millennium.

When *Malina* and *Three Paths to the Lake* appeared in the early 1970s, they were scarcely acknowledged by the West German women who would soon become feminists, for within the charged political climate of that time, reading novels was a sign of complicity with the bourgeois establishment. The West German student movement had emerged full blown after the June 1967 demonstration against the Shah of Iran, during which a Berlin student was killed. Many New Left activists of that period were convinced that students could become the vanguard of worldwide revolution, joining their efforts to those of their comrades in Third World countries such as Cuba, the Congo, and Vietnam. "A specter is haunting Europe, the specter of revolution," German author Hans Magnus Enzensberger proclaimed in *Kursbuch* in January 1968, and ten months later he declared, again in *Kursbuch*, that bourgeois literature was quite irrelevant to the tasks German revolutionaries then confronted: "In our situation, it is not possible to determine a significant social function for literary works of art" (7, 51). For, as Hazel E. Hazel has explained, that exuberant period around 1968 was "the time when literature was deemed superfluous and even in part was, since we no longer expected literature, but rather reality, to fulfill our desires" (129–30). Or as Michael Schneider put it, "Everyday life itself was to become a work of art within which the human instinct to play, freed from interior and exterior necessity, from fear, exploitation, and alienated labor, could finally realize itself" (147). But as the student movement waned, the New Left abandoned its earlier antiauthoritarianism, maintaining that the proper form of revolutionary self-organization was the highly disciplined cadre group organized along the Leninist model, and enjoined its adherents to go into the factories to organize the real revolutionary subject, the German proletariat. By subordinating individual needs to the purposes of the collective, the "K-Groups," which "around 1969/70 sprang up like mushrooms," as Schneider (151) later recalled, put an end to earlier New Left attempts to combine the personal and the political. The dogmatic and economistic appropriation of Marxism by the K-Groups throttled hopes for the development of an analysis and a form of political activism that would have demanded the transformation of both personal life and of the larger worldwide structures of domination that had originally called the New Left into being.

Objective and subjective factors combined to produce West Germany's much-heralded *Tendenzwende* (change of political direction) in the mid-1970s. An

economic downturn, the *Radikalenerlaß* (decree against radicals) of 1972, and
the subsequent *Berufsverbot* (ban on careers) later in the decade caused many
erstwhile revolutionaries to have second thoughts about the wisdom of their
commitment to revolution. The self-denial demanded by their commitment to
a doctrinaire Marxism now turned into its opposite, as Schneider has explained:
"If for five years they hadn't acknowledged anything else but the rigorous logic
of *Capital*, now they projected their loathing of their own rigorousness onto the
theorist of *Capital*, that is, onto Marxism. And of course in the same moment
they rediscovered their old love for beauty, for art, and for sensuality. . . . And
if for five years happiness consisted solely of socking it to the class enemy, now
happiness again consisted solely of the happiness of the individual" (155).

   This is the moment at which West German feminism emerged, simultaneously a critique of the male left's theoretical and practical subordination of
women and personal needs to its own purposes *and* an expression of the larger
cultural move away from politics to a new sensibility and new subjectivity. West
German women from the left determined that the study of Marx did not allow
them to address their own condition, as one woman from the socialist women's
group in Frankfurt, the Weiberrat (Dames' Council) recalled in the first *Frauenjahrbuch* (Women's yearbook): "So it came about that the longer we dealt with
Marxist theory, the less attention we paid to the fact of women's oppression"
(*Frauenjahrbuch* 21). Instead, West German women of the early 1970s increasingly organized in autonomous groups around issues of immediate relevance to
their lives: they joined the campaign against paragraph 218 (the antiabortion
clause of the Federal Republic's Basic Law), addressed issues of sexual preference, motherhood, and contraception, founded women's centers and *Selbsterfah-
rungsgruppen* ("self-experiencing groups," the German term for consciousness-
raising groups); organized *Frauenfeste* (large women-only parties); and celebrated
sisterhood. The striking political shift that the new politics of self-affirmation
and self-discovery represented was captured by a cartoon from the *Frauenjahrbuch* in which a female figure proclaimed: "The most wonderful day of my life
was the day I discovered my clitoris" (*Frauenjahrbuch* 77).

   For a variety of reasons West German feminists thus focused their political
analysis primarily on women's oppression in the private sphere and engaged in
political activities mainly in cultural areas. At its best, feminism made connections between gender issues, private life, subjectivity, sexuality, and every other
area of social life, a deepening and broadening of conceptions of the political,
visions of social change, and forms of political struggle. But when those connections were not made, some kinds of feminism, particularly those focused

only on improving individual women's personal lives, represented a retreat from politics, not an expansion of them. West German feminists' general suspicion of Marxism and other "male" theories hindered the development of an analysis that could have located their private sufferings in the context of its specific determinants within a larger social framework. Some 1970s feminists retained a commitment to left analysis and left practice, and the one major exception to feminist hostility to Marxism was the wages-for-housework debate of the late 1970s. But many other feminists (often those who came to politics after the decline of the left) now elaborated new forms of feminist theory, arguing that since the world-historical defeat of matriarchy, an undifferentiated patriarchy had been responsible for the oppression of women everywhere. Socialist feminism played an even smaller role in the West German women's movement than in the United States and in other West European countries, and the political stance of the early West German feminist movement as a whole resembled that of American radical feminism (Kulawik 77). Those politics dominated West German feminism into the 1980s, as Myra Marx Ferree explains: "The concept "feminist" generally means a radical feminist analysis, which takes oppression by patriarchy as its starting point, manifested in male control of the female body—in marriage, motherhood, sexuality, and the workplace. . . . Gender is viewed as the primary, fundamental difference; class and ethnicity are in contrast secondary qualities and competing forms of political identity. Even though class occasionally is used as an analogy and metaphor for gender, gender counts as the more fundamental criterion" ("Gleichheit" 289–90).

From the mid-1980s onward, however, West German feminist consensus about a radical feminist analysis and an autonomous political strategy was drawn partially into question both by the changes attendant upon the Christian Democrat accession to power in 1982 and by the activities of large numbers of women in the Greens and other political parties. The emergence of Afro-German women and other women of color as a constituency within West German feminism raised significant questions about the purported unity of interests of all women—questions only compounded after unification by the discovery of the extraordinary differences, manifesting themselves very swiftly as anger and hostility, between West German and East German women in life experience, self-definition, political priorities, and forms of organization. Nor were feminists immune to the larger shift in political atmosphere occasioned by the collapse of communism and the Federal Republic's absorption of the GDR. As Konrad Jarausch observed: "The defeat of communism has fundamentally transformed the conditions for the old ideological confrontation between Left and Right by discrediting the former and bolstering the latter. Newly confident due to their triumph over the East, various economic, moral, and national conservatives are trying to reclaim the ground they had largely lost to the new social movements after the cultural revolution of 1968" (10). In part because they lacked any supra-regional forms of organization that could defend women's interests on the national level, German feminists found themselves incapable of responding politically to conservative assaults on women's rights, assaults including the elimination of "socialist achievements" that had benefited GDR women and the decision of the Constitutional Court to overturn the Bundestag compromise on abortion legislation and declare that abortion in Germany was henceforth "illegal"—if also "free from punishment." A decade after unification the perception still prevailed that "women were the losers of German unification." Despite hopes to the contrary, the Social Democratic (SPD)/Green coalition government's accession to power in fall 1998 did not in fact represent an enormous lurch to the left. (An example of the coalition's break with what might earlier have been regarded as traditional Social Democratic politics can be seen in the comment of Peter Struck, then leader of the SPD parliamentary faction: "The old motto of a workers' party, taking from the rich to give to the poor, doesn't suit a modern society" [Germnews 10 August 1999]). Why the new coalition government did not bring about a sudden upturn in feminist fortunes is perhaps also suggested by remarks made by Doris Schroeder, the chancellor's wife, in a *Stern* interview of Summer 1999: "I like to be in the background," and "If you're good and reach people's hearts, it doesn't matter what your sex is" ("Frau Doris").

The analysis developed by feminist intellectuals (including writers and literary critics) in the late 1970s to justify and advance the politics of the autonomous women's movement in West Germany elaborated upon its basic principles. Gender was the most fundamental form of oppression; as Verena Stefan put it in *Häutungen* (Shedding) in 1975; "Sexism goes deeper than racism than class struggle" (34). Women everywhere and always were victims of men's violence, as Alice Schwarzer declared in *Der "kleine Unterschied" und seine großen Folgen* (The "little difference" and its big consequences, 1975): "Nothing, neither race nor class, determines a human life as much as gender. And in that regard women and men are victims of their roles—but women are victims of the victims" (178). (That portrayal of women as victims, Angelika Bammer has argued, was particularly attractive to German feminists, since it relieved them of the necessity of pondering women's complicity in National Socialism.) Women and men were fundamentally different from each other, and those differences should be preserved, not eradicated. Men's domination over women took the form of the oppression, suppression, and/or repression of femininity, a monolithic and all-encompassing patriarchy expressing itself most perniciously through its "colonization" of female consciousness and culture. Feminists believed they discerned preexisting alternatives to patriarchy in the past either of the human species (in prehistoric matriarchal societies or other preserves of women's culture) or of the individual (in preoedipal psychic organization or the prediscursive drives of the female body). Culture and consciousness thus became the main arenas of feminist social transformation. The task of feminism was to disrupt, deconstruct, and destroy patriarchal culture and to retrieve and elaborate alternative female forms for the future so as to create a new feminist culture that could promote the emergence of a new female subjectivity. After an initial flirtation with theories of matriarchy, many West German feminist literary scholars turned enthusiastically to a direction of feminist literary analysis that had begun to seep into Germany from France: French poststructuralist feminism. Drawing on that French theory, literary scholars looked for works by women that could disrupt the all-embracing phallogocentric symbolic order, recover a hitherto repressed femininity (sometimes defined as a dispersed, destabilized identity or that which eludes definition [Fraser, Introduction 7]), and create new forms for female subjectivity that would finally permit female otherness to speak.

By the end of the 1980s, a number of feminist academics (perhaps more frequently in the United States than in Germany) had raised some troubling questions about a radical feminist analysis. Economic and political changes over the course of the decade led feminists to question whether domination was really exercised mainly in the symbolic realm of culture, consciousness, or discourse. More complex ideas of how power functioned suggested that it was wrong to argue for the existence of only one single system of domination or to elide patriarchy with other structural forms of oppression (such as fascism, capitalism, colonialism, enlightenment). Some feminists questioned the utility of the term "patriarchy" (or "phallogocentrism") altogether, since it suggested that a single form of male domination was responsible for the oppression of all women. Similarly, they questioned the invocation of a female identity, female subjectivity, or femininity repressed by a dominant order, since it seemed premised on a belief in a transhistorical female essence, as if only one sort of woman had existed throughout all time and culture. Feminists increasingly rejected the argument that women were always victims of the dominant order and never agents of oppression themselves. Among other U.S. feminist theorists, Judith Butler, whose works enjoyed a surprising success in Germany in the early 1990s, questioned the stability and even the political utility of categories such as "woman," suggesting that "performance," "masquerade," or even at times "parody" better described manifestations of femininity. Such fundamental challenges to a paradigm that had predominated in feminist analysis for over a decade now left feminist literary scholars in some confusion about how to proceed—not the least in the area of Bachmann scholarship.

The analysis that would make Bachmann's prose accessible to German women had not yet emerged, of course, in the years before Bachmann's death when her last prose works were published. In the polarized political context of the early 1970s, *Malina* and *Three Paths to the Lake* could not help but disappoint (or even enrage) engaged readers, and, as Elke Atzler showed in a review of *Malina*'s reception, even mainstream reviewers lamented its "turning a blind eye to social constraints" (157). A review by Michael Springer in *konkret* was typical of the New Left response to *Malina*. Springer is quite willing to acknowledge the accuracy of Bachmann's portrait of her protagonist: "Doubtless the kind of private hell in which the main figure of *Malina* lives is reality for most good bourgeois housewives." But he protests the absence of two elements that really are missing from *Malina*: explicit social criticism and resistance. By failing explicitly to show how (or even that) her figure's suffering was embedded in and derived from the bourgeois society to which she belongs, Springer argues, Bachmann permits readings of her novel that do not draw that society into question: "Anyone who doesn't question the bourgeois lifestyle and the manners and manias with which it cages in women makes himself complicit in it." And Bachmann's portrayal of a woman utterly unable to defend herself against her tormentors suggests that her fate is inevitable: "Who is helped when it's shown that it's impossible that way [*daß es so nicht geht*], and when it's shown in such a way that dying in dubious beauty is the unavoidable consequence of these complications—as a tragedy?" (60).

Springer's was not the only left response possible in that period; Hans Mayer, indebted to a different kind of Marxist criticism (and a far better critic), wrote a sympathetic review of *Malina* that defended it against leftist misreadings: "In reviews people accused this 'heroine' and her author of being someone who, in the midst of bourgeois prosperity, is only striving for individual happiness. . . . Those who read that way have misunderstood the novel. The self-realization of the 'I' is prevented by the social conditions that always stand in the way of such fulfilled moments" (164). But there is no reason to believe that women of the New Left responded differently from Springer, and Sigrid Weigel has commented on "politically engaged women's lack of attention to Bachmann's novel *Malina* when it appeared in 1971" (*Stimme* 27).

But if politicized women of the early 1970s were uninterested in *Malina,* that was not at all the case for a more general female readership. Springer's review had suggested that the interests served by books like *Malina* were those of the *Kulturbetrieb* (culture industry): "By means of clever packaging this anti–Love Story was turned into a bestseller; the 'better circles' enjoyed the bitter taste, which by contrast sweetened their shallow lives" (60). Perhaps for that reason, *Malina* enjoyed an immediate, if surprising, popularity among readers who evidently did not measure it by New Left standards. As *Die Zeit* reported, its publisher, Suhrkamp Verlag, launched an exceptionally cynical public relations campaign that targeted women readers: "A mail-in campaign was begun last week to gain readers, not just buyers, for this book, which Suhrkamp's director Siegfried Unseld hopes will outsell Hildegard Knef's *Gift Horse.* The question posed on the dust cover, 'Murder or Suicide,' is to be answered on a mail-in coupon, with a one-sentence justification—and only women are allowed to participate. First, second, and third prizes consist of a skiing weekend with Unseld at St. Moritz" (P n.p.). Released in April, *Malina* reached third place on the *Spiegel*'s best-seller list by mid-May and, Vienna's *Wochenpresse* reported, on May 24 moved up to second place, just behind the American tearjerker *Love Story* ("Gut" n.p.).

It may be possible to regard the enthusiastic reaction to *Malina* as an indication of prescient readers' awareness of the impending sea change in German literary production that was soon to produce the "New Subjectivity" of the 1970s. Wolfgang Kraus, for instance, attributes some portion of the novel's success to the "rise of the 'soft wave,' a kind of new romanticism, which also pushes a different literary genre to the fore. If *Malina* had appeared two years ago, perhaps even a year ago, it's doubtful that it would have enjoyed the same resonance with readers as now" (n.p.). Perhaps, too, one could recognize in women readers' enthusiasm for *Malina* a response not so different from the feminist excitement several years later about Verena Stefan's *Shedding* and other semiautobiographical women's narratives of the 1970s: they believed they recognized their own lives in the story of *Malina's* "I." (Weigel suggested something of that sort a decade later when she deplored "the proliferation of a way of female reading that consists of identifying with the female figures of texts, understanding them as empirical subjects, and reducing these novels to the stories of women victims' love and suffering" [" Ingeborg Bachmann: Was folgt" 3].) If that is the case, *Malina* represents one of the bridges that links prefeminist to feminist consciousness in Germany. Yet that popular reading of *Malina* was not an altogether unproblematic one for feminism. On the one hand, *Malina* helped women readers to acknowledge the existence of male power over women and the central role it plays in women's lives—a gain over the response of *Malina's* mostly male reviewers and an important step in the direction of feminism. But in other ways the popular reading of *Malina* did not challenge the prevailing understanding of gender relations. The woman as victim is, after all, a central figure of many genres of bourgeois literature, and it was quite possible for women to read *Malina* as confirming traditional gender expectations: in that novel men and women are polar opposites; women's concern is the private realm and emotional life; women are consumed by their love for men, men mistreat and abandon women, and women suffer. Perhaps *Malina* allowed early women readers the pleasure of having it both ways: they could experience a feminist indignation at the power men hold over women and satisfaction that the full extent of women's degradation had been revealed without having to consider how their own lives might have to change to transform those unequal arrangements. In some ways, I am inclined to believe, Bachmann's early readers found and enjoyed in the novel exactly what Bachmann's critics accused her of writing, the story of an unhappy love affair, so that to them there really did not seem to be such a long distance from *Malina* to *Love Story.* This reading of Bachmann's novel as a narrative of male power and female victimization would continue to influence feminists' reception of *Malina* (and, later, of other "Ways of Death" novels) far into the 1980s.

In the earliest responses to Bachmann by feminist critics, however, the woman-as-victim model of feminism had not yet made its appearance. The first clearly feminist essay appears to have been written by Ursula Püschel, a GDR critic, and was first published in the West German journal *Kürbiskern* in 1978. Püschel is critical of both the mainstream and New Left reception of Bachmann and particularly indignant about critics' insistence on using Bachmann's biography as a criterion of their literary evaluation: "Who would dare to mention a male writer's friends or lovers in assessments of his literary potency?" (121) Probably under the influence of Christa Wolf, whose 1966 essay, "Truth That Can Be Faced—Ingeborg Bachmann's Prose," was reprinted as the afterword to a 1976 GDR edition of Bachmann's stories, Püschel attempts to counter criticism of Bachmann's work as politically *unverbindlich* (noncommittal) by arguing that Bachmann's writing was instead a response to the human deformations produced by her postwar society. In "The Good God of Manhattan," "Undine Goes," and *Malina,* those deformations are represented via "the constitutive human relationship, the relationship of man and a woman, one of the great themes of Ingeborg Bachmann," relationships that bear "the stigma of patriarchy" (113). And though Püschel concedes that *Malina* might give rise to the impression that men are responsible for all social ills—"as if their causes in this male society were the men themselves and not social cir- cumstances" (117)—reading the novel the way Bachmann intended it, as the entrée to the entire "Ways of Death" cycle, shows that the author is concerned with "investigating social conditions, of which the daily murder of humanity, the 'ways of death,' forms part." Bachmann's treatment of gender, Püschel maintains, precisely illustrates the charge she gives to literature in her Frank- furt lectures, to represent what exists and to present that for which the time had not yet come: "The limits of the possible and the reactions to transgressions of those limits become visible in the sphere of male-female relations" (116). Püschel is able to acknowledge the centrality of Bachmann's concern with gender and patriarchy while simultaneously embedding it in a specific social setting that is responsible for the particular forms these male-female relations assume. Püschel's essay represents a direction in which feminist scholarship on Bachmann could have developed but did not choose to go, and the essay has been virtually ignored in subsequent treatments of Bachmann.

Writing at about the same time as Püschel, the first West German critic to connect Bachmann to feminism in print was a man. In accounts of the aston- ishing transformation that Bachmann's reputation underwent in the decade after her death, an exchange between Peter Horst Neumann, writing in *Merkur* in 1978, and Gisela Lindemann, who answered Neumann in the *Neue Rund- schau* a year later, occupies a central position. Neumann reads "Undine Goes" as an anticipation of "the essential motifs of the later women's movement, . . . one of the most far-reaching of the intellectual and political movements of this period." But though he can accept Bachmann's "hatred of men" in that story, he rejects *Malina*, whose "whole message" had already been presented in "Undine goes." Yet he is confused, Neumann continues, by the fact that only men share his objections to *Malina*, its "garrulousness, lack of precision, triviality"—while women defend Bachmann's novel vehemently. Neumann concludes that *Weiblichkeit* (femininity) is the key variable: "I know that I may make a fool of myself using this word. But in my aesthetic judgments of this novel I am incapable of ignoring its constant appeal to a gender-specific sensibility. . . . I can't get over the feeling that, as a male reader, I have failed this book" (1134– 1135).

In her response to Neumann, Lindemann assumes a position that places her between the social engagement of the early 1970s and later feminists' blanket condemnations of patriarchy (a position Neumann already equates with feminism *tout court*). She is not prepared to claim Bachmann uncritically for feminism. Instead, comparing her with Doris Lessing's Anna Wulf in *The Golden Notebook*, Lindemann proposes that the flaws in Bachmann's writing may have socially occasioned, gender-specific causes: "Perhaps Bachmann's prose was indeed not capable of all her millennial theme demanded, so that the reviewers who were dissatisfied with her prose were right, but for the wrong reasons" (271). Yet she aligns herself with later feminists' universalizing tendencies when she extrapolates from Bachmann's and Lessing's novels and her own experience to conclude that women's sense of individual grievance is their most powerful emotional response to their oppression: "For reasons that are obvious and in the meantime have gradually become well known, for reasons that derive from the centuries-long subordination of women in patriarchal society, it's obvious—more's the pity—that the deepest feeling of which women are capable is not at all love or devotion or whatever else that nice stuff is called, but rather the feeling of being injured [*Kränkung*]" (273). What both disturbs and fascinates Lindemann is Bachmann's inability to move beyond "pure lamentation," her "tone of being betrayed" (274)—the aspect of Bachmann's writing that would engage ever more feminists in the subsequent decade.

In the early 1980s, a third West German feminist, also with some allegiance to the left, expressed dissatisfaction with the adequacy of Bachmann's formulations for feminism. Marlis Gerhardt discerns in many women writers of the 1970s an inability to disengage themselves from the gender polarities that had shaped literature and life in the nineteenth century: "Precisely in new literature by women, thus in that very literature that has something to do with the label 'feminism,' it's stereotypically a matter of the suffering of women and the actions of men, of female introspection and male room to maneuver" (128). The "I" of Bachmann's *Malina* cannot even hope that Ivan will love her as she desires, yet she continues helplessly to subjugate herself to him, while regarding the aspects of herself she projects onto Malina—rationality, autonomy, competence—as irreconcilable with her femininity. Gerhardt proposes that Bachmann's works demonstrate a "refusal . . . to step out of the poetic image that, in its own interest, a male culture has declared to be the 'nature' of woman" (140). To Bachmann's writing Gerhardt contrasts texts of other writers of the 1970s—Christa Wolf, Irmtraud Morgner, Sarah Kirsch, Barbara Frischmuth—who could imagine possibilities for women apart from those to which men had consigned them. Their works confront the same conflicts as Bachmann's but think beyond them to envision other alternatives—self-experiments—for women which will not include their self-destruction.

Bachmann's earliest U.S. feminist critics also sought female figures who were defiant, not victimized, and advanced a variety of interpretations to make Bachmann's texts correspond to their own needs: some were not prepared to read Bachmann's works as narratives of female subjugation at all; others criticized her for her failure to imagine more positive feminist solutions. Ellen Summerfield, who had written the first monograph devoted entirely to *Malina* before feminism reached German Studies in the United States, also presented at the 1977 Amherst Colloquium what was probably the first feminist address of Bachmann scholarship. There she argued that *Three Paths to the Lake* portrayed five modern women who had successfully achieved their independence from men— a conclusion with which subsequent feminist scholarship would soon take issue ("Verzicht"). Dinah Dodds and Ritta Jo Horsley presented papers on "A Step towards Gomorrah" at a session titled "Lesbian Themes in German Literature" at the Women in German conference, October 1979. Both praised Bachmann's daring choice of topic but criticized her for failing to create characters who could abandon hierarchical male models and envision an equal partnership of women. Margret Eifler, writing in German but for an American journal, *Modern Austrian Literature*, concludes that *Malina* is about women's unwillingness to remain subjugated to men: "The fundamental statement of this novel aims at saying no once and for all to the possibility of a relationship between man and woman" (379). The absorption of the "I" into Malina is for Eifler a willed act, "self-extinction of femininity for the sake of a doubtful self-preservation," with Malina's masculinity as "the least of all possible evils" (388). Eifler regards the disappearance of the "I" into the wall as the renunciation of "slavish love" (380) and as "militant self-assertion" (382) (a gesture also figured in Undine's return to the water). If the novel itself ends in solipsism, silence, and resignation, Eifler nonetheless hopes that the "expression of this epochal violence and mayhem can influence the course of human history" (390).

Most 1970s feminists in Germany and the United States treated Bachmann's prose texts as more or less realistic representations of female experience, measured Bachmann's figures according to feminist criteria, and assumed that a relationship existed between feminist scholarship and the task of feminist social transformation. But by the 1980s feminists were less inclined to insist upon an immediate connection between feminist literary analysis and feminist political practice (possibly because the new conservative governments in both West Germany and the United States made swift changes in feminists' interest much less likely). In that context, new feminist approaches could arise that asked quite different kinds of questions about Bachmann's work. Those approaches drew upon the assumptions of the new directions in feminism that had gained prominence in the late 1970s. Feminist Bachmann scholars now tried to read her work as an expression of repressed femininity, regarded previous negative responses to her writing as an unwillingness to engage with female otherness, and banished ideology criticism altogether from the repertoire of critical tools they applied to her writing. *The Book of Franza,* first published in 1978 in the four-volume edition of the *Works,* replaced *Malina* at the center of the feminist Bachmann canon and was often regarded as the Rosetta stone that provided the key to the feminist translation of Bachmann's other works. Following her cue in the preface to *Franza* that "the real settings" were "laboriously covered over by the exterior ones" (*W* 3: 342), many Bachmann scholars also shifted their attention from the content to the form of her work, now particularly interested in how she drew what they regarded as patriarchal structures and language into question. In its acceptance of essential differences between men and women, the new feminist response to Bachmann in some ways harked back to popular readings of *Malina* that likewise did not challenge gender dichotomies. But in its emphasis on the relationship of symbolic or discursive structures to questions of femininity and masculinity, the new approach also prepared the way for feminist poststructuralist analyses of Bachmann.

A widely read essay that Elisabeth Lenk published in 1981 in the feminist journal *Courage,* "Pariabewußtsein schreibender Frauen" (The pariah consciousness of writing women), featured Bachmann prominently in showing how the new approach could be applied to women writers. Lenk does not yet call upon French feminists as her authorities, yet many other elements of the new approach are already present in her essay. Women, Lenk maintains, are the outcasts, pariahs of all societies, like Jews, Indians, and gypsies—like Franza, who considers herself "of inferior race," "a Papua." Qualitatively different from and not subsumable into a dominant homogeneous order, women belong to another order altogether, "to the heterogeneous" (27): "The bloody or bloodless annihilation of woman, her exclusion from society, her reduction to a beast of burden, on which, as on its foundations, the society rests, was the precondition for the classical ideal, the equilibrium of the homogeneous" (34). Women face two choices: to participate in the dominant order at all, they must deny their heterogeneity and hate themselves; alternatively, they are compelled to embrace their heterogeneity—that is, develop a "pariah consciousness." Only those who stand outside society—like women writers—can give adequate expression to it. That, Lenk declares in conclusion, is Bachmann's accomplishment:

What else could the novel cycle "Ways of Death" have been but a description of the imperceptible, bloodless annihilation of the other within the human being, of the female "I," which isn't even allowed to say "I" any more: of an It over which men negotiate.

In the opinion of the champions of culture, this It should learn to disappear without remainder into a new homogeneous "I." Then the eternal source of disorder would be out of the way. At the end of Ingeborg Bachmann's novel *Malina* the female "I" has disappeared: a normal process, the process of female socialization. But what from the perspective of society looks like successful normalization becomes in Bachmann's hands, in the sense of pariah consciousness, an accusation against the whole society. "I don't have any sex, not any longer, they ripped it out of me." Female socialization is depicted as a crime against women, as a process of annihilation. "It was murder," reads the last sentence of the novel *Malina*. (34)

In Lenk's essay most of the components of the new feminism are present. She extracts the oppression of women from its historical determinants and projects it back into the beginnings of history, when all women became social outcasts for the same (biological) reason, all subject to the same kind of male power in the same way. Women are by definition outside of and victimized by the male order, hence without relationship to or responsibility for its actions. The dominant order has become so all-encompassing that it is impossible (hence not necessary) to imagine any concrete political steps that can be taken against it. Simply to change one's consciousness and articulate otherness in writing is already a mighty feminist act.

In the Federal Republic the first feminist analysis informed by the new approach which was devoted entirely to Bachmann was published by Ria Endres in 1981 in two somewhat different forms in *Die Zeit* and the *Neue Rundschau*. Endres draws on a different philosophical model to make arguments similar to Lenk's. Launching a frontal attack on efforts to connect literature and politics in the late 1960s and the 1970s, "a time of fetishized concentration on social phenomena," Endres also relies upon an understanding of patriarchy that encompasses (while extracting away from) all of human history, folding fascism into the grander structure of patriarchy by equating the Heideggerian *Angst* that derived from the "knowledge about the beginning of a new way of Being (patriarchy)" ("Erklär" 51) with the *Todesangst* (deathly fear) that Bachmann experienced when Hitler's troops invaded Klagenfurt. She too assumes the existence of diametrically opposed principles of masculinity and femininity, masculinity exercising its control via the "way of Being" of patriarchy, which had conquered an earlier matriarchy: "'Primary' Being ends at the latest at the time of the old Greeks; it is like the paradise of a lost world, in which there exists the possibility of matriarchy and thereby another way of Being" ("Erklär"51). Under patriarchy, language as well has been brought under male control, obscuring expressions of femininity: "Seen from the perspective of its origins, language is magical and bisexual. But in the history of patriarchy a secondary force field emerged. It is allocated to the father and saw to it that the female-matriarchal diminished or was so fully concealed that it could scarcely be discerned any more" ("Wahrheit" 82). Both "Undine Goes" and *Malina* show that "this contest over life and death was waged in the world of language." *Malina*'s absorption of the "I" at the end of Bachmann's novel is a dramatization of the "loss of female identity," and the Ungargasse is "the site of the defeat of femininity." Bachmann's accomplishment lies in her ability to convey "the essence of male cruelty and female martyrdom" ("Erklär" 51).

An essay of my own was (as I later regretted) the first to make an explicit connection between Bachmann, psychoanalysis, and French theory, and at least one of the first to treat Bachmann's writing as an anticipation of French theory. (It is reprinted as chapter 3 of this volume). In that essay, I read *Malina* through the theoretical lens of feminist poststructuralism, maintaining in the first sentence that the novel is concerned with the discursive status of female subjectivity: "Ingeborg Bachmann's *Malina* is about the absence of a female voice; in some respects it reads like an illustration of the feminist theory which has evolved since its publication to explain why, within Western discourse, women are permitted no voice and subjectivity of their own" ("In the Cemetary" 75). I situate Bachmann's concern in *Malina* with gender and language in the context of her statements about language, the dominant order, and challenges to the order in her essays and earlier works. Through a close reading of the text I try to show how the textual practices of the novel undermine its realism and thematize the relationship of femininity to representation. Despite my analysis of the text's symbolic structures, my essay still displays my very strong inclination to identify with Bachmann's protagonist (one of the reasons, I recall, that I had some trouble writing the article: in what voice does a female scholar write about the absence of a female voice?). My analysis of *Malina* places me squarely in the woman-as-victim camp. But I also understand Bachmann's project and my own to be both a deconstructive and constructive one in the service of feminism. Bachmann "found a language to write the story of women without language," I maintain, and I argue that feminists too "can read her novel as part of our struggle to challenge those categories within which we have no right to speak as women and to construct some other, more authentic female voice" ("In the Cemetery" 102, 76).

Christa Gürtler was the first German-language feminists to apply French theory to Bachmann. In her 1982 dissertation, *Schreiben Frauen anders?* (Do women write differently?), she investigated various feminist theoretical models of the early 1980s, including Cixous and Irigaray, at some length but had difficulty applying the theory because her analyses examined the themes rather than the structures of Bachmann's and the Austrian author Barbara Frischmuth's works: marriage, sexuality, female identity, patriarchy, female liberation. One of the dissertation's best chapters applies French theory to *The Book of Franza* (the first example of what would in the course of the decade become a small industry devoted to connecting French theory to *Franza*). Gürtler's interpretation of *Franza* brought French feminist theory into the mainstream of Bachmann criticism when it was published in revised form as the lead essay in Hans Höller's pathbreaking anthology *Der dunkle Schatten, dem ich schon seit Anfang folge* (The dark shadow that I've followed from the beginning—a collection that also included another feminist contribution by Karen Achberger, an examination of subtexts in Bachmann's writing that challenged patriarchal discourse, and an essay more skeptical of feminist approaches by Sigrid Schmid-Bortenschlager).

Gürtler was the first to read *Franza* as a novel about the encounter of two systems of thought: on the one side, Franza's husband's (male) "fascist thinking"; on the other, Franza's (female) *ver-rückter Diskurs* (dis-placed/crazy discourse, a fashionable pun of the period)—"the different image of a different woman, who speaks differently than we all learned to do and which we are used to" (82 citing Hassauer 56). Jordan, also portrayed as a colonizer who wishes to destroy all otherness, drives Franza into madness that expresses itself via the body, in hysterical symptoms of the sort French feminists had described as a substitute for the female voice. As Gürtler views it, "Franza's magical way of being (for Ingeborg Bachmann the female way) removes itself from rational (male) analysis and is threatening for the man. Ingeborg Bachmann insists on the difference of the sexes; for her woman is the other/second sex, for whom it isn't possible within patriarchy to be a human being, because here to be a human being means to be a man. But she also insists that the female way of life is the more human" (72). Gürtler also argues that Bachmann overcomes female speechlessness in her writing through the articulation of an alternative female voice and claims Bachmann for feminism by maintaining that in the "Ways of Death" she attempts "to describe the female experience of the world . . . in a very partisan way" (82). Gürtler's analysis is not a very systematic one, but her essay nonetheless shows the ease with which *The Book of Franza* accommodated and could be made to illustrate the prevailing feminist paradigms of the decade—doubtless one reason that in the next years *Franza* would move to the center of the feminist Bachmann canon. Her essay also illustrates the elision of a variety of systems of domination into one undifferentiated and all-encompassing system, of which the protagonists of the "Ways of Death" are victims. That elision would characterize feminist Bachmann interpretations for most of the rest of the decade.

Christa Wolf's enthusiasm about Bachmann's works in the early 1980s helped bring that new feminist reading of Bachmann to the attention of a wider German reading public. In 1966, Wolf had written a response to the Frankfurt lectures and *The Thirtieth Year* which in my view (see chapter 5) still counts as one of the finest essays on Bachmann's early prose. There Wolf maintains that Bachmann's prose texts address the state of human subjectivity under particular historical conditions (Ursula Püschel's position a decade later). She argues that Bachmann's concern with language in the early texts served a goal that was deeply and directly political, an effort to provide her readers with new categories of perception that would help them understand and change the world. Bachmann's influence on Wolf's writing has been apparent since the 1960s, and in the 1970s she began explicitly to acknowledge Bachmann as her mentor. Most significant for the purposes of this discussion is the evidence in Wolf's writing, beginning in the mid-1970s, of her growing allegiance to a model of feminist analysis that dominated Western feminist thought of the same period. The story "Self-Experiment" (1974) had already shown Wolf to be a quite early proponent of women's difference from and superiority to men. In her essays on the women Romantics she appeals to those women's experience to provide a still-compelling alternative to an instrumental rationality that had increasingly assumed control of bourgeois society. In her Büchner Prize speech, Wolf portrays woman as being outside the "citadel of reason" throughout human history, becoming subject to its laws only in the twentieth century, when she entered men's world and engaged in men's activities. Wolf begins the fourth of her Frankfurt lectures (held in spring 1982 at the University of Frankfurt and published a year later as *Voraussetzung einer Erzählung-Kassandra* [Conditions of a narrative: Cassandra]) with an explicit listing of some of the most popular Western feminist texts of the decade—including studies of matriarchy and patriarchy, goddesses and Amazons, femininity and writing, and Irigaray—texts, Wolf declares, whose influence over her she could compare only with her discovery of Marx. Wolf's reading of Bachmann in the fourth lecture is advanced under the influence of— perhaps even in the name of—that kind of feminism.

In that lecture, Wolf, like many contemporary Western feminists, also premises her analysis on the presumption of a matriarchal society organized along principles preferable to those of the present—that was overthrown in Greek antiquity by a system of male dominance that still continues without fundamental changes. Women do not fit into that society; they can sometimes articulate alternatives to it but mostly are its victims. That is the context within which Wolf locates Bachmann:

> I claim that every woman in this century and in our culture sphere who has ventured into male-dominated institutions—"literature" and "aesthetics" are such institutions—must have experienced the desire for self-destruction. In her novel *Malina*, Ingeborg Bachmann has the woman disappear inside the wall at the end, and the man, Malina, who is a part of her, serenely states the case: "There is no woman here."
>
> The last sentence reads: "It was murder."
>
> It was also suicide. (*Cassandra* 299)

Bachmann's "Ways of Death" cannot be pressed into conventional male aesthetic forms because (unlike, say, Flaubert's *Madame Bovary*) it derives its different morphology from Bachmann's female experience: "But Ingeborg Bachmann *is* that nameless woman in *Malina*, she is the woman Franza in the novel fragment *The Franza Case* who simply cannot get a grip on her life, cannot give it a form; who simply cannot manage to make her experience into a presentable story, cannot produce it out of herself as an aesthetic product" (*Cassandra* 301). Wolf's lecture culminates in a discussion of *Franza*, which she regards as evidence for her argument. Franza stands for those "who live magically (a description true, says Wolf, of every woman—"seeress, poetess, priestess, idol, subject of artworks" [*Cassandra* 304]—about whom her lecture speaks), and who are so great a threat to that representative of evil masculine, white, Western science that he must eradicate them. Wolf concludes with the novel's description of the power of white men to conquer with their spirit what they can not otherwise possess: "They will come in spirit if they can no longer come in any other way. And they will be resurrected in a brown and a black brain; it will always be the whites, even then. They will continue to own the world in this roundabout way" (*Cassandra* 305). That, she tells her readers, would be Cassandra's prophecy today. The consequence of Wolf's arguments on behalf of women, against the power that men have exercised over them and others, was, in some contrast to her project in *Patterns of Childhood*, to extract women from their own culture and exempt them from responsibility for it. Those are also the arguments that underlie Wolf's own novel *Cassandra* and are, in my view, responsible for some of its weaknesses.

Sigrid Weigel is the West German feminist literary scholar whose work most strongly influenced Bachmann criticism of the 1980s—and whose scholarly method Bachmann seems strongly to have influenced. Beginning with her widely read "Der schielende Blick: Thesen zur Geschichte weiblicher Schreibpraxis" (Double Focus: Theses on the history of women's writing), published in 1983, Weigel laid the theoretical foundations for a German feminist-poststructuralist criticism, a method that she often elaborated with reference to Bachmann's writing. In 1984, Weigel edited a special issue of *text + kritik* that featured her own essay "'Ein Ende mit der Schrift. Ein andrer Anfang': Zur Entwicklung von Ingeborg Bachmanns Schreibweise" ('An end to writing. Another beginning': On the development of Ingeborg Bachmann's writing style) as its longest contribution. Bachmann's writing and responses to it then helped to constitute the structure around which she built her book-length study of contemporary West German women's writing, *Die Stimme der Medusa* (The voice of the Medusa). Finally, the last chapter of her 1990 book, *Topographien der Geschlechter: Kulturgeschichtliche Studien zur Literatur* (Topographies of gender: Cultural-historical studies of literature) used *The Book of Franza* to define "the work of deciphering" (*Topographien* 252) as the task of feminist cultural critics.

"Double Focus," Weigel's earliest essay dealing with Bachmann, is much more historically and politically grounded than other essays on Bachmann of the early 1980s and uses Bachmann's work to support Weigel's own theses on the possibilities of women's writing. She praises *Malina* for its profound critique of women's condition at a particular historical point and understands its portrait of a diametrically opposed masculinity and femininity as illustrative of women's *present* difficulty in finding a place for themselves: "The incompatibility of the male and female principle is not thematized as an eternal inner conflict that obtains for men and women in the same way; rather, it is the expression of the experience of a woman living 'today'" ("Schielende" 123). The disappearance of the "I" at the novel's end is a mark not just of that irreconcilability but also of that figure's female resistance: "The disappearance of the 'I' should not just be understood as a homicide, but also as a separation from Malina, as a refusal to live a Malina-life" ("Schielende" 125). Weigel similarly reads "Undine Goes" as a *"refusal* of a fairy-tale role" ("Schielende" 129), a rejection of the projection of male needs onto female figures, a move that helps to anticipate women's freedom from male projections altogether. In "Eyes to Wonder" shortsighted Miranda represents for Weigel a different kind of resistance: willing to see only a world that meets her needs, Miranda cannot survive because she lacks the "double focus" (Weigel's guiding metaphor here) that would allow her to find her way in the real world.

In her *text + kritik* article, "An End to Writing," Weigel moves substantially closer to French theory, though the French thinkers on whom she draws for feminist writing strategies are Roland Barthes, Jacques Lacan, and Jacques Derrida rather than Irigaray or Cixous. Weigel now formulates Bachmann's concerns in less historically specific terms, maintaining, for instance, that "the gender motif" is "from the beginning integrated into the structure of occidental thought; it is a moment of history that can be described as an assault on nature and on humankind" ("Ende" 72). Following Barthes, on whose *Writing Degree Zero* Bachmann seems to have drawn to write her Frankfurt lectures, Weigel defines as a central project of Bachmann's prose texts the creation of a new *Schreibweise* (writing style, *écriture*) simultaneously destructive and productive. She traces through *The Thirtieth Year* the steps that in her view brought Bachmann to a conception of the relationship of language and the symbolic order to gender and argues that only in *Franza* was Bachmann able to devise a writing style that was "a deconstruction of the cultural order" ("Ende" 76), *Malina* functioning as a less radical, more realistic introduction to the problems that inform the "Ways of Death." The deconstruction or "decomposition" of *Franza* demands "the destruction of the symbolic father or of the conception of God which as an inscription within Franza corresponds to the real crimes outside" ("Ende" 83–84). The "composition" Bachmann accomplished in *Franza* derives from her ability to formulate "a third thing" that operates outside of binary oppositions and constitutes a female utopia within literature that would be, says Weigel in Bachmann's words, "an empire with unknown borders open towards the future" ("Ende" 91).

In *Die Stimme der Medusa*, Weigel's admiration for Bachmann's accomplishment leads her to lend a certain teleology to her account of the previous three decades of women's writing and reading. Although Bachmann anticipated concerns of feminism in works that Weigel calls "concealed women's writing" (*Stimme* 32), early feminists, she maintains, had not yet learned to read Bachmann in ways that enabled them to appreciate her. Conversely, Bachmann's writing functioned as a kind of critique of earlier writers and readers, who sought socially critical, realistic texts or authentic articulations of female identity or subjectivity. Here, too, Weigel views Bachmann's "Ways of Death" through a poststructuralist lens, seeing *Malina*'s "I" not as a woman but as "that form of existence that is sacrificed to the entry of woman into the symbolic order"

(*Stimme* 37–38). But, perhaps because of the subject of her book, Weigel's treatment of Bachmann here slides away from the formal concerns of the *text + kritik* essay back to Bachmann's status within a body of women's writing and her relevance to German feminists. She uses Bachmann's writing approvingly to exemplify a variety of possibilities for women's writing. Again Weigel praises Bachmann's ability to draw conventional narrative into question, both to convey in *Malina* the history of the "I" and to show why it is impossible to represent it. Weigel also praises Bachmann's treatment of the "paradox of love," a topic that reengaged feminist attention from the mid-1980s onward, "a fundamental motif of Bachmann's literature . . . that she explored in ever new variations" (*Stimme* 217). In *Malina,* Bachmann portrays love as destructive of but necessary for women situated within a dialectic of *Leben und* Über*leben* (life and survival) (*Stimme* 226). Like the feminists of the 1970s, "Three Paths to the Lake" suggests that women should keep their distance from men but also preserves the idea of love as utopian possibility. Portraying this aporia, "the affirmation of love as the negation of its social possibilities or, to put it the other way around, the impossibility in the real as the salvation of possibility" (*Stimme* 230), Weigel shows Bachmann able both thematically and formally to present both sides of an opposition that seems irreconcilable.

By the time of her 1990 book, Weigel's treatment of Bachmann, though still shaped by poststructuralism, has moved significantly in the direction of cultural studies. Here Franza is treated as a figure able to undertake the project of "deciphering," the task of a female cultural critic. Weigel's analytical model has become discernibly more complex, and she understands and uses Franza's journey to the desert as an illustration of the central metaphor of Weigel's own study, "as a *topography* of signifying, textual, and intellectual orders" (*Topographien* 254). Franza's story is now not just about femininity, Bachmann's text representing "the exterior traces of the destruction of (not just) female history" (*Topographien* 252). Weigel now acknowledges "the ambivalent location of the white woman, who often finds herself in a simultaneity of victim and perpetrator positions" (*Topographien* 263): Franza is not just a victim of "the whites," but white herself. And Weigel explicitly draws attention to "the psychic and linguistic involvement of women in the dominant order and thus their own interest in existing relationships" (*Topographien* 255).

In this book, two "burning problems" (*Topographien* 260) emerge for Weigel that are of great relevance for the Bachmann criticism of the 1980s. First, she points out the limitations of attempts to find alternative discourses and forms of representation for women outside the dominant order: "In general, the question of the otherness of woman has revealed itself to be a trap, since up to now it has just led to an extension of the gender polarity in which woman is fixed as the other/second sex" (*Topographien* 261). In this context, her criticism of efforts to place women writers outside of or embracing binary oppositions might be read as an effort to distance herself from her own portrait of Bachmann's writing style six years before. Second, Weigel radically draws into question a prior model of feminist analysis that had starkly divided the world into the opposition of men and women, masculinity and femininity. Now Weigel calls for an intensified concern with the relationship of sexual *and* cultural difference, "since every subject moves within a meshwork of social, cultural, ethnic, and gender-specific differences" (*Topographien* 264). Such an investigation would demand revision of much of the feminist Bachmann criticism that dominated the 1980s.

By the mid-1980s, variants of radical feminist and feminist poststructuralist approaches had conquered the field of Bachmann scholarship, as most clearly evidenced in two special journal issues devoted to Bachmann—Weigel's *text + kritik* volume of 1984 and a special Bachmann number of *Modern Austrian Literature* in 1985—as well as several MLA special sessions ably organized by Karen Achberger and Beth Bjorklund. Weigel's introduction to the *text + kritik* collection outlines the principles of that paradigm as they were applied to Bachmann and explains that now Bachmann's works are often regarded as "anticipatory concretization of poststructuralist theses," her "Ways of Death" revealing "a structural relationship between fascism, patriarchy, ethno- and logocentrism and the central role of language/writing for this context, within which the 'feminine' as the embodiment of the repressed other is subjected to a wide variety of ways of death" ("Andere" 5). But as many feminists now read them, Bachmann's texts also represent her effort to combat (often: to destroy or deconstruct) the dominant order; her works, Weigel argues, depict the structures "to which individuals are subjected and against which they—led by the author—mobilize their desperate longing for their own subjectivity, their own history, and a not yet occupied location of their own" ("Andere" 6). What Weigel maintains is not altogether true of her own collection: only her own, Christa Bürger's, Birgit Vanderbeke's, and one of Marianne Schuller's essays are significantly influenced by poststructuralism; several others do not thematize gender at all; and Helga Meise, Irmela von der Lühe, and I (in the essay published here as chapter 5) try to advance various other kinds of feminist approaches to Bachmann.

But the hegemony of a certain kind of French feminist theory is very striking in the *Modern Austrian Literature* volume, where more than half of the essays make at least an obligatory nod in its direction. To Angelika Rauch, for instance, "femininity" in Bachmann is a "counter model to the reified mode of experience and perception that was a consequence of a culture and society defined by rationality and patriarchy" (21); especially the dream chapter of *Malina* pushes in the direction of a "textual practice" that might produce "new models for female images" such as "deconstruction, *écriture féminine*, hysterical discourse, displaced/crazy discourse" ("Sprache" 48). Peter Brinkemper views *The Book of Franza* as a "paradigm of female aesthetics" that both thematically and formally addresses "the female experience of oppression as well as the destruction of personal, sexual, and social identity via the power of a symbolic order" (170). Renate Delphendahl sees "Undine Goes" as a "critique of patriarchal language" (199), and Karen Achberger speaks of a female subjectivity "incompatible with patriarchal culture" ("Beyond" 219). Ritta Jo Horsley argues that "Undine Goes" "anticipates French feminism and poststructuralism in its presentation and partial deconstruction of the fundamental cultural forms that shape our consciousness" ("Re-reading" 224). In this volume, even some dissenters from the dominant trend find it necessary to recognize the power of the paradigm, Leo Lensing pointing out that the "recent provocative feminist scholarship" neglected the Austrian literary tradition (53), while Sigrid Schmid-Bortenschlager tries to distinguish Bachmann's writing from the German *Frauenliteratur* of the 1970s and 1980s but nonetheless acknowledges the "surprising new orientation . . . particularly marked in the studies of the prose and of the 'feminist' Bachmann" ("Spiegelszenen" 39).

What probably demonstrates most clearly how feminism had moved to the mainstream of Bachmann criticism by the 1980s is the sympathetic treatment it has received from male Bachmann scholars from that point onward. As early as 1980, Bernd Witte, in two essays that still remain extremely useful, identifies gender as the central concern of Bachmann's work. Surveying "Ingeborg Bachmann Today" in 1983, Kurt Bartsch is prepared to give credit for what he terms "something like a Bachmann boom"—evidenced in the four Bachmann symposia held that year—to "the change in the expectations of literary criticism and scholarship in the second half of the 1970s, which among other things is due to the influence of the recent women's movement" ("Ingeborg" 281). Bartsch's Sammlung Metzler monograph, published in 1988, makes proper and generous use of feminist approaches to Bachmann's late prose while also attempting to illuminate other aspects of her work. The final "Ways of Death" chapter of Hans Höller's 1987 study of Bachmann is also indebted to a French feminist approach, while Peter Beicken's more chatty and less rigorous 1988 Beck series monograph takes the legitimacy of a feminist approach for granted. By the time that *Kein objektives Urteil—Nur ein lebendiges* (No objective judgment—just a living one), a retrospective collection of thirty-five years of Bachmann criticism, was published in 1989 by Christine Koschel and Inge von Weidenbaum, the editors of Bachmann's *Werke*, feminist approaches had become so important to the evolving body of Bachmann scholarship that essays by many of the feminist critics I have discussed here occupied a central and uncontroversial place. Even in the 1990s, at a time when some erstwhile feminists abandoned a gender perspective (as I show below), male scholars (with a few exceptions) continued to acknowledge, even insist upon, the importance of gender issues in Bachmann's writing.

From the high point of feminist Bachmann criticism at mid-decade, interest in Bachmann ebbed in the late 1980s, studies for a time mostly limited to dissertations written by younger women and frequently published by Peter Lang, a press very hospitable to doctoral theses. But in the 1990s three developments directed attention to Bachmann again. First, in 1990 Werner Schroeter released a controversial film version of *Malina*, based on a script by Elfriede Jelinek. Though Jelinek's adaptation followed Bachmann's novel quite closely, Schroeter had other ideas. As the *Vienna Standard* reported, Schroeter was more interested in the problems of *Malina*'s "I" than in her difficulties with individual or generic men: "Schroeter would have preferred to cut the sequence with the father; for him it was a matter of self-destruction" (Cerha Hozwath 10). But that reading of Bachmann's novel produced an outraged response from some feminist Bachmann fans (detailed below). The second development was the number of conferences organized around various aspects of Bachmann's works to which many established Bachmann scholars (the "usual suspects," in effect) were invited. These meetings drew those scholars back into Bachmann research, allowing (and compelling) them to address aspects of Bachmann's work different from those they had previously considered. Many of major conferences also produced volumes of their proceedings, including Saranac Lake, New York, 1991 (*Ingeborg Bachmann: Neue Richtungen in der Forschung?*); Münster, 1991 (*Ingeborg Bachmann—Neue Beiträge zu ihrem Werk*); Vienna, 1993 (*Die Schwarzkunst der Worte*); London, 1993 (*Kritische Wege der Landnahme*); Bern, 1993 (*Schriftwechsel*); Debrecen, 1993 (*Nicht [aus, in, über, von] Österreich*); Vienna, 1994 (*Ingeborg Bachmann and Paul Celan*); Brussels, 1996 (*Text-Tollhaus für Bachmann-Süchtige*); Saarland, 1996 (*Klangfarben*); and Binghamton, 1996 (*If We Had the Word*). Third, 1995 saw the publication of the mammoth four-volume critical edition of the *"Todesarten"-Projekt*, meticulously edited by Monika Albrecht and Dirk Göttsche, which made available for scholarly use and quotation large portions of the previously unpublished material that had resided in the manuscript collection of the Vienna Nationalbib-liothek. Because the critical edition confirmed some scholarly speculations and challenged others, it was immediately at the center of a storm of controversy which again brought Bachmann's name back into print in the German-language press.

Within this context, it is possible to discern three more or less separate devel-opments in Bachmann scholarship that have continued from the late 1980s to the present. Despite the fact that it had fallen out of favor in many sectors of academic feminism, a number of studies written as dissertations by younger women (among them, Bärbel Thau, Eva Christina Zeller, Ingeborg Dusar, and Mireille Tabah) or as books and articles by more senior scholars such as Karen Achberger and Manfred Jürgensen continued to pursue some variant of the radical or poststruc-turalist feminist approach to Bachmann that had claimed the field in the mid-1980s. Feminist studies by Ortrud Gutjahr, Inge Röhnelt, Saskia Schottelius, and Bettina Stuber pursued another connection influential in French-influenced scholarship: the utility of psychoanalysis for understanding the construction of female identity, language, and culture. Gudrun Kohn-Waechter's ambitious 1992 study *Das Verschwinden in der Wand* (Disappearing into the wall) continued and deepened the direction of analysis begun in the early 1980s and also initiated a controversy in Bachmann scholarship that rages to the present day. In *Malina*, Kohn-Waechter maintains, Bachmann had elaborated a "new language" that might have pointed the way beyond a Western rationality that suppresses femi-ninity, yet the position from which that writing style could be undertaken is eradicated when the "I" is murdered at the end of the novel. Since the novel fully discredits Malina's narrative position, Kohn-Waechter alleges that it would have been impossible for Bachmann to continue to write after the end of her only pub-lished novel, so that, even had she lived, there could have been no further "Ways of Death" narratives. Such arguments for *Malina* as the single novel Bachmann could have written (further elaborated by German feminist scholars such as Franziska Frei Gerlach and Edith Bauer but contradicted by statements Bach-mann herself made after *Malina* was published) seem to me to rest on the femi-nist postulation of an essential femininity, eternally antagonistic to masculinist domination, whose problems might be solved if a writing style adequate to its expression could be devised. Assertions like those of Kohn-Waechter, Gerlach, and Bauer also underwrite many of the attacks on the critical edition of the *"Todesarten"-Projekt*. Yet if the edition's editors are correct to argue that at the time of her death Bachmann was engaged in an ongoing literary project, Kohn-Waechter, Gerlach, Bauer, and others must concede that their own analyses of Bachmann's writing strategy are quite wrong.

Werner Schroeter's film of *Malina* provided one final opportunity for radical feminists to vent their anger against men who treated women and their cultural productions badly. Schroeter's adaptation produced, for example, an outraged response from Alice Schwarzer in the journal *Emma*, demonstrating that at least in her circles radical feminism was alive and well. Bachmann's great theme, Schwarzer maintained, had been men's brutality to women, and a close reading of *Malina* now revealed that the suffering of Bachmann's protagonist was a consequence of incestuous sexual abuse, the great radical feminist issue of the late 1980s. Schwarzer outflanked German feminist scholars by accusing them of diminishing the brutal crimes of men via arguments that made women complicit in their own subjugation: "Feminist, postfeminist, antifeminist, or whatever-else criticism dissects the novel with aesthetic and psychoanalytic methods. . . . Fashionably, it blames the victim, even insinuates that the victim enjoys suffering, even worse, some of the critics relegate what happens to the realm of a masochist's fantasies" ("Schwarzer" 19). She protested the violence done to Bachmann both by Schroeter's film and by her "feminist" critics, who failed to recognize that a majority of women will endure sexual assault during their lifetime and that incest survivors suffer lifelong symptoms like Bachmann's own. To support her position, Schwarzer reprinted an updated version of Jelinek's 1984 essay, "Der Krieg mit anderen Mitteln" (War By Other Means), which proclaimed men's treatment of women a continuation of the Nazi extermination of the Jews, viewing women as exiles from a culture in which they had no part and no voice and which was determined to destroy them.

A number of other feminist critics and scholars followed Schwarzer's lead—Iris Radisch, Dorothee Römhild, Kathleen Komar, Regula Venske—in denouncing the film (and at least one male scholar, Gerhard Austin, denounced the feminists' denunciations). But later in the decade, possibly as a radical feminist analysis loosed its hold, opinions moderated to the point that Ingeborg Gleichauf could maintain: "The film opens new interpretive possibilities for reading the novel" (222), and Margret Eifler, writing from a more historically conscious U.S. feminist perspective in 1997, even declares that the changes Schroeter made to Bachmann's text were necessary: "The progress of time dictated alternate forms of the same problem: feminism had moved into another generational perception, and the change to another medium demanded an alternate encoding" ("Bachmann" 223).

But even though feminist approaches with roots in the early 1980s continued to shape some analyses of Bachmann work up to the present, some discomfort with those sorts of feminist arguments also seemed apparent by the end of the

1980s. Thus a countertendency to feminist approaches emerged increasingly in the second half of the decade: often investigations of Bachmann by younger women scholars did not address the question of gender at all. In the *Women in German Yearbook* in 1992 ("Feminist"), I opined that gender was missing in those studies because Bachmann scholars wanted to pursue a range of aspects of her work other than those addressed by 1980s feminists and did not know how to do so in a way that also took gender into account. Now, I would not be so certain that there is a single answer to the absence of attention to gender in Bachmann scholarship. It may really be the case that some feminist scholars have not been able to elaborate a gender-based approach adequate to the questions they want to pose. (As my commentary to chapter 6 shows, for instance, it still is not clear to me how to explore whether the question of gender influenced Bachmann's reading of Wittgenstein.) On the other hand, the Bachmann criticism of the 1990s sometimes manifests the abandonment of gender as an analytic category even when its utility seems obvious and even in writing by scholars for whom gender formerly seemed to be a central concern. Thus the question arises whether the retreat from gender (particularly in Germany) might be read within the context of a larger move away from oppositional politics after German unification. The poststructuralist feminist model of the 1980s made it possible to examine femininity and writing in the rather ethereal context of high theory alone. But since many of the newer approaches to gender demanded that scholars simultaneously consider class, race, sexuality, and other social categories, 1990s feminists found it much harder to avoid more controversial social issues. The retreat from gender might thus be viewed both as a welcome repudiation of an earlier feminist model that seemed inadequate to address the new concerns of Bachmann scholarship and as a means to avoid topics that seemed quite out of fashion in the new and more conservative unified Germany.

A 1994 special issue of the Zurich monthly *Du* devoted to Bachmann displays both these tendencies. The issue's editor, Dieter Bachmann (no relation to the author), understands his project to be saving Bachmann from feminist and other extremists: "The one extreme: many (men) . . . constructed a myth out of the elements Undine and death drive. The other extreme: many (women) . . . transfigured her into their feminist ancestress and installed her as their principle of hope" (13). Similarly, Corinna Caduff, Sigrid Weigel's research assistant at the University of Zurich, protests that Bachmann has been "co-opted by the women's movement and elevated to their cult figure" (86), while Maria Gazzetti, reporting on Bachmann's Italian reception, warns that "the scholarly and artistic undertakings of a new women's movement could stand in the way of a deeper comprehension" of Bachmann, though, she happily notes, such misunderstandings scarcely ever occur in Italy (92-93). On the other hand, the issue of *Du* also evidences some of the problems that arise when discussions of gender are omitted in accounts of Bachmann's life and work. The magazine contains much new information including unpublished photographs, material from the Vienna archive, and reminiscences by friends. Yet except for a somewhat sexist recollection by Hermann Burger of an evening with Bachmann ("A woman of boundless openness for everything terrible, hard as a man in her tragic consistency, and yet helpless as a woman towards an overwhelming life" ([69]) and a commentary by Sigrid Weigel on Bachmann's "effort to combine work on the (im)possible location of a female position within the dialectic of enlightenment with the problem of representation in the aftermath of National Socialism" (["Urszene" 23]), gender is not discussed at all—though precisely an examination of the condition of being a woman intellectual in the aftermath of National Socialism in the 1940s, 1950s, and 1960s might help to explain some of the problems that Bachmann confronted and on which her friends and acquaintances comment.

Similar problems are evident in a later *text + kritik* issue devoted to Bachmann, published in November 1995 and obviously meant to replace the famous 1984 number that had first proclaimed "the other Ingeborg Bachmann." To be sure, in her article Ursula Krechel notes that earlier feminist paradigms have been abandoned for good reason: "The dichotomy exploiter-exploited, like that of perpetrator and victim, derived from the general political discourse of the 1960s and used by the new women's movements for gender difference, was replaced in the 1980s by differentiated analyses of the accountability and complicity of women in the patriarchal system, complicity which looks not at individual responsibility or guilt but rather at the social networks of gender dependencies" (15). With the exception, however, of an article by Susanne Baackmann, a young Berkeley-trained Germanist, none of the other essays— even those by such scholars as Sigrid Weigel ("Sie sagten") and Irmela von der Lühe ("Abschied"), who were represented in the 1984 issue—can be termed feminist in any sense or consistently employ a gender analysis, even when their topics cry out for an investigation of gender's relevance: responses to Bachmann's writing by younger women poets; Bachmann's literary and actual relationships to Max Frisch, Paul Celan, and Jean Améry; the degree to which Maria Callas and Bachmann are phenomena of the 1950s. It is difficult to avoid the conclusion that some Bachmann scholars find gender issues to be no longer opportune.

Indeed, in the popular media the rollback to a prefeminist era seems even more emphatic than a mere obliviousness to gender issues. In the 13 November

1995 issue of *Der Spiegel*, Sigrid Löffler—then a member of the ZDF's Literarisches Quartett, the former editor of the *Feuilleton* of *Die Zeit*, and herself an
Austrian woman—purported to review the new four-volume critical edition
of the "Ways of Death" but in fact reduced Bachmann's writing to a mostly
biographical account of her successes and failures with men. "At thirty she was
a myth," writes Löffler. "A myth for men. Fellow writers, readers, and critics all
succumbed to her morbid charm which combined girlish timidity and lyrical
power, shyness and poetic boldness. Half accursed princess, half wild, prophetic
conjuress, Bachmann [*die Bachmann*] moved as if transported from prize ceremony to prize ceremony, from poetic honor to poetic honor" (244). The less
positive reception of her prose Löffler attributes to the criticism of masculinity in *The Thirtieth Year*: "'Undine goes'—and curses men. Her community of
male adorers never forgave her that" (244). The main impetus behind the "Ways
of Death," Löffler intimates, was Bachmann's personal ressentiment resulting
from her "experience of a catastrophic and crisis-ridden love affair with Max
Frisch" (245), though her portrait of society "as the execution site of patriarchal
violence" won her a new readership: "As a myth for men she'd long been cast
aside; as a myth for women she made her posthumous career" (247). Pursuing
her trope with a vengeance, Löffler also metamorphoses Bachmann into a range
of mythological figures, portraying her as a spurned woman obsessed with
revenge against the men who have wronged her: "The poetic seeress and song-
stress turned into the herald of prosaic violence, the beautiful Melusine turned
into the male-hating virago. A transformation from ondine to banshee. The
lyrical water nymph, driven from her magic element, exploits the devastated
land of annihilated femininity. Undine goes. Undine has gone. She comes back
as a Fury" (247). Löffler's review signals a 1990s backlash against feminism as
she attempts both to trivialize feminist concern with women's treatment by men
in the private sphere and also, turning radical feminism on its head, to reduce
Bachmann's writing to that single issue.

Surprisingly, even Sigrid Weigel, the scholar probably most responsible for
directing feminist attention to Bachmann, seems to have moved significantly
away from feminist approaches in the comprehensive 600-page study of
Bachmann she published in 1999. In many ways, the book represents a breakthrough for Bachmann scholarship. Assuming that letters *from* Bachmann
would be found not among her own private papers—closed to the public until
2025—but in the papers of her correspondents, Weigel consulted archives in
Germany, Austria, Israel, and the United States to discover letters to and from
Gerschom Scholem, Theodor W. Adorno, Hannah Arendt, Paul Celan, Peter

Szondi, Uwe Johnson, Wolfgang Hildesheimer, Alfred Andersch, Hans Werner Richter, and Hermann Kesten, among others. Weigel can particularly document Bachmann's very grave concern with the aftermath of National Socialism in Germany and Austria and her connections to major Jewish figures of the period, and that indeed will change the way Bachmann scholars address her work. The conception structuring her book, Weigel explains in her prologue, is that of Bachmann as intellectual and participant in the debates and discussions of her day. "Resistance to a female intellectual" is what explains the negative response to her prose: "Literary critics never forgave her for breaking from a terrain that was defined with the help of the equivalence lyric = intuitive = female" (*Ingeborg* 16). Yet Weigel's book almost entirely fails to pursue that topic. In her prologue she is very critical of feminist scholarship, apparently not entertaining the possibility that feminist investigations can be carried out in varieties of ways: "To be sure, often only in the light of feminist and deconstructive literary theory were the more radical philosophical dimensions of [Bachmann's] thought and writing discovered; but at the same time in an abundance of seminar papers and theses her work has been misunderstood as the legacy of 'women's literature' and in presenting her so that she represents 'female identity,' they have once more obscured the profile of the author as an engaged literary politician, as a philosophically and historically informed thinker" (*Ingeborg* 16). But when the book addresses questions of femininity at all, Weigel falls back into the model of the 1980s (an approach that to me does not seem compatible with her historical emphasis): "Franza is figured as a woman who has no stable place of her own in the symbolic order"; the dreams of *Malina* "refer to the drama of the 'feminine' in the symbolic order under a 'law in the name of the father'" (*Ingeborg* 516, 538). Weigel rightly observes critically that "Germanists' interpretations quite frequently ignore the historical situations in which [Bachmann's] literature was located" (*Ingeborg* 17). We can hope that in subsequent studies Weigel will explore the possibility of elaborating a method that is both historical *and* feminist and add gender to the analytical categories she uses to understand the historical situations she so usefully explores.

Happily, not all Bachmann scholars either remain wedded to a radical or poststructuralist feminist method or decide not to address gender at all. Many studies of Bachmann's work include gender among the various issues they investigate, an approach that would be called feminist in the United States if not in Germany, and a number of younger feminist scholars—particularly though not only in English-speaking countries—have also begun to investigate the application of new kinds of feminist methods to Bachmann's texts.

Several essays in Andrea Stoll's very useful 1992 Suhrkamp volume of materi- als pertaining to *Malina* (*Ingeborg*) consider gender-related aspects, and Stoll's own overview of *Malina*'s reception ("Bruch") treats feminist approaches very evenhandedly. From earlier feminist studies, Maria Behre's essay very sensibly extracts three historically specific points for analysis—a description of con- temporary expectations of femininity, a historical investigation of their genesis and variability, and an examination of the utopian functions of descriptions of the other—proposing that the feminist question "Do women write differ- ently?" (*Schreiben Frauen anders?* is the title of Christa Gürtler's 1983 study) be transmuted into "Why did Bachmann write differently than her male con- temporaries?" (212). Almut Dippel's fine 1995 monograph situates the vol- ume *Three Paths to the Lake* very precisely at the time of its production, notes that Bachmann criticizes not only capitalist consumer society but also the "partial blindness of left circles in the 1960s and 1970s, who like Philippe [in "Three Paths to the Lake"] fight exploitation in the Third World, but don't see or don't want to see that they're exploiters themselves in their private lives. ... Remarkably," Dippel notes with some irony, "it was exactly this contradiction in the behavior of many comrades of 1968 that was the catalyzing moment for the constitution of a solid women's movement. The women in the *Three Paths to the Lake* cycle don't of course rebel or do so only inaudibly. Thus it remains for male and female readers to recognize the contradictions and draw conclusions from them" (127). In another excellent book on *Three Paths to the Lake*, Bettina Bannasch argues that even though Bachmann tried to distance herself from feminism (maintaining, for instance, "This is not a book for women, and also not one for men, it's a book for human beings" [*TP* 4: 11]), she was not success- ful, since, in contrast to the male perpetrators of crimes against women, none of her women figures becomes a persecutor of men (53). These books show that it is possible to consider gender relations as a central concern of Bachmann's writ- ing without making gender the central and overriding emphasis to which all other issues in the texts are subordinated.

The editors of the critical edition of the *"Todesarten"-Projekt*, Monika Albrecht and Dirk Göttsche, also take for granted in their textual commentaries that gender is a significant, though far from the only, issue addressed in the novel cycle (in my view one of the virtues of the edition). In their own scholarship, Göttsche and Albrecht emphasize gender themes and add a dimension frequently missing in Bachmann scholarship by assuming a critical stance toward her writing. Albrecht observes, for instance:

Just as Horkheimer and Adorno equate the beginning of enlightenment with that of world history, Bachmann seems to locate the origins of today's gender problematic in prehistoric times when myth developed. It seems, therefore, doubtful that Bachmann, as it has been claimed, does bring up for discussion the "incompatibility of the male and female principle . . . as an 'eternal' conflict that equally concerns man and woman." After all, in *Malina* she even goes one step further; in the last dialogue with Malina, just before the disappearance of the "I" in the wall, it is noted, in reference to Malina and the "I": "Something must have gone astray with the primates and later with the hominoids. A man, a woman . . .strange words, strange mania." ("A man" 133–34)

That critical perspective continues to inform their selection of scholarly essays in the three volumes titled *Über die Zeit schreiben* that Albrecht and Göttsche published as a kind of Bachmann yearbook in 1998, 2000, and 2004 and in their *Bachmann-Handbuch* of 2002. (In the interest of full disclosure, I should reveal that chapters from this book appear in German translation in all three volumes, and I also contributed several sections to the handbook.) In their call for papers for the second volume, Albrecht and Göttsche stress that Bachmann scholarship is changing and urge contributors to pay special attention to situating her works within history: "Contributors are welcome to choose their topics but should take into consideration that in the last few years a changing view of the historical period in which Bachmann wrote has been evolving. In the light of the emerging reassessment of the 1940's to early 1970's Bachmann scholars will have to pay even more attention than so far to the historical context of her writing, to her involvement with contemporary history and the critical (scientific, philosophical, social, literary) discourse of her time, and to the cultural implications of her works" (E-mail 18 May 1998). Interestingly, the three volumes feature a preponderance of U.S.-based scholars, and, as perhaps is appropriate for studies that have come into being "with the consciousness that Bachmann research is going through a time of upheaval" (Albrecht/Göttsche *Über* 8), many of the essays treating gender do so in ways critical both of Bachmann and/or of previous varieties of feminist scholarship. The scholarly revisions necessitated by the appearance of the critical edition also include, it appears, a reconsideration of Bachmann's own treatment of gender relations.

Finally, some of the most original and exciting feminist work on Bachmann to appear since the late 1980s has begun to apply to texts a range of new methods that foreground gender concerns and maintain gender as a central category of their analysis. In a subtle 1989 essay in *New German Critique*, Sabine Gölz adapts and revises Harold Bloom's theory of literary influence in order to understand Bachmann's own female theory of writing as rereading, advanced from her perspective as a woman poet positioned in opposition to the poetic Father Precursor. Though gender appears not to be an explicit concern of the poems Gölz discusses, she shows that gender is nonetheless inscribed in the poem in the way Bachmann distances herself from a male tradition that assured the coherence of the poem and "a reading that presumes it can 'know' its object" ("Reading" 31). Gölz's interpretive model opens up Bachmann's poetry, which had seemed to baffle feminists, to feminist analysis, allowing discussion about gender there without resorting to essentialist notions of what counts as female or feminist. Her book, *The Split Scene of Reading* (1998), expands on these insights by contrasting the relationship of Bachmann's stance—a "readerly" one that refuses closure and allows readers the freedom to make their own meanings—to the posture of other writers (Derrida, Apollinaire, Nietzsche, Kafka) who appear to undermine the reliability of signifying structures but finally retreat from their own daring critique to insist that they themselves can proclaim what meaning is.

From quite another standpoint, Constance Hotz's lively and very innovative *"Die Bachmann"* (1990), an examination of Bachmann's reception by journalists during her lifetime, uses reception theory, structuralism, and semiotics to examine the production of a journalistic discourse about Bachmann in which gender (among other issues) played a central role. Thus, for instance, she argues that the *Spiegel* cover that brought Bachmann her early fame derived some portion of its effect through its *contrast* with the usual portraits of women: "Erotic stylization is *de rigeur* for the *Spiegel* covers of the fifties that feature women; the attributes of makeup, jewelry, a neat hairdo, mouth opened to a smile, often décolleté, consistently present a femininity that directs attention to itself. Ingeborg Bachmann's face, however, is characterized by a significant lack of these attributes or by their negative presentation: short hair, an evasive glance, a covered neckline, a firmly closed mouth. The eroticism of this face is infused with a gesture of refusal"(46). Even the identification of female authors through the use of the definite article prescribed by Duden, the authoritative dictionary of the German language, Hotz argues, affected the way Bachmann would be read: "With the addition of the definite article in the case of female authors (cf. in contrast without articles: Goethe, Grass etc.) the neutral use of the name as a metonymic representation of the work is abandoned, and the personal aspect is emphasized before the work; and according to gender-specific usage demanded by grammar the personal aspect is always characterized by and as femininity. The category of gender (but only the female, not the male) is thus always connected to the reference to the work."(130). Via these and many other examples, Hotz contributes to an understanding of how and why the image of Bachmann as "the poetess" [die Dichterin] and "First Lady of the Gruppe 47" was generated and simultaneously establishes a new paradigm for feminist Bachmann scholarship.

Susanne Ruta's 1991 review of *Malina* in the *Village Voice*, written from outside the German feminist hothouse, brought a breath of fresh air to the entire feminist debate on Bachmann. "Bachmann's feminism," Ruta declares, "is always full of unresolved paradoxes," particularly as "she buys into the ancient misogynist division of humankind that equates the male with reason, logic, order, light, and the female with passion, chaos, confusion, and darkness." What interests Ruta as much as gender issues in Bachmann's novel are its politics: she views *Malina* as "a political novel about postwar capitalist society on the remake, and about cold war tensions and their hidden psychic toll. It's a cold war novel the way *le temps retrouvé*—as Bachmann demonstrates in her lovely essay on Proust—is a novel about World War I. In both cases polite society, with its furtive nastiness, concealed vices, and paraded vanities, is presented as a microcosm of the larger political scene" (66). Ruta's iconoclastic reading of *Malina* points in the direction of the approach to Bachmann's "Ways of Death" that is grounded in politics and social history that scholars writing since her review now increasingly pursue.

Most recently, feminist scholars often based outside Germany have pursued a variety of innovative approaches to Bachmann. Friederike Eigler, for instance, uses a Bakhtinian model to examine the "heteroglossia," the various voices within the figures of *Simultan*, in order to investigate the split relationship of women to dominant discursive forms. Helgard Mahrdt views Bachmann's writing through the lens of the Frankfurt School, emphasizing the deformations of subjectivity and sensuality that result from the penetration of instrumental rationality into the private sphere. Karen Remmler explores the affinities between Walter Benjamin's concept of remembrance (*Eingedenken*) and Bachmann's own treatment of history and memory. Gisela Brinker-Gabler proposes that Franza's identification ("I am a Papua") with the victims of colonization represents a renewed colonization of the colonized, since her assumption of their perspective does not leave room for a perspective of their own. And Monika Albrecht ("Sire"; "Postkolonialismus") and I ("White" and this book's chapter 10) pursue further the question of Bachmann's relationship to postcolonialism and critical exoticism. Ingeborg Majer-O'Sickey criticizes "post-structuralist theoretical paradigms" that "tend to ignore Bachmann's understanding of women's situation as a social phenomenon in historical contexts" (55), and she also raises the possibility that the split subject and multiple voices of *Malina* force readers to avoid totalizing readings and offer "an altogether new possibility for feminism" that simultaneously rejects 'representivity' at once as it retains a feminism of articulation" (68). Gudrun Brokoph-Mauch considers Bachmann's treatment of Austria a reason to allocate her writing to the Austrian tradition of "critical Heimat-literature." Rhonda Duffaut reads *Malina* through the perspective of nationality, arguing that in her ecstatic love for Ivan the "I" of *Malina* conceives of an alternative form of community beyond national boundaries but, when that love ends, "becomes reinscribed by gender roles that confine her to the kitchen, to the home, that function together with nationalism" (39). Reading "Undine Goes" through a Lacanian lens, Veronica Scrol maintains that "her oscillation between the imaginary and the symbolic" subverts dichotomies (24), while Margaret McCarthy, criticizing poststructuralist and psychoanalytic theory for its denial of female agency, maintains that the "I" typifies the alienated Lacanian subject but expresses her resistance via her performance of "excess." Also critical of French poststructuralist theory for its too easy acceptance of gender dichotomies, Stephanie Bird instead shows how different modes of responding to historical experience are central to definitions of the female subject. Karin Bauer applies categories of queer theory, as elaborated by Teresa de Lauretis and Judith Butler, to argue that the love relationship of two women in "A Step towards Gomorrah" fails because even Charlotte's fantasies are "censored images always already relegated to the realm of the reproduction and reiteration of the norm" (232). Finally, two essays by Elizabeth Boa from 1990 and 1997 display the transformation of feminist approaches to Bachmann in the 1990s. In the first, Boa still draws upon French theory, arguing that *Malina*'s "I" gives expression to the Kristevan semiotic, an expression of female desire that can be conceived of as simultaneously regressive and, in its challenge to the symbolic ruled by the law of the father, subversive. By 1997, in contrast, she discusses *Malina* "as expressing less the dilemmas of all women under universal patriarchy than of an intellectual woman in twentieth-century Austria" ("Reading" 271); she also addresses ethnocentrism in *Franza*, though she concludes that the novel can be defended against that charge "precisely because the Other is left largely blank" ("Reading" 286).

All these essays reveal both the proliferation of feminist approaches during the fifteen years 1990–2005 and the more general feminist move towards a more historically and culturally specific conception of gender inflected by a range of other social categories. And recent Bachmann conferences since the thirtieth anniversary of her death (Rome 2003, the papers published in a special issue of *Cultura tedesca*; Dublin 2004; Nottingham 2005; Vienna 2006; Ljubljana 2006) with the ensuing essay collections are producing yet more new and innovative feminist readings of Bachmann's texts.

A 1995 dispute in *German Quarterly* reveals what is at stake in this transformation of feminist methods over two decades and why, for academic feminists, such methods are of more than academic interest. In the fall number of *German Quarterly*, Albrecht Holschuh published an indignant response to an article by Susanne Baackmann on "Undine Goes" takes extreme issue with what he considers her misreading of Bachmann's text. To Holschuh, Baackmann is guilty of pressing the text into a predetermined interpretive schema, associating textual passages with random extratextual phenomena, appealing to the obligatory authorities to substantiate her shaky points, and looking for political relevance instead of literary understanding. Moreover, Holschuh claims, Baackmann's essay exemplifies a more widespread practice deriving from a new conception of the discipline that has become *German Quarterly*'s virtual program. "But the prevailing practice has disadvantages," Holschuh warns ominously, "and it's high time to get its effects under control" (430).

So what has Baackmann done to incite such wrath? In her *GQ* article, as in her essay in the 1995 Bachmann issue of *text + kritik* and in her book *Erklär mir Liebe* (1995), Baackmann employs an approach that is quite representative of Bachmann scholarship in transition (and also probably manifests the influence of her two most important teachers, Sigrid Weigel and Anton Kaes). On the one hand, she continues to draw on the French thinkers most influential for 1980s feminist theory—Irigaray, Cixous, Kristeva—and also still speaks of the place of femininity *tout court* in discourse or the symbolic order, as if this system and its definitions of femininity were not historically variable. But to the feminist poststructuralist method she adds a new historicist examination of other cultural materials illustrating "the representation of femininity and the presence of women in the 1950s and 1960s" in order to show, as she puts it, "that Bachmann thematically and via her writing style intervenes into the contemporary discussion of femininity and love and in what terms [*unter welchem Bedeutungshorizont*] this discourse circulated in the public sphere during the years in which Bachmann was working on *The Thirtieth Year*" ("Reply" 433). Baackmann's approach is premised on many of the assumptions that inform feminist investigations of the late 1990s: that literary texts are not beyond or exterior to the social order of a particular period, but are rather both products and producers of that society's discourses, toward which the text may take any variety of stances; that texts—and various readings of those texts—are thus in no sense politically neutral but can support, subvert, oppose, and so on, various aspects of that social order; that feminist readings (like all others) are partisan in specific ways and thus will necessarily stress those aspects that correspond to their particular feminist needs.

Holschuh regards all those methodological principles as illegitimate, but, as Baackmann's dignified "reply" underlines, his objections to her reading of "Undine Goes" are also founded upon unacknowledged ideological premises. By alleging that a literary text can be understood immanently, without reference to the society from which it emerges, and by maintaining that concepts such as "the absolute," "spirit," and "humanity" can have a meaning independent of the society that gave them rise, scholars blindly perpetuate the dominant values of the reigning order; by insisting that there is a single meaning of the text (perhaps guaranteed by the author's intentions) to which he alone has access, Holschuh seems to situate himself as the authoritative purveyor of a single truth and denies the polysemy and multivalence of the text and the multiplicity of subject positions assumed by the readers who appropriate it. Finally (and here I am assuming a more polemical position than Baackmann's own), Holschuh's military imagery—"I'm sorry that so to speak as a front soldier [Baackmann] has entered the line of fire" (430)—and his rhetoric in accusing Baackmann of "political correctness [das politisch Korrekte]" (432) suggest that his intervention should be understood as another volley in what, since the late 1980s, has been termed the "culture wars" or the "P.C. debates": the efforts of conservatives to roll back the methodological and curricular changes that were the academic consequences of the struggles for social justice on the part of the social movements of the 1960s. And certainly Holschuh does nothing to dispel that suspicion when he sarcastically claims of Baackmann's approach: "So with a good conscience and not too much effort the social sins of all times can be exposed and the scholar's existence at least virtually obtains that political-moral relevance that has glimmered on as a fantasy since 1968" (430). This apparently innocuous scholarly exchange thus reveals itself to be a small skirmish in a much larger struggle over what kind of social order will prevail.

Evidently, I understand my own work, and this book, to form part of that struggle. Since, as this chapter must have shown, feminism itself is far from monolithic, smaller disputes over strategy and tactics take place among feminists themselves, in places (among others) such as the displaced form of disagreements over readings of texts. Although over the past several decades I have myself advanced a number of different interpretations of Bachmann which were clearly not always consistent with one another, I have continued to plead for a historically grounded understanding of her work. I would argue now that the

German feminist appropriation of Bachmann in the 1980s did damage both to the understanding of her that is of most utility to feminism and to feminism itself. Bachmann's writing as feminists received it then encouraged them to ask certain questions about women's lives and ignore others, supported what was in effect a withdrawal from political contestation in the public arena by portraying issues of the private sphere as most crucial to women, and allowed feminists to advance a monocausal analysis of women's situation: all women always only victims of all men. Her work thus supported political tendencies which had by the late 1970s moved to the fore in many Western feminisms: a concentration on the private realm, culture, psychic structures, and interiority to the relative neglect of social structures and the public arena. In my view, those developments produced a depoliticization of feminism from which we may still have not completely recovered.

But as this chapter has shown, the 1980s feminist appropriation of Bachmann is not the only feminist reading of Bachmann possible. It appears to me that feminist readings of Bachmann from the 1990s onward (like my own) begin by making several assumptions about how to think about Bachmann in her historical context. First, feminist Bachmann scholars return to questions asked in the 1960s, exploring how the deformations of private life portrayed in Bachmann's writings are related to larger social structures—and this time not to an abstract, generalized, monolithic, and all-embracing patriarchy or phallogocentrism but to particular historical and social determinants of which gender is only one—and how those issues find representation in Bachmann's texts. That is, we attempt to return Bachmann to history and history to Bachmann. Second, we may view Bachmann's relationship to poststructuralism, for which indeed a good deal of evidence exists, as itself a historical phenomenon; we might even concede that Bachmann's affinities to French poststructuralist thought (or any other intellectual or literary tradition) may well tell us nothing at all about the "truth" of women but is evidence only of the fact that some (women) intellectuals wrote at approximately the same time, turned to the same intellectual precursors, and used them to arrive at similar conclusions. And finally, we have begun to abandon what Leslie Morris in conversation called our "wishful thinking" about Bachmann's politics, our attempt to make her conform to our ideas about what the proper form of feminist (or other) theory and practice should be. For as Hans Werner Henze told Morris in an interview conducted on 2 August 1988, though Bachmann was a committed antifascist, she was in fact—especially vis-à-vis the possibilities for political action the 1960s offered—not otherwise very politically engaged. Instead, we can now regard Bachmann's writing with a more dispassionate eye, consider her limitations as well as her virtues, and investigate her and her texts as products of a particular historical moment which is no longer our own. With this grounding in history as their starting point, feminist scholars can begin to appropriate and elaborate new methods of feminist analysis, ask new questions about aspects and areas of Bachmann's work other than those that 1980s feminists considered, and perhaps advance readings of Bachmann's works that could be of increased utility to feminist thought and practice in the first and subsequent decades of the new millennium.

The questions I myself ask about Bachmann's work and the assumptions I make about it derive, of course, from my own social and historical location and are generated by my own intellectual interests—among other things, my desire to elaborate a method for feminist scholarship that is adequate to the investigation of the relationship of historical situatedness, gender, and textuality; my commitment to a feminism that acknowledges and respects women's difference; and my continued allegiance to an anticapitalist politics. My present reading of Bachmann, like all others (including the quite different interpretations of her work that I myself have advanced over the past several decades), is one that grows out of my particular needs and accords with my own political agenda. That positionality produces, I hope, new kinds of insights into Bachmann's texts but is also, I am sure, responsible for other sorts of blindnesses. After twenty years of poststructuralism, I would not want to argue for a single truth of the text, nor would I wish to maintain that any reading (except perhaps one that willfully flies in the face of the evidence of the text), is false, wrong, or a misreading (though I might want to oppose it for other, political reasons). As Bachmann herself maintained in the passage that I have chosen as the first epigraph for this chapter, literary texts deserve and can accommodate many different readings, and we should be prepared to grant their legitimacy while recognizing that different interpretive postures will serve different and contending interests, including those that are non- or even antifeminist. Our feminist reading remains merely one among others; we as feminists have no special advantage that allows us to transcend our own historical situation or gives us special insight into the meanings of Bachmann's works. To vary my second epigraph, women readers, too, when they read, are readers of themselves. What we, like Bachmann's other readers, find in her texts will also inevitably be at least in part a mirror of our own concerns.

PART II

A History of Reading Bachmann

1981

"Around 1981," Jane Gallop observes in her book of the same title, "a good num-ber of feminist literary academics in this country were focused on the 'difference between French and American feminism,' on the question of psychoanalysis or deconstruction and their usefulness or danger. 'We' were not only American feminists like me who thought French psychoanalytic, deconstructive theory a great thing but also those who expended a good deal of energy attacking it. Around 1981, this conflict, this debate seemed central, and to many more aca-demics than me, to feminist literary studies" (3). Now, gazing back from the perspective of the early twenty-first century on the battles that then rent U.S. academic feminism, the distinctions between these two methods of feminist cul-tural analysis seem much smaller, and the course that American (academic) fem-inism has taken since its emergence in the late 1960s might even be understood as leading toward the convergence of the two approaches. In its earliest phases of both activism and analysis, the U.S. women's movement primarily agitated against men's sexist treatment of and discrimination against women. Socialist feminists (indebted to a Marxist, class-based paradigm) and radical feminists (who saw men's oppression of women as primary) sought a revolutionary social transformation, whereas liberal feminists wanted equality in a society otherwise unchanged, but all agreed that women possessed the same capabilities as men and deserved the same opportunities.

The earliest feminist literary scholarship focused, like Kate Millett in her groundbreaking *Sexual Politics* (1970), on male (and sometimes even female) authors' stereotypical images of women. Susan Koppelman Cornillon, for instance, declared in the preface to her anthology *Images of Women in Fiction* (1972) that her book addressed all of women's social roles, "beginning with the most desiccated and lifeless traditional stereotypes of woman as heroine and as invisible person, progressing through an awakening to reality, wherein the woman is treated as person, and ending with the newest insistence by women that we are equal in all respects to men"(x). But by the mid-1970s (perhaps under the influence of the new groups of women without experience in the social movements of the 1960s who now declared their allegiance to feminism), many academic and nonacademic feminists had arrived at a much-altered understand-ing of women's situation and the tasks that would be necessary to ameliorate it. As the influence of socialist feminism waned with the decline of the New Left, a new kind of radical feminist assumed leadership of the movement. Radical feminists now took the position that women were not only different from men but perhaps even superior to them, so that existing gender differences (which, some argued, included qualities that might be considered fundamentally female) should be preserved and elaborated, not elided or obscured. Some feminists attempted to determine qualities that could be identified as particularly, perhaps essentially female—attachment to life, peacefulness, capacity to form connections and embrace interdependency, cooperation, tolerance of ambiguity. Feminists of the later 1970s sought to discover in the past and elaborate in the present an already existent female counterculture. Culture thus became the appropriate realm for political activity, and the proper political practice for feminists increasingly came to be seen not as challenging male dominance in the public arena—a domain somewhat contemptuously relegated to liberal feminists—but as constructing autonomous or even separatist feminist institutions. No politically correct woman, radical feminists argued, would wish to enter into any sort of relationship with men, let alone assume an "equal" position in institutions dominated by them.

"Cultural feminism," as this feminist tendency came to be called in the late 1970s, loosed an enormous energy and creativity: the past accomplishments of women were rediscovered and celebrated and a wide array of new feminist institutions brought into being: battered women's shelters, rape crisis lines, women's centers, bookstores, restaurants, journals, publishing houses, record companies, rock groups, and even "the other MLA," as feminists in the seventies referred to a whole range of feminist counterevents within the official convention. Though early U.S. feminists had regarded psychoanalysis as a field dominated by sexist male analysts endeavoring to reconcile women to their traditional feminine duties, by the late 1970s, under the influence of scholarly studies such as Juliet Mitchell's *Psychoanalysis and Feminism* (1974), Dorothy Dinnerstein's *The Mermaid and the Minotaur* (1977), and Nancy Chodorow's *The Reproduction of Mothering* (1978), cultural (and other) feminists used psychoanalysis to provide an explanation for why and how girls relinquished their first love objects, their mothers, and learned to assume their proper position within a patriarchal order. In her influential *Signs* article "Compulsory Heterosexuality and Lesbian Existence" (1980), Adrienne Rich maintains that women choose male sexual partners and otherwise "collaborate" with men only as a consequence of male violence and situates all woman-identified experience on what she terms a "lesbian continuum." The paradigmatic work of cultural feminism in the late 1970s was Mary Daly's *Gyn/Ecology* (1978). Daly details the crimes of male culture (ruled by a single necrophilic principle which sometimes seems to derive from male anatomy), catalogues the multitude of ways in which all women can be perceived to be victims of all men, and, in a brilliant series of wordplays, attempts to recover original feminist meanings in a language debased by men. For Daly, the task of feminists is to repudiate, by an act of will, their identification with male culture, separate themselves from patriarchy, and join in a voyage toward a community of free lesbian women—Spinsters, Hags, and Crones.

Under the influence of cultural feminism, the question that dominated the work of literary scholars up to the early 1980s had been posed by Silvia Bovenschen: "Is There a Feminine Aesthetic?" As Elaine Showalter observed, the appropriate activity of feminist literary scholars was "gynocritics," defined as "the study of women as writers, and its subjects are the history, styles, themes, genres, and structures of writing by women; the psychodynamics of female creativity; the trajectory of the individual or collective female career; and the evolution and laws of a female literary tradition" ("Feminist" 248). From the late 1970s to the present the vast majority of feminist literary analyses have focused on writing by women. Within the various national literatures feminists attempted to retrieve lost and neglected women writers, to establish the canonical literary figures of feminism, to uncover a female countertradition, to identify the literary qualities that distinguish women's writing from men's. At issue was not merely feminist content but also form, for if the shape, the morphology of every aspect of female experience was different from men's, then that difference would inevitably also express itself in the aesthetic forms necessary to contain it. Or, as Sandra Gilbert and Susan Gubar emphasize in *The Madwoman in the Attic* (1979), if women writers are constrained to use men's methods and follow their rules, at the very least they succeed in embedding their own subversive message like a palimpsest in their texts, and those cryptic communications can be retrieved by a later generation of feminist scholars who have learned to read against the grain texts endeavoring to accommodate themselves to patriarchal norms.

Such feminist accomplishments in many areas of cultural analysis prepared the ground on which "French feminist" theory would flourish (battles between proponents of "French" and "American" feminism notwithstanding), and at least in the version in which U.S. feminist academics received French feminism, the two tendencies seemed to display many similarities. The French thinkers (of whom Hélène Cixous, Luce Irigaray, and Julia Kristeva were the most frequently cited) seemed to propose that some qualities were shared by all women, that those qualities had been suppressed by men (or a male-dominated system of signification), and that access to them could be achieved by attending to the specificity of the female body, the female unconscious, and female language. Whether in Kristeva's appeal to a presymbolic, "semiotic" realm of poetic languages deriving from the child's connection to the mother's body, Cixous's demand that we write in mother's milk, or Irigary's two lips speaking their *jouissance* or orgasmic pleasure, the maternal body and female eroticism were central to the release of that which a phallogocentric symbolic order had prevented from expressing itself. Culture was hence the most important realm within which to challenge patriarchy, since it had been systems of signification (often delimited by the adjective "Western," though adherents of this paradigm never investigated whether "non-Western" structures of representation might function differently) that were responsible for the systematic repression of femininity and hence must be challenged by finding some alternative voice in which women might nonetheless speak. By thus breaking the silence and claiming their right to a female subjectivity the possibility of whose existence Western discourse denies, women draw into question the premises on which Western symbolic systems rest and, as a revolutionary act, explode the entire phallogo-centric order. As in the analyses of the groups around the French journal *Tel quel*, the French feminist approach placed special emphasis upon the revolutionary potential of avantgarde literary texts, termed by the French feminists *écriture féminine* or sometimes *parler femme*. Via their appropriation of French theory, feminist literary scholars in the United States were able to arrive by a different route at the same conclusions (very flattering to their own discipline) to which United States feminist theory had led them: that literary texts by women and the feminist analysis of them constituted one of the most (if not the most) crucial sites of feminist intervention.

From the perspective of the early twenty-first century (and within the framework of this book), it may seem startling that I have been able to produce such a historical narrative of academic feminism without any reference to historical events that may have helped to shape it. It is also hard to understand how feminists of that era could have advanced analyses so breathtakingly unaware of women's historical situation and the various historically specific forces that interacted to produce it. Such obliviousness to history and culture, however, was itself characteristic of many feminists' self-understanding in this period, who were fond of quoting the assertion by Virginia Woolf in *Three Guineas*: "As a woman, I have no country." In retrospect, feminists' freedom to disregard the larger historical context seems itself historically occasioned, enabled by the moderate liberalism of the 1970s which allowed feminists still to imagine that they could preserve or establish women's spaces exterior to male power. And though cultural feminism was founded on assumptions that now seem demonstrably incorrect, for a time those premises were enormously productive for a particular group of white, middle-class women (arguably still the hegemonic group within academic feminism). The women's movement has probably never again recovered the vitality it manifested in the 1970s. Those premises were to be challenged "around 1981," though feminist literary scholars had perhaps not yet seen the writing on the wall.

In February 1981, Tom Hayden, writing in the *Nation*, declared: "What the conservatives called 'bleeding heart liberalism' finally hemorrhaged and died in

1980" (193). In "The Wraps Are Off," the first editorial of the *Nation*'s first issue in 1981, its editors drew the consequence:

> Let there be no illusions about the nature of the new Government of the United States, composed of Reagan et al. (and especially Al Haig), and the 97th Congress. Forget the Honeymoon. Dismiss the notion that the Presidency enobles. Prepare for the very worst. . . .
>
> On the evidence of the Cabinet choices and the radical policy formulations of the "transition," there seems little doubt about where Reaganism is heading. We had better start preparing to resist. The interlude of spurious hope is over. (3–4)

The hopes of the women's movement had been curtailed as well. In the context of a *Nation* series in November–December 1981 on the future of the women's movement, Frances Lear asserted tersely: "Feminism has had a generous share of heroes, but the 1980 elections proved that it does not have clout" (635). In the same series, Ellen Willis began her article by taking account of the changed circumstances: "The momentum of the movement has drastically slowed, and if it is to survive, let alone progress, it must regroup and begin a new offensive" (494).

Willis took particular aim at cultural feminism because of its damaging impact on the women's movement more generally:

> While cultural feminism has always been one tendency in the women's movement, in recent years it has become increasingly prominent and more aggressive in attempting to establish itself as the feminist orthodoxy. It has been a drag on the movement in two ways. First, it provides no intellectual basis for a concrete antisexist politics. If anything, it does the opposite, channeling female energy into counter-cultural projects, fantasies of restoring an alleged golden age of matriarchy, or moral crusades against male vice. It also reinforces oppressive cultural stereotypes, especially the assumption that men have a monopoly on aggression and active genital sexuality (cultural feminists often equate the two), while women are nonviolent, nurturing and more interested in affection than in sex. (495)

She and the other contributors to the *Nation* series called upon feminists to break out of their isolation and to reaffirm their allegiance to oppositional politics. Indeed, over the course of the 1980s, a new attention to women's historical situatedness would come to shape feminist activism, theory, and analysis. As I hope Part 2 of this book will show, over the decade the new feminist orientation would "trickle down" (a favored image of those years) to feminist literary scholarship as well.

CHAPTER 3
In the Cemetery of the Murdered Daughters
MALINA

> *Look, she said, but the pharaoh*
> *forgot that though he had eradicated*
> *her, she was still there. It can still be*
> *read, because nothing is there where*
> *in fact something should be.*
>
> —*Ingeborg Bachmann,* The Book of Franza

Ingeborg Bachmann's *Malina* is about the absence of a female voice; in some respects it reads like an illustration of the feminist theory which has evolved since its publication to explain why, within Western discourse, women are permitted no voice and subjectivity of their own. It may be that feminism is the collective struggle of women to constitute that voice, but that battle has barely begun. In what voice, then, does a female scholar write about the absence of a female voice? I have realized that my struggle with *Malina*, Bachmann's struggle to write it, and the struggle she describes in it are all part of the larger war in which we women (against our will and often without our conscious knowledge) are combatants—and which may have killed Bachmann. "Our bodies, falling, will dam that great river of sexism," Tillie Olsen said in 1979 at the MLA, "and over us others will pass." Feminist literary scholars still speak mostly with that sovereign (male) voice which explains the literary text to less astute readers. (What other choice do we have, particularly given our precarious position at the edge of academics? We have to play by their rules.) But *Malina* shows what women lose when they try to accommodate themselves to the categories of male subjectivity. Though Bachmann is without solutions herself, we feminists can read her novel as part of our struggle to challenge those categories within which we have no right to speak as women and to construct some other, more authentic, female voice.

Bachmann explained in a 1972 interview that her novel *Malina*, published the previous year, had provided solutions to problems of composition with which she had struggled for years. With *Malina* as opening or overture, she could proceed with her work in progress, a mammoth novel cycle titled "Ways of Death": "I wrote almost a thousand pages before this book, and these last 400 pages from the very last years became the beginning that I had always lacked. I didn't find the entrance to that book—and for me this has now become the book which makes my access to the Ways of Death possible" (*GuI* 96). How, the interviewer asks, did she happen upon the double figure of Malina and the "I" of the novel?

> For me it's one of the oldest, if almost inaccessible memories: that I always knew I had to write this book—very early already, while I was still writing poems. That I constantly searched for the main character. That I knew: it would be male. That I could only narrate from the standpoint of a male character. But I often asked myself: Why? I didn't understand, in the stories either, why I so often had to use a male "I." It was like finding my character to be able not to deny this female "I" and nonetheless to emphasize the male "I." (*GuI* 99–100)

Of all the authors mentioned in *Malina*, not a single one is a woman: for Bachmann, there is no female narrative voice. At the end of the novel, the female "I" disappears into a crack in the wall, and only Malina is left. "It was murder," reads the novel's last line (*Malina* 239). "Malina will be able to tell us," Bachmann explains, "what the other part of his character, the 'I,' left behind for him" (*GuI* 96). These are the "ways of death," told in Malina's male voice, experienced by the female "I" and the cause of her destruction.

The novel *Malina* itself has been badly received and ill-understood since its publication in 1971. Most recently [1980], Marcel Reich-Ranicki called it Bachmann's "late, incidentally weak and confused novel" ("Tageslicht" 387); in the latest installment of the *Kritisches Lexikon zur Gegenwartsliteratur* (Critical lexicon of contemporary literature) Bernd Witte gives probably the most accurate assessment of it yet, but in his limited space he must ignore most of the work's difficulty. But *Malina* is a difficult work, and its relative inaccessibility is tied very closely to its subject matter. Before her death, Bachmann published another volume of prose, the short story collection *Three Paths to the Lake*, which seems to be part of the "Ways of Death" cycle, since its characters appear also in both *Malina* and the cycle's unfinished novels. In 1978, four volumes of Bachmann's collected works appeared, including the mostly completed novel *The Book of Franza*, the novel fragment *Requiem for Fanny Goldmann*, and some longer fragments whose position in the larger cycle is not clear. The *Werke* also contain Bachmann's essays from the 1950s and 1960s. From these various writings it is possible to conclude a great deal about her purposes for the "Ways of Death" in general and *Malina* in particular, why these were subjects that concerned Bachmann from the time she began writing, and why, most specifically, the struggle to find a narrative voice to tell the "Ways of Death" realized itself in a text that took the shape of *Malina*.

Trained as a philosopher at the University of Vienna by Viktor Kraft, one of the last of the grand old men of logical positivism (*GuI* 82), Bachmann explored her concern with the possibilities of language from her student days onward. From the beginning, however, her examination of language was an idiosyncratic one, more akin to the concerns of present-day poststructuralism than to mainstream logical positivism, as her two 1950s essay on Ludwig Wittgenstein show. For what interests Bachmann most about Wittgenstein is not his analysis of what language *can* say, but what it can't: "The limits of my language mean the limits of my world." For Wittgenstein, a mystical appropriation of the world is also possible which does not participate in the limitations of language: "There is indeed the inexpressible. This shows itself; it is the mystical" (*Tractatus* 149, 187). What Bachmann finds in Wittgenstein is the possibility of a response to the world which transcends the categories of occidental reason, as she quite explicitly indicates in a radio essay:

> FIRST SPEAKER: Does Wittgenstein not in fact come to the same conclusion as Pascal? Let's hear what the author of the *Pensées* said three hundred years before him: "The last step of reason is the recognition that there is an infinitude of things that surpass it."
>
> SECOND SPEAKER: Wittgenstein took this last step of reason. He who says like Wittgenstein: "God does not reveal himself in the world" says also implicitly "Vere tu es deus absconditus." For about what should one keep silent if not about that beyond limits—about the hidden god, about the ethical and aesthetic as mystical experiences of the heart which take place in the unsayable. (*W* 3: 120)

Moreover, Bachmann pursues this line of thought in Wittgenstein's work into his later *Philosophical Investigations*, where she identifies his project as an attempt to abolish the language of philosophy, understood as a system of abstract categories, and substitute for it some other way of speaking which is closer to the texture of daily life: "It is Wittgenstein's conviction that philosophy has to be brought to rest by us so that it is no longer tormented by questions which place *it itself* in question, and he believed that we can silence the problems if our language functions well and sensibly, if it lives and breathes in use. Only where language, which is a form of life, is taken out of use, where it runs dry—and that happens, in his opinion, when it is used philosophically, in the usual sense—do problems come about. These problems are not to be solved but rather to be gotten rid of" (*W* 4: 124). Using metaphors which will emerge again in the "Ways of Death," Bachmann argues that Wittgenstein's philosophy will undertake a healing of the sickness that philosophical problems now represent: "And since language is a labyrinth of ways—as he terms it at another point—philosophy must take up the struggle against the bewitching of our understanding through language. Philosophy must destroy castles in the air and reveal the basis of language, it must be like a therapy, for philosophical problems are sicknesses which have to be healed. It's not a solution but a cure that he calls for" (*W* 4: 124). The implications of what Bachmann hints at here are far-reaching: she points towards fundamental and inherent defects of our present language (which is to say, of the entire mode of thought that we know), which her choice of metaphor allies with the human body or psyche ("therapy," "sickness") and which can be overcome only through some transformation in the present condition of language/philosophy—that is, of present human categories of thought.

But Bachmann's essays also identify ways of speaking already outside the categories of Western reason. Particularly interesting is her essay on Georg Groddeck, to whom her short story "Eyes to Wonder" in *Three Paths to the Lake* is dedicated. Groddeck, a psychoanalyst slightly older than Freud and loosely allied with him, originated the term "It" ("Es" in German, "Id" in English translations of Freud), which represented for him the speech of the body. For Groddeck, Bachmann explains, a physical symptom "is a production, like an artistic one, and sickness means something. It wants to say something, it says it by its particular way of appearing, running its course, and disappearing or ending fatally. It says what the sick person doesn't understand, although it's his most particular expression." Passionately, Bachmann speaks of Groddeck's recognition of the power of the It over the relatively powerless ego: "The *It* is a word he uses for lack of better, it's not a thing in itself but is supposed to mean something's there, it's there and stronger and much stronger than the ego, for the ego can't even intentionally intervene in breathing, in digestion, in blood circulation, the ego is a mask, a pretension with which all of us go about—and we are ruled by the *It*, the *It* does that, and it speaks through sickness in symbols" (W 4: 352). Important here are Bachmann's insistence that human desire cannot be contained, though its needs refuse the categories which the ego has accepted, and her allying of the speech (the attempt to signify) of Groddeck's It to artistic productions, where that which the ego had not wanted to say or known it was saying can break through into signifying material and speak itself behind the back, against the will, of the signifying subject.

Finally, a variety of Bachmann's essays from this earlier period as well as several short stories and her radio play "The Good God of Manhattan" address head on the role of Eros as source both of resistance to this social order and of the possible articulation of some alternative to it. The subversive power of Eros is also associated with the mysticism on which she had touched in the Wittgenstein essay, a mode of articulation beyond the borders of language. The influence of Critical Theory is apparent here, not simply Herbert Marcuse but also Ernst Bloch: love is a concrete utopia that points toward some future social order less hostile to human happiness. To understand the relevance of these utopian love affairs for the "Ways of Death," however, it is also necessary to recognize that they are antisocial, contravening fundamental social taboos, and that this dimension of the revolt of desire is exactly what constitutes their utopianism.

Bachmann's radio essay on Marcel Proust, whom she terms a "positivist and mystic" (*W* 4: 180), concentrates mainly on the theme of homosexuality in his work: "The latent revolt of the individual against society, nature against morality, led him to the conception of the 'homme traqué,' the hounded, surrounded human being of whom the invert is only an especially clear example" (*W* 4: 160). As Bachmann explains it, the love of Musil's Ulrich for his sister Agathe more clearly still elaborates a utopian alternative with explicit social relevance. This love is an alternative, ecstatic, quasi-mystical condition of mind which, though not itself applicable to a changed social order, fulfills its function in negating and disrupting the present dominant order: "It's true that the 'other condition' leads from society into absolute freedom, but now Ulrich knows that the utopia of this other life makes no prescriptions for the practice of life and, for a life in society, has to be replaced by the utopia of the given social condition—Musil calls it that of the 'inductive attitude.' But both utopias bring about the replacement of closed ideologies with open ones" (*W* 4: 27). Moreover—and this is of major importance for the "Ways of Death"—for Bachmann the order of thought that Ulrich's ecstasy opposes, those closed ideologies, has a direct and causal connection to war, a term which here includes not just the national conflicts of the twentieth century, but the general state of contemporary society: "Not only the case of Kakania has shown that thinking in closed ideologies leads directly to war, and the permanent war of faith is still the order of the day" (W 4: 27). A variety of Bachmann's earlier creative writings also locate a basic resistance to the dominant order of thought in love, so that to pursue this love would be almost to foment revolution, to change the world utterly: "A Step towards Gomorrah," "A Wildermuth," "Undine Goes" from *The Thirtieth Year*. But though with the exception of "A Step towards Gomorrah" these loves are taboo only in that they are illicit, what is important to notice with respect to the particular relevance of these stories to the "Ways of Death" is that the promise of satisfaction for which desire longs is embodied in women. In "The Good God of Manhattan," love is "another state of being" and "crossing a boundary" ("GG" 182), which Jan, the man, cannot sustain. He retreats to a corner bar, "lapsed. Routine stretched its hand out to him for a moment" ("GG" 96). Jennifer, the woman, keeps the faith and is blown sky-high by the Good God to reestablish his divine, patriarchal normality.

It is not clear (nor does it matter much) whether a coherent theory underlies these various concerns of Bachmann's earlier writing—though it is hard to believe that this erudite woman, with her particular interests in philosophy, psychology, and language, did not follow the latest developments in European thought in the 1960s and 1970s. In any case, that theory exists now (a theory that addresses the problem of coherence and incoherence) and can be used to explain the conjuncture of interests that meet in the "Ways of Death." For even the most superficial reading of Bachmann's late prose should make clear who is being killed in these various ways (and also that "death" can be the death of the spirit as well as of the body): women. Recent feminist theory, drawing particularly on the work of Derrida and Lacan, argues that the oppression of women is structured into the fundamental categories of our thought, which must be transformed if women are to achieve an autonomous subjectivity of their own. This order, as Derrida argues, is logocentric, predicated on the assertion of a logos, a central term or presence-to-itself (whose name has varied historically: God, essence, substance, consciousness, man, etc.) against which all other terms are measured. The laws of logocentricity which structure all our thought are learned through the child's appropriation of language and constitute its fundamental categories. But as Lacanian psychoanalysis maintains, through this entry into language infants are also constituted as gendered human beings: to take on language means to accede to the channeling of infant desire into socially appropriate expressions and to assume one's proper place in the gendered order. For women, this means to accept both the preeminence of the phallus, Lacan's "transcendental signifier," and the "fact" of their own castration. So long as they fail to revolt against this order, women logically and in fact will be associated with the negative term of a logocentric and phallocentric order: object, nature, other, absence, silence, lack. Derrida's endeavor is of course to deconstruct self-identity, presence-to-itself, by showing that it was never that which it asserted itself to be. Bachmann's intent in the "Ways of Death" and particularly *Malina*, I would like to argue here, is a similar one. This work, with which she struggled for so long, shows that the destruction of women—though it be a destruction they themselves accept—is a necessary consequence of the order in which they live. But even as they are destroyed, they speak, cry out, rebel: their desire will not be completely contained. The current women's movement barely existed when Bachmann died in 1973, and she can conceive women only as victims. Perhaps we are further than that today—but it is important that we know what she has to tell us.

The dilemma that Bachmann confronts and represents in *Malina* involves women's place in the symbolic order. How can it be possible for her, a woman, to write about women when exactly what she wishes to assert makes her own position as woman wielding the pen impossible? This awareness of oneself as a contradiction in terms traces its way through *Malina* in recurrent phrases which express both extraordinary pain and perseverance: "Those who have to live a Why can endure almost any How," and, most poignantly, in view of Bachmann's own death by fire, "Avec ma main brulée, j'écris sur la nature du feu" (with my burned hand, I write of the nature of fire). Damaged herself, she will insist on overcoming her injuries to write of their causes. But what voice does she assume? Monique Wittig, in her introduction to *The Lesbian Body*, addressed this problem of the lack of a female "I" in our language, pointing out that subjectivity is generically human, which is to say male, in Western thought:

"I" [*Je*] as a generic feminine subject can only enter by force into a language which is foreign to it, for all that is human [masculine] is foreign to it, the human not being feminine grammatically speaking but he [*il*] or they [*ils*]. "I" [*Je*] conceals the sexual differences of the verbal persons while specifying them in verbal interchange. "I" [*Je*] obliterates the fact that *elle* or *elles* are submerged in *il* or *ils*, i.e. that the feminine persons are complementary to the masculine persons. The feminine "I" [*Je*] who is speaking can fortunately forget this difference and assume indifferently the masculine language. But the "I" [*Je*] who writes is driven back to her specific experience as subject. The "I" [*Je*] who writes is alien to her own writing at every word because this "I" [*Je*] uses a language alien to her; this "I" [*Je*] experiences what is alien to her since this "I" [*Je*] cannot be "un ecrivain." If, in writing *je*, I adopt this language, this *je* cannot do so. J/e is the symbol of the lived, rending experience which is m/y writing, of this cutting in two which throughout literature is the exercise of a language which does not constitute m/e as subject. J/e poses the ideological and historic question of feminine subjects. (x)

Wittig drew attention to her problem by orthographic splitting; Bachmann's solution is analogous, as we will see.

Moreover, if another writing is necessary even to begin to examine the possibility of the female articulation of subjectivity, it is clear that, for us, another, different, reading will be entailed as well—as feminist critics, most brilliantly Sandra Gilbert and Susan Gubar, have begun to argue. For, Gilbert and Gubar point out, what traditional scholarship regards as the strangeness of women's writing may result both from their own difficulty in writing with a male "I" and from the necessity to transform male narrative to fit the forms of female lives:

> They [women writers] may have attempted to transcend their anxiety of author-ship by revising male genres, using them to record their own dreams and their own stories in disguise. Such writers, therefore, both participated in and . . . "swerved" from the central sequences of male literary history, enacting a uniquely female process of revision that necessarily caused them to seem "odd." . . . [W]omen . . . produced literary works that are in some sense palimpsestic, works whose surface designs conceal or obscure deeper, less accessible, (and less socially acceptable) lev-els of meaning. (*Madwoman* 73)

No doubt, many scholarly difficulties with Bachmann's writing result from the attempt to understand it in terms of exactly those categories that she is trying to subvert. Cited in the center of Bachmann's novel is the Ibsen play which also gives its title to Adrienne Rich's famous essay on female creativity. Rich's essay begins: "Ibsen's *When We Dead Awaken* is a play about the use that the male art-ist and thinker—in the process of creating culture as we know it—has made of women, in his life and in his work, and about a woman's slow struggling awak-ening to the use to which her life has been put." Women in the "Ways of Death" rarely awaken to an understanding of the male order (though they often cry out in their sleep), but a feminist reading of Bachmann's late works could be part of our awakening. Rich continues:

> Re-vision—the act of looking back, of seeing with fresh eyes, of entering an old text from a new critical direction—is for women more than a chapter in cultural history: it is an act of survival. Until we can understand the assumptions in which we are drenched we cannot know ourselves. And this drive to self-knowledge, for women, is more than a search for identity: it is part of our refusal of the self-destructiveness of male-dominated society. A radical critique of literature, femi-nist in its impulse, would take the work first of all as a clue to how we live, how we have been living, how we have been led to imagine ourselves, how our language has trapped as well as liberated us, how the very act of naming has been till now male prerogative, and how we can begin to see and name—and therefore live—afresh. ("When" 34–35).

This, evidently, is part of Bachmann's purpose in *Malina*.

To begin this strange book is already to be put off balance. The "Malina" of the title appears to be the first name of a woman but is identified in the initial cast of characters as the last name of a man. (There are in fact plenty of last-name Malinas in the Vienna phone book, yet it is clear that this confusion is intentional.) The "I," whose female identity emerges only slowly, has no name at all, though she shares some qualities with Bachmann herself: "born in Klagenfurt." But Malina too has some characteristics which, ironically transformed, are reminiscent of Bachmann: "Author of an apocrypha no longer available in bookstores, but which sold a few copies in the late fifties." Apocrypha: writings of doubtful authenticity or authorship. Malina's occupation puts him in his place once and for all: "employed in the Austrian Army Museum," to preside over the relics and mementos of past wars, of an empire and way of life which has already succumbed to history (*Malina* 1). (Elsewhere in the novel the "I" remarks of Vienna: "I am very glad to live here, because from this point on the planet where nothing more is happening, a confrontation with the world is all the more frightening, here one is neither self-righteous nor self-satisfied, as this is not some protected island, but a haven of decay, wherever you go there is decay, decay everywhere, right before our eyes, and not just the decay of yesterday's empire, but today's as well" [*Malina* 59].)

Though Malina is presented as an independent character and continues to be elaborated as one throughout the novel, it is clear early on that there is something odd about his relationship to the "I": "For years my relationship with Malina consisted of awkward meetings, absolute follies and the biggest possible misunderstandings—I mean of course much greater misunderstandings than with other people. Certainly I was *subordinate* to him from the beginning, and I must have known early on that he was destined to be my doom, that Malina's place was already occupied by Malina even before he entered my life" (*Malina* 5). Bachmann has made clear enough in a number of interviews that Malina is the double of the "I" (though, she says, the reader need not necessarily grasp the relationship to appreciate the novel) and that he represents male subjectivity, a position that a woman must occupy, a guise that she must assume, according to the rules of this social order, if she is to possess any subjectivity at all. It does not make sense within a Freudian paradigm to assert, as Walter Helmut Fritz does, that Malina is sometimes a superego for the "I" (24); among other things, he is far too nice to her. To be quite clear: Malina is the persona that women must assume when they enter the project world; they must become the genderless (that is to say, male), liberal, bourgeois subject, suppressing their female qualities. Malina is the voice in which Bachmann mostly narrates, the only voice available to professional and academic women, and the voice in which I am writing this essay, a borrowed voice, not our own.

Now it is apparent that the invention of Malina solves a good many problems for both Bachmann and the "I." In the voice of Malina, Bachmann can narrate the rest of the "Ways of Death" in a form apparently coherent, realistic, and accessible—as various reviewers (e.g., Wirsing) remarked with relief of *Three Paths to the Lake*. If Malina does not break with the categories of the order he depicts, he nonetheless gives account of the tragedies it occasions with kindness and compassion. Bachmann's fondness for her figure is evident in the Toni Kienlechner interview: "There is an important place in the book for me where the 'I' says that Malina is not out for the demasking that we know from literature, that x-ray glance at people which humiliates them, that Malina does not look through people but looks at them, that he's fair to everyone—for otherwise irony can easily lead to diminishing people" (Kienlechner 101). But though Malina moves in the direction of a nineteenth-century narrator, the moral burden of what he has to tell us is none the weaker for that; it is only that we must read the moral out of his narratives. In drafts for the figure of Malina, Bachmann makes his moral purpose clear. Observing, for instance, the wreckage of a civilization at the Frankfurt Book Fair, Malina thunders his wrath like an Old Testament prophet:

> You hear, I obey an old language and old concepts, I turn back like all people who gaze at what has happened and are turned to stone, and perhaps an angel will tell you in time, don't look back, and then you won't see Frankfurt consumed in smoke and brimstone, as I see it consumed today and twice every year, for vengeance has come. Not my vengeance, for I have come to tell and not to judge, but judgment haunts all the stories, and lamentation in the smoke when it rises to heaven and is told. (*TP* 1: 364)

Malina tells; we judge.

For the female "I" in Bachmann's novel, Malina is also a convenient figure, a kind of reality principle. He is the one who pays the bills, remembers appointments, keeps her affairs in order. He is also the calm and soothing voice of male reason, who comforts her when she awakens in terror from her nightmares. What would we do without him, especially in the middle of the night? It is foolishness, nonsense, forget it and go back to sleep. (Or, at least as often, the voice of a sovereign male reason which, in a sober and distanced way, tries to analyze the psychological motives for the terror which emerges in the dreams: "I'll get to the point. Why is your ring missing? Did you ever wear a ring? Or course you didn't" (*Malina* 144). Lina, the cleaning lady, who is a further splitting off from Malina, is also a useful figure; she is clean and orderly and can move furniture all by herself, that autonomous, if subservient, superwoman: "Men! gnädige Frau, we don't need any men for that!" (*Malina* 75).

But there are also disadvantages when a woman assumes a male persona, something like the "double consciousness" of black people which W. E. B. Du Bois described: we know who we are seen to be; we know what we assert ourselves to be; we have some idea of who we are—and those are not the same thing. The tension involved in holding together these disparate parts of the personality is difficult to sustain. What a fortune-teller reads out of the palm of the "I" is no surprise to her:

> She said that at first glance it shows an incredible tension, it's really not a picture of one person but of two people standing in extreme opposition to one another, it must mean that I am constantly apt to be torn in two; with configurations like these, if all the dates I had given were accurate. I asked hopefully: The torn man, the torn woman, right? If they were separated it would be livable, maintained Frau Novak, but scarcely the way it is, furthermore male and female, reason and feeling, productivity and self-destruction also appear in an unusual manner. I must have made a mistake with my dates, since she liked me right away, I'm such a natural woman, she likes natural people. (*Malina* 163)

Of course she is a natural woman, hanging on despite the fact that this tension has become second nature to us. But an even more critical disadvantage to asserting (and believing) ourselves to be generically human and not specifically female is that we have no access to the female side of ourselves. Subsumed in the male, we do not attend to it and cannot tell about it. It is in good part because Malina exists, as a dimension of the "I" to which she clings, that she has no narrative voice, as she sometimes recognizes: "Malina interrupts me, he is protecting me, but I think his wanting to protect me is preventing me from telling. It's Malina who isn't letting me talk [*erzählen*]" (*Malina* 175). As in Christa Wolf's story "Self-Experiment," for women to become men seems the most obvious solution to centuries of women's oppression. But it may also mean that women lose what is most important to them.

Yet to demonize men as somehow ontologically incompatible with the female is also too easy a solution. As it has been the burden of deconstruction to show, male subjectivity is not altogether unproblematic or identical with itself, either. How much more this must then be the case of a male subjectivity assumed by a woman! Examined more closely, Malina himself is a suspicious figure; perhaps it's for this reason that he can narrate the "Ways of Death" at all. As Rainer Nägele has pointed out, "Shuffled anew, the letters of the name produce an ANIMAL which, if you cut off its tail, spiritualizes itself into an ANIMA" (38). An "animal" is hidden in Malina, a metaphor which Bachmann also pursued in her short story "The Barking," where the old woman finally rebelling in her senility against her tyrannical son is overwhelmed by the imaginary barking of the dog her son had hated (it is also interesting that in her loving topography of Vienna's Third District, the one large landmark the "I" suppresses is the Tierärztliche Hochschule [Veterinary School], right around the corner from the Ungargasse). Malina also has a female double in the novel, Maria Malina, a Viennese actress much more famous than he, her name combining the two most popular stereotypes about women, sainthood plus carnality: Maria Animal. In the drafts for the Malina figure, Maria Malina, "who on stage was a dream, an animal," is revealed—by a male narrator—to be "unassuming" in real life: "a vehemence, a silence, a sob, a smile, those stooped shoulders and big feet and her nose was rather thick, she didn't have make-up on, she had a bad complexion and too thick a nose, and she wasn't thin and wasn't fat, a medium-sized body, not unrobust, and her hair was greasy, stringy, dishwater blond, that was the Malina woman" (*TP* 1: 346–47). A woman must be a consummate artist to meet men's expectations of her, and her reality is bound to disappoint them. Maria Malina is eaten by a shark at age thirty-four—or at least this was the report given by the man with whom she had traveled to Greece, the only witness to her death. Malina has experienced "ways of death," too.

The first encounter of the "I" with Malina is also an interesting allusion to his lack of self-identity and to the possibility of suppressed psychic qualities emerging into male bourgeois consciousness which could destroy all its achievements. If Bachmann's name itself reveals the split personality to which Malina gives expression, the "Bach," fluidity of the female, channeled by the masculine "Mann," it is a "Mann"—Thomas—whose themes *Malina* varies in displaying its own problems with a threatened and dying society to which no alternative seems to offer itself. The "I" first glimpses Malina in a scene which draws upon the experiences of Gustav von Aschenbach (who shares a portion of Bachmann's name and combines the fire and water motifs that trace their way through *Malina*): she waits for a streetcar on the edge of a park (the Stadtpark, which, as I show later, represents the allure and threat of psychic nondifferentiation), boards, and looks about for Malina, who has vanished. But of course the figures are reversed here: it is Malina who represents the firm male ego boundaries which will be confirmed at the end of this work, though dissolved at the end of Mann's. Malina is first observed with a newspaper in his hand: he has the access to the language of social communication (here some-what debased) which Aschenbach also possesses and which is lacking in this female "I." Moreover, this "I" will never even make it to Venice. Though it represents as for Aschenbach the promise of sensual fulfillment, the "I" must experience it as distinct and separate from herself, in the "cinema behind the Kärntnerring . . . where I first saw Venice, for two hours in extravagant colors and a lot of darkness, the oars beating the water, a melody accompanied by lights passing through the water as well, and its da-dim da-dam carried me along, all the way inside the figures, the coupled figures and their dancing. In this way I arrived in a Venice I would never see, on a clanking, windy winter day in Vienna" (*Malina* 11).

Of yet more central importance to *Malina* is the opposition, which is central to Thomas Mann's *Doktor Faustus*, of Beethoven and Arnold Schönberg: if Adrian Leverkühn's masterwork, "Fausti Weheklage" is written to rescind Beethoven's Ninth Symphony, to remand that joyful affirmation of a social order, Bachmann's "Ways of Death" cycle aims at the same intention. Across from the house where this silenced female "I" lives, Ungargasse 6, is Ungargasse 5, the Beethovenhaus, where the deaf Beethoven wrote his Ninth Symphony. Yet the central musical composition whose thematics shape Bachmann's work is by the figure whom Mann construed as Beethoven's negation, Schönberg. But as I explain in more detail below, the Schönberg work *Pierrot Lunaire*, on which *Malina* draws, not only negates current cultural categories like Leverkühn's composition but also hints simultaneously at some other, utopian possibilities for human happiness.

By far the most intriguing indication that Malina is more than he appears to be is found in a reference to the work by Bachmann's admirer Christa Wolf, whose writing circles about many of the same themes as Bachmann's own. In Wolf's *The Quest for Christa T.*, the one extended narrative which Christa T., that thwarted and utopian figure, is able to write is titled "Malina, die Himbeere" and involves a journey of a thirteen-year-old girl to Kalisch, then (in 1940) a district of Russian Poland occupied by the Nazis. The young narrator insists she is traveling to a foreign country, though her mother maintains it is German. The story breaks off with their arrival in Kalisch. "Now one ought to know why she stopped at this point," the narrator of *Christa T.* continues. "What was to be the outcome of the Polish strawberry [*sic*: *Himbeere* = raspberry]—Malina—for which she had raised the whole magic structure, with Brockhaus 1889, the journey to a foreign country which wasn't any such journey, her mother and herself, talking and replying . . . you asked what testimony I've got. Well: the tone of these pages of hers, for example. She speaks so you can see her" (Wolf, *Quest* 90).

To speak about and across borders which are not physical ones is a task of female writing, especially in a land occupied by a foreign invader, one whom Bachmann might even be inclined to define more precisely as fascist, as in Wolf's work. Christa T. couldn't write either; even the story "Malina" is unfinished, and she laments "the difficulty of saying I." Nevertheless, in Wittgensteinian terms, Christa T. does venture to cross some borders, and both the "I" of *Malina* and Malina himself come from the border, where the rigid boundaries each language sets become softened a little. This pressure on the limits of language is one of the themes and strengths of Bachmann's novel.

Yet perhaps this discussion of Malina has been somewhat misleading, for Malina is not, strictly speaking, whom the novel is about. The other and more overtly tyrannical figure in relationship to whom the "I" constitutes herself is Ivan, her lover, and it is this relationship that structures the novel: after a short introductory section, the first longer portion of the novel is called "Happy with Ivan" and gives an account of their love affair. The middle section, "The Third Man," consists mainly of her dreams of persecution, in which her father plays the major role. In the third section with its apocalyptic title "Last Things," the relationship with Ivan trails off and the disappearance of the "I" is prepared. As Bachmann pointed out in an interview, Ivan is also probably a kind of double for the "I" (*GuI* 88), which is to say, he also resides in the female psyche: he represents the tyranny of romantic love, of compulsory heterosexuality, whose laws women accept and interiorize. Like other lovers in Bachmann's works— Jan in "The Good God of Manhattan" and "You monsters named Hans!" (*TY* 177) in "Undine Goes"—Ivan is a "john," a more or less interchangeable male lover. That is why, unlike Malina and the "I," he is a signifier identical with his signified or, perhaps more accurately, a signifier without a signified, as the "I" remarks: "Despite all our differences, when it comes to our names Malina and I share the same timidity, only Ivan is completely enthused with his own name [*geht ganz und gar in seinen Namen ein*]" (*Malina* 52).

For the same reason Bachmann could assert in an interview (though what she says is not quite true), "We never learn: what did Ivan do before, what will he do later, what's going to happen at all, who is this man?" (*GuI* 88). In the final section of the novel, Bachmann makes extremely clear that for women, loving a john is a far from idyllic or utopian experience, nor does it allow women the exploration and elaboration of their own sensuality and eroticism. Men make love as suits their tastes, and their female partners must arrange themselves as best they can:

Sometimes one is lucky, but I'm sure most women are never lucky [*haben aber bestimmt nie Glück*]. What I'm talking about has nothing to do with the supposition that there are some men who are good lovers, there really aren't. That is a legend which has to be destroyed someday, at most there are men with whom it is completely hopeless and a few with whom it's not quite so hopeless. Although no one has looked for it, that is where the reason is to be found why only women always have their heads full of feelings and stories about their man or men. Such thoughts really do consume the greatest part of every woman's time. But she has to think about it, she needs to evoke feeling, to provoke feeling—and she can do this without harming herself—otherwise she could literally never bear being with a man, since every man really is sick and hardly takes any notice of her. (*Malina* 178)

"A legend" literally—love is an elaborate symbolic system, a game or dance, the responsibility for which falls on women, who nevertheless do not expect their sick male lovers to make them happy.

This illness leads to the heart of Bachmann's argument: all men are sick, and all women must come to terms with these diseased gender arrangements: "You could say the whole approach of men toward women is diseased [*krankhaft*], moreover each disease is so wholly unique that men will never be completely cured. At most it might be said of women that they are more or less marked by contaminations they have contracted by sympathizing with male suffering" (*Malina* 177). It is this sickness that Bachmann's "Ways of Death" is directed at revealing, as she has made quite clear in interviews. Thus, asked of *Malina*, "Then one should understand it as a document of contemporary existence, of human beings who are themselves destroyed by this destruction—as one of their 'ways of death'?" she replied, "Yes, there is a correspondence between their sickness and the sickness of the world and the society" (Kienlechner 104). A closer examination of the love between Ivan and the "I" will reveal the far-reaching implications of this sickness.

It is important to notice the absences in this love affair. Love itself is rarely mentioned; never do they say "I love you." Sex is never discussed and barely alluded to; this is not a relationship where a female subject discovers her *jouissance*. Even at the level of realism, it is obviously a miserable relationship, with the "I" steadfastly refusing to concede her own unhappiness; yet I would suspect that for most women this sexual dependency is quite convincing: of course she will not break with him, for she loves him. Or one might formulate this somewhat differently: Ivan is the presence that makes it possible to constitute reality, a "fix" which must be renewed for it to have its effect on her:

> I'm thinking about Ivan.
> I'm thinking about love.
> About injections of reality.
> About their lasting merely a few hours.
> About the next, more potent injection. (*Malina* 24)

For her, Ivan is "My Mecca and my Jerusalem" (*Malina* 23); "Everything bears Ivan's brand, from the House of Ivan" (*Malina* 13–14). In this relationship the "I" is thoroughly female: "My fräulein, we are, after all, very female," says Ivan (*Malina* 89). But this is a femininity socially defined, offering her no more access to an authentic female voice than the assumption of Malina's male subjectivity. Ivan is a father with two children, but he is "The Onlie Begetter" (*Malina* 59); the mother does not exist in this story. The children's names suggest some relationship to the original differentiation which makes language possible: Belá, Andras, b-a. But Ivan has accomplished this on his own; the woman is absent and unnamed. The "I" regards Ivan's function for her as the assurance of her entry into language: "For he has come to make consonants constant once again and comprehensible, to unlock vowels to their full resounding, to let words come over my lips once more, to solve problems and recreate connections long since disrupted, and I will not stray from him one iota" (*Malina* 15) Yet the language Ivan gives her to speak is one in which women are permitted to exist only in relationship to men and have no independent voice of their own at all.

Ivan places a variety of limits on the right and ability of the "I" to speak. The most frequent conversations reported between them are telephone calls (a *Verbindung*, connection, facilitated by the cord, always impossibly tangled, which connects her to him). At their best, the calls are banal and boring miscommunication—the "I" running gasping and desperate to answer the telephone, then maintaining, in a futile endeavor to protect herself from him, that she really has no time to talk. Usually the telephone conversations reported are not even complete sentences but completely inadequate vehicles for conveying her emotions, precodified sets of propositions: "example sentences," "fatigue sentences," "swearing sentences." By the time we arrive at that last, ominous set of sentences, the self-deception as the "I" asserts that she is "happy with Ivan" is quite clear, for he directs the terms at her which men have often used to express their terror and loathing of women: "witch," "beast [*Luder*]," bastard [*Aas*]." But Ivan insists that she nonetheless proclaim her happiness with him; in the language that it is given her to speak, all is well between men and women. (All the books in her huge library don't help the "I" deal with Ivan—those books are written by men. The one book she needs is missing: a cookbook.) Ivan explicitly forbids her to continue writing the drafts of the "Ways of Death" he has found in her apartment:

> In general he avoids questions, but today Ivan asks, what do these notes mean, since I've left a few pages lying on the armchair. Merrily [*belustigt*] he takes one and reads: DEATH STYLES [*TODESARTEN* = WAYS OF DEATH]. And from another piece of paper: Darkness in Egypt. Isn't that your writing, didn't you write that? Since I don't answer, Ivan says: I don't like it, I suspected something like this was going on, and nobody wants all these books lying around in your crypt, why isn't there anything else, there must be other books, like EXSULTATE JUBILATE, which make you mad with joy, you're always mad with joy yourself, so why don't you write like that. (*Malina* 30)

And the "I" vows obediently henceforth to rejoice in and write about the bliss which this affair has brought her: "[Ivan] told me: I'm sure you've already understood. I don't love anyone. Except my children, of course, but no one else. I nod, though I hadn't known, and it's obvious to Ivan that it should be so obvious to me. JUBILATE. Poised over an abyss, it nonetheless occurs to me how it should begin: EXSULTATE" (*Malina* 33). This "way of death" can't be written either.

Since the "I" accepts the rules for entry into the symbolic order of compulsory heterosexuality, she constitutes herself according to the social rules of femininity even away from Ivan. There is great and painful irony in the scene in which the "I," on her own, "fables removed from the men [*sagenweit entfernt von den Män-nern*]," nonetheless recreates herself as the woman the fashion industry has told her to become: "The result is a composition, a woman is to be created for a dress. In complete secrecy designs for a female are redrawn, it is like a genesis, with an aura for no one in particular. The hair must be brushed twenty times, feet anointed [*gesalbt*] and toenails painted, hair removed from the legs and armpits, the shower turned on and off, a cloud of powder floats in the bathroom, the mirror is studied, it's always Sunday, the mirror, mirror on the wall is consulted, it might be Sunday already" (*Malina* 86). The natural, independent woman: painted, powdered, dehaired, self-created as an image for the mirror on the wall, of which a woman asks—naturally?—"Who is the fairest of them all?" As John Berger argues, since women are born into a world which men control, they are constrained to become the observers of themselves, for how they appear determines how men will treat them. Women interiorize this doubleness and constitute themselves as comprising both "surveyor and surveyed": "The surveyor of woman in herself is male: the surveyed, female. Thus she turns herself into an object—and most particularly an object of vision: a sight" (47).

Or one might theorize this scene as Susan Gubar does: such female narcissism exists for lack of other expressive possibilities. Without language, female creativity is expressed through the female body itself—though still within a referential system that predefines what those possibilities for creativity may be. The "I" thus suffers from the dis-ease of misrepresentation—though it's the only representation she's got. We are warned not to believe anything she maintains about herself. It's clearly not the case that Ivan (or Ivan plus Malina) provides the solution to her problems, nor is, contrary to her assertions, the Ungargasse the home for which she has longed. For a reader sensitized to issues of sexual politics, the irony in the following passage is very strong:

> The tremulous anxiety, the high tension hovering over this city and presumably everywhere has almost completely abated here [between Ungargasse 6 and 9], and schizothymia, the world's schizoid soul, its crazy, gaping split, is healing itself imperceptibly.
>
> The only remaining excitement is a hasty search for hairpins and stockings, a slight quiver while applying mascara and manipulating eyeshadow, using narrow brushes on the lids, or while dipping flimsy cotton puffs in light and dark powder. (*Malina* 14)

Of course it is precisely this crack in the world into which she disappears at the end; the Ungargasse is not a refuge for her after all. Before meeting Malina and Ivan, the "I" had lived in the Beatrixgasse, where she, if—à la Dante—participating in the male order, nonetheless preserved a certain virginal inaccessibility. Now she has moved around the corner to the Ungargasse, which derives its name from the penetration of (Hungarian) foreigners into Vienna. Malina lives at 6, Ivan at 9; two men, simply inversions of one another, not different in quality. The "I" is "un-gar," unfinished, undone. Neither of these male voices permits her to express herself at all.

Yet this isn't the complete story of the "I" (if it were, we'd have a different text: a female *Bildungsroman*, perhaps, or a Gothic love story). It is to her credit that despite Ivan's urgings, she is not happy: she is not totally subsumed in the ideology of romantic love through which her identity had been constituted, and she does not write that book EXSULTATE JUBILATE. Her story speaks through her unhappiness, a sickness which moves toward madness. One is reminded of the statement by S. Weir Mitchell, cited as an epigraph to the second chapter of Gilbert and Gubar's *The Madwoman in the Attic*: "The man who does not know sick women does not know women" (45). It was, after all, Weir Mitchell's patient, Charlotte Perkins Gilman, whose protagonist in *The Yellow Wallpaper* also tries to disappear into the wall because her doctor, based on Weir Mitchell, has forbidden her to write. But what it is important to emphasize here is that the other story of the "I" *can't be told*: there is no language that this story can be told in. Like the female schizophrenics whom Luce Irigaray studied, there is no metalanguage for this dis-ease: "A woman in a state of madness does not have, for some reason, the means for elaborating a delirium. Instead of language being the medium of expression of the delirium, the latter remains within the body itself. The dominant element in feminine schizophrenia is corporal pain, the feeling of deformation or transformation of organs, etc" (74). Repressed, it must struggle to speak in spite of the proscriptions upon expression, here not so much through symptoms of the body (though this is the case elsewhere in Bachmann, for instance in "Eyes to Wonder") as in the dreams and parapraxes which Freud indicated to be the signifying material of the repressed. But there is no coherent narrative of the "I": to argue that there is would be to recuperate her own distress and misunderstand Bachmann's novel. Instead, we need to look for places where the "I" *mis*-writes herself—*sich verschreibt*, as Bachmann puts it (*GuI* 98). At best, we can indicate some areas in which that which she cannot say tries nonetheless to speak.

The narrative structure of the book itself is one of those places. The central thematic concern structuring the traditional novel, the relationship of the individual to the social world, is the one that's missing here, except for one short, funny examination of the vacation habits of the Viennese upper crust. (So inclined, Bachmann can write social satire with the best of realist novelists. But there's an ominous undertone even here; it's hinted that the brilliant, articulate women who oversee these social games have their dark side, too: "Antoinette is completely puzzled by every man"; "But what do you say to Christine's hysteria" [*Malina* 103–104].) If the lack of coherent plot development or even of an identifiable narrative stance has been responsible for some of reviewers' and scholars' problems with the book, it's also an assertion of the lack of coherence available to the "I." It is interesting, too, that this is the area of the novel which Bachmann identified as closest to experimental writing proper: "What I regard as experiments with prose the reader isn't bothered with, for my experiments land in the wastebasket—although I certainly need them. But I don't believe they're there to be published. In this novel, which isn't a seamless narrative—it isn't that at all—there are quite different elements, from the dreams to the dialogue to the musical score–like ending—I call those a no longer visible experiment with narrative possibilities" (Kienlechner 102). But one might also regard these failures of the text to constitute a seamless narrative, and even those opaque and mysterious allusions which remain resistant to interpretation, as a utopian hint—though only a hint—in the direction of another, less oppressive discourse which feminists could make use of. In this reading of the text we might explore Bachmann's suggestion with respect to the complexity of her novel, "how interconnected it is, so that there's almost no sentence which doesn't refer to another one" (*GuI* 96). This might be a logic of association and "both/and" rather than of causality and "either/or." This might be a subjectivity which does not do violence to itself by asserting its self-identity but concedes its disunity and nonsynchrony. For without (one hastens to add) giving up on reason altogether, a feminist voice, however it finally constitutes itself, will need to admit that which the binary oppositions of logocentricity haven't wished to permit within present patriarchal discourse.

"But at night, alone, is when the erratic monologues arise, the ones that last, for man [sic] is a somber being, only in the darkness is he master of himself and during the day he goes back to being a slave" (*Malina* 63). Most clearly we discover that which the "I" can't say in the middle or dream section of the novel. Bachmann told Kienlechner: "We learn nothing about the life of this 'I' or about what's happened to her—that's all in the dreams, partially concealed and partially expressed. Every conceivable kind of torture, destruction, harassment (*GuI* 97). As these are dreams, even though literary ones, we cannot expect to be able to interpret them completely; indeed, as Freud cautioned, "We must not concern ourselves with what the dream appears to tell us, whether it is intelligible or absurd, clear or confused, since it cannot possibly be the unconscious material we are in search of" (15: 114).

Nonetheless, as Bachmann suggests, not everything is concealed here, and some themes emerge which help us to understand the constraints of consciousness. The most obvious common element of these varied dreams is the father figure, who emerges again and again as the persecutor and tormentor of the "I." Bachmann has stated explicitly that this omnipotent father is the figure who is responsible for the destruction of the "I," her "murderer": "All the stories which are not included here because the 'I' is not permitted to tell anything about herself— for her doppelgänger forbids her to—they appear in the dreams, for instance the explanation for her destruction, for her almost having been annihilated by a prehistory brought about by this overpowerful father figure, about whom we discover that this figure is the murderer, and more precisely, the murderer whom we all have" (*GuI* 89). This is a patriarchal, an oedipal tragedy which strikes all of us. Under threat of the most terrible of punishments, the deprivation of our sexuality, we submit ourselves to the Law of the Father, which spells death to an independent desire expressing itself outside of socially prescribed channels.

From the first dream, from which I have borrowed the title of this essay, the crime for which the father is responsible emerges: its setting is "the cemetery of the murdered daughters" (*Malina* 114), and he is the perpetrator of the "ways of death." Murder (along with lesser offenses) is accomplished in the greatest variety of ways. In the second dream she is gassed in a gas chamber; later she is transported to Siberia with other Jews (more substantiation for Bachmann's association of patriarchy and fascism). She is frozen in ice and plunged into fire, subjected to electroshock, buried under an avalanche, electrocuted, and eaten by a crocodile. With yet clearer symbolism her dreams frequently refer to her incest with her father, a connection she regards with abhorrence, though Melanie, a recurrent figure who, analogous to Malina, is another of her doubles, is pleased enough at the advantages of the relationship. "Mela-Nie," thinks the "I." Her mother, who sometimes allies with the father, is a dog, "who completely submits to his thrashing" (*Malina* 124). Her father directs an opera: "My father has gone to the theater. God is a show [*Vorstellung*]" (*Malina* 118), in which she is prepared to sing a duet with a young man, yet she recognizes that "his voice is the only one audible in this duet anyway, because my father wrote the whole part for him and nothing for me of course, since I don't have any training and am only supposed to be shown" (*Malina* 123). In various ways he denies her speech: he will not permit delivery of letters to her friends and tries to gain control of the sentences dried on her tongue as she dies of thirst. But what is constant in these dreams is her resistance to her father and her refusal to be murdered: "Now and then I lose my voice. Nevertheless I have permitted myself to live. Sometimes my voice returns and can be heard by all: I am living, I will live, I claim my right to live" (*Malina* 151–152). By the end of these dreams, the "I" (with Malina's help) has understood that despite the apparently harmless ball scene from *War and Peace* which recurs in the dreams, what she has experienced here is only war, and the section concludes with this recognition:

MALINA: So you will never again say: War and Peace.
ME ["I"]: Never again.

It's always war.
Here there is always violence.
Here there is always struggle.
It is the eternal war. (*Malina* 155)

If "The Third Man"—the title of this section—prevents her self-articulation like the other two, the "I" is at least left with the possibility of refusing their definition of her: "In another language I say Ne! Ne! And in many languages: No!

No! Non! Non! Nyet! Nyet! No! Ném! Nein! No! For in our language, too, I can only say no, I can't find any other word in any language" (*Malina* 115).

The waking life of the "I" is also informed by a desire to write, to articulate herself, which cannot be fulfilled. Interspersed through the first and third sections of the book are letters by the "I" which represent her attempt to take up the pen. They are mostly written "in tremendous haste and anxiety," a recurrent phrase which also characterizes, as the "I" reported in the introduction, the unity of time—"Today"—in which she is compelled to live. If the letters are completed at all, they are signed "an unknown woman." At the beginning of the novel's third section, the "I" explains that these mysterious and cryptic letters are connected to her experience of a postal crisis concerned with the nature of the "privacy of mail [*Briefgeheimnis*]." Her own meditations on the "privacy of mail" and the unmailed letters mostly written deep in the night are released by the case of the letter carrier Otto Kranewitzer in Klagenfurt who, suddenly struck by the enormity of his postal duties, was no longer able to deliver the mail. For this crisis, the "I" asserts, is one with immense existential and ontological implications:

> After the Kranewitzer case I burned my letters of many years, then began writing completely different letters, mostly late at night, till eight in the morning. I didn't send all these letters, but they're the ones that concern me. Over these four, five years I must have written ten thousand letters, to myself alone, letters which contained everything. I also leave many letters unopened, in my attempt to practice privacy of mail, in my attempt to approach the height of Kranewitzer's thought, to comprehend what could be unlawful in reading a letter. (*Malina* 160).

No doubt the "privacy of mail" is illuminated by a multilingual pun, the overlapping of the two meanings of letter/lettre in English and French. For the "I" had betrayed the secret earlier in the book to her baffled and frustrated interviewer Herr Mühlbauer, saying, "I will tell you a terrible secret: language is punishment" (*Malina* 60).

Nonetheless, there are moments when, despite herself, that which the "I" is forbidden to say breaks through into her waking language as well. The "I" recognizes (and tips us off to) the parapraxes that allow the repressed to emerge in this book: "That's when I also started distorting everything I read. Instead of 'Summer Fashion Exhibition' [*Sommermode*] I would read 'Summer Fashion Execution' [*Sommermorde*]. That's only one example. I could name hundreds of others" (*Malina* 137). Thus, it seems, we are also to look at the language of this book for that which is not supposed to be there. Reading closely, one can find, below the apparent narrative, some subterranean themes that tell a different story from the one the "I" intends. The *Pierrot Lunaire* motif to which I have already referred is one of these. The first line from the last poem of that cycle, which recurs through *Malina*—"O ancient scent from far-off days"—points in the direction of archaic reminiscences which the "I" has repressed and to which she now barely has access, having constituted herself in a different time, a present, "Today," "a word that only suicides [of which, it appears, she is one] ought to be allowed to use" (*Malina* 2). (The dreams in contrast deny synchronism altogether: "The Time is not today. In fact, the Time no longer exists at all, because it could have been yesterday, it could have been long ago, it could be again, it could continually be, some things will never have been" [*Malina* 113]). Yet it seems that the "I" is able to resist these men at all only because of her archaic reminiscences of an original satisfaction now denied. The "I" first hears her Schönberg song sung by a "chalkwhite Pierrot . . . in a cracking voice" (*Malina* 4) in the Stadtpark, to which neither Ivan nor Malina wish to accompany her and of which she herself is afraid, for it is a place of "shadows and dark figures," that is, a site of night and dreams: "Only in the darkness is man master of himself" (*Malina* 87). The Stadtpark also seems to be the site of an original polymorphous perversity where in the immediate postwar period illicit sex of all varieties took place: "You could hardly meet anyone who hadn't seen everyone with someone else" (*Malina* 181).

For the "I," the Stadtpark is associated as well with water and with the fear of drowning, from which her men in the Ungargasse save her: "I wasn't sure of myself but am again insured [*in Sicherheit*], no longer walking past the Stadtpark at night, jittery as I walk along the walls of houses, no longer on a detour through the dark, but already a little at home, already docked safely at the Ungargasse, already safe and sound in Ungargassenland, with my head even a little out of water. Already gurgling the first sounds and sentences, already setting forth, beginning" (*Malina* 88). The "I" flees water, which may suggest to her the "oceanic feeling" before psychic differentiation and the more fluid ego boundaries of the female. Instead, she's chosen to associate herself with Malina, whom she imagines to be a phallic hero creating order out of watery chaos, allowing, so the legend has it, Klagenfurt (a ford of lamentations?) to arise from suspiciously female swamps—Klagenfurt, the city where she was born: "but I liked him best as Saint George who slew the dragon so that my first city could be born, so that Klagenfurt could arise from the barren swamp" (*Malina* 7). Yet the *Pierrot Lunaire* motif recurs throughout the novel: in the Beatrixgasse, at a moment of despair in Vienna society; as a reprise at the end of the novel before the "I" vanishes into the wall. That ancient scent wafts a promise of happiness which can't be completely forgotten.

Perhaps this can help us understand the one extended narrative, running in italics through *Malina*, of the Princess of Kagran, which the "I" seems to have written and which anticipates her love affair with Ivan. The princess comes from a region near the Danube where St. George had triumphed over the floods. When the princess has to decide between the floods and the fearsome willows, she allows herself to be rescued by the stranger in the dark coat who prefigures Ivan. What other possibilities did she have, what other narrative could she have written? She has to tell this story: there is no other way for her to imagine the satisfaction of her desire. But this does not mean that her utopian vision is altogether wrong, only that it must be channeled into the language which is given her to speak. The transformation she longs for is a vision of *luxe, calme et volupté*, which nonetheless draws upon her own specifically female desire. Bernd Witte has argued this most persuasively:

> Attached to the fairy tale, also characterized externally as connected by the same italics, are further fragments of a vision of a perfect society in later portions of the first chapter. "A day will come when all women have redgolden eyes, redgolden hair, and the poetry of their sex, their lineage will be recreated . . ." The return of the golden age here emanates quite obviously from women. Only several pages later, when this sentence is repeated, is the word "women" replaced by "mankind," while the arrival of paradise is linked to the condition that "their hands will be gifted for love." (*Kritisches*)

Counterposed to and subversive of Malina's patriarchal subsumption of women is a feminist utopia of sensual pleasure and erotic joy. It is from this narrative that Bachmann herself read when asked for her own vision of utopia: "A day will come when people will have goldblack eyes, they will see beauty, they will be freed from dirt and from every burden, they will rise into the sky, they will dive into the sea, they will forget their calluses and their wants. A day will come, they will be free, all people will be free, even from the freedom they had intended. There shall be a greater freedom, beyond measure, a freedom to last a whole life long" (*GuI* 92).

Now what are feminists to make of this? The vision is beautiful but scarcely realizable; the patriarchal reality, terrifyingly familiar and concrete. The story the "I" tells about of Marcel, a clochard of Paris (and, it seems, a compatriot of Proust), comes to mind; like the "I," he is one of the "wounded," and he simply dies when a well-meaning social worker tries to redeem him "for a new life which does not exist" (*Malina* 187). As the feminist scholar Myra Love once remarked to me, Bachmann lacked the context. But we might derive some comfort and assistance from the single vow of the "I." Having passed the *Rigorosum* (oral examination) of the University of Vienna, she swears upon its staff and, armed with this knowledge, triumphs over both the waters and her father's might: "And with a handful of sand that is my knowledge, I cross the water, and my father cannot follow me" (*Malina* 122). Perhaps we need not, like Leda, put on patriarchal knowledge with his power. Perhaps there is another and more liberating use to make of knowledge; perhaps, from within the cemetery of the murdered daughters, men's knowledge can be turned against them. Bachmann is neither the "I" nor Malina; she found a language to write the story of women without language. We know this now. "One who expresses herself completely does not cancel herself out," wrote Christa Wolf of Bachmann in 1980 in her Büchner Prize speech. "The wish for obliteration remains as a witness. Her part will not vanish" ("Shall" 10).

READING BACHMANN IN 1981

Published in early 1981 (with a publication date of 1980) in a special issue of *Studies in Twentieth-Century Literature,* this essay is a paradigmatic example of many qualities of feminist literary scholarship around that time. As I noted in chapter 2, I believe it is also the first to apply this sort of cultural feminist analysis to Bachmann's work, an approach that would become virtually de rigueur by 1984–85, responsible for producing what Sigrid Weigel termed "the other [feminist] Ingeborg Bachmann" ("Andere" 5). As the essay's title already underlines, its approach is premised on a notion of woman as victim—*all* women, including the "I" of Malina, Bachmann herself, and (with quite a dose of self-pity) me. (The "we" of this essay—e.g., "'We' have to play by their rules"—is a common rhetorical gesture of the period, invoking all women's commonality. My evident identification with Bachmann and her figure, enabled by cultural feminist assumptions, is also a very common feature of Bachmann scholarship during this period.) In this essay, men's (*all* men's, or, alternatively, "Western" men's) domination over women is a phenomenon of the cultural realm where women are denied a voice and a subjectivity; thus if women ("we") nonetheless speak, it is only because we have uneasily assumed the subject position (a term that would not have been used at that time) of men. This I then took to be the "message" of *Malina*, which—as I along with many, many other Bachmann scholars of the period insisted—can be read as an anticipation of the theory now used to explain it.

For feminists, then, the immense value of Bachmann's novel derives from its ability to delineate women's situation before the advent of the second wave of feminism and to point us ("us") in the direction of our preeminent feminist task, the elaboration of an authentic voice for women. In the essay I understand Bachmann's lifelong concern with questions of language as her effort to grope in such a direction via her rejection (like that of the French theorists) of totalizing theories, her allegation of a connection between reason and totalitarianism, and her advocacy of possibilities of signification other than those that existing philosophical systems allow. Such possibilities are enabled by Eros, non-normative sexuality, the body, or the unconscious. The essay draws upon French poststructuralist theory to shore up its cultural feminist approach (discerning no incompatibilities at all between the two methods): women, I maintain, accommodate themselves to the patriarchal system both because they must yield to the strictures of compulsory heterosexuality and because they must subject themselves to the law of the phallus to enter the symbolic order. The struggle between men's attempts to contain female subjectivity (and the language in which it would be expressed) and women's efforts at deconstruction/destruction of the male philosophical/cultural/linguistic order is, I allege, the war of which *Malina* speaks. The experimental quality of *Malina* derives from Bachmann's endeavor to probe the limits of language as she represents this bellicose contest. Her texts are thus shown to manifest precisely the kind of feminist politics that were most en vogue in the U.S. women's movement of the time, and Bachmann proves herself a woman writer worthy of adulation by feminists and supremely fit to enter the feminist pantheon of German literature.

The cultural/French feminist approach proved very satisfying to feminist literary scholars and Bachmann fans, since it revealed the limitations of the male critics who had earlier responded negatively to Bachmann's texts because, it now appeared, they were simply not theoretically au courant. Conversely, this reading of Bachmann's texts provided powerful support for the cultural feminist tendencies that had mostly dominated the West German women's movement from its outset, allowing that direction of feminist analysis now to be substantiated by vanguard theory. Within West (and possibly even East) German feminism, Bachmann early took on the role of iconic figure akin to that played by Virginia Woolf (or possibly a combination of Woolf and Sylvia Plath) within Anglo-American feminism. I am inclined to believe that the immense prestige of Bachmann's work within German feminism and the apparently perfect congruence between her works and the cultural feminist theory of the early 1980s provided a powerful substantiation for the cultural feminist approach within Germany, helping it to maintain its legitimacy there long after it had been drawn into question in Britain and the United States.

To be sure, even in its heyday, cultural feminism was never without its feminist critics in the United States. I discern in this essay no effort at all to distance myself from the theoretical paradigm elaborated by cultural feminists or French feminists in 1981. But (to come to my own defense for a moment) in the same year I also formulated (in "The Female Aesthetic and German Women's Writing," one of the first feminist articles published by *German Quarterly*, thanks to Ruth Klüger Angress, then *GQ*'s editor) a critique of some of the major limitations of that approach:

> As the [French feminist] analysis has been received outside of France, it has intersected with and reinforced certain "essentialist" tendencies in German (and American) feminism which argue that the historical facts of women's difference are ontological qualities instead. Likewise, female subjectivity is taken to be capable of articulating itself fully in its radical otherness outside of male discourse when feminist women only open their mouths. . . . Thus, what spoke in the many autobiographical accounts of recent German feminism was at best a woman no more than the inversion of male categories, subjective in the sense of private, emotional, irrational, and receptive. No doubt there is already something liberating in women's daring to objectivate in writing female experiences which have never been so expressed before. But to assume that a pristine woman exists underneath

female socialization, only silenced but not fundamentally shaped by her social experience, has a retarding effect for feminism, for it ignores the enormous political and personal changes which feminists must still undertake. ("Trends" 64)

I am pleased to discover that over two decades ago I was already convinced of the importance of historical analysis and of praxis (a holdover, no doubt, from my earlier training in historical materialism). But like many other feminists of the period, even in this relatively critical account of flaws in the feminism of the early 1980s, I was not then able to raise the kinds of objections to cultural feminism that would emerge over the course of the coming decade: that in fact no basis exists on which to postulate the commonality of the very different kinds of women in the world; that to comprehend women's situation gender was certainly a necessary yet always also a far from sufficient category; that women cannot be perceived as universal victims but are always implicated in the social circumstances of which they are part and may quite willingly contribute to the perpetuation of the oppression of others (including other women), though they may be subordinated themselves. Only later in the decade would such insights begin to inform the analyses of feminist literary scholars—including my own.

1983

By 1983, as a consequence of developments outside of and within the U.S. women's movement, the limitations of the cultural feminist analysis had emerged more clearly, and challenges to its founding premises were raised on a variety of fronts in feminist theory and practice. In June 1982 the Equal Rights Amendment went down to defeat because it had failed to achieve ratification by the requisite number of state legislatures. The "New Right," arrayed under the banner of the "Reagan revolution" and proclaiming a pro-family, "right-to-life" (i.e., antiabortion) politics, concentrated much of its energies on rolling back gains made by women in the 1970s. Women continued to earn only fifty-nine cents for every dollar earned by men, and they were so hard hit by the Reagan administration's cuts in social benefits that social commentators began to speak of the "feminization of poverty." In 1976 the Hyde Amendment denied poor women Medicaid funding for abortion, and many state legislatures followed suit. In the second half of the 1970s, the dispirited liberalism of Jimmy Carter had still allowed cultural feminists a certain free space in which to operate and other women to make moderate inroads into various male domains. But in the context of the vastly changed politics of the Reagan era, it began to seem ludicrous for white, middle-class women to assert that retreat into a separate female sphere was an adequate solution to all women's problems or to maintain that women would burst the bonds of a phallogocentric culture if they could only elaborate a specifically female voice. Feminists who had defined power as male and any struggle in the political arena as reformist now saw naked political and economic power exercised against themselves and, without an adequate theory or analysis to explain current developments, watched with horror as women's rights were eroded and ever more women sank into poverty.

In addition, the right-wing upsurge under Reagan brought with it a new heightening of Cold War tensions, as Reagan set about to demonize the "Evil Empire" of the Soviet Union and demanded new expenditures for weapons systems to protect an America that was once again "standing tall." The huge military build-up that the Reagan regime initiated included plans for tactical nuclear war and the deployment of cruise and Pershing II midrange missile systems, to be stationed in Western Europe and directed toward the Soviet Union. These initiatives spurred the resurgence of a post-Vietnam peace movement in the United States and Europe; half a million people demonstrated, for instance, in New York City on 12 June 1982. The dangers of nuclear war also encouraged feminists to address issues of global and national politics and launched a feminist peace movement that turned the cultural forms elaborated in the 1970s to the cause of peace. In November 1980 and 1981 the Women's Pentagon Action developed an elaborate set of two-day rituals focusing on "Mourning, Rage, Empowerment, and Defiance" (they included encircling the Pentagon and weaving its doors shut with yarn) to express "their fear for the life of this planet, our Earth, and the life of the children who are our human future," as their Unity Statement put it. Modeling their action on the 1982 Women's Peace Camp at Greenham Common in England, in 1983 at Seneca Falls, New York, feminists established a Women's Peace Encampment to protest the nuclear weapons stored at the Seneca Army Depot. Though it is unlikely that any of these actions had any practical political effect, they signaled the beginnings of a new feminist understanding of the necessity of public engagement with "male" political power.

Beginning in the late 1970s, protests by women of color speaking from within the women's movement itself also began to unsettle the dominant paradigms of U.S. feminism by challenging white feminists' assumption of female commonality across race, class, and culture and their blithe willingness to say "women" but describe only their own white selves. Many conferences of this period ended with shouting, bitterness, and tears, and by 1982 the National Women's Studies Association had decided to focus its entire national conference on the topic "Women Respond to Racism." In a widely read open letter to Mary Daly that illustrates the vehemence of these exchanges, black lesbian poet Audre Lorde attacked *Gyn/Ecology*'s appropriation of the experiences of women of color merely to advance the argument of Daly's book: "Mary, I ask that you be aware of how this serves the destructive forces of racism and separation between women—the assumption that the herstory and myth of white women is the legitimate and whole herstory and myth of all women to call upon for power and background, and that non-white women and our herstories are noteworthy only as decorations, or examples of female victimization. I ask that you be aware of the effect that this dismissal has upon the community of Black women, and how it devalues your own words. . . . Should the next step between us be war, or separation? Assimilation within a solely western-european herstory is not acceptable" (96). The early 1980s saw the publication of a series of important books by feminist women of color that addressed the specificity of their experience and its difference from that of white women: Angela Davis, *Women, Race and Class* (1981); bell hooks, *Ain't I a Woman: Black Women and Feminism* (1981); Cherríe Moraga and Gloria Anzaldúa, editors, *This Bridge Called My Back: Writings by Radical Women of Color* (1981); Gloria T. Hull, Patricia Bell Scott, and Barbara Smith, editors, *All the Women are White, All the Blacks Are Men, But Some of Us Are Brave: Black Women's Studies* (1982); Barbara Smith, editor, *Home Girls: A Black Feminist Anthology* (1983). White feminists were thus compelled to recognize the implicit racism of an analysis that assumed that categories derived from the lives of white women could describe all women; that alleged that gender oppression was the most primary and fundamental problem of all women; that called upon women of color to repudiate their connections to their brothers, forged in the struggle against racism, to bond with potentially racist white women; and that assumed that the same strategies of resistance were appropriate for all women in all cultures and contexts. For academic feminists, the challenges raised by U.S. and international women of color have been the factors most crucial to the elaboration of present-day academic feminist paradigms, "conflict over race" becoming, as Jane Gallop put it in *Around 1981*, "a decade later [i. e., 1991] the point of densest energy in academic feminism" (6).

The battle between radical/cultural feminists and others (including socialist feminists, somewhat revitalized in the 1980s) was also joined via debates over the relationship of feminism to sexuality. Cultural feminism had argued that pornography, butch/femme lesbian relationships, consensual sadomasochistic relations, perhaps even heterosexuality itself were expressions of patriarchal society's violence against women and—should women also engage in, even enjoy, such forms of sexual behavior—evidence of their brainwashing by patriarchy. By the early 1980s that position (sometimes termed "anti-sex" by its opponents) had expressed itself in a quite powerful antipornography movement that sometimes made common cause with the New Right. At a contentious conference at New York's Barnard College in 1982, that analysis was challenged by a group of mostly academic feminists who denounced cultural feminist positions as simplistic and dreary, insisted that fantasy and play should not be conflated with reality, and demanded their right to sexual agency and sexual pleasure. Debates surrounding the conference had consequences that extended far beyond its topic. Probably the conference was a signal of a more far-reaching discontent with cultural feminist analyses and led, like the race debates, to an emphasis on women's difference from one another and on the possibilities of female agency as well as female victimhood. Even more important, conference organizers began, as Carol Vance formulated it in the conference's "Concept Paper," "from the premise that sex is a social construction which articulates at many points with the economic, social, and political structures of the material world" (39). This conception of sexuality demanded the elaboration of categories sufficient to understand it and pointed feminists in the direction of the creative combination of poststructuralist and post-Althusserian Marxist categories that would characterize feminist and other forms of cultural analysis in the 1990s. Like the race debates, then, the controversy over sex in the women's movement marked at least the beginning of the end of cultural feminism's hegemony over academic (and probably nonacademic) feminism.

The changed climate of early 1980s feminism did not translate immediately into new paradigms of literary analysis, however. Instead it produced confusion and incoherence, for some feminist literary scholars perceived at least dimly that the neat frameworks of American and French feminist analysis did not exactly correspond to altered circumstances, yet they were at a loss for an alternative model. In 1982 in *Writing and Sexual Difference* (a volume of feminist essays, edited by Elizabeth Abel, that had appeared in *Critical Inquiry*), prestigious feminist scholars continued to speak of "the woman writer"—though women of color are represented by Mahasveta Devi's "Draupadi," translated and analyzed by Gayatri Chakravorty Spivak, whose method is explicitly that of deconstruction. Whether indicating the "difference between the sexes" or "the difference within sex" (Gallop, "Critical" 285), the "sexual difference" of the book's title refers to solely men and women, or masculinity and femininity, and many of the contributors to this volume are concerned with the relationship of femininity or the female body to writing—of sexuality to textuality—often with the help of French theory. Some essays explore the relationship of women's to men's writing, thus locating women's cultural production in the context of cultural practices in general rather than in a separate female sphere, but only Carolyn Allen's "Critical Response" objects to the lack of attention to "the contemporary plurality of cultures based on differences of race, class, sexual preference, age, religion, and geography, to name only some of the variables" (300).

Feminist journals of the period directed a self-critical gaze at academic feminism's earlier omissions, a *Signs* editorial of autumn 1982 inquiring, for instance: "True, feminism challenges the disciplines with questions relating to women, but to what extent are those questions still bound by the values and viewpoints of the dominant cultural group? Are the questions those of a privileged, white, heterosexual middle class, and does their language, while reflecting some women's experience and knowledge, leave others totally invisible?" (Gelpi 2). But the literary analyses in those journals often limp somewhat behind their historical and social-scientific studies. (It is worth noting, however, that in spring 1983 *Signs* published an article on women under National Socialism by Gisela Bock which is now regarded both as somewhat scandalous and as a prime example of the woman-as-victim paradigm within historical scholarship. There Bock maintained that German women, both "Aryan" and Jewish, were victims of Nazism because they were targets of Nazi eugenicism.) Janice Radway, now one of the influential figures of feminist cultural studies, published an early article on women reading romance novels in *Feminist Studies* in spring 1983, and Paul Lauter explored "Race and Gender in the Shaping of the American Literary Canon" in the next issue. Nevertheless, in essays on mythmaking in American women's poetry (Ostriker, "Thieves"), on representation in recent women's fiction (Homans, "Her"), and on H.D. and Adrienne Rich (Friedman, "I go"), *Signs* remained firmly committed to various versions of the amalgam of the older American and French feminist model. The disaggregation of women had for the most part not yet taken place in literary criticism, and several more years would be required before feminist literary analysis could develop a methodology adequate to the challenges posed to feminism in the early 1980s.

CHAPTER 4

Christa Wolf and Ingeborg Bachmann

DIFFICULTIES OF WRITING THE TRUTH

Man can face the truth.
—Ingeborg Bachmann, Werke

*I*n the West German edition of Christa Wolf 's essays, *Lesen und Schreiben* (1980; translated into English as *The Reader and the Writer*), the two oldest essays, dating from 1966, deal with the works of Bertolt Brecht and Ingeborg Bachmann. Along with the East German author Anna Seghers, Brecht and Bachmann count among authors whose writing Wolf respects most, and the presence of those essays in *The Reader and the Writer* provides a useful metaphor for understanding Wolf's own work: one might maintain that it exists in a tension between those two poles, Brecht and Bachmann. For all the differences between Wolf and Brecht, they evidently share certain convictions and concerns: Wolf too is a socialist, deeply committed to social change and to creating a literature that promotes it. Brecht's example encouraged Wolf to develop other literary forms appropriate to the problems of her own age, as she explained in 1966: "The possibility of applying Brecht's art and his theory of art lay not in simple imitation, . . . but in encouraging people to make their own discoveries" (*Reader* 58). Yet if in this sense Wolf's project continues Brecht's own, one can sometimes detect in Wolf's remarks on Brecht a hint of impatience, as if the model provided by this now classic GDR literary figure could also have a retarding effect on the literary discoveries Wolf wishes to undertake—might even, one suspects, share some complicity in the problems Wolf's work has increasingly sought to critique. Pursuing in detail Brecht's influence on Wolf and her growing distance from him would be a fascinating enterprise; however, it is one that

I explore here only indirectly, as I investigate instead Wolf's attraction toward that other pole, the writing of Ingeborg Bachmann.

The nature of Bachmann's influence on Wolf is less easy to grasp and, though Bachmann's name recurs again and again particularly in Wolf's writing of the 1970s and 1980s, scholars with some rare exceptions (e.g., Klemens Renolder) have not addressed the relationship of these two major women writers, no doubt in some part because Bachmann's own work has proved so difficult to comprehend. With the elaboration of feminist theory and a methodology for feminist literary scholarship, Bachmann's work has become more transparent for us, though it may be that we still do not possess a conceptual apparatus capable of understanding completely what connects Wolf to Bachmann. That is an investigation I would like to begin here. I want first to outline the qualities of Bachmann's work which Wolf identifies and admires in the 1966 essay, relating them to themes in Wolf's work from the mid-1960s onward. Then I want to trace some parallels between Wolf's work and Bachmann's which might be regarded as conscious allusions or even as homages to Bachmann on Wolf's part. Finally, I want to look closely at Wolf's most recent writing, examining her work on the women Romantics, her Büchner Prize acceptance speech, the Frankfurt lectures, and *Cassandra* to show that in the late 1970s, encouraged by Bachmann as well as by events of recent history, Wolf arrived at a standpoint very similar to Bachmann's in her last writing, the novels of the "Ways of Death" cycle. I maintain that the 1970s saw a movement in Wolf's writing away from Brecht and toward Bachmann, as Wolf increasingly challenged the received truths of Marxism and, from the perspective of a woman within European society, both insider and outsider, grappled with the difficulties of expressing another truth that would question some of the most basic assumptions on which European culture rests and on which Marxism itself also relies.

Certainly this critique was not fully elaborated in 1966, when Wolf wrote her Brecht and Bachmann essays; yet already the title of the Bachmann essay, "Truth That Can Be Faced [*Die zumutbare Wahrheit*]"—Ingeborg Bachmann's Prose" deriving from an essay of 1959 by Bachmann, "Man Can Face the Truth [*Die Wahrheit ist dem Menschen zumutbar*]," shows that Wolf had grasped something of Bachmann's philosophical project, her struggle to formulate a different epistemology, to articulate a different model for truth. More impressionistic than analytic, Wolf's early essay does not provide, probably could not have provided, handy categories for understanding Bachmann's prose. But two themes are striking. First, Wolf emphasizes that Bachmann aimed to provide her readers access to a truth they had not seen before: "To become seeing, to make people see: a fundamental motif in the work of Ingeborg Bachmann" (*Reader* 85). Bachmann seemed to suggest that humans might not even successfully grasp the nature of their own suffering, might lack the categories enabling them to recognize it at all. "For it is time," Bachmann had written, "to understand the voice of man, the voice of a chained creature not quite able to say what it suffers from" (quoted in *Reader* 85). On the other hand, failing to challenge conventional truths might mean not only individual pain but complicity in the world's evils altogether: "the haunting temptation to join hands—through conformity, blindness, acceptance, habit, illusion or treachery—with the deadly dangers to which the world is exposed" (*Reader* 84). As Wolf viewed it, Bachmann's endeavor was to hold fast to the legitimacy of her own experience and to find a language that could accurately express it: "It is her cause to have the courage to create her experience anew in herself and to assert it in the face of the truly overwhelming mass and discouraging dominance of empty, meaningless, ineffectual phrases" (*Reader* 85). And this explained Bachmann's concern with a new language, which critics had too often understood as only aestheticism. Quoting Bachmann herself, Wolf emphasized what Bachmann sought in her quest: "To seek 'a new language,' 'a thinking that desires knowledge and wants to achieve with and through language. Let us call it, for the time being, reality'" (*Reader* 94).

As its second structuring theme, Wolf's essay insists—remarkably enough for a Bachmann study written at this time—that Bachmann intended her writing to be deeply and directly political. In the 1950s and 1960s, Bachmann's lyric poetry was generally thought to be the beautiful, if somewhat obscure, expression of the personal experiences of the poetess, timeless and generally applicable to the human condition, whereas her prose was regarded as unsuccessful, weak, and confused by some, although enthusiastically and positively received by others. But Wolf had read carefully Bachmann's essays, particularly her Frankfurt lectures of 1959–1960, observing there the centrality of Bachmann's insistence that literature should promote social change, and Wolf was able to use those essays to illuminate qualities of Bachmann's imaginative writing that other readers had not grasped. Epigraphs from Bachmann's essays begin each section of Wolf's own essay and document her emphasis on the connectedness of Bachmann's concern with language and consciousness to a society she wishes to transform. Thus, for instance, the third section of Wolf's essay begins with a quotation from the Frankfurt lectures: "But what in fact is possible is change. And the changing effect of new works educates us to new perception, new feeling, new awareness" (*Reader* 89). Wolf emphasizes, too, that Bachmann understood literature to derive from a particular historical period and to address historically specific problems, as she had again maintained in her lectures: "'Writing does not take place outside the historical situation'" (quoted in *Reader* 89). If this is the case (as Wolf obviously believes it to be), Bachmann's works need to be read both as written from the perspective of her own historically specific experiences and as addressed to quite specific, if far-reaching, problems of her society. The categories of perception she wants to encourage in her readers would be those enabling them both to understand and to change the world. Simultaneously, the insufficiencies and weaknesses of her works—as well as the difficulties of her own life—can be understood as having historical causes, too. For Christa Wolf, then as now, "the historical situation is such that the question of the possibility of man's moral existence must be at the center of all writing. This approach is one of the main drives in [Bachmann's] prose—often in curious disguises, not immediately recognizable, as a subjective reflex, as fear, doubt, a feeling of menace: 'Hanging on to the high-voltage current of the present'" (*Reader* 89).

But if social change is the central emphasis of Bachmann's prose, the literary strategies she chooses could scarcely be more different from those of Brecht, who exemplified the engaged, experimental writer: neither the arena she identifies as crucial for change nor the techniques she employs resemble Brecht's at all. Instead, Wolf emphasizes, Bachmann's stress is on the human subject, its "self-assertion," even its "spreading" of itself [*Selbstausdehnung*] (*Reader* 85–86). For Bachmann, as later for Christa T., it is important to be able to say "I," "without arrogance but with head high" (*Reader* 87). But this is a subject that also finds itself deeply imperiled, and its salvation might come through reasserting human power to comprehend the object world: "To regain a sovereignty lost through submission. To master it by designation" (*Reader* 86). "It may stimulate her," writes Wolf, "to conquer banality in the course of writing" (*Reader* 89). "Banality," a noun that could not be used carelessly after Hannah Arendt's 1963 book on Adolf Eichmann, suggests even in this early essay some connection between the crisis of the subject and National Socialism, a theme that Wolf's and Bachmann's later works would pursue in great detail. For Wolf, most important in Bachmann's work is her defense of that subject itself against the many forces that threaten it: "She defends no outlying regions but 'regions of the heart.' Man's right [*Anspruch des Menschen*] to self-realization. His right to individuality and to unfold his own personality. His longing for freedom" (*Reader* 91). Defending those human capacities, Bachmann's work begins to make it possible for new subjects to be created: "brave, deeply moving picture[s] of a new man" (*Reader* 95).

Bachmann's concentration on the subject rather than on events in the external world is, for Wolf, not a quality to be understood only, or even primarily, negatively. From the perspective of Wolf's later work, clearly her description of Bachmann's prose is not really intended as criticism: "One will often seek in vain for concrete situations or for a realistic presentation of social processes. What we have here are stories of feelings" (*Reader* 89). Bachmann's prose reveals the movements of subjectivity: "taking up her own position, showing her own weaknesses, being hit, rising again, attacking the enemy at its center, constantly in danger at the very heart of life, . . . self-assertion as a process" (*Reader* 86). When Bachmann portrays the external world, it is a world made luminous and transparent by the subject's comprehension of it, a vision of its hopes and its dangers. Another frame of reference produces another reality: "This, subordinated to a surprising system of references, is the irrepressible and insatiable longing to penetrate into the natural and social environment with the help of human standards" (*Reader* 86). What "system of references"? "Unnamed," says Wolf, "probably not thought out. Literature as utopia" (*Reader* 95). The pursuit of that "system of references"—or "viewing lens," as Wolf termed it most recently in her own Frankfurt lectures—is what draws Wolf back repeatedly to Bachmann's work.

To be sure, Wolf's response to Bachmann in this essay is not solely positive. She perceives obscurities and inadequacies in Bachmann's writing, but those often derive from Bachmann's real situation: she felt she lacked an audience who could understand her and was deeply pained by that. And since she could not foresee any mediation between her fantastic visions and their realization in the world, the resolutions her stories achieve sometimes also seem abrupt and unmotivated:

> If it accords with no social movement the radical claim to freedom becomes a ravaging longing for absolute, unlimited and unreal freedom, complete despair about what steps to take next turns into illusionary demands "to set up a new world" by "abolishing all that exists." And the departure from this radicality, a return to normal activities and attitudes to life is either regarded as capitulation or remains unmotivated and without foundation, as in "The Thirtieth Year": "I say to you: Stand up and walk! No bones are broken!" (*Reader* 92)

In 1966, Wolf seemed still able clearly to distinguish her position as a socialist writer in the GDR from Bachmann's. Bachmann stood for the furthest extreme of integrity and resolution one could reach in a capitalist society. Wolf wanted to hope that socialist writers, learning new lessons from Bachmann, could also provide the setting to bring them to concretion. "Only then," says Wolf, "on a new social foundation, can the 'defence of poesy' begin" (*Reader* 95).

Yet one of Wolf's observations in the Bachmann essay points beyond her confidence in GDR socialism toward a position she herself would come close to assuming in the coming decades. The fourth section of her essay begins with a quotation from Bachmann's story "The Thirtieth Year": "But a few drank the cup of hemlock unconditionally" (*Reader* 94). Without access to a social movement radical enough to realize the social changes her works had envisioned, Bachmann is inclined to withdraw her characters from society altogether instead of making them pay the price necessary to survive in it. In this gesture, she joins others in the history of German literature: "Some refused to be bought, to be won over by temptation or forced by blackmail; they preferred death to self surrender, in order to remain alive in their own time and to have an effect on the future. Ingeborg Bachmann appears to be trying to hold on to these, to their moral example" (*Reader* 94–95). In Bachmann's prose of this period, the most striking example of nonconformity is Undine in the last story of *The Thirtieth Year*, "Undine Goes." (Appropriately, Wolf's essay from *The Reader and the Writer* was reprinted as the afterword to *Undine geht*, the East German edition of Bachmann's stories published in 1973.) Wolf understands fully how radically Bachmann had rejected the achievements of an entire culture: "Weariness of civilization and doubts about progress are most strongly marked in 'Undine Goes': total alienation of man from himself and his like and romantic protest against it" (*Reader* 92). She grasps as well that this is a protest advanced against a male world from the standpoint of a female figure who stands outside it, "accusing a man's world in the barely disguised voice of the author" (*Reader* 93). Given Wolf's recognition of the extremity of the positions Bachmann assumes in this story, it is all the more startling to observe how closely Wolf's description of Undine corresponds to figures in her own work, particularly Christa T. and Karoline von Günderrode: she is "also romantic in attitude, the comparison of commonplace utility thinking with 'a spirit that is destined to no use.' . . . Since [Undine] sees no possible way to take up the struggle, she retreats before the unacceptable demands of society in the hope that she can thus preserve herself. But this retreat always ends in surrender of self, since separation from the practices of society also wears away the individual's inner powers of resistance" (*Reader* 92–93). "The acceptable [*zumutbare*] truth" that the (woman) writer can provide, should she withstand "the unacceptable [*unzumutbare*] demands of society"—this dilemma threads its way through Wolf's work to the present.

Although Wolf did not explicitly acknowledge Bachmann as a mentor until the late 1970s, a careful reader of her work can clearly perceive her indebtedness to and acknowledgment of Bachmann much earlier. Wolf's literary-theoretical essay of 1968, "The Reader and the Writer," reveals great debts to Bachmann's writing in general and more specifically to the concerns in Bachmann's work on which Wolf had commented earlier. Remarkable in the 1968 essay is its attempt to pose its concerns in Brechtian terms while moving at least in some respects ever further from Brechtian literary models. Though Wolf, like Brecht, places her considerations "in the scientific age," the science she stresses is that of Einstein and Heisenberg, where scientific regularity and reliability have given way to relativity and imprecision. In the wake of these scientific changes and given the continuation of Brecht's project, she calls for a new "epic prose." But in contrast to epic theater, Wolf's epic prose is produced and consumed by single individuals; indeed, here she expressly criticizes Walter Benjamin's assertion that the individual author as producer was as inevitably fated to disappear as the individual entrepreneur, "crushed between the institutions producing on a mass scale" (*Reader* 207). Moreover, epic prose does not undertake to show its readers a world "changing and changeable" into which they—cool, critical, and dispassionate—can intervene; instead, it offers to address and transform those readers' very subjectivity itself: "Epic prose should be a genre which undertakes to penetrate along paths not yet traveled into the inner regions of this individual, the reader of prose. Into the very inmost part, where the nucleus of the personality develops and consolidates" (*Reader* 201). As Wolf had argued in her "Interview with Myself" published in the same year as "The Reader and the Writer," the achievement of the real basis for socialism in the GDR meant that socialist literature could, indeed should, now concern itself with human subjectivity, comprising emotions as well as reason (*Reader*). As a socialist writer, Wolf thus turns to the elaboration of precisely those dimensions of human experience virtually excluded in Brecht's work.

Wolf's shift reveals the influence not just of Bachmann but also of Ernst Bloch—the thinker whom Bachmann in the Frankfurt lectures had proposed, along with Wittgenstein, as a central impulse for contemporary writing. The last of Bachmann's Frankfurt lectures was titled "Literature as Utopia"; from "The Reader and the Writer" and *The Quest for Christa T.* onward, Wolf also places her own work (as Andreas Huyssen has shown) in the service of the Blochian principle of hope. Her writing, like Bachmann's, projects an unrealized vision and reveals the desires and disappointments beneath the surface of the present, employing epic prose to project, as she maintained in "The Reader and the Writer," "the future into the present" (*Reader* 201). Wolf argued eloquently in that essay that formulating utopias should be the most important function of socialist prose, indispensable in a socialist society:

> [Prose] can keep awake in us the memory of the future that we must not abandon on pain of destruction.
>
> It helps mankind to become conscious subjects.
>
> It is revolutionary and realistic; it entices and encourages people to achieve the impossible. (*Reader* 212)

In 1968, what still distinguished Wolf's utopias from Bachmann's was of course Wolf's ability to imagine a society in which they might be realized—a hope she long, against mounting evidence to the contrary, tried doggedly to maintain. One might suggest that Wolf's use of Bachmann is what Benjamin would have termed redemptive: rescuing the most radical elements in her work from misunderstanding and oblivion, making it accessible to the present, in order to bring about her visions in reality.

In Wolf's writing until the late 1970s, one can detect a series of parallels with and allusions to Bachmann's writing too obvious, particularly in the case of the names Wolf chooses, to be anything but deliberate. To readers familiar with Wolf's Bachmann essay, the words with which her narrator introduces the short story "June Afternoon," for instance, recall the description of Bachmann's prose. The last two clauses ("A vision perhaps, if you understand what I mean" [Herminghouse 113]) reveal the narrator's expectation that, as was the case with Bachmann's work, the vision that this difficult story comprises is not immediately evident. What the story reveals, beneath an exterior that could not be more banal—a family afternoon in a weekend garden plot outside Berlin—is the fantastic texture of subjectivity underlying it. On the one hand, the garden itself, not unlike other literary gardens, stands as a container for "the immoderate desires, always held in check" of the Bachmann essay. This very real garden, says the narrator, also contains within it the dream of its own perfectibility: "In all the time we have known it, . . . it has never had the opportunity to show what it is capable of. Now it turns out that it was the dream of being a green, rampant, wild, and lush garden, no more, no less. The archetype of a garden. Garden incarnate" (Herminghouse 113). Simultaneously, the banal everyday is filled with vague and ominous threats—"Husband's Corpse Found in Bed Cabinet" (Herminghouse 117) reported in the newspaper, the lost ropes needed to tie up the roses, the dismembered dead in a train wreck, the fear of death itself: "After all, who is to say that the hand which will pull one away from everything is already set to pounce?" (Herminghouse 129).

Although the story, drawing conventional conceptions of reality into question, never moves altogether into the realm of the fantastic or the surreal, it succeeds in undertaking nonetheless the epistemological experiment Wolf began to describe in "The Reader and the Writer," questioning the immutability of a physical and a social world exterior to human subjects. Readers, recalling Wolf's comments there on Newtonian "celestial mechanics" (as well as the imagery of her novel *Divided Heaven*), will apply them to the narrator's remark in "June Afternoon": "We were suddenly overcome by a sense of insecurity about the reliability of celestial landscapes" (Herminghouse 116). Instead, in this vision, reality is often constituted through the creative use of language; the family engages in spontaneous play with words that brings into being that which has never existed before: "wormghost and crookrain and nightjail and duckworm and jailluck and nightrain and duckcrook" (Herminghouse 121). But to their creativity is contrasted the attitude of their neighbor, the engineer, of whom the narrator remarks, "He goes by printed matter in general" (Herminghouse 119). The danger the engineer represents is his attractiveness for the thirteen-year-old daughter, who regards him as "modern," "chic." On this ordinary afternoon, two models for the future compete for the allegiance of the next GDR generation.

Such themes evidently continue into Wolf's next creative work, *The Quest for Christa T.* Critics have remarked on some similarities between Christa T. and Bachmann, or at least Bachmann as Wolf describes her (Stephan 122). Christa T. too formulates fantastic visions, longs to be useful, and laments "that I can only cope with things by writing!" (*Quest* 34). For Christa T. also, "seeing" is a key term: "*Sehnsucht* comes from *sehen*, to see, and *Sucht*, craving. This craving to see, and this was her discovery, accorded with actual things in a simple but irrefutable way" (*Quest* 88). But the most striking concrete parallel between this work and Bachmann's can be found in the single extended narrative written by Christa T. within Wolf's novel, a narrative that bears the same title as Bachmann's longest prose work—"Malina." Assuming that even the deep affinities between these two writers could not have caused them to arrive independently at this same and unusual title for a prose work, I risk the assertion that Wolf meant the title as an acknowledgment of Bachmann's work and her influence on *The Quest for Christa T.* (Alternatively, as I suggested in chapter 3, Bachmann may have intended the name "Malina" as an *hommage* to Wolf—or the two authors may of course indeed have arrived at the same title independently.) Christa T.'s "Malina" presents puzzles similar to those of Bachmann's writings: an apparently realistic narrative whose purpose is unclear but which touches on the themes of National Socialism; a mother who encourages her young daughter to accede to the assertions of a dominant order; a journey over a border to a destination simultaneously foreign and not foreign (recalling Bachmann's metaphoric use of the both real and Wittgensteinian language border from which she derived), and a text a female narrator fails for unknown reasons to conclude. "Now one ought to know why she stopped at this point," writes Wolf's narrator (*Quest* 90). But we can assume that Christa T.'s inability to continue, despite the vital importance to her of writing, is deeply connected to the larger dilemma of women (and particularly women writers) in this time, the dilemma that both this work and Bachmann's writing are devoted to exploring.

The complex eighth chapter of *Patterns of Childhood* then pursues explicitly the connection of the most important themes of Wolf's writing to Bachmann's work. In this novel again the somewhat unusual name, Jordan, had already revealed affinities between *Patterns of Childhood* and Bachmann's work: the family whom Wolf chooses to illustrate the functioning of "everyday fascism" shares its name with central figures of "The Barking" from *Three Paths to the Lake* and of the novel *The Book of Franza*, published first in 1978 but from which Bachmann had given readings in the late 1960s. Wolf's chapter eight, which, her narrator tells us, had long been intended to deal with the topic of war, becomes explicitly structured around references to Bachmann's work when the narrator learns through a radio broadcast on 19 October 1973 that Bachmann had died from burns. "With my burned hand I write about the nature of fire" (*Patterns* 163) is the epigraph from Bachmann that heads the chapter, and, like the "I" of *Malina*, the narrator broods over all-pervasive war; however, war here is not just metaphorical, as it sometimes seems in Bachmann, but real—in Poland, Vietnam, the Middle East, and in Chile, where in 1973 Allende had just been murdered. The connections to Bachmann's female "Ways of Death" are underlined also in the links the narrator establishes between Goebbels's declaration, "At last the Teutonic Empire of the German Nation has come into being," and young Nelly Jordan's mournful assertion to her mirror image: "Nobody loves me." "How can anyone be made to understand," the narrator asks of her character, "that these two completely unrelated sentences are, in your opinion, somehow connected?" (*Patterns* 164–165). In this dark chapter the despair that led Bachmann to her death is comprehensible, though staggering to the narrator:

> The military junta in Chile has forbidden the use of the word *compañero*. There is, then, no reason to doubt the effectiveness of words. Even when someone on whose serious relationship to words you have counted for a long time can no longer make any use of them, who lets go of herself and records these days with the

sentence: With my burned hand I write about the nature of fire. Undine goes. Make with the hand—with the burned hand—the sign for finality. Go, Death, and stand still, Time. A solitude into which no one follows me. It is necessary, with the echo still in the mouth, to go on and to keep silent. Be prepared? For what, then? And not overcome by sadness? Explain nothing to me. I saw the salamander go through every fire. No fear threatens him, and he is pained by nothing. (Wolf, *Kindheitsmuster* 233–234; passage omitted from English translation)

But the temperamental or historical differences between Wolf's narrator and Bachmann reassert themselves: "To regain oneself after a brief stumble, caused by the increased burden on one's shoulders. It is necessary to talk" (*Kindheitsmuster* 234; passage omitted from English translation). Bachmann's 1953 script for a radio broadcast on Wittgenstein, "*Sagbares und Unsagbares*" (The speakable and the unspeakable; *W* 4: 103–127) very early had maintained that it was altogether impossible to speak about that which was most important. For Wolf, however, this position is not at all sufficient, and her narrator responds to Bachmann's death by maintaining, "One must eventually break the silence about difficult things" (*Patterns* 178). And this narrator also recognizes the small concrete utopias of everyday life, as Bachmann sometimes recognized, too; consider, for example, the Bachmann quotation with which this dark chapter ends: "The most beautiful thing under the sun is being under the sun" (Wolf, *Patterns* 197).

Wolf's writing since *Patterns of Childhood* can be regarded as centrally concerned with the dilemma posed by Bachmann's death: whether the (woman) writer can have faith enough in the hope of remedying the evils she details, of realizing the visions she projects, to preserve her from despair. The eighth chapter of *Patterns of Childhood* had already described Nelly's mother as the figure with whom Wolf's more recent work is concerned, the prophet whose words are not heeded: "Always expecting the worst. Cassandra, behind the counter in her store; Cassandra aligning loaves of bread; Cassandra weighing potatoes" (*Patterns* 165). For instance, in an interview published in 1982, Wolf explained that this problem informed *No Place on Earth*—written after the East German songwriter Wolf Biermann's expulsion from the GDR: "I wrote *No Place on Earth* in 1977. That was a time when I found myself obliged to examine the preconditions for failure, the connection between social desperation and failure in literature. At the time, I was living with the intense feeling of standing with my back to the wall, unable to take a proper step. I had to get beyond a certain time when there seemed to be absolutely no possibility left for effective action" ("Culture" 89). In "The Shadow of a Dream," the foreword to her edition of Karoline von

Günderrode's writing, Wolf uses Bachmann's term to describe the generation of young Romantics to whom history offered no hope: "German life stories. German death styles" [*Todesarten* = ways of death] (*Author's Dimension* 135). The metaphor of the injured hand also threads its way through the story of Günderrode's ill-fated love for a married man not her equal.

Wolf's clearest response to the dilemmas posed by Bachmann's life and death, however, is found in her Büchner Prize acceptance speech, which circles the issues posed in Bachmann's last published poem, "No Delicacies" (*Storm* 187–188). In that poem, first published in the 1968 issue of *Kursbuch* that proclaimed the death of literature, Bachmann declares her unwillingness henceforth to seek beautiful words to adorn her writing at this time of grave social crisis. In yet more dire times, Wolf, too, expresses great doubts about the efficacy of writing, in which she continues to believe nonetheless. Bachmann's writing, even in its despair, gives precise expression to the extremity of a state of consciousness that we would not have known so well without her description of it, showing us more clearly what conditions unworthy of human beings we need to combat. In this time, Wolf explains, "all, nearly all products of our age must bear within them, or at least within their invented opposites, the seed of self-destruction. Art can-not transcend itself as art, literature not as literature" ("Shall" 10). Bachmann had concluded "No Delicacies" by renouncing her vocation: "As for my part, let it vanish" (quoted in "Shall" 9). In the Büchner Prize acceptance speech, Wolf does not accept that resignation: "One who expresses herself completely does not cancel herself out: the wish for obliteration remains as a witness. Her part will not vanish" ("Shall" 10). In a 1982 interview as well, Wolf, herself unresigned, seemed to promise that she would not choose Bachmann's way out: "But many readers also see that by probing deeper and deeper into the wounds of our times, which are also my wounds, I don't intend to give up" ("Culture" 96).

It remains still to be asked what these wounds of our times are that occasion responses so dark from these writers and in what senses they, women writers in central Europe in the last third of the twentieth century, arrived at a corresponding understanding of themselves and their culture. Now, looking back on Bachmann's writing, we can see that she sought from the beginning, in her prose writing at least, to understand the causes of the troubles of her time. Although her explanations seem now too vague, too imprecise, or too restricted to the realm of ideas, those defects may derive from Bachmann's lack then of an appropriate theoretical vocabulary or framework—a lack that theory writing of the last twenty years, including that of feminism, has helped to address. Elsewhere I have argued that it is possible to observe in Bachmann's essays insights into the structures of Western thought akin to those of contemporary French poststructuralism (see chapter 3): she discerns both the limitations of Western discourse and the connections between Western thought and Western history. In one essay on Wittgenstein, for instance, Bachmann emphasizes that Western thought is unable to speak, to formulate meaningful propositions, about precisely what is most important to human beings, which nonetheless is available to us as "the mystical," about which nothing can be said. This "negative" dimension of Wittgenstein's philosophy, as she terms it, interests Bachmann most and makes Wittgenstein represent for her the insoluble dilemmas at which Western thought, indeed Western culture altogether, has arrived. "These efforts may permit us to call Wittgenstein the great representative thinker of our time, since in him are expressed the two extreme tendencies of the intellectual trends of the West. He occupies the pinnacle of scientific thought of the age—that thought which accompanies and precedes the development of technology and the natural sciences; and yet it is precisely he who reminds us of the quotation by the nineteenth-century Austrian playwright Johann Nestroy: 'The altogether unique aspect of progress is that it appears to be much greater than it really is'" (W 4: 116–117).

An Austrian writer in the late twentieth century, Bachmann obviously understood the danger of challenges posed to reason, particularly within a German context. But simultaneously, she insisted on the necessity of questioning a destructive form of reason that could not transcend the limitations of scientism and positivism. Moreover, even Bachmann's early essays indicate her clear awareness that the problems she was addressing were not merely those of the realm of thought but were, on the contrary, expressions in thought of the real cul-de-sac at which our culture seemed to have arrived. Her radio essay on Simone Weil (W 4:128–155) pursues the deep connection in Weil's work between structures of Western thought and the misery of the proletariat—a misery against which a Marxism that fails to repudiate its roots in the Western philosophies from which it derives is also powerless. In Bachmann's essays on Robert Musil she also stresses that his *The Man without Qualities* addresses the same cultural problematic, showing, as Bachmann herself wants to maintain, that its logical outcome is war: "It is not the Kakanian [the term Musil used to refer to the Austro-Hungarian empire on the eve of World War I] situation alone that has shown that the thought-processes of rigid ideologies lead directly to war" (W 4: 27).

Read from this perspective, Bachmann's creative writing and particularly her prose reveal themselves as concerned from the beginning, if sometimes somewhat obliquely, with the destructiveness at the heart of our culture, the flaw at its core. Her story "The Thirtieth Year" attempts a far-reaching critique of all hitherto existing cultural structures: "The renunciation of every traditional view and every traditional condition, of states, churches, organizations, means of power, arms, education. The great strike, the instantaneous stoppage of the old world. The cessation of work and thinking for this old world. The dismissal of history, not for the sake of anarchy, but for the sake of a fresh start" (*TY* 56). "A Wildermuth," recalling Wittgenstein's *Tractatus* and Hofmannsthal's "Lord Chandos Letter," deals with the impossibility of talking about a truth that is more than facts (*TY* 139–176). As Wolf had recognized, the last story of the collection makes Bachmann's point with the greatest clarity and finality: Undine goes, repudiating the monstrous male world that is incapable, for all its achievements, of grasping human happiness. As Bernd Witte has perceptively observed, Bachmann's writing from the mid-1960s onward pursues the insights first expressed in "Undine Goes": "Ingeborg Bachmann hints already in this anti-fairy-tale at the central motif of her later prose works by attempting to combine in thought the catastrophic course of world history and her own self-alienation as a woman. She locates their common cause—she blames the thoughts and actions of men" (Witte, "Ingeborg" 27).

In those late works Bachmann shows us her "ways of death" directly: women mentally or physically destroyed, often themselves unaware of how their condition is connected to a social order that makes a happy and autonomous female subjectivity impossible. In *Malina*, the female "I" disappears into a crack in the wall, leaving her male alter ego to tell her story; "It was murder," says the narrator (225). In "Gier" (Greed), the central female figure is literally murdered by her husband; in *Requiem for Fanny Goldmann* (*Franza*), Fanny dies mysteriously after a man betrays her; and the women in the stories of *Three Paths to the Lake* suffer all manner of psychic and physical distress. Bachmann's argument is made most decisively and completely in the unfinished novel *The Book of Franza*: here the causes for Franza's madness are linked explicitly to both National Socialism and European imperialism; they aim to extend their totalitarian grasp over the entire world, colonizing minds they cannot control through physical violence. Like the other "Ways of Death" women, Franza is destroyed, but in this case she recognizes that she is a victim of the white culture to which she belongs, and she dies resisting, cursing the whites: "[The whites] should be damned" (*Franza* 142). Given these far-reaching and devastating recognitions, then, it must be no surprise that there is no way out for Bachmann's characters. If white history culminates in fascism and imperialism, in murder and destruction, then how can a white woman, excluded from that history but part of no other, find another place to stand? By the time of her death, Bachmann was thus left with an increasingly more radical and more clearly formulated analysis of the major failures of our culture—a critique so far-reaching that only that culture's abolition could have seemed adequate response to the abuses she detailed. But virtually nowhere in her work do we find expressed even the hope for her culture's transformation, scarcely even the hope that that to which she gives expression will be understood.

Wolf's Frankfurt lectures on poetics (*W* 4: 182–271) make it possible to maintain that the position toward which her writing of the 1970s moved increasingly resembles Bachmann's, both in the radicality of her cultural analysis and to some degree in its pessimism as well. As early as the stories in *Unter den Linden*, published in 1974, the critique of scientific positivism and instrumental rationality—to which GDR functionaries were only too clearly not immune—became a central theme of Wolf's work. Although she reveals the deep-reaching consequences of technocratic thought, however, a reading of her stories generous to the GDR might still understand them as attacking social abuses there, not the fundamental orientation of her country or even of Marxism altogether. But in Wolf's essays on the Romantics, written after the expulsion of Biermann as a thinly veiled examination of conditions in her own country, the varieties of ways in which she takes issue even with Marxism are scarcely concealed; Marxism continues rather than breaks with the structures of thought and action that had led civilization to its present pass.

In the letters of Bettine Brentano and Karoline von Günderrode, Wolf finds, for instance, an alternative to the instrumental reason about to conquer all of Europe—triumphant, Wolf clearly believes, to this day: "An alternative, yes. An alternative which was conceived and proposed at the very moment when the society switched irreversibly onto the track of the exploitation of nature, the twisting of ends into means, and the oppression of every 'feminine' element in the new civilization" (*Author's Dimension* 212). Contrasting Bettine's sympathy with and tenderness toward nature with Faust's attempt to subdue the Earth Spirit, Wolf shows herself willing to reverse an entire orthodox Marxist tradition of the appropriation of the cultural heritage within which Faust, unbounded in his energy and ambition, is a paradigmatic figure, a culture hero: "What a different scene from Faust's confrontation with the Earth Spirit! Not a declaration of war to the death, not the unconditional subjugation of nature; not the hubris of the Faustian man who, casting aside Faust's doubts, gains knowledge by putting nature on the rack, forcing confessions out of it with screws and irons. Hers is a different kind of progress. A different kind of magic from the diabolic sort for which Faust sells his soul, and which destroys him, a man become a stranger to himself (*Author's Dimension* 213). Wolf obstinately rejects a model she also identifies as male, and Bettine joins Undine in the female opposition: "How different an adversary was created by God the Father when he made Mephisto to incite man to ambivalent creation than was bred by Mother Nature when she made her army of witches, nymphs, and sprites—those beings who now, in the Faustian age, were repressed, accursed, and labeled taboo, and whose ranks Bettine, their latter-day descendant, joined trembling with emotion" (*Author's Dimension* 213). Wolf's Büchner Prize acceptance speech only makes completely explicit and pursues to its final, most contemporary consequence what had been clear already in these essays: committed in East and West to its destructive course, a culture based on principles that alienate human beings from nature, each other, and themselves, now stands poised to destroy itself altogether.

What is not so clear in the essays on the Romantics, however, is the exact object of Wolf's attack; there it might still be possible to regard that attack as limited to residues of bourgeois thought—the Romantics, after all, produced their counterproposals at the moment when bourgeois industriousness and utilitarianism triumphed. Yet even in these essays there are indications that Wolf's analysis of the flaws of Western civilization might reach as far as Bachmann's imprecations against "the whites." In "The Shadow of a Dream," for instance, Wolf praises Bettine and Karoline for their discovery of models other than those of classical Greece, other than those of Europe: "Powers which derived from the mother's womb instead of from the father's brain, that is, the head of Zeus, like Pallas Athena: an alternative to the sources of classicism, a turn toward archaic, partially matriarchal models. They reread mythology—not just the Greek, which had dominated the study of myth in the past, but prehistoric myth and the teachings of India, Asia, the East. Eurocentrism had been breached, and, with it, the exclusive rule of the conscious mind" (*Author's Dimension* 155–156).

With the Büchner Prize acceptance speech Wolf aligns herself more clearly with the analysis of Max Horkheimer and Theodor Adorno's *Dialectic of Enlightenment*, tracing the destructive tendencies of the present back to the Greek beginnings of Western culture; and her recently published [1983] narrative, *Cassandra*, reveals in its fullness, often with virtually explicit allusions to Bachmann, the extent of her critique. Here Wolf returns to the roots of our culture to tell of its origins from the perspective of a woman who, like the figures of "Ways of Death," is simultaneously inside and outside that culture, destroyed because of her complicity in it. Surely, as in *The Book of Franza*, one must understand the real events of this story as internal to the female psyche, an illustration, perhaps, of Freud's remark that Greek culture—that is, the oedipus complex—stood in the way of the analytic discovery of an earlier layer of civilization, the Minoan-Mycenean preoedipal phase so crucial for femininity (21: 26). For Cassandra, a "seer," as for Bachmann, seeing is primary, and her own insights deepen as the narrative progresses, but, like Bachmann, she is fated not to be understood. Indeed, Cassandra laments, "They did not even understand the questions to which I was seeking an answer" (*Cassandra* 48), and she will perish as a consequence of what she recognizes—"to give birth to what slays me" (quoted in *Author's Dimension* 157), as Karoline von Günderrode had written. Cassandra, also, writing with her burned hand: "I was noted for my endurance of pain. For my ability to hold my hand over the flame longer than anyone else" (*Cassandra* 31).

What does Cassandra see, and how does that correspond to Bachmann's visions? Wolf explained the new position at which she had arrived and explicitly acknowledged her indebtedness to Bachmann in her Frankfurt lectures, held in May and June 1982 at the University of Frankfurt and titled *Voraussetzungen einer Erzählung: Kassandra* (Conditions of a narrative: translation published as *Cassandra: A Novel and Four Essays*). Her lectures begin by explaining, with some irony, why she herself has no poetics of her own, a new poetics according to her *Classical Antiquity Lexicon* coming into being via an oedipal struggle with one's fatherly precursors: "'Poetics' (the definition reads): theory of the art of poetry, which at an advanced stage—Aristotle, Horace—takes on a systematic form, and whose norms have been accorded 'wide validity' in numerous countries since the age of humanism. New aesthetic positions are reached (the book says) via confrontation with these norms (in parentheses, Brecht)" (*Cassandra* 141). From that warlike patriarchal lineage that ends with Brecht, from that entire literary-theoretical tradition, Wolf here distances herself altogether: "I have never felt the raging desire for confrontation with the poetics, or the model, of a great writer (in parentheses, Brecht). This has only struck me in the last couple of years, and so it may be that, incidentally, these essays will also treat a question that I have not been asked: the question of why I do not have a poetics" (*Cassandra* 141). Advancing another model, "a fabric [that] . . . is an aesthetic structure, and . . . would lie at the center of my poetics if I had one" (*Cassandra* 142), Wolf attempts in the lectures to explicate the complicated and subjective process whereby she arrived at the Cassandra narrative. Her first and second lectures deal with her trip to Greece; her third, a "Work Diary," records "the vise grip between life and subject matter"; the fourth explores, with explicit and detailed reference to Bachmann, the "historical reality of the Cassandra figure" and the "conditions for the woman writer past and present" (*Cassandra* 142). The fifth lecture is the narrative *Cassandra* itself.

In the fourth lecture Wolf declares that the discoveries she has made in writing *Cassandra*—the epistemological changes forced upon her, still difficult even to describe—are comparable only to the transformation of her vision to which her discovery of Marx had compelled her thirty years before:

> With the widening of my visual angle and the readjustment to my depth of focus, my viewing lens (through which I perceive our time, all of us, you, myself) has undergone a decisive change. It is comparable to that decisive change that occurred more than thirty years ago, when I first became acquainted with Marxist theory and attitudes; a liberating and illuminating experience which altered my thinking, my view, what I felt about and demanded of myself. When I try to realize what is happening, what has happened, I find that (to bring it down to the lowest common denominator) there has been an expansion of what for me is "real." Moreover, the nature, the inner structure, the movement of this reality has also changed and continues to change almost daily. It is indescribable; my professional interest is wide-awake and aims precisely at description, but it must hold back, withdraw, and it has had to learn to want and to bring about its own defeat. (*Cassandra* 278)

The title of this lecture draws our attention to those epistemological concerns that had already served as the basis of Wolf's original essay on Bachmann: "A Letter, about Unequivocal and Ambiguous Meaning, Definiteness and Indefiniteness; about Ancient Conditions and New View-Scopes; about Objectivity" (*Cassandra* 272). And the essay's epigraph comes from Bachmann's *The Book of Franza*: "For the facts that make up the world need the non-factual as a vantage point from which to be perceived" (*Cassandra* 272)—the same sort of vision, that is, that Wolf had detected in Bachmann's early prose.

And indeed, insights learned from Bachmann, the epistemological changes forced upon her by her reading of Bachmann, form the structuring principle of this lecture. As Wolf began to think about Cassandra, she explains, as she began to pose to herself the question: "Who was Cassandra before anyone wrote about her?" (*Cassandra* 273), she began also to meditate upon the meaning of the Bachmann poem she had cited in the eighth chapter of *Patterns of Childhood*, "Tell Me, Love." Wolf devotes several pages to explicating the poem, stressing the concern of the poem's speaker with her status as thinker, which might preclude her from love. Says Wolf, "'Must someone think' may perhaps mean: must a man—or a woman— think like that? So—exclusively? In a way that excludes love, and what is lovely" (*Cassandra* 274). But the poem simultaneously offers another model of thought and feeling: "Reflecting on this, regretting it, even lamenting it, the poem itself gives an example of the most precise indefiniteness, the clearest ambiguity. Things are this way and no other way, it says; and at the same time (this cannot be thought logically) things are that way, a different way. You are I, I am he, it cannot be explained. The grammar of manifold simultaneous relations" (*Cassandra* 276).

Wolf had begun this lecture/letter by telling her friend A., the addressee of the letter, about the "mountain of books" she had taken to the country with her, listing almost half a page of works of mostly feminist scholarship from Western Europe and the United States. From feminism, from Euro-American women's conscious refusal to accede to the structures of men's reality, she begins to derive her explanation of that new model, as she had often hinted in earlier works and stated clearly in her third essay: "To what extent is there really such a thing as women's writing? To the extent that women, for historical and biological reasons, experience a different reality than men. Experience reality differently than men and express it. . . . To the extent that they stop wearing themselves out in trying to integrate themselves into the prevailing delusional systems" (*Cassandra* 259). In the fourth essay, Wolf pursues women's status in classical works, especially in Aristotle and Goethe, tracing women's loss of the authority they had possessed in European prehistory and linking it to the triumph of a mode of thought that was to culminate in the technological nightmare of the present. "To put it in simplified terms," Wolf tells us, "this one-track-minded route is the one that has been followed by Western thought: the route of segregation, of the renunciation of the manifoldness of phenomena, in favor of dualism and monism, in favor of closed systems and pictures of the world; of the renunciation of subjectivity in favor of a sealed 'objectivity'"(*Cassandra* 287).

But thinking men still need women to preserve them from the limitations of their own rarified thought: "They need cunning little devices to avoid dying of the cold. One of these devices is to develop women as a power resource. In other words, to fit them into their patterns of life and thought. To put it more simply, to exploit them" (*Cassandra* 294). Leaping unabashedly 2,500 years to show in what that thinking culminates, Wolf quotes a few sentences of dialogue from Marieluise Fleisser's "Tiefseefisch" (Deep sea fish). The setting is Berlin in the 1920s; the speakers are Wollank, a former bicycle racer, and Tütü, head of a literary clique, obviously modeled on B.B.—Brecht. Wollank maintains, "These women are dreadful, the way they swarm around you and each one dies to perform a different service." But Tütü asserts in reply, "I don't see why I shouldn't take what I can get. I have turned it into a system. Everything that is able to stimulate me is brought to me without my having to lift a finger.

. . . My energies," he continues, "are freed for what is essential" (*Cassandra* 295). How, asks Wolf, can this be an aesthetic that women writers could use to free us from the West's destructive thinking?

And the woman who starts to speak in her own voice, to say "I," faces enormous obstacles. "I claim," Wolf asserts, "that every woman in this century and in our cultural sphere who has ventured into male dominated institutions— 'literature' and 'aesthetics' are such institutions—must have experienced the desire for self-destruction" (*Cassandra* 299). Her example is the unnamed female "I" of Bachmann's *Malina*. Bachmann, Wolf maintains, had succeeded in naming what had happened to women in the course of the development of Western civilization, their "ways of death," and had also consciously chosen an aesthetic different from that of "Goethe, Stendhal, Tolstoy, Fontane, Proust, and Joyce" to do so (*Cassandra* 300). But Bachmann found also that her experience as a woman scarcely allowed itself to be pressed into form at all: "Whichever direction you look, whichever page you open the book to, you see the cave-in of the alternatives which until now have held together and torn apart our world, as well as the theory of the beautiful and of art. A new kind of tension seems to be struggling for expression, in horror and fear and tottering consternation. There is not even the consolation that this is still capable of being given form; not in the traditional sense" (*Cassandra* 301).

What is the "this" of this sentence? Wolf asks, and she looks for an answer in *The Book of Franza*, where Franza's brother asks a similar question: "What could have destroyed her in this way?" (*Cassandra* 302). Concluding her lecture, Wolf offers a reading of that unfinished novel, quoting passage upon passage to underline her own argument that real women, like Franza, have been colonized by a culture culminating in National Socialism which destroys them and itself. Franza dies cursing the whites; Wolf 's final words in this lecture come from *The Book of Franza*, and they are, she says, what Cassandra would say today,

> mocked, of course, not heard, declared abnormal, ejected, turned over to Death.
> She says:
>> The whites are coming. The whites are landing. And if they are repulsed again, they will return again once more. No revolution and no resolution and no foreign currency statute will help; they will come in spirit if they can no longer come in any other way. And they will be resurrected in a brown and a black brain, it will still always be the whites, even then. They will continue to own the world in this roundabout way. (*Cassandra* 305)

The Cassandra metaphor is almost as bleak as those of Bachmann's novels, and one stands sobered and aghast before so devastating an assessment of our contemporary condition. In the third lecture Wolf had asked herself, "How can you teach younger people the technique of living without alternatives, and yet living?" (*Cassandra* 251). In the Cassandra image Wolf gives with one hand the possibility of Euro-American women's providing that alternative, only to take that hope back with the other hand—like Bachmann in that respect, whose late works offer almost only "ways of death." It might be, of course, as a male East German writer, Heiner Müller, suggested in a recent interview, that there is no answer for Euro-Americans because the proletariat on whom Marx and Brecht counted can no longer be relied upon to redeem the system that created it. If one has really grasped what Bachmann and Wolf have said in its materiality and historicity, it is hard not to come as close to despair as they. Quotations from Wolf, however, spring to mind. In *No Place On Earth* she had written, "If we cease to hope, then that which we fear will surely come" (117). Or her words on Bachmann in the Büchner Prize acceptance speech: in describing clearly the historical dilemma at which we have arrived, in advancing, at least as vision, an alternative, these women writers may, we can hope, help to forestall the worst. Or perhaps they may not. Wolf's third lecture began with that fear: "The literature of the West (I read) is the white man's reflection on himself. So should it be supplemented by the white woman's reflection on herself? And nothing more?" (*Cassandra* 225).

To these depressing notes let me add, however, a coda, drawing on a recent essay [1982]on Brecht and Bachmann by Gerhard Wolf, Christa Wolf's husband. Käthe Reichel, one of Brecht's female collaborators, had preserved a copy of *Die gestundete Zeit*, Bachmann's first poetry volume, that she had brought from West Germany to give to Brecht. (One recalls the comment Wolf quoted from Fleisser's dialogue: "Everything that can excite me is brought to me.") Reading the volume *an einem kleinen Nachmittag* (On a little afternoon)—the title of Gerhard Wolf's essay—Brecht had undertaken to make corrections in Bachmann's poems, so that they became linear, pointed, didactic, political, like his. "We"—Gerhard Wolf fails to specify to whom, apart from himself, that pronoun refers—travel to visit Reichel and record her impressions of that arrogant Brechtian undertaking, so illustrative of his aesthetic, political, and human failings. But Reichel's judgment of Brecht is more differentiated. His commitment to those ordering principles was, she maintains, also a way of managing his own pain at the world he saw around him, a poetry written with tightly pressed lips. Bachmann's advantage as a woman, though it brought her greater pain, was to pursue that suffering to its depths, with open mouth. In this she joins another lineage, another tradition: "It will be written on a new page that here speaks a woman whom one regards today in a line of tradition: Else Lasker-Schüler—Nelly Sachs—Bachmann—Sarah Kirsch—the open mouth!" (Gerhard Wolf 180). Into which sisterhood of German women poets, Christa Wolf, though not herself a poet, may also be admitted, to write upon that new, unwritten page.

READING BACHMANN IN 1983

This essay was written in spring 1983 for the volume titled *Responses to Christa Wolf: Critical Essays*, edited by the late Marilyn Sibley Fries (though not published until 1989). It displays some of the methodological heterogeneity of the early 1980s, as feminist literary scholarship hesitated between a cultural feminist paradigm and something to come that had not yet been elaborated. Perhaps somewhat paradoxically, I wrote it at almost exactly the moment that Christa Wolf herself emphatically declared her allegiance to the very feminist paradigm that U.S. feminists were beginning to draw into question. In May 1982, in connection with the lecture series on poetics hosted by the University of Frankfurt which Bachmann's own Frankfurt lectures had inaugurated in 1959–60, Wolf delivered four lectures titled "Conditions of a Narrative," intended to explain the political and literary considerations that led her to write her novel *Cassandra*. The fourth lecture had just been published in *Sinn und Form* when I began work on this essay, and *Cassandra* appeared as I was writing it.

It is in lecture four that Wolf lists the feminist works that brought about a "decisive change," as she terms it, in her "viewing lens," comparable only to her discovery of Marxist theory thirty years previously. Most of the texts she cites are by feminist writers who in the main can be consigned to the radical or cultural feminist camp: *"The First Sex. Mothers and Amazons. Goddesses. Patriarchy. Amazons, Warrior Women, and He-Women. Women—the Mad Sex? Women in Art. God-Symbols, Love-Magic, Satanic Cult. Male Fantasies. Female Utopias—Male Casualties. Women and Power. The Sex Which Is Not One. The Secret of the Oracle. Utopian Past. Outsiders. Cultural-Historical Traces of Repressed Womanhood. Mother Right. Origin of the Family, Private Property and the State. Woman's Wild Harvest. The White Goddess. Woman as Image. A Room of One's Own. Womanhood in Letters"* (*Cassandra* 273). In her increasing concern since the mid-1970s with "the self-destructiveness of male dominated society" (Kuhn 178 quoting Rich, "When" 35), then manifesting itself in the superpowers' stationing of nuclear missiles in Central Europe, Wolf also seemed to align herself with cultural feminists' new concern in the early 1980s with issues of peace and ecology. In the *Cassandra* lectures Wolf read Bachmann through that lens, contrasting Bachmann's writing to the masculinist politics and poetics of Bertolt Brecht—and providing me with the framework for my own essay, Brecht versus Bachmann.

Despite these avowed allegiances, Wolf was mainly not read as a cultural feminist by her U.S. feminist audience, probably consisting mainly of Germanists at least until the publication of *Cassandra*. Many Germanists of my generation, products of the student movement and trained by Marxist-influenced professors (at *das rote Wisconsin* [red Wisconsin], among other places), had turned to GDR literature because focusing on the GDR made it possible for us to con-join our professional careers and our commitment to socialism. To those of us who became feminists in the late 1960s and early 1970s, the extraordinary texts of GDR women's writing that blossomed in that period (exactly as U.S. social-ist feminism became enmired in ever more tortured [and boring] attempts to force women's experience into the categories of Marxist economics) allowed us to keep alive the hope of combining the most creative and visionary possibilities of Marxism and feminism in a society that would both provide for basic human needs and promote subjective self-realization ("This coming-to-oneself—what is it?" as Wolf put it in the motto to *The Quest for Christa T.* [*Quest* 1] which she had borrowed from Johannes R. Becher). Many socialist feminists of the 1970s had elaborated a position (somewhat indebted to Herbert Marcuse) that allowed us, while not relinquishing our commitment to a far-reaching transformation of the entire society, to repudiate an equal-rights feminism that sought only to give women men's prerogatives and to embrace cultural feminism's celebration of superior female qualities. Excluded from the instrumental world of work, women, we maintained, had preserved alternative, more humane modes of human interaction that could be embraced "after the revolution" by all of human-kind—much the same argument Wolf makes in her short story "Self-Experi-ment." In Christa Wolf's writing I and others thus believed that we had found an example of the socialist feminist model we were seeking. In the years between Erich Honnecker's accession to power and Wolf Biermann's expulsion (1971–1976), it also appeared to us that the GDR offered the real possibility of bringing into existence a society based on such a model (in some contrast to the very abstract demands of the U.S. left or feminists for a revolution that seemed, as the 1970s progressed, increasingly improbable). Though our hopes were cer-tainly much dimmed by the crackdown that followed Biermann's expulsion, Christa Wolf's work nonetheless encouraged socialist feminists within the dis-cipline of German Studies to continue to assert a Marxist-influenced analysis through the 1970s and early 1980s that would then assume renewed relevance in the Reagan era.

Wolf's still very Marxist 1966 essay on Bachmann, published both as an afterword to a GDR edition of Bachmann's writing and in Wolf's own essay collection, *The Reader and the Writer*, suggested strongly that Wolf had derived from Bachmann the fundamentals of what we U.S. feminists read as her social-ist feminism. Simultaneously, the 1966 essay asserted that Bachmann could nei-ther realize her vision nor even articulate it very clearly because she lived and worked in a capitalist society where such far-reaching changes were almost liter-arily inconceivable; that is, Wolf took the position that the situation of women (and, consequently, of women writers) was shaped by the specific social condi-tions of the society from which they derived, not just from a patriarchy that had oppressed women since the beginnings of human history (as many of the texts in Wolf's feminist library seemed to maintain and as one might also reasonably conclude from *Cassandra*). From the beginning to the present, Wolf's 1966 essay has strongly influenced my appropriation of Bachmann. My reliance on it in this 1983 essay may be regarded as a somewhat tentative effort, born of my residual socialist feminism together with a growing discontent with cultural feminism, to wrest Bachmann not only from earlier male critics who had considered her writing a manifestation of timeless beauty but also from the kind of feminism that Wolf now espoused. As well, as the critique of white racism became increasingly central to U.S. feminism, I had been very moved to discover *The Book of Franza*'s focus on the crimes "the whites" had committed against the other peoples of the world and was quite thrilled to discover that Wolf had also stressed this aspect of Bachmann's work in her fourth *Cassandra* lecture. As was the case with my earlier interest in the GDR, it now seemed to me that in focusing on these two writers, I could address a topic of importance within the field of *Germanistik* and simultaneously pursue what had increasingly become my central political priority: elaborating an antiracist feminism. (Indeed, while I was writing this essay I also presented a paper, "Towards an Anti-Racist Feminist Theory," at a conference on the intersection of Black Studies and Women's Studies.) The question of white women's support for racism almost inevitably directed the attention of U.S. feminist Germanists to the issue of German women's support for National Socialism, despite German feminists' vehement insistence that German women had only been Nazism's victims. (Claudia Koonz's *Mothers in the Fatherland: Women, the Family, and Nazi Politics* [1987], which argued for the centrality of women's participation, within their own female sphere, in the success of National Socialism, settled this question to the satisfaction of U.S. feminists, but for some time its conclusions continued to be vigorously opposed by German feminists.) On this count, Wolf's courageous examination in *Patterns of Childhood* (1977) of her own quite enthusiastic involvement in National Socialist youth activities seemed to me to place her on the side of those feminists prepared to concede that women had not been *just* victims for all of human history.

Nonetheless, despite my enthusiasm for this topic because it seemed to point beyond some of the impasses at which the feminism of the early 1980s had arrived, I think my essay itself mainly rests on principles that do not deviate significantly from those of cultural feminism (in part, of course, because it was much shaped by the mostly cultural feminist perspective through which Wolf read Bachmann). I structured it around the notion of a fundamental difference between men and women: Brecht versus Bachmann. It is "gynocritical," focusing on two preeminent women writers and attempting to establish a countertradition of female literary production that would link them. Like cultural feminists, I consider the violence of the contemporary social order to be a consequence of its control by men (*tout court*), and I treat women (*tout court*) as the implacable foes of that order and as almost entirely excluded from it. If there is hope for such a death-driven civilization at all, Wolf and I imply, it is to be found in the interventions of women, and literature is to be one of women's primary weapons, since it is in literature that women writers (*tout court*) can give expression to their alternative vision of human relations which derives from their (common) female experience, epistemology, and aesthetics. If contemporary society is to survive, this essay seems to suggests, it will be solely as a consequence of the contributions of women alone (an expression of cultural feminism's new interventionist stance of the early 1980s). Thus, though this is an essay of which I am quite fond and that does, I think, correctly represent the relationship of Wolf to Bachmann, it also very clearly displays, despite some superficial evidence to the contrary, its fundamental indebtedness to a feminist paradigm about which I and other scholars of the period had grown increasingly dubious, yet to which we had not yet found an alternative.

Much of this 1983 work, then, is founded on principles that do not significantly differ from those of the cultural feminism of the day, possibly inflected to some degree by ecofeminism. Beginning my essay with Brecht signaled not only my own (as well as Wolf's) allegiance to socialism but also my feminist distance from certain varieties of it, a question I had already pursued in a 1978 article on Brecht and women. There and in this 1983 essay I took the cultural/ecofeminist line (a position similar to Wolf's own and one I may have in part derived from her as well as from the Frankfurt School) that an increasingly hegemonic instrumental, project-oriented, productivist rationality was inimical both to feminist ends and to the welfare of the world altogether. Like Horkheimer and Adorno in their *Dialectic of Enlightenment*, I assumed that such a form of rationality could be traced back to what I then considered the origins of European history or the European tradition in Greece (a construction that now seems in need of interrogation), from which point it had progressively grown in intensity and in the increasing array of human activity under its sway. Marxism I considered to be of a piece with this tradition, not a rupture with it. (During this period a member of my women's group who had visited Cuba sent me back a postcard with a picture of a huge poster hung from a Havana high-rise bearing the words "Productividad! Productividad! Productividad!") I clung tenaciously to the claim (clearly authorized by Bachmann's and Wolf's texts) that it was men who were the agents of such forms of rationality and women its implacable foes. Characteristic of much literary and other scholarship of the early 1980s, I think, is my unwavering conviction that the culture of our era could be conceived of as a single, coherent, malevolent piece, a position I now believe to be a holdover from Cold War theories of totalitarianism, and the unremitting idealism (in its philosophical sense) of my (*and* Wolf's *and* Bachmann's) arguments: rather than assuming a reciprocal (not to say dialectical) relationship between thought and action, we postulated that it is structures of thought or ideologies that are responsible for how individuals and societies behave.

I suggested in chapter 2 that in the early 1980s Wolf's attention to Bachmann in her Büchner Prize speech and the *Cassandra* lectures helped to popularize the new feminist reading of Bachmann. My own essay, which for a range reasons first appeared in English only in 1989 and was then reprinted in German in 1992 (in a collection originally intended to introduce U.S. feminist literary scholarship to the GDR, though history overtook its editor, Ute Brandes), acceded and lent authorization to that feminist reading long after I myself had ceased to advance it. It is thus a particularly good example both of the historical specificity of feminist readings and, a little paradoxically, of their nonsynchronicity. As in this case, the vagaries of publishing may be responsible for the simultaneous circulation of feminist analyses that derive from quite different historical moments and may potentially support positions long since abandoned in practical feminist politics.

1984

Even feminists themselves sometimes recall the mid-1980s as a period of decline for the U.S. women's movement. One of the longtime feminist activists that Nancy Whittier interviewed for her *Feminist Generations*, for instance, characterized those years as "a time of this horrible backlash, a fear-producing, economically self-motivating time, when lots of stuff was driven out of the visible realm into the personal again" (85). Certainly it is true that during this period funding for feminist projects was cut, numbers of shorter- or longer-term feminist organizations and initiatives folded, grassroots feminist activism waned, and the influx of younger women into the movement slowed. And such developments delighted many media commentators, who could allege that the "postfeminist" younger generation disdained the women's movement because they had now successfully "made it" in all the arenas to which feminists had sought access.

But this waning support for feminism's goals and activities is only part of the story. It is also possible to regard the Reagan era as a time when feminist strategies and tactics were reconfigured in response to the new political landscape. As early as 1982 the journal *Feminist Studies* had called upon feminists to "dig in" and confront these changed political circumstances by building institutions and forming alliances. The exuberant countercultural practices of feminism in the 1970s no longer sufficed as a response to the new conditions. "After a decade of experience," the editors observed soberly, "we realize that a magic sisterhood cannot sustain a woman's movement, especially through hostile and shifting circumstances." Particularly, they argued, "we feel it essential that our ties to the 'movement' acquire the solidity and specificity of alliances" (Ryan iv). Often quoted in this period were the words (cited at greater length in my introduction) that Bernice Johnson Reagon (civil rights activist, Smithsonian Institute anthropologist, and founder and lead singer of the a cappella group "Sweet Honey in the Rock") had directed at participants in a (mostly white) lesbian feminist music festival in 1981: "In a coalition you have to give, and it is different from your home. You can't stay there all the time. You go to the coalition for a few hours and then you go back and take your bottle wherever it is, and then you go back and coalesce some more" (359).

As a consequence both of the changed political context, which seemed to demand coalitions and alliances, and of debates around differences of race, class, and sexual practice among women, many feminists of the mid-1980s moved into more generally left-of-center political activities, bringing their feminist political priorities with them. One of Whittier's activists mused: "I haven't forgotten the women's movement. But to me it's a piece of this larger issue, in which we need to think about how all people can be empowered, as who they are. It's the feminist criticism, I think, that has expanded our consciousness to the point where we can even see that there's a problem. But I guess I don't see feminism as my guiding call anymore. It's sort of part of the whole picture" (99).

Although large political demonstrations for peace subsided after the stationing of cruise and Pershing missiles in Europe in November 1983, feminists continued to be active in organizations for peace and against militarism and nuclear weapons, particularly under the aegis of the National Nuclear Weapons Freeze Campaign. CIA subversion of the leftist Sandinista regime that had come to power in Nicaragua in 1979 and U.S. support for the right-wing regime in the civil war in El Salvador called into birth a range of support organizations for Central America. (Margaret Thatcher's war over control of the Falklands/Malvinas in 1982 and Reagan's invasion of Grenada in October 1983 showed that these new right-wing leaders were quite prepared to use military force to ensure constellations of power favorable to their interests in the rest of the world.) Campaigns urging institutions to withdraw their investments from firms that did business with South Africa's apartheid regime achieved significant successes in the mid-1980s. Of long-range importance were coalitions of feminists and black electoral candidates that coalesced under the umbrella of the Rainbow Coalition, first formed to support black progressive Mel King's campaign for mayor of Boston in fall 1983. Many feminist groups participated in the August 1983 March on Washington, commemorating the twentieth anniversary of Martin Luther King's 1963 march. In 1984 these coalition efforts converged in Jesse Jackson's candidacy for the Democratic Party's presidential nomination. Like those of Rainbow Coalition mayoral candidates, Jackson's platform included strong feminist planks written for him by his feminist supporters. The Jackson campaign inspired widespread feminist enthusiasm and left in its wake broad coalitions prepared to work for progressive political change at the local level.

Except for cuts in research funding, feminist scholarship was probably less affected by the Reagan era than feminist activism, but it is possible to discern research trends that to some degree parallel political transformations outside the academy. On the one hand, the broadening of feminist emphases to include a wider range of political concerns was, possibly under the influence of ecofeminists and women in the peace movement, accompanied by quite grand efforts to theorize the connections of women's oppression to everything else—not so different from the arguments made by Christa Wolf. The autumn 1983 issue of *Signs*, for instance, focused on women and religion and alleged in its prefatory editorial that religion was, as Virginia Woolf had commented of science, "not sexless; she is a man, a father, and infected too" (Woolf 139). The editors of the issue continued: "The infection of both science and religion does not lie in masculinity itself but in the infusion of masculinity with dominance. As [Hilary] Rose points out [in an article in this same *Signs* issue], an ideology of dominance twists scientific investigation into the study of the means of control over nature, with an accompanying loss of feeling for the sacredness of all life." Indeed, the editorial goes on to allege, exactly such qualities may in fact constitute "the central malaise of Western culture: one in which conflict for dominance, beginning with dominance over women, becomes obsessive. Such conflict, when it finds its expression in international politics, makes nuclear armament the 'business' of science, as Rose points out" ("Editorial" 1983 1-2). Such grand and all-encompassing theoretical models revealed their indebtedness to cultural feminism particularly in their effort to portray the oppression of women as primary and as prior to all other forms of domination.

In some contrast to attempts to elaborate large theoretical paradigms, however, other feminist scholars called for much more careful attention to historical and cultural specificity in order to acknowledge diversity among women. In that same issue of *Signs*, black feminist Gloria Joseph, reviewing Angela Davis's *Women, Race, and Class*, remarks: "Mainstream white feminists must realize that feminist theory, feminist organizing, women's conferences, and women's studies courses generally lack an ideological philosophy capable of systematically encompassing the histories, experiences and material need of Black and working-class women" (136). Such observations necessitated a fundamental rethinking of certain basic feminist premises. Some U.S. scholars followed the lead of British feminist Michèle Barrett in maintaining that even the use of the term "patriarchy" obscured significant differences in the way male dominance was exercised transhistorically and -culturally (Van Allen 85). Others maintained that the use of the analytic category "women" confused more than it clarified, Marilyn Power arguing in *Feminist Studies* with respect to Reaganomics, for instance, that "women cannot be analyzed as a sexual class. To understand the impact of Reagan policies on women, and the implications for political activity by women, we must remain aware of class and race differences among women" (31). And Roger Gottlieb, writing in *Socialist Review*, convincingly demonstrated the inability of psychoanalytic feminist theories such as Chodorow's and Dinnerstein's to account for historically specific psychic structures. Many articles in feminist journals, particularly those written by historians and anthropologists, now concentrated on the wide varieties of female experience in the world. Increasingly, feminist conferences focused on differences among women worldwide and in the United States: for example, the University of Illinois conference "Common Differences: Third World Women and Feminist Perspectives" and the pathbreaking Five College conference on the intersection of Black Studies and Women's Studies, both held in April 1983. On the other hand, despite pious disclaimers like that of the *Signs* editorial in the spring 1983 issue focused on "women and violence"—"Yet we should remain mindful that women are participants in violence as well as victims of it and note that feminist scholars up to this point have given little attention to this fact" (Freedman/Gelpi 399), feminist scholars nonetheless seemed to remain loath to concede that some women might really be fundamentally antagonistic to the goals claimed by feminists and other progressives. Examinations of even the most unlikely groups (women of the Moral Majority [Pohli], women missionaries seeking "to convert heathen savages" [Grimshaw], Mormon women in polygamous marriages [Dunfey]) continued to discover that they too displayed at heart a germ of true feminist consciousness.

In some articles written in 1983-1984 it was nevertheless possible to discover faint traces of a paradigm shift that would not be fully evident until the late 1980s. Though Gayle Rubin (sex radical as well as anthropologist) had first proposed the examination of women's lives in the context of a "sex/gender system" in a 1975 article, it was only in the mid-1980s and particularly in connection with the sex debates that feminists more generally began to discuss the necessity of understanding femininity as a reciprocal term always defined in relationship to masculinity, the assumption on which the term "gender" rests. As well, feminist scholars began in this period to investigate the "social construction" of gender and sexuality, again in the context of the debates around sexuality. As Kate Ellis put it, "The question is: does sexuality begin as an unmediated 'it' that is later constructed by societal input, or is sexuality like language, only brought into being through the process of 'learning' it?" (119). Ellis also suggested that the social construction of sexuality and femininity is the notion that fundamentally divides cultural and socialist feminists, and it seems to me that it was indeed social constructionism that pounded the final nail in the cultural feminist coffin.

It is not surprising that Michel Foucault entered feminist discussion at about this moment, particularly via the sex debates. From him, feminists began to acquire a new conception of power not just as repressive and negative but as productive and positive—a notion that would be central to the elaboration of social constructionism. In feminists' attention to Foucault it is possible also to discern some stirrings of suspicion about the utility of grand theory and totalizing models altogether: Biddy Martin, for instance, one of the earliest U.S. feminists to emphasize the importance of Foucault for feminist scholarship, argues that conceptions of capitalism and patriarchy as "total theories of monolithic control or power held by a clearly identifiable and coherently sovereign group" have made it impossible "to get at the operations of power and the possibilities for resistance in modern Western societies, to comprehend the constitution and the transformation of power relations at the level of the local and everyday" (5). Yet in the mid-1980s, as the tensions of the Cold War were reinvigorated by a president who saw America "standing tall" again, a conception of power disseminated from the top downward seemed after all not so far-fetched, and it may be that the collapse of communism and the end of the Cold War would be necessary before Foucault would find final favor with feminists.

Finally, though feminist literary scholarship made no great leaps forward in the period up to 1984, some hints of things to come could be detected in that arena. In 1982 Stephen Greenblatt had first coined the term "new historicism," a method which was at that point was, and for several years to come would remain, astonishingly oblivious to gender issues yet which nonetheless served as a harbinger of the new, more historically based approach inflected by cultural studies, cultural materialism, and Foucault which feminists would embrace in the 1990s. In a 1984 report in *Signs*, "Towards a Feminist Literary History," Marilyn L. Williamson pointed feminist literary scholars in a similar direction. Williamson proposes that, rather than attempting to add great women writers to the canon, feminists should abandon the notion of the canon altogether. Instead, they should seek to examine women's non-traditional writing, and for that they would need to draw upon the conclusions of other disciplines and develop an interdisciplinary approach: for "providing a cultural setting for non-traditional works through the study of history and ideology may be a more effective method than one governed by purely literary concerns" (137). More-over, she proposed to abandon a concept of the autonomous text set against the backdrop of its context in favor of understanding how each helped to configure the other: "The ideological approach, moreover, will not privilege aesthetic dis-course: it will not see social and economic conditions as a background reflected in literary products. Instead such an approach will view literature as part of a general discourse produced by a given culture, all aspects of which at once create and reflect its value system" (143). (Louis Montrose would later famously cap-ture Williamson's insight in the chiasmus "the historicity of texts" and "the tex-tuality of history" ["Professing" 20].) In the light of things to come in feminist literary scholarship, Williamson's conclusion is remarkably prescient: "And so it appears that as contemporary theories gradually transform our curricula and habits of mind, the historical, ideological study of women's nontraditional writ-ing will take its place among many accepted ways to organize and study a great variety of texts" (147).

CHAPTER 5

Gender, Race, and History in
The Book of Franza

> *Philosophical problems are illnesses that*
> *must be healed.*
>
> —Ingeborg Bachmann, Werke

Though *The Book of Franza* was uncompleted at the time of Bachmann's death, it was begun as the first of the "Ways of Death" novels. As the editors of the *Werke* explain, Bachmann had conceived her plan for the novel cycle even before she completed *The Thirtieth Year* and originally intended "Ways of Death" as the title for the novel which was to become *Franza*. In 1967, after having written the portions that have now been printed, she laid *Franza* aside, to begin work on *Malina*. She explained in a 1971 interview that only *Malina* had made access to the world of the "Ways of Death" possible for her: "I wrote almost 1,000 pages before this book, and these last 400 pages from the very last years finally became the beginning that I had always been lacking" (*GuI* 96). One can understand the importance of the novel *Malina* for a novel cycle which was to be narrated by a male figure; that first published novel explains why there could be no female narrative voice for the "Ways of Death." But, perhaps because of its subject matter, that difficult first novel of the "Ways of Death" cycle was badly received, and only now are we beginning to grasp all that is responsible for the destruction of the "I" of *Malina*, that, as Bachmann put it, "the sickness of the world and the sickness of this person is the sickness of our time for me" (*GuI* 72). Should Bachmann have completed and published *The Book of Franza* before *Malina*, the misunderstandings to which *Malina* was subjected might have been fewer, for *The Book of Franza* more explicitly and concretely locates the female "ways of death" of which her cycle speaks in a social and historical context. The reading of *The Book of Franza* I offer here is thus intended both as an interpretation of this daring, complex, and fragmentary novel and also as an attempt to illuminate, via an understanding of *Franza*, Bachmann's intentions for the entire "Ways of Death" cycle.

I consider this endeavor of particular importance because in my view Bachmann's work, after her rediscovery and reinterpretation by feminist literary scholars of the late 1970s, now faces the danger of a second dehistoricization and *Verharmlosung* (domestication). Several recent scholars have shown how Bachmann's fame as a poet in the 1950s was purchased at the cost of the extraction of a social context from her work. Bernd Witte argues, for instance, "For secret conservatives of all hues her moderate modernism thus became the appropriate contemporary continuation of pure poetry" (*Kritisches*). Such preconceptions continued to shape the reception of her later fiction—with which critics seemed powerless to come to terms. Now the feminist rereadings of Bachmann, particularly facilitated by the works of the French feminist theorists Luce Irigaray and Hélène Cixous, have given us a lens through which to view that late fiction, showing us how Bachmann's "Ways of Death" investigate the psychic states of women in a world dominated by men. These new feminist interpretations have permitted extraordinary insights into Bachmann's work, and we now understand dimensions of it which without feminism we perhaps might never have seen at all. Nonetheless, it has seemed to me recently that there is an inclination in feminist literary scholarship in general and in Bachmann scholarship in particular to use gender as the single category through which to understand works by women writers. Encouraged by French and American psychoanalytic feminist theory and by the influential American literary scholars Sandra Gilbert and Susan Gubar, such scholarship often treats the category "woman" as if it were one that did not vary historically and culturally, as if gender were the only source of oppression from which women have ever suffered, and as if all women were only innocent victims of male power, not also members of classes and cultures in which they possess (some) privilege and power, including the power to oppress other women and men. At a point at which Bachmann's deep concern with the status of human (and particularly female) subjectivity *in the contemporary world* is only beginning to be grasped in its fullness, such ahistorical feminist interpretations seem to me, despite their contributions, once again to do violence to her works, by truncating the breadth of their politics and depth of their suffering and depriving them of their full radicality.

In this essay I want thus to stress what I believe to be *The Book of Franza*'s most central theme, the location of the "ways of death" suffered by contemporary European women within the trajectory of European and world history. Fundamental to my analysis is an understanding of the course of European history which draws heavily upon Critical Theory: I assume here (and document in *The Book of Franza*) that Bachmann also believes European history to be characterized by increasing tendencies toward domination and control, accomplished particularly through the eradication of the qualitatively different, the other. These efforts manifest themselves not just through the use of overt violence and force but also through the management of consciousness. In the realm of human thought the eradication of otherness takes the form of the domination of the abstract and interchangeable over the specific or unique, what Horkheimer and Adorno, following Weber, call the disenchantment of the world, the elimination of magical thinking. To create the human beings who are the agents and the objects of this domination, violence also had to be done to the human psyche, as Horkheimer and Adorno remark: "Men had to do fearful things to themselves before the self, the identical, purposive, and virile nature of man, was formed, and something of that recurs in every childhood" (33). Only a repressed residue remains that can express itself in dreams, parapraxes, neurotic symptoms, and madness. Language as well is complicit in domination, subsuming the particular under the rule of the concept; with the increasing separation of science from poetry, nonliterary language is employed to control the object world, not to be like it or to know it in its otherness. Women (or at least those women lacking a "manly character") cannot be the agents of domination: they are included among the others, an "image of nature, the subjugation of which constituted that civilization's title to fame." On the other hand, alone of all the dominated object world, women are allowed to participate in the human world, to enjoy the spoils of domination if they agree to accede to their oppression and to celebrate their masters' accomplishments: "Woman herself, on behalf of all exploited nature, gained admission to a male-dominated world, but only in a broken form. In her spontaneous submission she reflects for her vanquisher the glory of his victory, substituting devotion for defeat, nobility of soul for despair, and a loving breast for a ravished heart" (Horkheimer/Adorno 248–249). This is mostly the situation of the women Bachmann depicts in the "Ways of Death."

What is missing from *Dialectic of Enlightenment* and from most of Critical Theory is what Bachmann, building on this understanding of history, brings to *The Book of Franza*. Horkheimer and Adorno wrote from the perspective of what they believed to be the world-historical triumph of domination: National Socialism in Germany on the one hand, the culture industry of the United States on the other (developments that obviously concern Bachmann as well). But they virtually ignored the most obvious of enlightenment's efforts at domination: Western imperialism and neoimperialism, which surpass National Socialism in their brutality if not in their efficiency. In a parallel omission, Horkheimer and Adorno also fail altogether to acknowledge that there are cultures in the world which operate according to quite different rules, still at least in part outside the grip of enlightenment. Western history is not the whole of human history, and one suspects that in omitting any mention of that which is not subsumed by the West, Horkheimer and Adorno show themselves to be entrapped in the very dialectic of enlightenment that their book details. In *The Book of Franza*, however, Bachmann pushes the logic of their analysis further, particularly as regards Western women and also as regards their possibilities for liberation. The questions this novel poses are ones that it is central for feminism to address. If Western women are implicated in enlightenment, simultaneously its victims and its beneficiaries, what standpoint can they assume to struggle for their own liberation, and what will be the relationship of their struggles, within the West, to the struggles of other victims of the West who stand outside of it? Can history take a course which is not just that of increasing domination? Do white women have a place in such a history, or is their fate inextricably tied to that of the West? Where does their own story (told in the "Ways of Death") fit in? To these difficult and painful questions Bachmann has only the beginnings of answers, but her novel attempts to explore these dilemmas in their full complexity, revealing the truth to her readers—a charge she had set herself as a writer, for "Man can face the truth [*Die Wahrheit ist dem Menschen zumutbar*]" (*W* 4: 275-277).

The historical event central to *The Book of Franza* provides a concretization of the quandaries white women face. In flight from the white man in Vienna who had tried to drive her mad, Franza, in the company of her brother Martin, finds herself in Luxor, Egypt, on 14 May 1964. They had, we are told, "traveled into a historical event" (*Franza* 105, translation modified). On that day Nikita Khrushchev, Gamal Abdel Nasser, and three other Arab presidents—Ahmed Ben Bella of Algeria, Abdel Salam Arif of Iraq, and Abdullah al-Salal of Yemen—"standing on a granite bluff high over the site of the Aswan Dam Project, pressed a button . . . setting off a dynamite charge that opened a channel to divert the waters of the Nile," reported the *New York Times* of 15 May 1964 on its front page. "The explosion marked the completion of the first stage of the billion-dollar power and irrigation project which is designed to remake the face of this ancient and undeveloped land" (Walz 1).

The ramifications of this event for the themes of the novel are great. The story of the building of the Aswan Dam is centrally entwined with the activi-

ties of the whites in Africa. Perhaps the dam itself can be regarded as an image
something like the grand technological plans for progress at the end of *Faust II*,
for, as the *Times* reported in another article of the same day, "a gigantic high
dam that would harness the Nile became the dream of Egyptian reformers"
(Mohr 3)—European technology used to channel the powers of nature, turning them to human purposes. In the 1950s, the United States, Britain, and
the World Bank initially agreed to finance the building of the dam. President
Nasser, objecting to their condition that the Egyptian economy be supervised
during the dam's construction, began negotiations with the Soviet Union. When
the Americans withdrew their offer, Nasser seized the internationally owned
Suez Canal Company, and the Israelis, French, and British invaded Egypt in
retaliation, an act many regarded as blatant imperialism, bringing the world to
the brink of war.

In the novel, Martin and Franza pass through Suez and allude to that crisis,
though Suez shows no trace of such momentous events: "Suez was a surprise,
for no immediate drama presented itself to the eyes, nor any trace of a past
war" (*Franza* 90). Instead, the Soviets financed the building of the dam: Egypt
chose a course of development not that of Western Europe but one that might
nonetheless be regarded as the culmination of enlightenment thinking. As
Khrushchev pointed out during his visit (a visit which, the novel tells us, Martin followed avidly in the newspapers), the dam can be regarded as a "symbol
of peaceful cooperation" and "proves that through socialism there is progress"
(Walz 1). Indeed, the dam will achieve for Egypt the inundation and fertility
which Franza, as I show below, is unable to find: the *Times* notes that the dam is
"designed to raise the Nile nearly 200 feet. It will store water in a lake 300 miles
long. The lake will enable Egypt to increase tillable acreage from six million to
eight million acres" (Walz 3). On the other hand, the day on which the statesmen loose the Nile waters is the same day on which Franza is buried alive in the
hardening Nile mud. She says: "What have I seen? A limousine, a ship, and rose
petals. Then they will open the sluices, the water will come out. History will
dub it the Day of the Water. And I was buried alive" (*Franza* 106-107). Probably
this history is preferable to that of outright colonial exploitation, though it is not
clear that such progress leads in the direction of human liberation. It is also not
at all clear what this larger course of history has to do with Franza's own story,
for the history made by the statesmen of the Second and Third World is not one
that she shares. Or, as she asks: "My story and the story of all those who make
up the larger history, how do these find a place within the whole of history?"
(*Franza* 107).

In this novel Franza's story has three parts, which stand simultaneously for different cultural locations, different points in history, and, most important, for different regions of the psyche or stages of psychological development, as Bachmann explained in her draft of a preface to the novel: "The settings then are Vienna, the village of Galicien and Carinthia, and the Arabian, Libyan, and Sudanese deserts. The real settings, the interior ones laboriously concealed by the external, are elsewhere" (*Franza* 4). The different locations of the novel allow Bachmann both to explore the development of Franza's illness and also to interrogate its causes, to pursue the reasons for Franza's death: "The book, however, is not simply a journey through an illness. Ways of death also include crimes. This is a book about a crime" (*Franza* 3). For, as Bachmann goes on to explain in the preface, "the virus of crime . . . cannot have simply disappeared from our world twenty years ago [i.e., in 1945]" (*Franza* 3). Instead, in our society, the attitudes of mind which produced National Socialism now exercise their brutality in the realm of consciousness: "Crimes that require a sharp mind [*Geist*], that tap our minds and less so our senses, those that most deeply affect us—there no blood flows, but rather the slaughter is granted a place within the morals and customs of a society whose fragile nerves quake in the face of any such beastliness. Yet the crimes did not diminish, but rather they require greater refinement, another level of intelligence, and are themselves dreadful" (*Franza* 4).

The novel's second chapter, "Jordanian Time," explores, as I detail below, how these destructive practices are most commonly carried out within European culture (only apparently not at war) in the domination of women by men. To demonstrate, however, that male dominance (or domination altogether) is neither an ontological nor a historical constant, Bachmann shows in the novel's first chapter, "Return to Galicien," that there existed a time, a culture, and a point in psychological development—now all irretrievably lost—when peace was possible. In the novel's final chapter, "The Egyptian Darkness," Franza flees Europe in search of a cure for the madness into which her husband, agent of the crimes of her culture, has driven her. In North Africa, however, she discovers the extent of the crimes of Europe. Her imprecations are thenceforth delivered against "the whites" as well as against her husband, her dying words: "The whites should. They should be damned. He should" (*Franza* 142). Franza finds in the North African desert no cure for the situation of women in contemporary Europe, no standpoint from which she can assert an alternative to the cultural dominance of the white fathers—though she may have learned there at least how to break out of the psychic structures imposed upon her by European men, and perhaps even how to rebel against them. But the novel seems to conclude with the suggestion that if there is a solution for humankind, it may not be one that would include white women like Franza. To explain fully the relationship of Franza's story to "the whole of history," the remainder of this essay investigates these points at greater length.

Franza's "case" begins in contemporary Vienna, the site of *Three Paths to the Lake* and the other "Ways of Death" novels, whose characters appear again in this work. Here, as elsewhere in Bachmann's work, geography and landscape have a paradigmatic, sometimes even symbolic function. The elite social stratum Bachmann describes in Vienna embodies some central qualities of the *grande bourgeoisie* in contemporary Europe, and her Vienna recalls Balzac's Paris in its emphasis on social success, in its cold-blooded opportunism, in its constantly shifting liaisons, in the dirty or vicious secrets that lie beneath its polished surface. But simultaneously, Vienna (or more generally, Austria), because it is now no longer central to the course of European history, provides Bachmann a privileged perspective from which to view events elsewhere, as she remarked in a 1971 interview: "It [Austria] differs from all other small countries today in that it was an empire and it's possible to learn some things from its history. And because the inactivity to which one is compelled there enormously sharpens one's perspective on the big situation and on today's empires. Those who have declined themselves know what that means" (*GuI* 106). As "interior setting," Vienna stands for the psychic structures demanded and imposed in contemporary Europe, in Franza's case a feminine psyche as her culture constructs it. To succeed in Vienna, Franza must be *gleichgeschaltet* (forced into conformity), obliterating her provincial eccentricities and other nonsynchronic residues of her past; she must learn and accept her place in the social and linguistic order, where she is the object, not the subject. Talented at languages, Franza learns the language of her domination well, becoming a "young lady [who] had changed her hairstyle and dropped the Galicien accent, exchanging it for a different accent in Vienna, walking through Herrengasse and through the Kohlmarkt as if she had never walked over the Matchstick Bridge at home" (*Franza* 22). The sites at which Bachmann locates Franza in Vienna are significant: sipping coffee in the Café Herrenhof, strolling through the Herrengasse, Franza has agreed to acknowledge men as her masters. To be able to enjoy the privileges available to the wife of her husband, to become "Frau Jordan, who was used to being admitted" (*Franza* 126), Franza has been obliged to become feminine, following an almost classically Freudian model: "She was twenty-three, about to give up her studies, allegedly having fainted [*ohnmächtig geworden*] in a hall of anatomy, or in an equally romantic tale she fell into the Fossil's [Jordan's] arms" (*Franza* 9).

Anatomy teaches her her powerlessness (*Ohnmacht*): she cannot become the doctor but must marry someone who is—Leopold Jordan.

Though Martin terms Jordan a fossil, Franza knows that is wrong: "Why did you call him the Fossil? Oh, no, you're wrong, for he's more contemporary than I am, he is the type that rules today, that succeeds today, that attacks and lives to do so, for I've never seen a person with so much aggression" (*Franza* 79). An esteemed psychoanalyst, Jordan can be regarded as an administrator of consciousness, responsible for discriminating between sanity and madness and for restoring those who deviate to normality. Like the agents of domination whom Horkheimer and Adorno describe, Jordan uses his science to reduce his patients to that alone which his categories can contain: "He dissected everyone until nothing more was left, nothing remaining except a finding that belonged to him. . . . [H]e couldn't allow any person to deviate from the norm he established for them" (*Franza* 73). Martin uses the term fascism to describe a form of rationality which has turned into its opposite, and here Franza concurs: "He must be crazy. And there's no one who seems more rational" (*Franza* 76). Jordan's great work, a study of the medical experiments done on concentration camp victims (a preliminary study for the work mentioned in "The Barking," titled "The Significance of Endogenous and Exogenous Factors in Connection with the Occurrence of Paranoid and Depressive Psychoses in Former Concentration Camp Inmates and Refugees" [*Paths* 106]), is thus a model for and description of his own practice. Jordan prefers particularly those who willingly and completely give themselves into his hands, his wives: "He didn't like women, and yet he always had to have a woman in order to provide him with the object of his hatred" (*Franza* 72). "Why was I hated so much?" asks Franza, and corrects herself, "No, not me, the other within me" (*Franza* 62), the otherness of women that escapes the parameters of male control.

The accomplishment of this novel in the area of gender relations, then, is its dramatization of how a woman accedes to and is destroyed by a man's power. In two respects this novel is different from the other "Ways of Death" works: first, because rationalized male power is embodied in a figure deliberately and calculatedly brutal, and second, because Franza, probably alone of all the "Ways of Death" figures, is allowed to come to consciousness of her own condition. Franza discovers that Jordan has intentionally set about to manipulate and destroy her: "He was working on me, he was working on me as his case study. He hounded me" (*Franza* 82). She succumbs, falling prey to hysterical attacks of coughing and breathlessness, phobias, and paralyzing anxieties. Object of his scientific calculation, Franza is an experiment, like those of the concentration camps, as she explains bitterly: "A magnificent experiment was made on me. To put it vulgarly: How much can a person stand without kicking the bucket?" (*TP* 2: 62, passage omitted in translation). Jordan's omission of her name from even the foreword to his great work represents an attempt to remove her from discourse altogether: "He wanted to erase me. My name should simply disappear in order that I could disappear for real later on" (*Franza* 63). And in contrast even to the concentration camp victims, there are no words to describe what is being done to her, no one to whom to appeal, no allies against this sort of fascism:

> I was suddenly no more a co-worker, no longer married. I was separated from society with my husband, living in a jungle in the middle of civilization, and I saw that he was well armed and that I had no weapons at all.
>
> But what am I saying? I'm missing the central point. No, no, I wasn't in any jungle, I was in the middle of civilization, along with its definition in the dictionary, and its verbal ability to handle any situation. (*Franza* 81-82)

The turns of phrase obliterate her actual situation, will not allow her to tell the story of her victimization by the male subject of this civilization.

In Vienna, what reveals Franza's real situation to her are her dreams. Those dreams speak in the language of the unconscious, which refuses to acknowledge the rules of gender and discourse as culture imposes them but articulates in its own language its desire and distress. "When you learn this in the same manner within yourself, on the trip through the tunnel in the night, then you know it's true" (*Franza* 79, translation modified). (This is, it appears, the same metaphorical tunnel through which Martin passes at the book's beginning, a creative process drawing on the unconscious which produces the words on paper, the truth of this novel: "The words line up together, and brought along out of the darkness of the tunnel passage . . . the originals and the copies roll on, the illusions and the true conceptions rolling into the light, rolling down through the head, emerging from the mouth that speaks of them and asserts them and is reliable because of the tunnel in the head" [*Franza* 9, translation modified].) Franza's dreams tell her the story of patriarchy and power: "the dream . . . presenting you with your own great drama, your father and a henchman named Jordan together in one person as equally important as any great figure. . . . Your free-floating fear, for which you have no basis, presents a story that assaults your sight and hearing, and you know for the first time why you feel such angst. I saw a graveyard at sunset, and the dream told me: that is the Graveyard of the Daughters" (*Franza* 78). Both this dream and the dream of being gassed in a gas chamber ("and Jordan held the knob and was letting the gas in" [*Franza* 70]) appear also in

Malina. Here is the explanation for the "ways of death" endured by Bachmann's women, stories that can be told only outside a cultural framework that regards such treatment of women as natural and legitimate.

Her dreams let Franza generalize from her own oppression to that of other victims of this culture's power: "What I have realized is that I am from a lower race. Or perhaps it's a class" (*Franza* 79). She stresses particularly the affinities between the power exercised against her and that which white imperialism has directed against nonwhite peoples: "He stole all of my goods. My laughter, my tenderness, my capacity for joy, my compassion, my ability to help, my animal nature, my shining rays, for he stomped out everything that rose up until it could no longer rise again. Why someone does that I don't understand, but it's incomprehensible why the whites took all the goods from the blacks. Not just the diamonds and the nuts, the oil and dates, but also the peace in which such goodness grows, and the health without which one cannot live" (*Franza* 80; translation modified). Like the Papuas, she is dying of "deadly despair": "I am a Papuan," she proclaims (*Franza* 80). Only in the third chapter do we learn that Franza finally left Jordan because he had also taken her only child from her, forcing her into an abortion conducted by "a sterilized surgeon dressed in a snow-white uniform," a white scientist, an "authority" like Jordan. Franza foresees that the aborted fetus will be thrust, like the Nazi victims, into the cremation ovens. Falling on her knees in the operating room, revealing the real authority relationship in effect, she begs that the child be preserved (analogously to the Egyptian mummies) in a canning jar, or that she be allowed to reincorporate it into herself, to eat its heart (like Isis and Osiris in Musil's poem discussed below). It is Franza's behavior, of course, that is judged to be mad, while the men who control her are regarded as normal. Despite her psychic state, Jordan decrees that her expropriation continue: "Jordan, the psychotherapist in charge, knew best whether there was any cause for concern, and Jordan the authority assured him authoritatively: There's no need to worry" (*Franza* 94). For in the language of this white science, one need not worry about the fate of the victims, and the victims are unable to speak in their own behalf.

To be able to tell her own story, as Franza succeeds nonetheless at least partially in doing, two conditions seem to be necessary. First, she must have some way of moving outside the limits European thought sets her. She does so in her dreams but also geographically: the second chapter, "Jordanian Time," takes place on shipboard, under way from Genoa to North Africa, within the boundaries of no land at all (a situation somewhat analogous to the dream also in its relationship to water). Second, she seems to need a sympathetic listener;

she needs to be able to turn the analytic relationship against the aims of psychoanalysis that Jordan represents, using it to gain access to events and meanings that Jordan refuses to acknowledge, to create a history for herself different from Jordan's history. Even before their trip, Martin had noticed that inducing Franza to speak of her experiences helped her to combat the hysterical attacks which overcame her—precisely the same discovery Freud had made with his own hysterical patients. Thus what needs to be asked here as well is the status in the novel of this sympathetic listener and interlocutor, Martin. Is he the lost brother/lover whom women seek? What does the relationship of Franza and Martin tell us about the possibility of understanding and love between men and women in this culture?

As even the linguistic similarities of their names indicate, Martin plays in this novel a role somewhat similar to that of Malina in the novel of that name (Martin/Malina; cf. Jordan/Ivan). Martin and Franza as children, before each accepted the gendered rules for adulthood, spoke the same language (or sometimes no language at all), and hence could understand each other. But in the present time of this novel, Martin has also succeeded in the Viennese high society of the "Ways of Death," which means he has become a successful man. The novel's first sentence suggests that his relationship to Franza is almost as proprietary as Jordan's: "The Professor, the Fossil, had destroyed his sister for him" (*Franza* 7; translation modified). Martin also possesses other characteristics of men in this society, sometimes even a caricature of their qualities. He regrets, for instance, his sister's illness particularly because it interferes with his carefully calculated love affair with Elfi Nemec, the model who will become Jordan's next wife after Franza's death. In a rather comic scene Martin tries, in analogy to Jordan, to understand Franza's illness using geological categories, the only science he knows (and here portrayed as a particularly positivistic one): "His sister was cut through by pain and by something he was unable to explore, given his specialty, for he had no desire to describe or identify the grind [*Schliff*] of his sister, which was from the Modern Era and not from the Mesozoic" (*Franza* 29; translation modified). Even outside Europe, in the desert, "the immense sanatorium" (*Franza* 89), Martin mostly fails Franza; he cannot understand what she is trying to say, even when she is dying, and at the end of the novel returns to Vienna apparently untroubled, "a white man among white people" (*Franza* 145; translation modified). He came "home," Bachmann tells us, "where he felt at home again, there in the third district, and went to sleep and never thought this way again" (*Franza* 146).

Why does Martin fail Franza? His fascination for Breasted, an Egyptologist (to whom Franza is indifferent!), provides a clue. James Henry Breasted was the author of *The Dawn of Consciousness* (1933), a work that Freud used to support his argument in *Moses and Monotheism* (1937–39) that Moses was actually an Egyptian, not a Jew. According to Freud, Moses derived the monotheism he introduced to the Jews from the Egypt of Amenhotep IV (better known as Akhnaton) of the Eighteenth Dynasty. Amenhotep IV forced monotheism on his Egyptian subjects, says Freud, a religion that was "contrary to their thousands-of-years old traditions and to all the familiar habits of their lives." It was a strict monotheism, Freud continues, "the first attempts of the kind, so far as we know, in the history of the world, and along with the belief in a single god religious intolerance was inevitably born, which had previously been alien to the ancient world and remained so long afterwards" (23: 20). The roots of monotheism go back to the reign of Thothmes III (also known as Thutmose), who was responsible for making Egypt a world power. "This imperialism," Freud says, "was reflected in religion as universalism and monotheism" (23: 21). Thothmes III was the successor (and also half-brother and husband) to Hatchepsut, the first female queen in Egyptian history, and tried to eradicate every trace of her, a fact upon which Franza remarks when she visits Hatshepsut's temple in the novel's third chapter. Freud of course connects monotheism, the worship of a universal, all-powerful Godfather, to the internalization of patriarchal values resulting from the successful traversal of the oedipus complex. Martin's admiration for Breasted can thus be read as a kind of shorthand on Bachmann's part, an indication of how Martin—as a successful young white man—is also inheritor to a system of values that rest upon universalism, abstraction, imperialism, and male power (as well as a conception of linear progress from the past to the present)—while Franza is the victim of these values, at their mercy. Thus Martin, like Malina with the "I" and despite his evident love and sympathy for Franza, is also part of the order which is destroying her; hence, he cannot really understand her or come to her aid. At the beginning of the novel Martin believes that he has understood Franza's "message [*Mitteilung*]" (the telegram she sends him appealing for help), that he could be a Champollion for Franza, like the translator of the Rosetta stone, "the first to shed light on a forgotten form of writing [*Schrift*]" (*Franza* 7), finding an equivalent in his language. But Franza cannot be translated into Martin's language, as the "I" cannot be into Malina's.

Bachmann suggests, however, that Martin and Franza were not always so estranged, and the novel's first chapter, "Return to Galicien," returns to a time in human psychological development and in European history before the reign of terror (to which "Jordanian Time" testifies) held such complete sway. In this section, as elsewhere in Bachmann's writing, the Austrian province Carinthia plays an important role as a nonsynchronic alternative to contemporary Vienna, scene of the crimes of the "Ways of Death." Because it is in the "language triangle" [*Sprachdreieck*] or on the border, Bachmann also seems to regard it as an area where the limits of language are not drawn so firmly, whence transgressors of boundaries (*Grenzgänger*) derive. This aspect of Bachmann's work, its productive use of an Austrian tradition, has only begun to be investigated, but I can advance here at least some initial observations. The Galicien to which Martin and Franza return home is an imaginary village near the real town of Villach on the Gail River in Carinthia. But "home" seems also to be the site of an original, nonalienated relationship of man and woman to each other, to culture, and to nature. In this respect, of course, Bachmann's attempt at a "return home" recalls Ernst Bloch's *The Principle of Hope*, a work that she identified in the Frankfurt lectures as a major influence on contemporary writing. In psychological terms, the young Franza and Martin demonstrate the possibility of love between the sexes before they have assumed their role in the patriarchal order as adult man and woman. Alone, without parents, they have avoided the oedipal "family romance" and can love each other as equals; because their love precedes the institution of the incest taboo, it is also erotic, and it is possible that Martin and Franza become lovers in Egypt. This erotic and maternal older sister–younger brother relationship traces its way through Bachmann's published work from the poems (especially "The Game is Over") to "Three Paths to the Lake," an alternative to the present-day "tangle and confusion, the discrepancy inherent in all relationships" (*Paths* 175) between men and women.

It is because Martin is also psychologically not of a single piece, because he also preserves archaic recollections of other possible relationships between men and women "beneath" the psyche he has acquired as an adult male, that he can respond to Franza at all. In their childhood, Martin recalls, he called her "girl" in a different language, "For that's what he had called her, 'Gitsche,' the Windish word for girl, 'Gitsche,' who was the essence of all the Gitsches" (*Franza* 21–22). Because of their prepatriarchal connections, Martin and Franza can sometimes communicate across space and time, without words. Thus expressly "against all reason [*Vernunft*]" (*Franza* 18), Martin knows that Franza, in flight from Jordan, would have gone home to Galicien.

In a manner somewhat analogous to Freud himself, who used the metaphor of an earlier civilization, the Minoan-Mycenean, chronologically anterior to Greece, to explain the existence of a preoedipal psychic phase especially important for women, Bachmann appeals to Egypt to explain the nature of this preoedipal sibling love. The "special saying [*Kult-Satz*]" of the siblings, which Martin recalls only imperfectly, derived from a poem of Robert Musil's, "Isis und Osiris": "Among a hundred brothers there is one. And he ate her heart. . . . And she ate his [*Unter hundert Brüdern dieser eine. Und er aß ihr Herz. . . . Und sie das Seine*]" (*Franza* 58). Bachmann alludes here of course to the love of Ulrich and Agathe in *The Man Without Qualities*. She quoted the Musil poem for the first time in a radio essay written sometime after December 1952, explaining there how Ulrich and Agathe's love was a failed attempt to achieve a "different condition [*anderen Zustand*]" through love, a utopia intended as an attack on "the dominant orders, in which every thing is solely a singular example of its possibilities" and also an alternative to the impending war, "which initiated the collapse of culture and thinking about culture" (*W* 4: 100, 102). Musil's importance for Bachmann needs still to be investigated, for here as in other respects there seem to exist deep affinities between their writings, and Bachmann has acknowledged his work as one of her most important literary influences (*GuI* 56).

In *The Book of Franza,* however, even more important is Bachmann's allusion to the Isis and Osiris myth itself. As Freud recounted in *Moses and Monotheism*, the religion of Aten (associated by Freud with imperialism, abstraction, and the power of the father) kept "complete silence about the god of the dead, Osiris, and the kingdom of the dead" (23: 24). According to Breasted, traditional Egyptian thinking "was always in graphic form. The Egyptian did not possess the terminology for the expression of a system of abstract thought; neither did he develop the capacity to create necessary terminology, as did the Greek. He thought in concrete pictures" (7-8). Hieroglyphic writing (or the "royal cartouches" to which Bachmann refers) exemplifies Egyptian concreteness, and it is also of course according to Freud the technique the unconscious uses to construct a dream: "The dream-work makes a translation of the dream-thoughts into a primitive mode of expression similar to picture-writing" (15: 229). In the earliest Egyptian thinking, Osiris is identified with the Nile, with water in general, and sometimes also with the land; he is in general a god of fertility. After Osiris was killed by his evil brother Set, his faithful wife Isis retrieved the dismembered parts of her husband, and he was revived to rule over the kingdom of the dead; according to Sir James Frazer, both Isis and Osiris can be regarded as corn deities. Though Martin, apart from his love for Franza, bears little resemblance to Osiris, Bachmann hints that Franza has qualities in common with Isis. Martin recalls Franza in her girlhood, "who went around with lighted pumpkins, who in the afternoon had climbed the ladder to the hayloft with Martin to tunnel through stacks of hay, who had taught him how to carve pumpkins and roast corn and to live stretched out in the hay as if that was all he would ever need to live" (*Franza* 21, translation modified). Recalling how she had rescued him from drowning in the Gail, Martin calls her "a mythic figure" (*Franza* 20). From these hints and suggestions (Franza's age, thirty-three, also alludes to deities who die and are born again), one can begin to surmise what Bachmann intends with the Isis and Osiris myth. It performs a function something like the myth of matriarchy in feminism, indicating a time in personal and human history before the patriarchal estrangement of the present, when thought was still magical and concrete and those of different sexes could still love each other as equals. *Franza's* third chapter, "The Egyptian Darkness," will undertake, then, to explore the possibilities of retrieving this psychic and historical Egypt in the present.

To understand, however, why Egypt cannot answer Franza's needs, one must look at another dimension of the "Return to Galicien" chapter which is intertwined with Bachmann's investigation of prepatriarchal psychology. Galicien also stands for a time in the history of Europe before domination had achieved its present guises, for alternative forms of social relations that, though lost, are preferable, despite their problems, to the present. The relationship of their grandparents Nona und Neni, whose wedding portrait hangs over the beds in Galicien, if not a happy one, was far more desirable than any contemporary relationship of men and women in Bachmann's works: "Nona was undefeated, gazing across at the picture of Neni, . . . though he too was undefeated and under attack only by the picture opposite, whose face was not ready to sign any armistice in a silent marriage war that they would end together, and out of which each would emerge the victor. They were both the unvanquished, the two of them up there, and Franza said without a smile, that was her opinion too" (*Franza* 52; translation modified). Nona and Neni died at the end of World War II. It was not this sort of marital battle, between equal antagonists, in which she was engaged, Franza insists.

The incident with which Martin's and Franza's time in Galicien concludes suggests that out of Galicien a possibility might have come for saving Franza. On the last evening before the departure for Egypt, Franza tries to drown herself in the Gail, an attempt that can be read as an endeavor to stay in Galicien or, perhaps more accurately, as an effort to withdraw, like Undine, from the deadly world of men altogether to return to her original watery realm. Franza is retrieved from the water by a mysterious "man from Müllnern," an "experienced, knowledgeable, schnapps-besotted rescuer who lightly swayed, but who, like a rider in the Wild West, clamped the motorcycle between his thighs and, as ever, headed his horse in the right direction" (*Franza* 56). This incident recalls the utopian tale from *Malina*, "The Secrets of the Princess of Kagran," in which the Princess (and her horse) are likewise saved from the water by a mysterious knight whose appearance prefigures the possibility of the erotic love and happiness between men and women for which the "I" longs.

Within *Franza*, the incident also alludes to the images Bachmann uses to indicate a real historical course that Galicien could have chosen after 1945, a peace that might have prevented the "ways of death" that her works lament. For Franza recalls (though Martin cannot remember) the "most beautiful spring" of May 1945, when peace came to Galicien in the person of another knight, an English captain, Sir Perceval Glyde, an innocent man. For Franza, aged fifteen, left virtually alone in Galicien when the peasants flee the village, the peace, the extraordinary spring, and her own awakening sexuality intertwine, and she waits in Galicien for a "miracle, . . . that's what she called her sense of restlessness," heralded by the air force squadrons overhead, the "heavenly hosts" (*Franza* 38; translation modified). If, as Franza contends in the third chapter, Jordan later eradicates her sexuality, here she experiences the coming of peace with an erotic intensity expressed nowhere else in this novel: "Franza had fallen into such a state that there was hardly any more room in her body for such excitement" (*Franza* 39). In the charming and archaic English she has learned in school she hands Galicien over to the man who stands for peace: "Sire, this village is yours. We have no arms. . . . We have no Germans and no SS. The people has left (was that right, or was it lived?) the village, because of fear" (*Franza* 41). Unlike even her brother, this man understands, despite their different languages: "And Sire and the peace, this king and this first man in her life, realized what she meant and continued to understand even when she stopped shaking. . . . And the miracle continued" (*Franza* 41-42; translation modified). From this man, her first love, Franza receives her first kisses, which she terms "the English kisses." Later, she protests vigorously when Jordan tries to convince her that this description is a parapraxis, that she had meant not "English" but "angelic," yet she insists on the real-worldly content of her first encounter with love and peace. But Sir Perceval leaves Galicien, and when Franza, grown up, encounters him later at a conference in London, he is part of Jordan's world, a promise of peace that has been betrayed, to whom Franza could no longer offer her love and her body: "For it was a long way from the onset of peace to the middle of an extended peace, and amid the latter there was nothing one could do, . . . the peace having become a mirage" (*Franza* 48).

If, however, peace has been betrayed, if the fascism virus continues in the postwar period, if, as the "I" of *Malina* observes, "It is the eternal war" (*Malina* 155), Franza does not forget the promise of a peace that would save her. On her way to the desert she remembers peace and asserts, "Sire, I arrive" (*Franza* 90, translation modified). She remembers peace again when during a hashish experience she achieves an "other condition" and proclaims, "I want to fly again, I want to arrive, Sire, I want to arrive" (*Franza* 117, translation modified). But the "ways of death" result from Europe's failure to eradicate domination with the military defeat of fascism. Until fascism in this broader sense is overcome, European women like Franza will not find the peace that could make them happy.

If, for a moment, peace, the liberation from fascism in all its guises, seemed possible in Europe, why is it not realized? In part, this is the subject that the third chapter addresses. One suspects that Bachmann, in turning to the Third World, is attempting to assert that domination of the rest of the world is essential to the West, to enlightenment as a system, hence impossible to abandon on a worldwide scale, despite the eradication of domination in its most extreme political forms in Europe. Like "Return to Galicien," the novel's third chapter, "The Egyptian Darkness," can be understood as functioning on several separate if intertwined levels. On the one hand, the settings are again interior ones, and the journey to Egypt may be understood as an attempt to arrive at a layer of the psyche uncolonized by twentieth-century European structures of thought. Franza and Martin's father dies in the battle of El Alamein, one of the turning points of the Second World War. Egypt thus stands for the defeat of fascism and the death of the father. But on the other hand, Egypt in this novel is not just a metaphor for Franza's (or white women's) prepatriarchal psychic strata. (Indeed, to make it such would represent a kind of imperialist arrogance of the sort Bachmann is here critiquing—nothing allowed to exist which is not of relevance to the European subject.) It also literally represents the Third World with its victims of white domination in the form of European imperialism. Vis-à-vis the Third World Franza is part of the oppressor culture, not its ally. Both in its past and its present, Egypt is a land that is foreign to Franza, within which she is a white person (though also a victim of white men). Thus the Egypt of this novel reveals itself to be neither a possible site of refuge nor a source of healing for Franza, though it enables her to envision, for a utopian moment, a world that would permit her to live rather than die. It is this second aspect of the third chapter I would like to consider first, and then the consequences for Franza's psyche of the estrangement of this white woman from the nonwhite world.

As Franza travels farther into Africa, she first recognizes with relief her growing distance from the whites: "The whites. Finally they were nowhere to be seen. Here she no longer had to turn around and hear them behind her and be afraid of being strangled, pressed against a wall in fear, pushed from a car into the snow" (*Franza* 95). She stops wearing her underwear, "the sweaty nylon and lace, . . . since they had left Europe behind them, there being no reason for her to remain a white woman with habits, taboos, and residues of the past" (*Franza* 97), and with an almost mystical fervor embraces the—somewhat romanticized—customs of the nonwhite world. "Who here feared the bacteria catalogued by the whites? Who washed out a cup? Who boiled water? Who disinfected the lettuce leaves? Who closely examined the fish? Hunger, thirst, discovered once again. The danger, discovered once again. The ears, the eyes, were sharpened, directed toward the outer world, a sense of purpose having been regained" (*Franza* 98). Believing that other laws obtain here, Franza proclaims confidently, "I am discovering my rights" (*Franza* 102). But of course she remains a white woman, and curious Arab children touch her "reddish-brown arm again and again, since it still looked white compared to theirs" (*Franza* 110). And she discovers that the whites are not so easily evaded, that they, or their way of thinking, are almost everywhere: "The whites are coming. The whites are landing. And if they are driven back, then they will come again. No revolution or resolution can prevent it, nor any controls over the currency. They will come again in spirit if there's no other way for them to come. And they will resurrect themselves in a brown or black brain, which will become white once again. They will take over the world through such indirect means" (*Franza* 112). Further, it is not at all clear to her that the customs she encounters are any more humane than those she had left behind, and she is haunted by images of a camel slaughtered at a wedding, a belly dancer, a madwoman in Cairo bound by her hair. As a white woman she is, like the woman in Cairo, bound to Jordan, her fascist husband: "I am bound and tied. I never escape" (*Franza* 132).

At the level of her psychic development, Franza also expects that the desert will cure her. As Sigrid Weigel has argued, one can view Franza's recourse to the desert as an effort of decomposition or deconstruction, an attempt to destroy psychic structures of domination as a first step toward the establishment of new structures beyond the "ways of death" ("Ende"). The desert is termed "the immense sanatorium" and "the great padded room of the sky, light and sand all about me," or, alternatively, "the immense inescapable purgatory" which will burn away the dross of this existence (*Franza* 89–90). Franza hopes here like Undine to be able to return to the water, to the original Nile of Isis and Osiris. But she is in Egypt in May, at the worst time for that fruitful inundation, and access to the water is blocked by monsters, jellyfish and

snakes. Instead of flowing into the Nile, she finds herself covered with hardening Nile mud, unable to move or speak or scream ("I wanted to scream, I kept
wanting to scream. But I simply wasn't able to scream" (*Franza* 107); she was
"buried alive" as in Vienna (*Franza* 106). And she also finds she cannot escape
the European God (her father, her husband), who appears to her in a vision.
Though she has vowed never again to bend her knee to anyone, again as in the
operating room she falls to her knees before this image that wants to eradicate
both her and her otherness:

> She remained lying there, suffering convulsions as she had in the hallway in
> Vienna, on a parquet floor, a linoleum floor, a hospital bed, and again on the sand,
> on the sand bloodied by a camel, as she laughed and laughed and laughed—her
> laughter providing the opening for the decomposition that began: Who am I?
> Where did I come from? What's wrong with me? What am I looking for in this
> desert? Something happened and yet did not happen, since nothing can happen,
> only something stepped on her and alongside her walked something else, part
> death, part consciousness, part animal, part human, part of the five senses, one
> a sister, the other a woman, the flesh directed by the sun toward ruin, en route
> toward something that is unrecognizable. (*Franza* 119)

If deconstruction is Franza's necessary first step, she cannot escape entirely the
European patriarch who has colonized her head, and the desert cannot save her
from dying.

Franza's death, and its cause, follow then with a deadly logic from her experiences in the desert: it is appropriate to the course of events in the novel, perhaps even inevitable. Martin wishes to climb the Great Pyramid before they
leave Egypt; as he climbs, Franza walks around the pyramid, wading through
the sand. She encounters there a white man who, while masturbating, hits her
with his stick and then, returning, rapes her. Franza recalls that Jordan had also
raped her in their library in Vienna: "When she wanted to escape he had shoved
her against the hard edges of the shelves and done it" (*Franza* 139). After the
rape, in a gesture that is in part self-destructive, in part rebellious, she brings
about an injury that causes her death: "Then she hit the wall, smashing her
head, slamming it with full force, her head smashing against the wall in Vienna
and the stone wall in Giza" (*Franza* 140). Franza had agreed to visit the pyramid to please Martin, telling him, with great unconscious irony, "You've already
missed so much" (*Franza* 137). Martin's ambition to climb this enormous edifice,
his desire to conquer it through his human effort, is surely intended to refer to
such general habits among white men. The *Blue Guide* to Egypt [1983] reports
that "because of the frequency of accidents climbing the pyramids is forbidden

except with special permission" (Seton-Williams and Stocks 399); it is significant that Martin, unlike Franza, can break the rules with impunity. At another
level the Great Pyramid, as Hegel argued, can represent the body of the sign,
the beginning of an alphabet which is nonhieroglyphic: hence the discourse
and language within which there is no place for Franza (Derrida, "Pit"). That
sexual violence should occasion Franza's death is fitting, since violence deriving
from definitions of gender (including the violent attempt to eradicate Franza's
sexuality: "I have no sex, no longer, it was ripped out of me" [*TP* 1: 278; passage
omitted in translation]) is in a more general sense responsible for the "way of
death" that Bachmann describes in this novel. Finally, it is not surprising that
Franza's last injury should be self-occasioned, since the order responsible for her
destruction is, as Bachmann underlines, one of which she is the victim but one
to which she has also acceded.

If this were the full story of Franza's death, however, she would be no different from the other victims of the "Ways of Death." It is what Bachmann adds
to Franza's story, her rebellion and resistance, that makes this novel so remarkable. Franza's initial response to her rapist is an acceptance of such violence
done to her as necessary and inevitable. Again she does not cry out against what
is killing her:

> Perhaps she should yell for help. She only had to let loose a scream, but why call
> for help? He was already at the corner. What was the point of screaming, why do
> it? The poor devils, they need to do it, to frighten someone.
>   She smoothed flat the linen dress behind her. It's nothing, nothing happened,
> and even if it did, what did it matter? (*Franza* 139)

Then, however, she breaks loose from those structures of thought that legitimate domination, rejecting (as she smashes her head against the stone) the violence committed against her in Egypt and Vienna: "Her thinking broke off, and
. . . her other voice returning, she said aloud: No. No" (*Franza* 140, translation
modified). Her last words, then, are an assertion of the destruction of the categories of domination and an imprecation against the whites and against a "he"
who carries out the white will:

> All conceptions shattered.
> The whites.
> My head.
> The whites should.
> They should be damned. He should. (*Franza* 141-142; translation modified)

The ability of Franza, virtually alone among the "Ways of Death" figures, to rebel derives from a highly significant encounter with an oppressor figure from which she does emerge the victor. Seeking some alleviation of her suffering, Franza is directed to consult a "doctor who worked miracles," "one of those Germans, you know the type" (*Franza* 124-125). Franza recognizes this doctor, SS-Hauptsturmführer Dr. Kurt Körner, in fact Viennese, from her husband's great work: he had participated in the Nazi euthanasia program for the mentally ill, "the eradication of undesirables" (*Franza* 129). "I know who you are," Franza tells Körner, and demands also to be eradicated (*Franza* 127). That is, acknowledging his power, Franza accedes to her destruction, seeking only to speed it along. Körner of course refuses, outraged and indignant. But to her astonishment when she next visits Körner, Franza discovers that he has vanished, afraid of her; she has vanquished him by confronting him:

> Körner had really left because of her, because he was afraid of her. Someone had been afraid of her, for the first time afraid of her rather than her being afraid of someone.
> On the drive to Giza [to the Great Pyramid], she said to Martin in the taxi:
> He—she corrected herself—Jordan was never afraid of me. He was so sure that I would tell no one, that I would rather die first (as well as until death did us part). He never once displayed any kind of uneasiness. But I still have made someone afraid. One of them. Yes, that I have done. (*Franza* 136)

What she has to say, however, is something Martin of course cannot, does not want to hear; this is a rebellion which he also must subdue: "Martin saw that her fists were balled up. He didn't understand her remarks, for the discontinuity of such sentences made it hard. In order to pull her out of her trance he took her hand and gently opened her fist and talked casually about something else" (*Franza* 136). Nevertheless, Franza's capacity not just to revolt but to revolt effectively, to put "one of them" to flight, suggests a strategy for women like herself which might move them beyond victimhood: to refuse this deadly order, actively to challenge their oppressors. (That "three muscular, older Dutch women" "pick up [*aufheben*]" Franza after her rape suggests how such a refusal might be carried out collectively, while their nationality hints that there may exist a Germanic people who refuse collusion with fascism or even actively resist it [*Franza* 140]). This strategy might move such white women not backward, into an imagined prepatriarchal past, but forward, past the crimes of whites in the present toward a future which is their own.

But this does not, of course, happen in the novel. Even if, as the imagery of this novel sometimes hints, Franza's "fall" (her "senseless fall [*Sturz*]," as Martin terms it [*Franza* 142]), has also a religious meaning, there is no grace for her, and she dies unredeemed. Thus the final question this novel addresses is whether, within the trajectory of human events that the novel describes, within human history, there can be a solution for women like Franza. I would like to propose here that, though this is a problem broached in the novel, Bachmann did not, perhaps could not, resolve it, and this is at least one of the reasons *The Book of Franza* remained unfinished.

European history, history as progress, is implicated in Franza's destruction. her horror at how the whites have treated Egyptian graves ("The whites. They violated the . . . , they didn't allow the dead to rest in peace" [*Franza* 109]) strongly recalls Walter Benjamin's "Theses on the Philosophy of History." "Only that his-torian will have the gift of fanning the spark of hope in the past," says Benjamin, "who is firmly convinced that *even the dead* will not be safe from the enemy if he wins. And this enemy has not ceased to be victorious" (255). The history written by the enemy regards as significant only those events that contribute to the pro-duction of the present—a present that the enemy controls. *This* history has no place for Franza's history, indeed, has eradicated it (whereas, says Benjamin, "a redeemed mankind receives the fullness of its past," a "past citable in all its moments" [244]). Franza and Martin are astonished at the effort taken by the third Thothmes (associated with the introduction of abstraction and monothe-ism) to destroy any evidence of the reign of Hatshepsut, Egypt's first queen— "this urge to destroy, . . . this desire to erase a great figure" (*Franza* 110)—but Franza consoles herself with the recognition that Hatshepsut's absence also speaks: "Look, she said, but the pharaoh forgot that though he had eradicated her, she was still there. It can still be read, because nothing is there where in fact something should be" (*Franza* 109). As a queen, Hatshepsut occupied the loca-tion of a man, even calling herself a king and wearing a false beard—thus becom-ing memorable within a history that is a history of domination. In the case of Franza and of white women like her, there is the danger that history may not even remark her absence, that she will be extinguished altogether. On the other hand, if Franza exists in the present only as part of white history, the history of domination, it is not clear how her story can in the future become part of the his-tory of the former victims. She belongs neither to the Second nor to the Third World, responsible for fruitful inundation at Aswan, and her own history may not intersect at all with the "historical event" she observes at Luxor.

If there is hope within history for Franza, it is given expression in the curi-ous fragments of chapter three included at the end of the *Franza* volume in the

Werke (passages omitted from the translation but located within the "Wüsten-buch" in volume one of the *"Todesarten"-Projekt*). The editors of the *Werke* tell us that these sections were intended to be inserted between the first and second parts of the third chapter: "In the typescript of part I a page follows with the handwritten note: Here a piece is missing with the stations Aswan and Wadi Halfa, before the return of the siblings to Cairo" (*W* 3: 561). That Bachmann intended an integration of those sections is indicated by the novel's conclusion, which refers back to them in a manner extremely significant for a final interpretation of this work.

The section with which these fragments begin, set in Luxor, is further substantiation for an interpretation of this novel through the lens of Critical Theory, for the passage suggests that in Egypt, Franza finds a nonreified relationship to the world of production: here both the producer and the consumer retain a human relationship to things, a relationship irretrievably lost in advanced capitalism. Franza remarks: "Luxor: all artisans' shops are open, I see for the first time how a shoe is made, again for the first time since childhood how bread is baked. The cobbler doesn't make a beautiful shoe but a durable one, the two men work all day in plain sight of everyone, they smile when you sit down with them, they don't let me pay for the tea that I fetch for them, every customer gets to sit down, in the shadows, gets tea or coffee to drink and gets to watch while they're working" (*TP* 1: 253). Bachmann goes on to specify, in almost classically Marxist fashion, the consequences of a way of life in which we have lost an organic relationship to the products of human labor: "It's not fondness for the simple life but rather merely the thought that we no longer see anything of how things come to be, which we need, that our children might again know where their food, their clothing comes from, that toys are palmed off on them that abuse the imagination so that it's all wrong from the outset, that their knowledge has no foundation" (*TP* 1: 253). Similar passages may be found in Bachmann's work as far back as *The Thirtieth Year*, but this one may represent Bachmann's clearest statement anywhere that the developments in the realm of thought which her works chronicle and lament have both a material basis and historical causes.

Yet more significant for the interpretation of this novel are Franza's experiences at Wadi Halfa, a town on the Nile in the Sudan, just south of the Egyptian border. The original Wadi Halfa will be submerged under the waters of Lake Nasser when the Aswan Dam is completed, a destruction that is a consolation and solace to Franza: "I'm traveling to Wadi Halfa. I can hang on to that. For it will perish [*untergehen*]" (*TP* 1: 278). On the one hand, for Franza,

Wadi Halfa has a meaning similar to that of the desert ("Oh, it is also there, the desert, what else should be" [*TP* 1: 279], she says), standing for the eradication of white thinking. Here the destruction of white thought takes the specific form of a refusal to recognize white symbols of exchange and communication (metaphors, it appears, for language altogether): at the closed post office, stamps are beautiful ("pretty stamps, a whole set") but useless, and a sign reads "tele-grammes are for delay." "Nobody needs telegrams here," Franza recognizes, "nobody ever needed them, as little as the stamps, the seals, the file folders" (*TP* 1: 279). Outside of Egypt and farther south, Wadi Halfa as interior setting may represent a layer of Franza's psychology antecedent even to the deconstruction of conceptions she achieves in the desert. But one may also regard Wadi Halfa as a utopian projection "forward" in that it represents the response of a community that is not white to white thought and a revenge on the whites: "gentle revenge, unconscious, on the whites is the legacy that stares back at them" (*TP* 1: 279). The question that then remains is that of Franza's relationship to that community.

In Wadi Halfa, for a moment, Franza finds that connection to a community in a setting that is almost religious, a kind of last supper. She drinks, like the Arabs, from the communal jug, finally finding her way to the water: "I have to drink, it tastes just like water, it's Nile water, the gnats don't matter" (*TP* 1: 280). Led by an old Arab to a house at the edge of the town, Franza there silently, without language, eats from a bowl of beans, her hands dipping into the bowl along with those of the Arabs and Nubians. For Franza this is a moment of total awareness and total peace: "It's the most conscious moment, the most natural, the first and only meal has taken place, is taking place, it is the first and only good meal, would perhaps remain the only meal in a lifetime that was not disturbed by barbarism, indifference, greed, thoughtlessness, calculation, by none at all" (*TP* 1: 282). Franza refers to this meal in specifically religious terms: she seems to view it both as confirming the possibility of comprehending the world "magically" (that is, non-instrumentally), as she has attempted to do, and simultaneously suggesting that it is possible to grasp that magic mode differently than she, in her madness, had hitherto been able to do: "I knew that the ingredients, the magic ones, of my world were given preference by my superstitions, I knew that the ingredients could be changed, but the experience of their variability was nothing less than a revelation" (*TP* 1: 282). The meal in Wadi Halfa thus (like John the Baptist, preaching in the desert, baptizing in the River Jordan, preparing the way for a savior whose time is not yet come) holds out the promise of a redemption for Franza on the far side of the world of the whites: "Thus I came to a sermon that nobody spoke and that was not held under a temple roof, to a sermon of the desert and unformulated laws, to mouthfuls of water and bites of food, ways of walking and sleeping, which waited under a thin crust of another kind of comprehension for their hour, for the mystical connection of breathing in and breathing out, of moving and resting, for the hallelujah of survival in nothingness" (*TP* 1: 283). With nonwhite people, Franza discovers that secular mysticism that traces its way as a utopian image through Bachmann's work from the beginning.

For Franza, of course, that image is only utopian. Though she succeeds in her efforts of destruction, there is nothing more she can attain, as the novel's last sentence indicates: "The Egyptian darkness, that one must grant her, is complete" (*Franza* 146; translation modified), and after her death Wadi Halfa is submerged as well, as Martin, returned to Vienna, learns from Viennese newspapers. The novel's difficult final paragraph suggests other consequences, though it is not altogether clear what we are to conclude from them. The communion of Wadi Halfa is continued, Bachmann tells us, but celebrated now only by nonwhite people, the hands of the white woman expressly excluded from that communal bowl. "But one can assume that the post office . . . was evacuated on schedule, despite an unscheduled delay, and that the brown and black hands would find themselves together again, reaching into a dish of beans in a new settlement further south. But Franza's white hand could no longer reach into a bowl in search of another morsel, and the silent woman near the wall would never learn that she had prepared the meal that had tasted better to her than all others" (*Franza* 146). If there is a historical realization of this utopia, it is not one in which a white woman like Franza participates.

On the other hand, the image with which this paragraph concludes is one of hope for history, though only in the most general of senses. A beacon remains at Wadi Halfa as a promise: "Even if it were forgotten by the departing refugees, there was a light in Wadi Halfa that would be lifted up by the Nile." With emphasis, Bachmann underlines the Hegelian term *aufheben*—to cancel, to preserve, to raise to a higher stage— to which she here makes recourse: "It wouldn't be swept away, for nothing can be swept away. It couldn't be dragged under, for it drags nothing down. Lift up [*aufheben*]. The inundator" (*Franza* 146; translation modified). What Bachmann's image does not clarify here is for whom the promise of the lantern is *aufgehoben*, or for whom it will be redeemed. If history, the passage of time, or nature itself (for we cannot tell how Bachmann wishes us here to understand the flooding of the Nile) will not solve the problem of domination, what hope is there for the Franzas of this world, for us? The example of Franza's resistance, the utopian image of human community beyond domination, and the promise of historical change may be as close as this novel can come to an answer to the problems of white women that it so carefully details.

READING BACHMANN IN 1984

This essay was first published in German in 1984 in the special *text + kritik* issue on Ingeborg Bachmann guest-edited by Sigrid Weigel; it appears here for the first time in English. Written in the spring of 1984, it was strongly influenced by contemporary debates both inside and outside of feminism. The two-year-long Fund for the Improvement of Post-Secondary Education–sponsored Five College faculty seminar on the intersection of Black Studies and Women's Studies, culminating in a major conference in April 1983 (Karcher), made a profound impact on me which has lasted to the present. Apart from discovering that I knew virtually nothing about black women, black history, and black culture in general (a gaping hole in my knowledge that I have tried to fill since then), I was brought into confrontation with two further aspects of black life that would cause me to reconsider my own feminist premises. First, it was impressed upon me that, whereas white feminists lamented their powerlessness and, as a solution, counseled retreat into preserves where men could not bother them, black history in contrast revealed (most obviously, of course, in the civil rights movement) a black determination to confront white power in order to gain for black people what was rightfully theirs. That recognition occasioned a transformation in both my theoretical and practical understanding of how feminists might contend with male power. Among other things, I drew upon the black example to encourage myself to become more feisty when I dealt with men, and that is why, in the essay, I am so pleased that Franza discovers it is possible to stand up to, even say no to, white men.

Second, a quite spectacular row in the seminar compelled me to acknowledge that the perspectives and modes of interaction elaborated by white feminists might not be the only forms opposed to those of dominant white men; that, indeed, the assertion of the superiority of white feminist models (with respect to how to conduct a seminar discussion, say) might itself be seen as an expression of white racial privilege. From these somewhat heated interactions I derived two far-reaching insights that would have a long-term impact on my conception of feminism: first, that white women (or "women" in general) are not inevitably on the "right" side; and second, that white women, even white feminists, can —quite unknown to themselves—think and act in ways that perpetuate their racial and class privilege (as in Marx's "social being determines consciousness"). In loose association with the faculty seminar two colleagues and I cotaught a rather large and somewhat disastrous undergraduate course called "Feminism, Black Nationalism, Marxism" in which, to my great dismay, the inadequacies of feminist analyses (and my own rhetorical skills) emerged in stark relief. (The French feminist paradigm was a particular casualty of the course.) The upshot of these experiences for me was quite a lot of confusion (not to say downright skepticism) about the validity of the assumptions I had hitherto relied upon to found my feminism.

But like many other feminists of this era, I had other, very compelling political concerns to occupy my time. In spring 1984, Jesse Jackson's campaign for the Democratic presidential nomination, waged under the banner of the Rainbow Coalition, called forth an astonishing cross-racial, cross-class coalition in the area of western Massachusetts where I live: academics and local townspeople of all races, ethnicities, and ages; Democratic Party politicians; trade unionists; students. I became cochair of the Five College Faculty and Staff Committee for Jackson (my greatest accomplishment a full-page signature ad in the local paper the Friday before the primary); the Students for Jackson committee was organized by students in the interdisciplinary program I direct, the Social Thought and Political Economy Program. The campaign produced both an exuberance and a sense of hope and wonder (particularly at seeing such an unlikely grouping of people assembled in one room working for the same end) that I had not experienced since the 1960s. The day of the primary, as I was driving voters to the polls, I recall seeing an old white man dressed in polyester pants hobbling slowly up the sidewalk to the polling place. "Jackson's for the poor," he said cheerfully. "I've been poor all my life. I'm voting for Jackson!" My deep admiration for the image of community that Bachmann invokes in the novel as Franza's white hand, brown hands, and black hands dip silently into a common bowl at Wadi Halfa derives from my own experience of community in the Jackson campaign. As well, the distress felt by Jews associated with the campaign after Jackson was reported to have said that he was going up to "Hymietown" forced me for the first time to confront the importance of ethnicity in American life, my own white Protestant Northern European ethnicity having shielded me hitherto from registering that ethnic background was of great importance to other Americans, including other feminists and, to my surprise, many of my friends, though not at all to me. The struggle and pain that emerged from this aspect of the Jackson campaign reinforced my commitment to the now not just theoretical but obviously also very practical urgency of addressing the question of differences among women.

Somewhat to my own astonishment, I wrote this essay in the spare moments I could steal from my work on the Jackson campaign: the intensity of the political work seemed to fill me with such buoyant energy that even academic writing came easily. In addition, I felt strongly that I was addressing at the level of my intellectual work many of the same issues that I confronted in my practical politics, and that made the essay take on a significance to me somehow akin to the importance of helping Jesse win. By this time, I had come to an understanding of Bachmann's work very like that of Christa Wolf's 1966 essay: all of Bachmann's writing, but the "Ways of Death" with greatest success, could be understood as an effort to illuminate the condition of (female) subjectivity at a particular place and in a particular period of human history—a reading quite different from that of chapter 3, "In the Cemetery of the Murdered Daughters," and one obviously called into being by the new attention to difference among feminists and among women in general and by the fascinating historical and anthropological investigations into the specificity of gender arrangements across time and culture appearing in recent feminist journals. Like probably all feminist Bachmann scholars, I had been dismayed by male scholars' condescending dismissal of her in the period before the advent of the second wave of feminism, but I had also grown concerned about her reception by feminists, since (as I suggest in chapter 2), they seemed to view Bachmann through a feminist lens that itself treated gender so ahistorically that the political dimensions of her undertaking disappeared. My essay here was an effort to draw on what I had learned in the 1980s from debates inside and outside of feminism in order to advance a new, more historically specific model of analysis.

Looking back on the essay now, it appears to me to be informed by two not very compatible feminist discourses, both of which were current in U.S. academic feminism at the time it was written. As I've already suggested, the new feminist attention to race and my own experiences in addressing questions of race were obviously factors motivating my writing of this essay. (At the time, I did not know that the use of the term *Rasse* was problematic in German because of its association with the Nazis' racial policies.) To the best of my knowledge, this is the first essay in Bachmann scholarship to deal straightforwardly with questions of race and the non-Western world (that is, to treat Franza's imprecations against "the whites" as not merely a metaphor for something other than race), and I believe it is among the first in feminist German Studies altogether to thematize the question of race (a topic around which something of a cottage industry has developed in the meantime). My own struggles with my position vis-à-vis racism also prevented me from regarding Franza only as a victim and exempting her from complicity in the culture she is trying to escape (an unusual position for those days), and I ask in this essay whether Franza's history is inevitably linked only to the history of the racist/imperialist West, a question of very grave concern to white feminists in general. I was at the time quite smug about being the first to whom it occurred to investigate the "historical event" that Martin and Franza encounter in Egypt and thus to be able to develop a whole historically based strand of argument that links the siblings specifically to First and Second World neoimperialism. (Now, I would also want to point out how that event emphatically situates Franza within the context of cold war tensions.) By turning to Critical Theory, I avoided an argument that uses gender as its single analytical category, though I was also sensitive enough to Eurocentrism to recognize that *Dialectic of Enlightenment*'s failure to discuss the non-Western world was a serious theoretical limitation. Finally, the alert reader will notice that even in 1984, this essay only uses the term "patriarchy" a single time.

Nevertheless, I think this essay still displays a recourse to totalizing theories with (white) women at the center which recalls the "Women and Religion" special issue of *Signs*. My appropriation of the Frankfurt School here is scarcely distinguishable from the Christa Wolf of *Cassandra* and is quite compatible with cultural/ecofeminist analyses or at least does not break with their founding premises. In *Dialectic of Enlightenment*, Horkheimer and Adorno identify a single, all-encompassing system of domination presided over by (possibly ruling-class) white men responsible for the subordination of everyone and everything else; the alternative to this model of thought is "magical thinking" of the kind that Franza displays. Within such a system, as Horkheimer and Adorno also suggest, the (white) woman-as-victim plays a central role. I would now consider theories making such grandiose claims to be examples of precisely the tendencies they believe they are challenging, displaying the hubris of a Western reason that believes its categories can adequately comprehend everything within its sway, that simultaneously elevates Western women to central status (thus merely the mirror image of the Western male subject) and lets them off the hook by maintaining that they are the innocent objects of a system for which men alone are responsible. (At best, they have access to the spoils "only in a broken form," as Horkheimer and Adorno put it [249], once they have submitted to their masters.) Moreover, in its assertion of the possibility of an uncontaminated, non-alienated existence temporally or spatially outside the system (an allegation central to many varieties of Western theory, not the least to psychoanalysis), this theory (like cultural feminism) makes exactly the claim that Foucault refuses (in *The History of Sexuality*), that some fundamental areas of human experience escape social construction to which humans could potentially retreat as a gesture of resistance or refusal. (Within the novel, Franza's hysterical symptoms and her flight to a location where she believes she can escape the whites perform this role.)

In general, this essay is far too dependent on psychoanalysis to be genuinely historical or attentive to cultural difference, for, as Stuart Hall has observed, psychoanalysis "addresses the subject-in-general, not historically determinate social subjects, or socially determinate particular languages. Thus it is incapable, so far, of moving its in-general propositions to the levels of concrete historical analysis" (46). My reliance on the Frankfurt School to found a historically based analysis is in general a little paradoxical, since in their attempt to discern broad trends within a historical tradition that appears to begin with the *Odyssey* the Critical Theorists are almost as cavalier about historical detail are as subsequent poststructuralists. Moreover, though I treat Bachmann as a writer concerned with historical problems that extend beyond gender alone, I do not examine Bachmann and her texts as historical phenomena themselves. At that point, I believe, a feminist methodology did not yet exist to pose such questions, and that is of course the main project of this book. Finally, I now detect in this essay a quality that I have discerned in a great deal of "gynocritcal" feminist scholar-ship: my analysis of Bachmann's writing is not only not critical of her but con-cludes by determining that she represents a position precisely in accord with what was most au courant in the feminist analysis of the moment!

Despite my criticisms of today, however, I remain quite pleased with this essay. I continue to believe that its analysis of Bachmann's own utilization of Frankfurt School theory is correct, and I believe that opened up some important areas of research into Bachmann that other scholars have since pursued. Yet somewhat to my dismay, my call for a more historically based Bachmann schol-arship did not immediately find a response or even, I think, much initial under-standing of what I was trying to do (as reviews of the journal that brushed over my essay seemed to show). On the contrary, I think, partially as a consequence of the position I had taken in "In the Cemetery of the Murdered Daughters," I was first assumed to be a proponent of the tendencies that dominated feminist Bachmann criticism in 1984. As I also note in chapter 2, this essay first appeared in the landmark issue of *text + kritik* which proclaimed the existence of the "other Ingeborg Bachmann," whose texts could be regarded as an anticipation of feminist poststructuralism, particularly its assertions about the repression of female otherness by a phallogocentric culture/discourse. Though this was pre-cisely the dehistoricizing tendency with which my own essay was contending, I suspect that by publishing it in that context I in fact lent support to precisely the political direction this essay had attempted to challenge.

1985

The caesura that separated 1984 from 1985 was Ronald Reagan's landslide victory in the November 1984 election. The lopsided results turned the euphoria of progressives who had participated in the Jackson campaign into deep gloom. The title page of the January–February 1985 issue of *Socialist Review* bore the caption (borrowed from Ntozake Shange's play) "For Leftists Who Have Considered Suicide When the Rainbow Is Enuf," and the Socialist Scholars' Conference in April 1985 was titled "The Left in Crisis." Despite the Democratic Party's nomination of the first-ever female vice presidential candidate of a major party, Geraldine Ferraro's candidacy had not especially inspired women to vote the Democratic ticket. Perhaps that was in part because the campaign managers for presidential candidate Walter Mondale, targeted as the candidate of "special interests" ("women, trade unionists, blacks, Hispanics, gays, and environmentalists—that is, seventy to eighty per cent of the population," remarked one commentator wryly [Altman 10]), did not allow Ferraro to appeal specifically to women voters until shortly before election day—far too late. And despite a 4 to 9 percent gender gap that divided men's and women's support for the Republicans, a majority of U.S. women as well as men backed Reagan (Riddiough 24–25). The *New York Times* quoted a thirty-year-old woman from Ferraro's New York neighborhood as saying: "Reagan is a true capitalist, and so am I. I really don't care about social programs. Reagan cares about strength, power, spending for the military just like I do" (Altman 8). The so-called New Deal coalition seemed to have collapsed, and only black voters, including those newly registered by the Jackson campaign, remained a reliably Democratic constituency.

Feminists also were shaken by the Reagan win and by a more general sense of feminism's lack of political effectiveness. Though they conceded that liberal feminism had made gains for women, within Reagan's America those changes were minuscule compared with the complete transformation of everything that radical and socialist feminists had originally envisioned. A panel of eminent socialist feminists, asked by *Socialist Review* to comment on the state of socialist feminism, proclaimed its demise (somewhat ironically, since only a few years later it would be reincarnated, at least in the academy, as "materialist feminism"). Deirdre English commented: "I don't feel very comfortable calling myself a feminist anymore, because socialist-feminism is dead, my version of radical feminism is dead, and the mainstream feminist movement is just barking up the wrong tree" (English et al. 104). Not surprisingly, recriminations and soul searching were the consequence both outside and inside the academy. Cultural feminists and "difference" feminists of all sorts took a beating in academic feminist journals, since the emphasis on women's difference from men was now seen as racist, classist, and of potential utility to the right. The editors of *Feminist Studies* noted, "We suspect that the very category of 'difference,' to the extent that it implies biologically based distinctions between women and men in cognition and capacity, may prove finally to impede rather than to further the quest for knowledge and for equality" (Vicinus/ Rosenfelt 5). In summer 1985 the editors of *Signs*, printing the papers of the 1983 *Signs*-sponsored conference "Communities of Women," apologized for the limitation of their topic: "We did not realize, until courteously yet explicitly advised of our failure of insight, that this focus might be seen to limit the topic's appropriateness to the interests of middle-class white women in their struggle against the dominance of white men. When women and men are oppressed because of class or race or both, women's autonomy may not be a relevant issue" ("Editorial" 1985, 634).

Among the critiques of feminist methodology advanced by those papers, most striking was Joan Ringelheim's account of how a cultural feminist perspective had led her to ask the wrong questions about women's experience in the Holocaust. "Cultural feminism," she now declared, "developed not simply as a tactic for battling the antiwoman line in a sexist world, but as a way to detour around it without violent revolution; without confronting the state, family, marriage, or organized religion, and without eliminating institutions intent on keeping women in their place. . . . [C]ultural feminism substitutes a political activism that was risky and offensive for another that, accidentally or not, conveniently disallows risk" (754). "My use of cultural feminism as a frame (albeit unconsciously)," she continued, "changed respect for the stories of the Jewish women into some sort of glorification and led to the conclusion that these women transformed 'a world of death and inhumanity into one more act of human life.' But the Holocaust, she concluded, "is a story of loss, not gain" (756–57).

Other feminist scholars developed similarly scathing critiques of cultural feminism. Anthropologist Micaela di Leonardo, for instance, debunked the notion of woman as peacemaker which had underwritten cultural feminist participation in the peace movement. The articles in the book she was reviewing, she explained,

> reflect a certain radical feminist perspective that envisions women as innately more peaceful than—and thus morally superior to—men, thus lodging this analysis in an imagined matriarchal past. This perspective leads authors to make statements that are historically and anthropologically inaccurate. They assert that "women are the first victims of the patriarchal state of war," and declare that "pre-Patriarchal cultures believed that, because women alone brought forth life, women therefore held the secrets of nature and the keys to wisdom." This last claim would come as a considerable surprise to the foraging African Pygmies and Australian

aborigines. Such counterfactual assertions, misreading ethnographic and historical evidence, are the despair of feminist anthropologists. (606)

Carol Gilligan's theory of women's different moral sensibilities were not just
based on insufficient empirical evidence, members of a feminist study collective
argued, but could also be used to support arguments like those of conservative
Phyllis Shlafly for the separate interests of women and men—"a conviction," they
maintained, "that contributed to the defeat of the Equal Rights Amendment"
(Auerbach et al. 159). Wendy Chapkis even cast aspersions at Susan Brownmiller's insistence on clinging to the feminist "uniform" of the 1970s—unshaven legs,
no makeup, functional clothing, trousers, flat shoes: "[Brownmiller's book] *Femininity* reads like the statement of a woman weary of the struggle and unable to
find inspiration for a new female esthetic that allows for play and pleasure" (111).
(Such a remark documents a striking sea change pointing in the direction of the
flirtation with gender performance that would characterize the queer politics of
the 1990s.) Even literary scholars denounced the cultural feminist or French feminist lens that had been directed at women's literary texts: in the spring 1985 *Signs*
issue, for instance, Alicia Ostriker protested a conception of poetry advanced in
an article by Margaret Homans which, drawing on French theory, portrayed
women's experience as inexpressible in men's language.

While thus displaying the influence of the reconsideration of feminist political strategies in the political arena, feminist scholarship simultaneously moved
toward the elaboration of alternative paradigms that might avoid what they
now perceived as earlier errors. In feminist journals, articles exploring the
enormous range of female possibilities across culture and history proliferated:
anarchist women in the Spanish Civil War (Ackelsberg); black women in the
Sanctified Church (Gilkes); contemporary Iranian women (Higgins); Jewish
immigrant women in New York and the 1917 food riots (Frank); women workers in the Shanghai cotton mills from 1919 to 1949 (Honig); German feminists
before World War I (Ann Taylor Allen); women in the Israeli army (Yuval-
Davis); Bedouin women (Abu-Lughod); women workers in the Yale clerical
union strike (Ladd-Taylor), women in the new Nicaragua (Molyneux). Authors
of articles on such topics developed increasingly more careful ways of theoretically and practically differentiating among women, Maxine Molyneux arguing, for instance: "Although it is true that at a certain level of abstraction women
can be said to have some interests in common, there is no consensus over what
these interests are or how they are to be formulated. This is in part because
there is no theoretically adequate and universally applicable causal explanation
of women's subordination from which a general account of women's interests
can be derived" (231).

As followed from the critique of cultural feminism's emphasis on women's
separate sphere, feminist scholars also began to problematize their strategy of
examining women's undertakings independently from those of men. Kathryn

Kish Sklar observed, for instance: "One of the most important questions asked by historians of American women today is, To what degree has women's social power been based on separate female institutions, culture, and consciousness, and to what degree has it grown out of their access to male spheres of influence, such as higher education, labor organization, and politics?" (659). In accord with critiques raised against various sorts of feminists in the political realm, feminist scholars also criticized the practice as well as the theory of feminists who perpetuate an existing system of domination in the course of pursuing what they believe to be feminist ends: Susan Schechter and Michelle Fine, for instance, drew attention to what they termed a "feminist hegemony" in the battered women's movement, "the imposition of a feminist way and a feminist set of values on women who live and work in these shelters" (Fine 402). Rather than predicting women's automatic opposition to oppression, scholars examined how they actually negotiated conflicting pressures and how ideologies as well as actual conditions guided their choices (Lamphere; Ferree, "Between"; Zavella). Particularly in texts focused on sexuality, scholars began to underline notions of the "social construction" of all aspects of female behavior (Caulfield).

Literary scholars also demonstrated a greater awareness of both political and social conditions and strategies of literary representations as barriers to understanding a female author as a voice unproblematically giving expression to the concerns of a female subject. Margaret Homans began an article on women's love poetry by remarking, "This essay assumes that poets are shaped as much by the literary forms and the conventions of language they inherit as they are by the social and political universe in which they have their historical being" ("Syllables" 569). Scholars commented as well on the difficulties of politics, positioning, and representation that intrude between a feminist scholar and her subject matter (Minnich). Leslie Rabine's analysis of Harlequin romance novels continued to move feminist literary analysis beyond canonical texts into interdisciplinary methodologies by arguing that recent Harlequins treat the theme of sexuality in the workplace as a means to envision "an end to the division between the domestic world of love and sentiment and the public world of work and business" (40), thus helping readers to manage conflicts in their own lives. A feminist critic of Shakespeare (a field where much pathbreaking literary scholarship was undertaken in the 1980s) proposed a feminist reading of Shakespeare's texts as a site at which discursive contradictions could be interrogated: "For generations Shakespearean critics lamented the marriages that end these plays as tacked on and conventional; recently feminist critics have described them as strategies that circumscribe female revolt and power. I would suggest instead that the plays expose contradictions between the enactment of repressive social structures manifested in genre (courtship and marriage) and the representation of powerful female protagonists" (Newman 602). In the best literary analyses of 1985, feminist scholars gave expression to their efforts to reach beyond the (frequently mainly formalist) training they had received in their own fields and also investigated developments occurring in other fields of cultural studies as they inched toward the major transformation of their field that would begin later in the decade.

Most indicative of the new directions in which feminist scholarship was moving and the rupture with earlier feminist paradigms that they would represent (as well as the emergence of a new version of socialist feminism) was Donna Haraway's article "A Manifesto for Cyborgs: Science, Technology, and Socialist Feminism in the 1980s," first published in the March-April 1985 issue of *Socialist Review*. From the perspective of the development of feminist thought, Haraway clearly elaborated her cyborg myth in response to the implosion of the category "woman." "Woman," she explained, is itself a fictional construction imposed on us by our enemies: "There is nothing about being female that naturally binds women. There is not even such a state as being female, itself a highly complex category constructed in contested sexual scientific discourses and other social practices. Gender, race, or class consciousness is an achievement forced on us by the terrible historical experience of the contradictory social realities of patriarchy, colonialism, and capitalism" ("Manifesto" 72). Instead, the cyborg is the "fiction" Haraway wishes to use to characterize women. In contrast, say, to the woman as cultural feminism understood her, cyborgs are hybrid and heterogeneous postmodern creatures that refuse those binaries which structure Western thought: arising out of a confusion and transgression of boundaries, they are both nature and culture, both organic and crafted, products of both imagination and material reality, both public and private, a conglomerate of races, beyond gender, neither deriving from a single lineage nor originating at a moment of prelapsarian wholeness. Haraway explains:

> An origin story in the "Western," humanist sense depends on the myth of original unity, fullness, bliss and terror, represented by the phallic mother from whom all humans must separate, the task of individual development and of history, the twin potent myths inscribed most powerfully for us in psychoanalysis and Marxism. Hilary Klein has argued that both Marxism and psychoanalysis, in their concepts of labor and of individuation and gender formation, depend on the plot of original unity out of which difference must be produced and enlisted in a drama of escalating domination of woman/nature. The cyborg skips the step of original unity, of identification with nature in the Western sense. ("Manifesto" 67)

When such concepts are drawn into question, theories based on ontology and teleology such as classical Marxism and classical psychoanalysis—and cultural feminism—become impossible as well. As Haraway observes: "Catherine MacKinnon's version of radical feminism is itself a caricature of the appropriating, incorporating, totalizing tendencies of Western theories of identity grounding action. . . . It's not just that 'god' is dead, so is the 'goddess'" ("Manifesto" 77, 81). But the consequence of the loss of such constructions that also motivated political action for socialist feminists, Haraway underlines, need be not cynicism or despair but rather opposition and a contestation for meanings that cannot predict in advance what the outcome will be. "We do not need a totality in order to work well. The feminist dream of a common language, like all dreams for a perfectly true language, of perfectly faithful naming of experience, is a totalizing and imperialist one. In that sense, dialectics too is a dream language, longing to resolve contradictions." Writing (in contrast to an originary, self-identical speech) is preeminently the technology of cyborgs, and "Cyborg writing," says Haraway, "is about the power to survive, not on the basis of original innocence, but on the basis of seizing the tools to mark the world that marked them as other" ("Manifesto" 92, 94). Haraway argues here for a theory and practice based on a feminism without guarantees, an aleatory strategy that squarely confronts the bleak present but, opting (like Brecht) for the "bad new" rather than the "good old," nonetheless continues, as a new sort of socialist feminism, to hope and work for a transformation of the future.

CHAPTER 6

Bachmann and Wittgenstein

> Not just the case of Kakania showed that
> thinking in closed ideologies leads directly to war,
> and the permanent war of faith is still ongoing.
> —Ingeborg Bachmann, Werke

welve years after her death, literary scholars are slowly beginning to understand the author whom Sigrid Weigel has termed "the other Ingeborg Bachmann." As Weigel explains, "The stimulus of feminist cultural criticism and poststructuralism was necessary before Bachmann's late work could be understood and the more radical dimension of her writing grasped" ("Andere" 2). The new Bachmann scholarship has been remarkable, producing several impressive recent volumes and finally enabling us to begin to comprehend Bachmann's profound and difficult texts. Yet despite the accomplishments of the new scholarship, it too runs some danger of again distorting Bachmann's works by extracting them and Bachmann herself from their cultural context, the mid-twentieth-century Austria which her fiction so carefully anatomizes. It is certainly the case that Bachmann participated in the intellectual debates of the European intelligentsia of the postwar period, thus also knew and was influenced by, among other things, the developing poststructuralist theory of the 1960s. As evidence of her familiarity with issues under discussion by European intellectuals, one might, for instance, consider the names of the other members of the editorial board of a proposed international literary journal on which Bachmann was also chosen to serve, including in 1963 Hans Magnus Enzensberger, Günter Grass, Helmut Heißenbüttel, Uwe Johnson, Martin Walser, Roland Barthes, Michel Butor, Michel Leiris, Italo Calvino, Alberto Moravia, and Pier Paolo Pasolini (*W* 4: 376). In Bachmann's own contribution to the first number of the journal, however, she cautions against the creation of a common

European "supermarket of the spirit" and urges instead that literary production be rooted in the particularities of language and culture: "Only now can one safely ponder what one can say and contribute oneself, each from his own province, from his own place at which the world (that is, the other provinces) washes up" (*W* 4: 70–71). At this point in the development of the new Bachmann criticism it may be most productive to follow Bachmann's own advice and, while preserving the insights gained via the use of poststructuralist theory, to investigate Bachmann's roots within the specificity of Austrian history and the Austrian cultural tradition.

As a contribution to that effort I would like to explore Bachmann's indebtedness to the works of Ludwig Wittgenstein, who, despite the efforts of Allan Janik and Stephen Toulmin in *Wittgenstein's Vienna*, is also almost invariably extracted from his Austrian background. Unpublished material from the Bachmann papers as well as Bachmann's published essays on Wittgenstein show that many of the concerns that inform Bachmann's late fiction were present, at least in germinal form, in her work from the beginning and can be traced to her encounter with Wittgenstein. Using Janik and Toulmin, I first briefly examine Wittgenstein in the context of the Austrian intellectual tradition, stressing particularly his relationship to the Vienna Circle, the perspective from which Bachmann, under the influence of her dissertation director, Viktor Kraft, first treated him. Then I trace Bachmann's own development as a young philosopher, from her critique of Heidegger—undertaken mostly from the perspective of logical positivism—to her growing engagement with the work of Wittgenstein, whom she increasingly distinguished from the logical positivists. Finally, I examine Bachmann's two published essays of the 1950s on Wittgenstein and argue that her encounter with his posthumous *Philosophical Investigations*, which she read after writing the first and before the second of her essays, was of key importance to her subsequent intellectual development, the themes she emphasized in the second essay remaining central to her own writing until her death.

Janik and Toulmin point out that Wittgenstein's concern with what language is able to say—in the *Tractatus Logico-Philosophicus* (1921) as well as the *Philosophical Investigations* (1953) and the various other collections of aphorisms, remarks, and lecture notes published after his death—is rooted in both the neo-Kantian atmosphere and the general spirit of cultural crisis of pre-1914 Vienna. His work needs to be understood as an attempt to secure the first principles of human thought at a time when it was increasingly unclear on what founding principles the culture rested. Wittgenstein, Janik and Toulmin explain, was born in 1889 as "the youngest son of Vienna's leading steel magnate and patron of the arts" (13). Within that intellectual milieu, of course, not only philosophers deliberated the principles through which language corresponded to the object world; for figures such as Karl Kraus, Arthur Schnitzler, Adolf Loos, Oskar Kokoschka, Arnold Schönberg, and Sigmund Freud, along with many others, questions about communication and representation were critical, finding their most drastic expression in Hugo von Hofmannsthal's "Lord Chandos Letter." Because the Wittgenstein household was, Janik and Toulmin argue, both a cultural center and also a site of generational conflict, "Wittgenstein was personally exposed to the crises in art, morality and even family life that were the central sources of cultural and ethical debate in prewar Vienna" (174). Wittgenstein (like Robert Musil and Albert Einstein) began his own intellectual life with the study of engineering, which required at that time also a thorough grasp of theoretical physics and mathematics, and his early thought was influenced by debates in those fields. Ernst Mach insisted, for instance, that all knowledge can be reduced to sensation and that physical theories are merely simplifications of experience which are more or less efficient and useful. Max Planck, however, maintained that Mach's theory was still enmired in metaphysics and argued instead (not unlike Kant) that the physicist "creates the physical world by imposing form upon it" (Janik and Toulmin 138). On matters of ethics and aesthetics, Janik and Toulmin argue that prewar Viennese thinking was informed by the very unscientific thought of Arthur Schopenhauer, Søren Kierkegaard, and Leo Tolstoy, demonstrably figures who also helped to shape the work of Wittgenstein. As a philosopher and a Viennese, Wittgenstein faced the problem of reconciling contemporary thinking on physics with that on ethics.

The *Tractatus*, which Wittgenstein completed while fighting in the Austrian army during World War I, thus draws upon his training in physics to argue that language uses an a priori system of logic to make "pictures" (*Bilder*) that describe the facts of the world. Such propositions can be empirically verified. Propositions that are neither tautological nor empirically verifiable are literally meaningless or non-sense. By far the larger part of the *Tractatus* is devoted to the details of its author's critique of language. The sixth and seventh sections of the book, however, concern the nature of ethics, a realm which is "higher" and "transcendental" and about which one cannot speak at all, as Wittgenstein explained in the work's final sentence (which Bachmann never tired of citing): "What we cannot speak about we must pass over in silence" (*Tractatus* 151). As Wittgenstein tried to explain to friends (e.g. in a letter to Ludwig von Ficker), what he had not said in the book was its point: "The meaning of the book is an ethical one. I once wanted to put a sentence into the foreword which now in fact isn't there but which I will now write to you because it will perhaps be a key for you. I wanted to write, my work consists of two parts, of the part that's here, and of all that I didn't write. And precisely this second part is the important one" (*Briefe* 35).

Believing the *Tractatus* to be the final solution to the problems of Western metaphysics, Wittgenstein gave up philosophy until 1929, when he returned to Cambridge, where he had earlier studied with the British philospher Bertrand Russell, and worked for the rest of his life on the ideas that would be published after his death (and that are discussed in greater detail below). In the English-speaking world, where Wittgenstein's work has received most attention, he has been viewed mostly through the lens of Cambridge as an analytic philosopher on the order of Gottlob Frege, Russell, and C. E. Moore. In Vienna, Wittgenstein's early writing influenced the work of the Vienna Circle, formed in the 1920s around Moritz Schlick, who held the chair for philosophy of the inductive sciences (established for Mach) at the University of Vienna. Relying on Mach's sensationalist theory of knowledge, the members of the Vienna Circle used the *Tractatus* to provide the basic logical structure for their own philosophy. As the Vienna Circle was dispersed in the 1930s by death, academic departures, and persecution, Wittgenstein's work came also via this route into international currency. "Nicely domesticated," as one Wittgenstein scholar has put it (Edwards 2), Wittgenstein's works became a subject of consideration by professional philosophers and social scientists, whereas their relevance to the historical issues of his time was scarcely examined.

Bachmann apparently also came to Wittgenstein via the Vienna Circle, writing her dissertation under the direction of Viktor Kraft, of whom she said in a later interview: "There were very few professors back then; I think the students were more or less on their own until I then happened on one of the last old men of this 'Vienna Circle,' the Vienna neopositivists, from whom I may really have learned something" (*GuI* 82). Kraft, born in 1890, had been a member of the Vienna Circle while still a student of Friedrich Jodl and may be the only member of the group to have remained in Vienna until after 1945 (Johnston 189). In a work published in 1951, *Der Wiener Kreis*, Kraft detailed the history and philosophical positions of members of the group, remaining, as he explained steadfastly if somewhat apologetically, committed to their principles:

> To be sure, those who seek from philosophy a confession of personal wisdom about the world or life, of subjective interpretation of world or life, or those who seek from it the speculative construction of an otherwise veiled and inaccessible ground of being or the conceptual poetry of a novel about the world—such people

can certainly understand philosophy as the Vienna Circle understands it only as an impoverishment. For it excludes everything that can't be obtained in a scientific way. But only then can one move beyond subjective difference and variability, only then can one claim universal validity and lasting results. (10)

That Bachmann's own philosophical position at the time of her dissertation corresponded to Kraft's is evident not just from the dissertation itself (analyzed in further detail below) but also from two unpublished essays in her papers, apparently written in the period immediately after she completed her studies. In what seems to be the first of the two, "Philosophie der Gegenwart" (Philosophy of the present), Bachmann briefly summarizes phenomenology, contemporary metaphysics, existentialism, idealism, and historical materialism, but ten of the essay's eighteen pages are devoted to the Vienna Circle, an emphasis she justifies in the introduction: "The special attention to the 'Vienna Circle' can be explained by the consideration that neopositivism displays the most radical break with traditional philosophy and the path toward scientific philosophizing is taken most convincingly" ("Philosophie" 1). Her discussion of the Vienna Circle follows the structure and content of Kraft's book and often also borrows his language without acknowledgment. Her treatment of Wittgenstein in this essay stresses his relationship to the work of the Circle: she emphasizes that neopositivism's concern with language derives from the members' interest in logic as a tautological system, and that their investigations of language are inquiries into its possibilities as a "system of representation [Darstellungssystem]." Because one must use language to speak about language, she explains, Wittgenstein came to the conclusion that one could not speak meaningfully about language at all: "But finally all philosophical questions led back to this analysis. Philosophical problems thus revealed themselves as pseudo-problems. Wittgenstein draws the conclusion from that and concludes his work with the explanation that his own remarks make no sense, for: What we cannot speak about we must pass over in silence" ("Philosophie" 11). This is a significantly different explanation of the conclusion to the *Tractatus* than Bachmann would later give to it.

In contrast, Bachmann continues, Rudolf Carnap argues that philosophy could evolve a "metalanguage" to analyze language. He considers the task of philosophy to be metalogical or semiotic analysis of the language of science, investigating linguistic symbols pragmatically, semantically, syntactically, and independently of their content. One of the sticking points of neopositivism, however, became the verification of propositions. Wittgenstein's solution in the *Tractatus* to the problem of verification "pointed the way ahead," Bachmann explains. There he insists that all general statements must be reducible to individual

empirical statements ("all men are mortal" being thus identical with the assertions "X is mortal" plus "Y is mortal" plus . . .) to be meaningful at all. Later
some of the neopositivists came to the conclusion that it was impossible to reach
ultimate verification and that statements must be regarded as more or less prob-
able hypotheses. The pragmatism to which the neopositivists were now compelled enabled them to address broader areas than before, though, says Bachmann, perhaps exactly because their earlier dogmatism allowed them to clarify
the bases of philosophy's claim to scientificity. But she concludes her essay by
maintaining, like her teacher, that still no answers to humankind's most fundamental questions can be expected from philosophy: "The expectations of many
that they will find instructions on how to lead their lives or access to understanding the world can't and won't be fulfilled here. Scientific philosophy—and
it is the task of philosophy to be a science—is, unlike religion or literature,
unable to console, to assist, or to give insight into thinking that may lie beyond
the experiential, but rather it must make order, must investigate the knowledge
that various sciences convey to us, uncover logical relationships and bring them
into a useful system" (18).

Bachmann's second unpublished essay on this topic is "Der Wiener Kreis:
Logischer Positivism—Philosophie als Wissendchaft" (The Vienna Circle: logical positivism—philosophy as science). This radio essay, first broadcast on 14
April 1953 by the radio station Hessischer Rundfunk, was not included in the
Werke, the editors explain, because "in places Bachmann followed to the letter
Viktor Kraft's book *Der Wiener Kreis*" (*W* 4: 406). Although its style is less
labored and the essay is more clearly oriented around the *Tractatus*, Bachmann
still interprets Wittgenstein here through the lens of the Vienna Circle, and the
essay does not differ in perspective from "Philosophie der Geganwart." Yet a
subtle shift in Bachmann's own position is apparent. Although she praises the
Vienna Circle for the resistance it offered to the irrationalism and subjectivism
of its time, no longer does she claim that the only philosophy possible is the sort
the Vienna Circle undertook. Through the voice of a critic Bachmann is able to
articulate objections to the Circle's position more clearly, and by explaining that
its endeavor initially was to create a "unitary system" via an analysis of language,
she is able to show how it continues to be implicated in the project of Western
metaphysics. Most important, Bachmann's radio essay, after discussing the later
fortunes of former Vienna Circle members, concludes by asking "Where should
the lever be applied today? Perhaps with Ludwig Wittgenstein, who still must
be discovered, the greatest and at the same time most unknown philosopher of
our epoch. There are statements on the last pages of his *Tractatus logico-phil-*

sophicus that could bring the turning point, the end of positivism, without having to give up its insights." She continues:

> For he says, before he revoked all his words into silence:
> (Professor/reading) "The facts all contribute only to setting the problem, not to its solution.
>
> We feel that even when all *possible* scientific questions have been answered, the problems of life remain completely untouched.
>
> Of course there are then no questions left, and this itself is the answer.
>
> There are, indeed, things that cannot be put into words. They *make themselves manifest*. They are what is mystical.
>
> My propositions serve as elucidations in the following way: anyone who understands me eventually recognizes them as nonsensical, when he has used them—as steps—to climb up beyond them. (He must, so to speak, throw away the ladder after he has climbed up it.)
>
> He must transcend these propositions, and then he will see the world aright."
> ("Wiener Kreis" 25)

If at this point in her development Bachmann could not yet think beyond the philosophical solutions of the Vienna Circle, this radio essay displays clearly both her desire for other sorts of answers and her recognition that Wittgenstein too pointed beyond the limitations of the philosophers who had learned so much from his work.

Bachmann's dissertation, "Die Kritische Aufnahme der Existentialphilosophie Martin Heideggers" (The critical reception of the existential philosophy of Martin Heidegger), completed in 1949, can begin to reveal both the kinds of philosophical questions the young Bachmann passionately wished to address and why neither Heidegger nor the Vienna Circle could provide the answer to them. Later interviews indicate that in some contrast to the Heidegger enthusiasts of the 1950s, Bachmann took Heidegger's early support for the Nazis seriously and was also prepared to connect his political opinions to his philosophy. In a 1973 interview she declared that she had refused to write a poem he had requested from her for the *Festschrift* on the occasion of his seventieth birthday, and it was still with some glee that she reported her certainty that her dissertation had demolished his philosophy: "Because back then, at twenty-two, I believed I was now going to bring this man down!"(*GuI* 137). To the end of her life she stood by the critique of Heidegger she had formulated in the dissertation. Until Bachmann's personal papers become available in 2025 we will not know why, given her political reservations about Heidegger, she chose nonetheless to write her dissertation on him. On the basis of evidence in it as well as in the body of her work, however, one might surmise that she was powerfully drawn to the kinds of questions Heidegger was asking but also realized that his answers were historically and politically inadequate; for all their alleged challenge to Western metaphysics, they were still deeply enmired in those ways of thinking which had led to the crimes and cultural crises of Europe in the twentieth century.

For my purposes, what is most important about Bachmann's dissertation is the *kind* of critique she directs at Heidegger. The dissertation is structured as a sometimes rather cursory survey of Heidegger's reception by various twentieth-century German-speaking philosophical schools: logical positivism, historical materialism, neo-Kantianism, idealism, phenomenology, existentialism, neo-Thomism, and so on. The two critiques with which Bachmann begins seem to be the most important determinants of her own position. Included first is logical positivism, and Bachmann outlines in some detail Rudolf Carnap's analysis of the meaninglessness of Heidegger's central argument in "What Is Metaphysics?" Heidegger wants to explore the status of "nothing" in the following passage: "What should be examined are beings only, and besides that—nothing; beings alone, and further—nothing; solely beings, and beyond that—nothing. What about this nothing?" (*Kritische* 20; Heidegger 97). Carnap insists that grammatically the "nothing" of this sentence cannot be a "name of an object"; hence, the question is literally meaningless and there is nothing to investigate. (Bachmann was evidently quite taken by the conclusiveness of this argument and repeated it in "The Vienna Circle" as well as in her two published essays on Wittgenstein.) The specific argument is of course illustrative of Carnap's general critique of Heidegger, "that science could not involve itself with a tangle of illogical questions, as Heidegger demands from it" (*Kritische* 22). Nor is metaphysics adequate for the expression of a "feeling about life [*Lebensgefühl*]," for even in this instance metaphysics takes the form of a theory which attempts to speak of truth and falsehood. "The result of the investigation is: Metaphysics could be only an insufficient substitute for art and deceives itself when it believes in its theoretical content. That is true not only for Heidegger but for every speculative or intuitional metaphysics, every ethics or aesthetics as normative discipline but also for a metaphysics that begins with experience and on the basis of some kind of conclusions or other maintains it can recognize that which lies behind or beyond experience" (*Kritische* 24). In her initial argument Bachmann has thus shown why philosophy is incapable of answering any of the questions she cares about. Though logical positivism leaves a space for art, it is also at the cost of art's claim that it can speak truly about the world.

The second perspective on Heidegger that Bachmann investigates in the dissertation is that of historical materialism, basing her analysis on a book by Theodor Hartwig, *Der Existenzialismus*, published in Vienna in 1948. For Hartwig (as evidently for Bachmann), there is a connection between Heidegger's existentialism and fascism. Quoting Hartwig, Bachmann explains: "That shouldn't be understood as the claim that existentialism was born from fascist ideology, but rather both ideologies grew out of the same sociopolitical fundament; they sprang from a social climate of conviction that developed out of the general economic crisis and the existential insecurity related to it" (Hartwig 9, *Kritische* 25.) She continues, paraphrasing Hartwig: "Existentialism is not a philosophy but rather a revolt of the threatened petty bourgeoisie in the guise of philosophy, which in its despair emphasizes all subjective values in order to work against modern collectivizing tendencies and to hold up the inexorable course of history" (*Kritische* 12). That this ideological reading of existentialism corresponds generally to Bachmann's own is suggested by her statement on existentialism in "Philosophy of the Present," this time in her own voice: "We are concerned in the main here with the transitory expression of European *Angst* that is rooted in the misery and distress of our continent after two world wars" ("Philosophie" 6).

To have thus ideologically comprehended the historical reasons for the appeal of existentialism has not, however, assuaged "European *Angst* . . . after two world wars." In a brief summary at the end of the dissertation Bachmann attempts to arrive at her own conclusions about Heidegger. She is compelled to conclude from her own logical-positivist perspective as well as from the others she examines that Heidegger's philosophy cannot legitimately make any claims to truth. Instead, she maintains, "the result will always be the dangerous half-rationalization of a sphere that can be addressed with the words of Wittgenstein: 'What we cannot speak about we must pass over in silence'"—and yet this conclusion has obviously not solved the problems for Bachmann, for she continues, "The fundamental experiences with which existentialism is concerned are in fact alive in the human being and demand expression" (*Kritische* 115). At most they can find their expression in art, which can make claim to neither science nor truth. Her dissertation concludes on a deeply subjective note (recalling in this respect Christa T.'s master's thesis in Christa Wolf's *The Quest for Christa T.*) by citing a "linguistic testimony to the most extreme representational possibilities of the communicable": Baudelaire's sonnet "Le gouffre." In its expression of horror before the ever-threatening void ("tout est abîme,—action, désir, rêve, Parole!") as well as its powerlessness to escape a rationality which cannot address the void ("Ah! ne jamais sortir des Nombres et des Etres." "'Nombres,' 'Etres,'" Bachmann adds in a footnote, "are things that have no consciousness but exist only numerically" [*Kritische* 117]), Baudelaire's poem particularly gives voice to dilemmas Bachmann confronted upon completion of her dissertation, for she had proved there were no answers to the questions most important to her. In this respect her position on Heidegger corresponds to Wittgenstein's own, revealed in a discussion in 1929 with members of the Vienna Circle: "I certainly can imagine what Heidegger meant by Being and *Angst*. The human being has an instinct to fight against the limits of language. Think for example of the astonishment that something exists. That astonishment can't be expressed in the form of a question, and there also isn't any answer at all. Everything that we'd like to say can a priori only be nonsense. Nevertheless we fight against the limits of language" (quoted in Waismann 68).

Grasping that this was Wittgenstein's dilemma (though we have no evidence that she was familiar with his specific comments on Heidegger), Bachmann thus stressed not his logical analyses but his ethical concerns, and his interest in "the mystical" about which we cannot speak, when she came to write about Wittgenstein directly. In her essay "Ludwig Wittgenstein—Concerning a Chapter of the Most Recent History of Philosophy," first published in the *Frankfurter Hefte* in July 1953, she stressed that the Wittgenstein of whom she wrote was not the British language philosopher who had shaped analytic philosophy but an unknown Austrian: "Now, he wasn't well known at all, he was in fact the least well-known philosopher of our time, a man to whom the words of his compatriot Karl Kraus apply, who once said about himself, 'I'm famous, but it hasn't gotten around yet'" (*W* 4: 12). Many sections of this essay are borrowed from writings already mentioned: the discussion of the Vienna Circle from the unpublished "Philosophie der Gegenwart" and "Der Wiener Kreis" and Carnap's critique of Heidegger from the dissertation. The standpoint Bachmann represents here, similar to that of the radio essay "Der Wiener Kreis," was probably written at about the same time. In this published essay, however, she places the work of the Vienna Circle and Wittgenstein more clearly in its Austro-German historical context as an endeavor to hold fast to an increasingly imperiled reason as the guiding principle of human activity. In 1929, she explained, the same year that the Vienna Circle declared itself publicly, "the second edition of Heidegger's *Being and Time* appeared, which seemed to show that the group was right in its struggle against the irrationalism which was spreading out from Germany, the land of depression. Conjoined to this in Vienna, and this was necessary, was the bitter opposition of the group to Austrian clericalism, for instance in the form of the doctrines of the state philosopher Othmar Spann" (*W* 4: 13–14).

Particularly important here also is her perceptible impatience with the philosophical poverty of the Vienna Circle, which "in its passion for the whole truth
can only offer the dry, formulaic, 'eternal' truth of logic" (*W* 4: 21), and her probing of Wittgenstein's work for possible alternatives. In the *Tractatus*, however,
there is no solution, if "the world is the totality of facts" and "the limits [*Grenzen*]
of my language mean the limits of my world." "We stand, think, speak on this
side of the limit/border," Bachmann tells us; "The way over the border is blocked
to us." We cannot utter ethical statements, "since a sentence cannot express anything higher," and we cannot act ethically in the world, "for the world [as a totality of facts] is independent of our will." She thus concludes correctly that "it
[Wittgenstein's philosophy] cannot answer any of the questions that we are accus-
tomed to direct to philosophy. With the question about the 'meaning of being' we
are left to our own devices" (*W* 4: 20–21).

Bachmann recognizes in this essay that this solution was no more adequate
for Wittgenstein than it is for her: "'God does not reveal himself in the world'
(6.432) is one of the bitterest propositions of the *Tractatus*" (*W* 4: 22). Thus she
wonders (though she finds it unlikely) whether Wittgenstein's posthumous
papers might reveal that he had taken the leap of faith to a certainty that reason
did not allow him. For it is clear that in the *Tractatus*, Wittgenstein, writing out
of his historical situation, was seeking ultimate truth and that no less would do,
as Hanna Fenichel Pitkin has eloquently explained:

> Confronted with the modern predicament, with a universe in flux, lacking cen-
> ter or meaning or stability, the *Tractatus* is essentially a failure of nerve, a retreat
> to what seems the only remaining solid ground, the one fortress that still seems
> defensible, ruthlessly abandoning whatever is outside the walls. If language
> defines our world, then for that world to retain any kind of stability language
> must be a system of fixed, exhaustive, systematic rules. If we stay within those
> rules, we will be safe, will save meaning and sense and reality. Of course, much
> will have to be given up. For all of art and esthetics, all of religion and ethics, all
> really of judgment, sensibility, and affect will have to be abandoned outside the
> fortress. Those things cannot be talked about, and if men continue to experience
> them they must do so in silence and therefore in isolation, in the wordless private
> world of dreams. Our language and our common life must be confined to the
> lucid, ordered crystal palace of mathematics, logic, science, a world secured
> against all ambiguity. That, I think, is the spirit of the *Tractatus*. (336–37)

As a philosopher the young Bachmann could not think beyond this cul-de-sac
either, and Pitkin describes her dilemma as well as Wittgenstein's. But Bachmann's
essay provocatively concludes with a sentence which the *Tractatus* could not

authorize (since there language is either empirical description or a tautological system independent of human use) but which suggests that she understands Wittgenstein's historico-cultural situation to be the real source for a text such as the *Tractatus*: "Or did he also conclude that we have forfeited our language because it contains not a single word that matters?" (*W* 4: 23).

Yet the sentence also points more perceptively in the direction of the kinds of answers Wittgenstein would explore in the *Philosophical Investigations*. Before Bachmann wrote her final Wittgenstein essay, a radio essay composed in 1953 and first broadcast on 16 September 1954 (*W* 4: 377), she was able, at least cursorily, to read that posthumously published work. As we know, Wittgenstein did not become a believer—on the contrary. But what Bachmann grasped, unlike the majority of Wittgenstein commentators, is the larger continuity of concern between his two works, despite the far-reaching critique to which Wittgenstein subjected the *Tractatus* in the later book. As James C. Edwards has explained, "There are at least two ways in which Wittgenstein's lifework is a unity: the later writing is an attempt to take the measure of the earlier, and hence of the tradition which it culminates; and the later work tries to recast, to transmute, the ambition that gives rise to the tradition itself, to fulfill that ambition in spite of itself. . . . In both periods his essential ambition is an ethical one: to locate the sense of life; to answer the question of human being" (4). Or, as Bachmann put it in the radio essay, "The experience that lies at the basis of Heidegger's mysticism of Being may be similar to that which allowed Wittgenstein to speak of the mystical" (*W* 4: 114).

In the *Philosophical Investigations,* Wittgenstein moved beyond Western metaphysics, addressing the problems of philosophy by showing that those problems were simply wrongly conceived. He recognized that in the *Tractatus* he had posed the question falsely—"A picture held us captive" (48)—misunderstanding the nature of language altogether. Language is not a perfectly coherent system that is true either because it is tautological or because it corresponds to empirical reality. Instead, language is primarily speech, and "speaking of language is part of an activity, or of a form of life" (11), deriving its meaning from whatever "language game" the speakers happen to be playing. Such language games are multiple and varied with no necessary coherence among them but, like the very different tools of a toolbox (another of Wittgenstein's metaphors), nonetheless allowing humans to operate successfully in the world. To use Lévi-Strauss's and Derrida's formulation, Wittgenstein has given up the perfectly coherent and abstract model of the engineer, within which every part can be explained as a component of a single system (the ambition of Western metaphysics since its beginnings), for the heterogeneity of bricolage (Derrida, "Structure" 255–56). As Edwards has explained, Wittgenstein's concern with language is really a concern with guaranteeing "rationality as representation," another way of explaining the central problem that has plagued Western philosophy since the Greeks: "The Socratic-Platonic answer to the question of human being stressed our capacity for *thinking*, conceived as accurate representation of the real: knowledge is (our) virtue, and knowledge is knowledge of universal definitions, representations of the eternal Forms of which we here and now see only the shadows" (20). Some version of this project was still Wittgenstein's ambition in the *Tractatus*, but in the *Philosophical Investigations* he abandoned the entire endeavor to find that intersubjectively verifiable, coherent, ultimate Truth, and, as Pitkin explains, he substituted "partial overviews, developed ad hoc where they are needed, for the older vision of a single, dominating politico-theoretical system" (326).

In her second essay on Wittgenstein, Bachmann shows that she understands exactly what was at stake in the *Tractatus*. According to the *Tractatus*, she explains, we are able to talk about reality at all, use "signs that mean something without having anything in common with that which is signified," because reality and language share "the logical form" (*W* 4: 110). Language can talk neither about this logical form itself nor about anything nonlogical—"outside logic everything is accidental" (*Tractatus* 137)—that is, not about the particular case, the nonessential, the specific, the contingent, or, of course, the ethical, the aesthetic, or any of the other questions of most crucial moment to humans. Thus, Bachmann asks, what has Wittgenstein actually accomplished? "He gives us the answer on one of the last pages of the *Tractatus,* which first allows us to grasp the adventure, the risk in which this book involved itself: 'nothing at all'" (*W* 4: 113). He asserts a similar answer in a passage from the *Philosophical Investigations* which Bachmann also cites: "A whole cloud of philosophy condensed into a drop of grammar" (*Phil. Investigations* 222; *W* 4: 123). As Bachmann perceives, the move beyond the *Tractatus* in the *Philosophical Investigations* is to show "that the problems of philosophy are problems of language, that so to speak the misfirings of language create philosophical problems" (*W* 4: 123). By reconceiving how language functions, by abandoning the abstract level on which he analyzed language in the *Tractatus*, she continues, Wittgenstein can do away with the problems altogether: "He believes that we can silence the problems when our language functions well and sensibly, when it lives and breathes in *use*. Only where language, which is a form of life, is taken out of use, when it comes to a standstill—and it does that in his opinion when it is used to philosophize in the conventional sense—do problems arise. These problems are not to be solved but rather eliminated" (*W* 4: 124). Language in use can be heterogeneous, multiple, nonsynchronous, particular, and in that practice and play of language the metaphysical problems which have plagued the West are revealed, indeed, to be meaningless.

Bachmann concludes her Wittgenstein essay by drawing from the *Philosophical Investigations* provocative citations and images that will resonate through the rest of her own work. Language is simultaneously a "system of signification" and a "multiplicity [*Mannigfaltigkeit*]" (*W* 4: 124), an almost Kristevan recognition of the multivalencies of language upon which particularly the "Ways of Death" novels draw. Language is "a labyrinth of paths" and an old city: "a maze of little streets and squares, of old and new houses, and of houses with additions from various periods; and this surrounded by a multitude of new boroughs with straight regular streets and uniform houses" (*Phil. Investigations* 8; *W* 4: 124)— images that point toward Bachmann's own later fascination with symbolic topography and her (and Freud's) interest in archaeology as a metaphor for the layers of the psyche. She emphasizes as well Wittgenstein's insistence that philosophy "must be like a therapy, for philosophical problems are illnesses that must be healed. He demands not a solution but a healing" (*W* 4: 124). Encouraged by Wittgenstein, Bachmann thus seems to have grasped very early what has become a central insight of poststructuralism, that the psyche is constituted through language, Wittgenstein's language games, a point she also made in a 1961 interview discussing "Youth in an Austrian Town": "The children—they entered into a game that somebody else was putting on. The I [of the story] leaves the game, unmasks the game as game; he or she has lost the innocence of these movements" (*GuI* 26). Moreover, present in germinal form in this Wittgenstein citation is also Bachmann's later concern with the connection of absolutist ideological systems to the Western (male) psyche, the same sorts of men of whom the "I" says in Malina: "the whole approach of men toward women is diseased, moreover, each disease is so wholly unique that men will never be completely cured" (*Malina* 177).

Finally, what Bachmann understands as Wittgenstein's particular kind of mysticism, his "points of invasion of that which shows itself or is experienced with belief, which affects what we do and leave undone" (*W* 4: 124), seems very close to what she has described (or shown) elsewhere in her work as the utopian, a vision of an almost-not-yet-imaginable, different way of being in the world. In this respect Wittgenstein succeeds in thought in moving beyond the limits/borders of the West, the analogues in thought to the terrible and terrifying practices of our time, as Bachmann also recognized in this essay: "It is true that he like no one else recognized the solidifying antagonisms of thought of his century: irrationalism and rationalism, held his own against them in his work, and already overcame them" (*W* 4: 126–127). If this is the case, Wittgenstein's thought might represent for Bachmann the hope that the nightmare triumph of Western political and cultural imperialism she envisioned in *The Book of Franza* might not have to come true after all: "The whites are coming. The whites are landing. And if they are driven back, then they will come again. No revolution and no resolution can prevent it, nor any controls over the currency. They will come again in spirit if there's no other way for them to come. And they will resurrect themselves in a brown or black brain, which will become white once again. They will take over the world through such indirect means" (*Franza* 112). Wittgenstein, after all, suggested in the introduction to his *Philosophical Remarks* that the spirit of his work "is a different one from that of the grand stream of European and American civilization in which we all exist" (7), and he prefaced the *Philosophical Investigations* with an epigraph from Nestroy: "Progress has altogether the quality that it looks much bigger than it is ([*Überhaupt hat der Fortschritt das an sich, daß er viel größer ausschaut, als er wirklich ist]*" (*Phil. Investigations* viii). In an essay on Musil, also written in the 1950s, Bachmann remarked, "Not just the case of Kakania showed that thinking in closed ideologies leads directly to war, and the permanent war of faith is still ongoing" (*W* 4: 27). Wittgenstein's philosophy, beyond the closed systems of Western metaphysics, may offer the hope and the possibility that the ever present war of the "Ways of Death" might cease.

But a further affinity between Bachmann and Wittgenstein may also exist, not in these essays but in their lives and work. In the *Philosophical Investigations* Wittgenstein said, "It [philosophy] leaves everything as it is," and similarly in *Bemerkungen über die Grundlagen der Mathematik* (Remarks on the fundaments of mathematics): "The illness of a time is healed by a change in human beings' way of living, and the illness of philosophical problems can only be healed by a changed way of thinking and living, not by a medicine that a single person invented" (57). About literature, Bachmann made much the same point in the Frankfurt lectures: "With a new language reality will always be encountered there where a moral, cognitive movement happens and not where someone tries to renew language all by itself. . . . A new language must have a new gait, and it has this new gait only when a new spirit inhabits it" (*W* 4: 192). Missing for both Wittgenstein and Bachmann was the practice which would enable their thoughts and images to guide an almost inconceivable transformation of the world; indeed, their works were so distant from a practice that most of their readers could not grasp that these works dealt with transformation at all. Wittgenstein stated gloomily in the introduction to the *Philosophical Investigations* (a passage which Bachmann quoted in her last essay): "It is not impossible that it should fall to the lot of this work, in its poverty and in the darkness of this time, to bring light into one brain or another—but, of course, it is not likely" (*Phil. Investigations* vi; *W* 4: 122). Despite the few moments of utopian harmony in the "Ways of Death"—the "Secrets of the Princess of Kagran" in *Malina*, the silent meal at Wadi Halfa in *The Book of Franza*—Bachmann too can scarcely imagine a mediation between the far-reaching critique of the later work and what she sometimes termed, borrowing Musil's words from *The Man without Qualities*, "the other condition," a world where it would be altogether different. In one of her last interviews Bachmann addressed this problem:

> And I don't believe in this materialism, in this consumer society, in this capitalism, in this monstrosity that's taking place here, and people who enrich themselves on us without having any right to do so. I really do believe in something, and I call it "A Day Will Come." And one day it will come. Well, probably it won't come, because it's been destroyed for us so many times, for thousands of years it's always been destroyed. It won't come, and I believe in it nonetheless. For if I weren't able to believe in it, then I couldn't write any more. (*GuI* 145)

But what Pitkin wrote about Wittgenstein's philosophy is also true (as Bachmann knew) of literature: "Where philosophy succeeds, it reveals our conceptual system as it now exists, not its trivial and evanescent details, but its deep necessities. For philosophy is concerned with precisely those concepts that reflect our most central forms of life. To change these concepts, our forms of life would have to change; and that is not accomplished through philosophizing" (298). Inspired by Wittgenstein's philosophy to understand the world differently, Bachmann also shared his gloom about changing it, as her work and her life reflect. Like the main character of *Malina*, Bachmann could not compose a book titled *Exsultate Jubilate* either, but instead wrote "Ways of Death."

READING BACHMANN IN 1985

This essay was written in summer 1985 and published in a special issue of *Modern Austrian Literature* devoted to the "other," feminist Bachmann. In that issue my essay was one of the few that did not address feminism or gender questions. As I observed in chapter 2, I believe now (though I probably would not have said so at the time) that my lack of attention to gender there expressed my general discontent with the cultural/French feminist reading of Bachmann that had by then become virtually hegemonic in Bachmann scholarship—a discontent that would become more general among feminist Bachmann scholars toward the end of the decade. I commented in chapter 2: "As in my own case, I am inclined instead to think that gender is missing in these studies because Bachmann scholars (who otherwise may well have identified themselves as feminists) wanted to pursue a range of aspects of her work apart from those addressed by 1980s feminists and did not want to make use of the feminist methodology that had come to dominate Bachmann studies. Because feminist scholarship had not yet elaborated alternative methods that permit other kinds of literary-critical questions to be asked in gender-specific ways, these young Bachmann scholars did not know how to address the issues they wished to consider in ways that also took gender into account." In August 1984 I had spent a month in Vienna consulting Bachmann's papers in the Nationalbibliothek, researching a project that I called "Philosophical Backgrounds to the 'Ways of Death,'" one of the earliest versions of this book. Though I found virtually nothing in the archive useful for my project (if such material exists at all, it is in the personal correspondence and other materials in the portion of the archive closed until 2025), my focus here on Wittgenstein grew out of that complex of concerns. Though I am at present committed to the position that all experience is gendered, I would still today find myself at something of a loss for a method that could allow me to demonstrate definitively what was gender-specific about Bachmann's reception of Wittgenstein. Two decades later, feminist scholarship has still not, I think, solved all its methodological conundrums.

My discontent with feminism in 1985 was not limited to Bachmann scholarship. That spring, I had written an article on the current U.S. women's movement for the collection *Frauen Literatur Geschichte* (Women literature history), edited by Hiltrud Gnüg and Renate Möhrmann. My argument there is a harsh one: I assert that feminists of the 1970s had taken positions that led the movement into the cul-de-sac of feminism in the mid-1980s. I maintain particularly that the separatist strategies of cultural feminism were predicated upon the class and race privilege of its participants, who did not have to concern themselves with securing resources to assure their basic survival and could focus on transforming their own lives rather than the larger society. This privilege, I continue, was also responsible for their lack of interest in, if not contempt for, campaigns of liberal feminism that focused on, say, assuring working women equal pay with men. The retreat from contestation in the political arena was precisely what had left feminists without strategies to combat the national and international developments that they now observe with growing horror. After a lengthy disposition on the theoretical and literary variants on cultural feminist positions, I conclude by directing attention to the many English-speaking women writers who deny that their works are primarily concerned with women's issues, who even go so far as to maintain—like the white South African writer Nadine Gordimer—that the problems of white women are not the most important in today's world. Attempting to end my article on a positive note, I look for sources of inspiration for renewed feminist struggle from feminists now working in the Rainbow Coalition or supporting striking coal miners in England, from Third World women or women in trade unions who say, "I'm not a feminist, but . . ," anywhere but from within the women's movement itself. Given that attitude toward U.S. feminism, it is no wonder that I do not address feminist issues in my essay on Bachmann and Wittgenstein.

Yet though this essay scarcely mentions feminism or gender, it could not have been written without the developments in feminist scholarship chronicled in my commentaries on previous chapters. First, this chapter was an experiment in methodology. I complain in both "Gender, Race, and History" (chapter 5) and this essay that feminist Bachmann scholars do not pay sufficient attention to history and culture. It was also clear to me that training in U.S. literary studies, at least, did not prepare one to do so. Under the influence of New Criticism, the school of formalist criticism that flourished from the 1940s to the late 1960s, and the various formalisms into which New Criticism mutated, including the literary reception of poststructuralism by the Yale School (Paul de Man, Geoffrey Hartman, Hillis Miller, Harold Bloom), literary scholarship had been defined as literary criticism: a sensitive mind produces a reading of a text unconstrained by the conditions of the text's production (the "genetic fallacy") or the author's intentions for it (the "intentional fallacy"). Particularly under Barthian and Derridean influence, that seemed to come to mean "anything goes," the wilder and more ingenious the better. Clearly, historians had different standards of evidence, as feminists' historical studies in feminist journals had showed me. Backed into a corner by many feminist poststructuralists at the conference "Feminist Studies: Reconstituting Knowledge," held at the University of Wisconsin–Milwaukee in April 1985, feminist historian Linda Gordon had maintained: "It is wrong to conclude, as some have, that because there may be no objective truth possible, there are not objective lies" (22). Moreover, as I attended to the arguments about the importance of recognizing other women's difference, I had increasingly come to feel that ripping a text out of the context of its historical and cultural conditions of production did violence to its author by failing to respect either the project she had set herself when she wrote it or the various social factors that informed her and her production. (I had been very indignant about an MLA talk by Sandra Gilbert addressing Zora Neale Hurston's *Their Eyes Were Watching God*, which removed Hurston from the context of black culture and anthropology to make her conform to the thesis of Gilbert's book.) In this essay, therefore, I try to understand both Wittgenstein's thought and Bachmann's use of it as undertakings motivated by the concerns of their time. (Such a historically based approach is not in much favor among U.S.-trained philosophers and political theorists, who often treat theoretical texts as if they all existed simultaneously in some ethereal realm detached from time and space.) My main secondary sources in this essay were thus written by intellectual historians. I also wanted to treat the thought of both figures as ideas that evolved over time, and I use my close reading skills (one aspect of U.S. literary training that still serves us well) to trace steps in Bachmann's own intellectual growth as she interacted with Wittgenstein's texts. In this regard I think the essay is true to the feminist goal of exploring women's specificity as well as my own attempt to reinsert Bachmann into her own history and culture.

But even more important, I think it was the development of feminist thought up to this point that allowed me to understand the rupture in the tradition of Western thought that Wittgenstein's work represented and why it was so important to Bachmann. Clearly, Wittgenstein was struggling with the problem that gained more currency when it was raised again by poststructuralism: how to guarantee the correspondence between reality and representation, how to anchor truth and morality securely. He concluded in the *Tractatus* that it was not to be done, that true statements can be made only about areas and aspects of human experience that are not very important. With this conclusion he bade a philosophical farewell to the theories we have come to call metanarratives (say, Marxism, Critical Theory, psychoanalysis, cultural feminism): there exists no "scientific" basis on which they could put in a claim to truth. Trained in logical positivism, Bachmann understood Wittgenstein's argument, as well as his anguish about not being able to address in any way the issues that most urgently confronted him. But—and this is what feminists such as Donna Haraway helped me to grasp—Bachmann also understood the dangers of those imperializing, totalizing theories (all "irrational" by definition, since they could not be proved "scientifically"), and that explains the vehemence of her rejection of Heidegger. It is a theme her works continued to pursue until her death. I am also pleased that even at this point, in emphasizing Bachmann's condemnation of "the whites," I understood the connection of totalizing theories and imperialism that postcolonial studies would later stress. (So one might argue that the cultural feminist appropriation of Bachmann is a profound misrecognition of one of the issues she found it most important to pursue.) And what Bachmann also seems to have learned from the *Philosophical Investigations* is that possibilities exist beyond the constraints of total systems—though she could imagine that alternative only as a utopia quite detached from any mediation that could move from the present to the future. That is also a quality which derives from Bachmann's historical situation and is a point at which it is up to feminists like Donna Haraway and like us to think beyond the point to which Bachmann herself was able to go.

Finally, I think the conclusion of this essay shows that I never repudiated my materialist roots—and still adhere to the 1966 historical materialist analysis advanced by Christa Wolf. Whatever the brilliance of their insights, neither Wittgenstein nor Bachmann could change the world by ideas alone. To translate theory into social transformation (Marx said in an early text, "Theory itself becomes a material force when it has seized the masses" [Tucker 60]), a social agent engaged in social practice is necessary. As Donna Haraway suggested in her cyborg myth, as I believed then (and probably still believe today), it's not impossible that feminists might join with others to become such agents. Or, to echo Bachmann, to be able to write and act at all, I have to continue to believe that that will be possible.

1987

Reagan's popularity continued unabated into his second term, and the Democratic Party seemed incapable of mounting any substantial opposition to Republican policies. One commentator observed: "By 1986, the White House and Senate were in Republican hands, and the Supreme Court was gradually shifting rightward. The House of Representatives, though controlled by Democrats, agreed with the administration's agenda more than half the time" (Kazin 115). Without significant outcry in response, Reagan successfully bombed Libya in April 1986, continued to lobby for financial support for the Nicaraguan contras, and sought billions of dollars for his "Star Wars" or Strategic Defense Initiative, a laser system intended to destroy incoming Soviet missiles in space which no one, including the military, was convinced would ever work. Increasing numbers of homeless people appeared on the streets of U.S. cities, a response to Reagan's shifts in national priorities: cuts in social services, the deinstitutionalization of the mentally ill, and the growth of unemployment and poverty (Peter Marcuse). A new discourse on race emerged that focused on "reverse discrimination" against white men. As David Wellman commented: "The new political language certainly resonates with the tenor of the times. . . . Resentment is high and all-white bars and living rooms are thick with tales of 'qualified' Euro-American males losing jobs to 'the special interest' of 'affirmative-action candidates.' There is good reason to believe that attacks on inequality are not politically feasible during periods of belt-tightening" (58). Reagan's reputation was tarnished only by the Iran-contra scandal—a system of covert operations begun in the first days of the Reagan regime but revealed only in late 1986—which involved an elaborate National Security Council scheme to sell arms to Iran in order to obtain funding for the contras. The congressional committees investigating the scandal were, however, never able to determine what the president himself knew and when he knew it.

On the other hand, left-wing activism was not entirely dead during the period. The academic year 1985–1986 marked a high point in the national campaign urging universities to divest themselves of their stock in companies doing business with South Africa, and in 1986–1987 students began to organize against CIA recruiting on campus. In April 1986 the founding convention of the National Rainbow Coalition was attended by nearly eight hundred delegates amid speculation about whether Jesse Jackson would again mount a campaign for the presidency. A number of large demonstrations took place in Washington,

DC: a rally supported reproductive rights in spring 1986; in April 1987 demonstrators marched there and in San Francisco to oppose U.S. policy in southern Africa and Central America; and in October 1987 a huge National March for Lesbian and Gay Rights was addressed by speakers Eleanor Smeal of the National Organization for Women (NOW), Cesar Chavez of the United Farm Workers, and Jesse Jackson. A similar coalition of women's groups, minority organizations, and labor united in fall 1987 to defeat the nomination of Judge Robert Bork to the Supreme Court. In an article called "A New New Left on Campus," Maria Margaronis wrote: "The Reagan era isn't over yet, and the children of the 1980s have a great deal to work out before they can build a national movement, for themselves and with what's left of the left. But as the times begin to lean toward changing, such efforts deserve all the support they can get" (757).

Meanwhile, feminists were beset by external and internal political problems of their own. The far right exacerbated the Reagan regime's assaults on a range of social programs benefiting women by intensifying their opposition to women's access to abortion: in May 1987 a nationwide campaign called "Operation Rescue" was launched to picket, blockade, and ultimately shut down abortion clinics, while other right-wing groups were responsible for clinic bombings and arson. Conservative trends could also be discerned within the women's movement itself: cultural feminists Andrea Dworkin and Catherine MacKinnon made common cause with conservatives in order to pass ordinances banning pornography in Minneapolis and Indianapolis, arguing that "pornography reveals that male pleasure is inextricably tied to victimizing, hurting, exploiting" (Pally 795 citing Dworkin, *Pornography*). In a notorious sex discrimination case against Sears, Roebuck, one woman historian enraged many other feminist scholars by declaring that it was not necessarily Sears's discriminatory policies but women's commitment to traditional female values that explained why so few women held the higher-paying sales commission jobs: "Working women who are married are likely to put family and children first," she argued, "and therefore, as the survey evidence of the Sears work force shows, are less willing to work evenings and weekends than men—evenings and weekends which are required of commission salespeople" (Wiener 178). Feminists were also increasingly forced to wrestle with a phenomenon that journalists had christened "postfeminism." "Most frequently," Deborah Rosenfelt and Judith Stacey explained, "journalists use this term to describe views expressed by relatively affluent and ambitious women in their late twenties and early thirties about the difficulties they face in attempting to combine satisfying careers and family life under present social and economic conditions. More broadly, postfeminism demarcates an emerging culture and ideology that simultaneously incorporates, revises, and depoliticizes many of the fundamental issues advanced by Second Wave feminism" (341). Rosenfelt and Stacey viewed postfeminism as, among other things, indicative of a crisis in feminism occasioned by its inability to find adequate solutions to the changed political and personal situation of feminists and other women in the Reagan era: "Defeats in the political arena coincide with significant shifts in the personal needs and priorities of many who were in the vanguard of Second Wave feminism, and together the public defeats and the personal changes have taken their toll on the confidence, vision, and solidarity of the left feminist community in the United States" (342).

For academics, the second Reagan administration also marked the beginning of what would later be termed the "culture wars" or the "p.c. debates," the right-wing assault on the changes in canons, curricula, methods, and topics of research that had been instituted by participants in the social movements of the 1960s as they took on positions of responsibility in universities and colleges. The offensive was launched in 1984 in *To Reclaim a Legacy: A Report on the Humanities in Higher Education*, written by William Bennett, the Reagan-appointed chair of the National Endowment for the Humanities and later secretary of education. Bennett "argued that the classic texts of Western civilization were being replaced by works of lesser value in an attempt to produce a more inclusive curriculum and that as a result, American students were being deprived of their 'legacy'" (Ginsberg/Lennox 178). "Accuracy in Academe"—founded in 1985 as a spin-off of Reed Irvine's self-proclaimed media watchdog organization "Accuracy in Media"—recruited classroom spies and began to compile a database on professors the organization considered "left-wing propagandists" (Diamond 91–92).

The year 1987 seemed to initiate a more intensified phase in the conservative campaign against changes in the academy. For example, it saw the founding of the first nationwide organization of right-wing faculty, the National Association of Scholars (NAS), which proclaimed that policies such as affirmative action and curricular focus on categories of "race, gender, and class . . . involve either the application of a double standard or the repudiation of appropriate intellectual criteria" (National Association of Scholars 8) and called for their abolition. The analysis advanced by the NAS was also promoted by two widely read conservative texts published in 1987, E. D. Hirsch's *Cultural Literacy* and Allan Bloom's *The Closing of the American Mind*, which attacked the recent "trendy relativism" in higher education as being responsible for the abandonment of what they regarded as enduring cultural values. Though multiculturalists are the main target of Bloom's invective, feminists, the "latest enemy of the vitality of the classic texts" (Bloom 65), also figure prominently on his list of major villains, and he observed in a 1988 *Time* magazine interview: "Radical feminism tends to be present in the universities more than within the general society. . . . This is an agenda, and it has entered the university as a huge theoretical network. It is overwhelming in its power and its very angry passions" ("Most" 74, cited in Ginsberg/Lennox 180).

Of course such claims were quite absurd: Marxists, feminists, and multiculturalists were very far from assuming control of any campuses whatsoever, nor had universities jettisoned classical and canonical texts for those deemed more "politically correct"—though a range of previously neglected perspectives and works had indeed been *added* to the curriculum since the late 1960s. Clearly, the NAS and its friends were not wrong to discern that far-reaching (and to them deplorable) changes had taken place in the academy, nor in choosing 1987 as the year in which they began their major assault on their antagonists. By 1987, even scholars less hostile to the social changes initiated in the 1960s had noticed that, at least in the humanities, a sea change had taken place as a consequence of the encounter of a rather attenuated British Marxism with French poststructuralism (especially Foucault). Describing the genealogy of new historicism, Louis Montrose, for instance, observed: "In various combinations and with varying degrees of consistency and effectiveness, the intellectual forces identifiable as new historicism or cultural poetics, cultural materialism, feminism, and revisionist forms of Marxism have been engaged in redrawing the boundaries and restructuring the content of English and American literary studies during the past decade" ("New Historicism" 392). Hillis Miller, a leading Yale deconstructionist and then MLA president, devoted his presidential address (published in the May 1987 issue of *PMLA*) to decrying what he called "the resistance to theory" in the new directions he discerned in literary scholarship: "As everyone knows, literary study in the past few years has undergone a sudden, almost universal turn away from theory in the sense of an orientation toward languages as such and has made a corresponding turn toward history, culture, society, politics, institutions, class and gender conditions, the social context, the material base in the sense of institutionalization, conditions of production, technology, distribution, and consumption of 'cultural products,' among other products" (283).

With even more alarm, in the lead article of the same issue of *PMLA*, Edward Pechter declared (echoing, of course, the *Communist Manifesto*), "A specter is haunting criticism—the specter of a new historicism." Moreover, Pechter observed, "The new historicization of literary studies is equally a new politicization, with interpretation judged as an expression of the political interests of the audience." And though he conceded that many different and even contradictory critical practices were represented in new historicism, he maintained that "it is at its core—or, better, at its cutting edge—a kind of 'Marxist criticism'" that is, moreover, "instrumental to social change, part of the project of making the world a better place" (292, 299). One might view the emergence of this new historical, Marxist-influenced methodology (committed, as Jonathan Dollimore and Alan Sinfield put it, "to the transformation of a social order which exploits people on the grounds of race, gender, and class" [viii]) as a somewhat displaced response on the part of a particular generation of academics to the depredations of the Reagan regime. Montrose notes that "the reorientation in the field under way since at least the beginning of the 1980s is largely the work of critics whose values were formed while they were students during the culturally experimental and politically turbulent 1960s," and he goes on to observe, "In general, these critics responded to the radically altered sociopolitical climate of the 1980s—and, perhaps, for some of them, to the uneasy comfort they had now achieved within its academic establishment—with work that confronted ideologies and cultural politics of other times and places but resisted the articulation of its own assumptions and commitments" ("New Historicism" 393).

The feminist scholarship of this period still mostly held these new historical methodologies at arm's length, as male neo-Marxists also continued to pay rather little attention to gender. In an article first published in *Cultural Critique* in July 1988 and widely reprinted, Judith Lowder Newton even denounced new historicism's failure to acknowledge properly its real genealogy: "Barely alluded to in most of the histories of 'new historicism' so far are what were in fact the mother roots—the women's movement and the feminist theory and feminist scholarship which grew from it" (153). Certainly, feminism played a central role in the challenge to universalist founding assumptions which culminated in the new methodologies of the 1990s. But I think Newton overstates feminism's contribution to the emergence of this specific approach, which was more attentive to historical context and reading strategies than much feminist literary analysis of this period and was in the early 1990s itself appropriated for feminist purposes. During Reagan's second term, however, feminist scholars themselves were also embarked on the search for new methodologies. In *Signs*, Linda Alcoff explored the conflict between cultural feminism and poststructuralism and showed how major feminist thinkers such as Teresa de Lauretis and Denise Riley had been able to reconceptualize femininity so as to avoid essentialism while preserving the political utility of the category "woman." Alcoff's article also advances the important concept of "positionality," which, as she elaborates it , has two dimensions: first, "that the concept of woman is a relational term, identifiable only within a (constantly moving) context; but, second, that the position that women find themselves in can be actively utilized (rather than transcended) as a location for the construction of meaning, a place from where meaning is constructed rather than simply the place where meaning can be discovered (the meaning of femaleness)" (434) (As the introduction to this book shows, "positionality" was to become a concept very important for my own thinking.)

In a paper first presented at the American Historical Association convention and later published in the association's journal, Joan Scott similarly elaborated the ways in which the concept of "gender" could be "a useful category of historical analysis":

> "Gender" as a substitute for "women" is also used to suggest that information about women is necessarily information about men, that one implies the study of the other. This usage insists that the world of women is part of the world of men,

created in and by it. . . . In addition, gender is also used to designate social relations between the sexes. Its use explicitly rejects biological explanations, such as those that find a common denominator for diverse forms of female subordination in the facts that women have the capacity to give birth and men have greater muscular strength. Instead, gender becomes a way of denoting "cultural constructions"— the entirely social creation of ideas about appropriate roles for women and men. It is a way of referring to the exclusively social origins of the subjective identities of men and women. (32)

One consequence of such advances was a more emphatic feminist insistence in empirical work that the received categories of male dominance and female victim-hood did not match up with historical or contemporary reality, Niara Sudarkasa observing, for instance, "that a 'neutral' complementarity, rather than a super-ordination/subordination, more accurately describes the relationship between certain female and male roles in various precolonial African societies" (101), and Barbara Harlow maintaining that the situation of Third World women throws into question the "convenient feminist categories of race, class, gender as well as 'unified' women's experience" (Milkman/Stansell 450–451). As well, the new analytical models permitted a much more complex understanding of the produc-tion and function of femininity, now conceived to be always inflected by other social categories, as Elizabeth Fox-Genovese, reviewing three books on women in the American South, observed: "The personal lives of southern women were profoundly political, that is, they were inscribed in a distinct social system that they also helped to shape and for which they bear the responsibilities of their gen-der-, class-, and race-specific contributions" (162). Equally important, books like Claudia Koonz's *Mothers in the Fatherland* showed how a definition of women as always part of men's world and defined in relationship to men could resituate women as figures also possessing human agency and making their own gender-specific contribution to history, whether for good or—as in the case of Koonz's examination of women's role in National Socialism—for very ill.

The new feminist paradigms elaborated in the late 1980s slowly began to shape literary analysis as well. In a *Feminist Studies* essay reviewing five surveys of feminist literary theory and criticism published in 1985, June Howard identi-fied the process by which this transformation took place. The definition of "difference" was the terrain of struggle in those texts, she explained: did it refer to the constitution of meaning through difference, as French theory would have it; to differences among women, a primary concern for Americans; and/or to the feminist project of "making a difference" and which form of feminist lit-erary analysis would best promote that end? "These books," Howard observes, "are true to their moment, in presenting the relations between Anglo-American and French feminist criticism as a confrontation, even an impasse. But they also provide evidence that the moment is already passing, perhaps that it has already passed" (169). A perspective that Toril Moi's influential *Sexual/Textual Politics* did not pursue, Marxist feminism, is in Howard's view most likely to point the way out of a "static Anglo-American/French confrontation," for (quoting Moi) "Marxist feminist cultural criticism enables the critic to link the literary work 'to a specific historical context in which a whole set of different structures (ideological, economic, social, political) intersect to produce precisely those textual structures' and opens up the possibility of 'studying the historical construction of the categories of gender and . . . analysing the importance of culture in the representation and transformation of those categories'" (Howard 175–76 citing Moi 94). Howard particularly praised the "materialist feminist" approach of Judith Newton and Deborah Rosenfelt's *Feminist Criticism and Social Change*, which, as they themselves note, "has much in common with 'the new Marxist cultural theory and the work of [the Marxist literary scholars] Tony Bennet, Fredric Jameson, Michael Ryan, and Terry Eagleton'" (Howard 184 citing Newton/ Rosenfelt xxiv). The difficulties of attending to all the areas emphasized by the new materialist feminist approach are "vertiginous" and "formidable": feminist literary scholars writing from a materialist feminist perspective must focus on "the power relations implied by gender and simultaneously of those implied by class, race, and sexual identification; an analysis of literature and an analysis of history and society; an analysis of the circumstances of cultural production and an analysis of the complexities with which at a given moment in history they are inscribed in the text" (Howard 186 citing Newton/Rosenfelt xix). "It is not surprising," Howard notes, "that brilliant critics like [Gayatri] Spivak and [Cora] Kaplan have published relatively fragmentary work over the past decade (186).

Certainly, I might add, that is also the case for those of us far less illustrious, who also struggled throughout the 1980s to find an adequate method. By 1987, however, it seems to me that the corner had been turned. Spurred to counterassault (at least within the academy) by the right-wing gains of the Reagan era, a range of progressives that included feminists had begun to elaborate analytical approaches that allowed them to address the "rainbow coalition" of concerns that had posed themselves in the 1980s, cobbling together a method that was historical and materialist and attentive to the theoretical advances of the past decades. Under the influence of Newton, Rosenfelt, and a host of other feminist scholars who had once called themselves Marxist feminists and socialist feminists, feminist literary scholars increasingly termed their own variant of that method "materialist feminism." As Howard presciently observed from her vantage point of 1987, "Both in its content and in its style, materialist feminism seems to me to offer the best hope for an approach that resists both the glamour of high theory and the comforting certainties of political correctness and common sense, for an approach that is theoretically rigorous, historically specific, and politically engaged" (186).

CHAPTER 7

Bachmann Reading / Reading Bachmann

THE WOMAN IN WHITE IN THE "WAYS OF DEATH"

*Sometimes it takes a coincidence,
sometimes intuition, to recognize the true stories
that are happening behind the play-acting.*

—Ingeborg Bachmann, "Todesarten-Projekt"

Only one single, brighter episode interrupts the dismal narrative of Ingeborg Bachmann's unfinished novel, *The Book of Franza*: Franza's recollection of May 1945, "the most beautiful spring." *The Book of Franza* mostly details Franza's husband's deliberate attempt to drive her mad, her escape from him into her brother's care, their trip together to northern Africa, and her subsequent decline and death there. But Franza also remembers Austria's liberation in May 1945, a month whose burgeoning splendor coincided with the unrest and excitement of her own adolescent body. The "miracle," as she terms it, means peace, freedom, and hope for Franza, brought to her small village in the person of an English captain, Sir Perceval Glyde, "the first man in her life" (*Franza* 42). She joyfully accompanies her captain on his journeys through the countryside and receives her first kisses from him as he leaves to return to England. "With that, Franza's first love came to an end" (*Franza* 45), Bachmann's narrator tells us, apparently this bleak novel's only example of a heterosexual romance that will not result in destruction and death—the "Ways of Death" of Bachmann's final novel cycle.

Thus it is all the more surprising to discover that Bachmann had found a prior literary model for her romantic captain in a figure seemingly quite his opposite. For "Sir Perceval Glyde" is not a name original to Bachmann's novel: before his appearance in *The Book of Franza*, Sir Perceval figures as the oppressively masculine villain of Wilkie Collins's *The Woman in White*, a Victorian "sensation novel" which also otherwise shares many similar themes and structures with *The Book of Franza*. The comparison of their similarities (as well as their striking differences) that Bachmann herself seems to have invited will reveal a good deal about Bachmann's reading habits and her methods of composition, and it can also clarify some puzzling aspects of both *The Book of Franza* and *Malina*. As well, the presence of this disguised allusion to another literary work may caution Bachmann's readers to be alert for other significant, if occluded, literary models for her fiction and in general to be aware of the importance of intertextuality for her own literary creations.

Like both *Malina* and *The Book of Franza*, *The Woman in White* is about gender, love, and politics, about sexual and social identity, about multiple doppelgängers and hints of incest, about male dominance and female submission, about confinement and madness. The novel's author, William Wilkie Collins (1824–1889), was a prolific writer of thrilling, suspenseful, and carefully plotted Victorian popular fiction intended—like that of his friend and associate Charles Dickens—for middle-brow, middle-class audiences. *The Woman in White*, his best-known work and one of the most widely read novels of the Victorian era, was published serially in Dickens's *All the Year Round* from 26 November 1859 to 25 August 1860 and first appeared in volume form on 15 August 1860. As was the case with many other "sensation novels" as well, questions of gender stand at the center of *The Woman in White*, and the concern of sensation novels with the role of women is now acknowledged to be one of the main reasons for the genre's success (Helsinger et. al 122–145). But, scholars argue, Collins, like other Victorian novelists, displays a deep ambivalence about the situation of women: "On the one hand, he creates characters, situations, and symbolic structures that implicitly indict a society that oppresses women. On the other hand, through his ambivalent depictions of those characters and situations, he stops short of acknowledging the basic premises of Victorian society" (Barickman 148–149). Unlike Bachmann's novels, Collins's novel ends with the villains vanquished, evil properly punished, and the legitimate order of (benevolent) male dominance restored. Elaine Showalter, author of one of the first book-length feminist studies of the British novel, can thus regard *The Woman in White*, along with Collins's other novels, as a mere apology for the system of gender relations Victorian men desired: "Like Dickens, Collins invariably ends his novels with sentimental happy marriages of patient woman and resolute man, marriages whose success is validated by the prompt appearance of male offspring" (*Literature* 162–163). But Bachmann's reading is more subtle and differentiated. To grasp how she appropriated this novel, we must read it, with her, "against the grain" to understand how she expands and explores the openings in the social and sexual order with which Collins tantalizingly plays, instead of closing them as Collins does in his conventionally Victorian happy ending.

Collins's four positive characters bear affinities to the central figures of both *Malina* and *The Book of Franza*. Three women stand in his novel's center, all evidently aspects of a single figure. Laura Fairlie, a blond, beautiful, childlike, and submissive heiress, is the central love interest. Anne Catherick, the "Woman in White," mysteriously resembles Laura (and is eventually revealed to be Laura's half-sister via a liaison between her father and a housemaid) but is congenitally weak-minded and deranged, one symptom of which is her insistence on always clothing herself in white. Marian Halcombe, Laura's half-sister on her mother's side, is as dark and ugly as Laura is fair, so that the viewer, we are told, is "almost repelled by the masculine form and masculine look of [her] features" (Collins 25), but she is endowed in return with masculine talents and a masculine assertiveness uniformly admired by the novel's other characters. Mad Anne dies; Laura marries, unhappily and then happily; Marian acts, is even permitted, in contrast to Anne and Laura, to narrate a section of the novel via her diary entries but in return is denied femininity and sexual fulfillment. The three half-sisters thus represent three irreconcilable possibilities for women. One might view these three partial women as a splitting of female possibilities like that displayed in the three major characters of *Malina*, the "I" representing female disruption and madness; the "I" in relationship to Ivan, a male-centered love; and the "I" in relationship to her doppelgänger Malina, ungendered, rational competence.

Affinities between Collins's major positive male figure and Martin, Franza's brother in *The Book of Franza*, are even more apparent. Though he is no blood kin to the sisters, the three disguise themselves for a time as siblings to escape villainous detection, and, until the time that his love for Laura is permitted to reveal itself, he describes his relationship to the sisters as brotherly. His name, Walter Hartright, tells all: like Martin, he is the *good* brother, nursing the deranged woman and protecting the weak; like Martin, he tells most of the story and attempts to unravel its mysteries. Yet, like Martin as well, he poses no threat at all to the order of male dominance and patriarchal inheritance: as must have been more apparent to Bachmann than to an English-speaking readership, Walter's function is, benevolently, to *walten*, to administer and control. By the end of the novel, Walter has become the proper husband for the proper Victorian heroine, and the book concludes with the birth of Walter's and Laura's son, another little Walter, proclaimed in the novel's penultimate paragraph as the legitimate masculine successor to *Laura's* properties—"the Heir of Limmeridge" (Collins 584). Like Walter, Martin is given the task of restoring threatened arrangements of male dominance, but Bachmann's treatment of the good brother is more daring and complex. Hinting at an incestuous attachment of the siblings (a relationship borrowed from Musil), Bachmann presents Martin as a figure once Franza's friend and equal but now a man like any other. Yet because Martin is Franza's brother by blood, he cannot marry her to restore the patriarchal order, Bachmann thus showing that a man cannot be both equal and husband to a woman. But if Martin does not succeed in reinserting Franza into patriarchy, he can easily enough forget the disruptions she represented: He "came home," Bachmann tells us, "where he felt at home once again, there in the third district, and went to sleep and never thought this way again" (*Franza* 146, translation modified).

Apart from Sir Perceval's name, Bachmann's most obvious borrowing from *The Woman in White* are the two motifs around which Collins's novel is structured, conflated by Bachmann in *The Book of Franza*. Like Franza, Anne Catherick, the "Woman in White" of the title, is a woman unjustly confined to a private asylum by an evil man, that very Sir Perceval Glyde: "I have been cruelly used and cruelly wronged," says Anne (Collins 22). Like Franza, Anne escapes, attempts to elude her male persecutor, and seeks the assistance of the kindly brother figure; indeed, it is her chance encounter with Walter as she flees which initiates the series of events with which the novel is concerned, just as Franza's escape from the spa in Baden near Vienna into Martin's care introduces *The Book of Franza*. Though Anne appears to be a secondary figure, both her appearance in the title and her function as a double to Laura underline, even at the novel's commencement, the significance there of madness and confinement for the fate of women.

The mysterious meaning of the madwoman in white within the logic of Collins's book is clarified by a second confinement and escape midway in the novel upon which Bachmann also appears to draw for her account of Franza's fate. In sorry financial straits, Sir Perceval realizes he will inherit his wife's estate upon her death; because of her resemblance to Anne, he is able to imprison her in the asylum in Anne's stead and arrange for Anne's death, passed off as Laura's. By the time Marian has accomplished Laura's escape and entrusted her to Walter's care, Laura herself is sorely weakened and deranged by the ordeal: her husband had wished to kill her and had almost succeeded in driving her mad—that is, in imposing Anne's fate upon her. As well, her suffering has now so transformed her that she cannot be visually distinguished from Anne (for, as Walter had commented earlier, "If ever sorrow and suffering set their profaning marks on the youth and beauty of Miss Fairlie's face, then, and only then, Anne Catherick and she would be the twin-sisters of chance resemblance, the living reflexions of one another" [Collins 84]) and has no way of proving who she really is.

Sir Perceval has thus stolen not just Laura's possessions and her sanity but her very identity; as Nina Auerbach has put it, the "plot against Laura's identity is a terrifying reminder of the jeopardy of any Victorian woman's selfhood once she has attained the socially approved but psychically and legally menacing position of wife" (141). This is the second motif Bachmann seems to have drawn from *The Woman in White*: the evil husband who is not satisfied merely to control his wife but, to serve his own purposes, wants entirely to eradicate her. As Franza laments of her own husband, Leopold Jordan: "He took my goods away from me. My laughter, my tenderness, my capacity for joy, my compassion, my ability to help, my animal nature, my shining rays, for he stomped out everything that rose up until it could no longer rise again" (*Franza* 80, translation modified). Though both wives escape, they are permanently marked and unbalanced by their husbands' persecution.

Bachmann's "Ways of Death" gives us every reason to believe that she found such oppression and tyranny, variously exercised, to be the normal state of heterosexual relations under the present order of male dominance: men seek to destroy women, whose existence is evident only through their absence, as Franza herself commented of an Egyptian king's effort to destroy all traces of his female predecessor: "Look, she said, but the pharaoh forgot that though he had eradicated her, she was still there. It can still be read, because nothing is there where in fact something should be" (*Franza* 109). Somewhat remarkably, a very similar opinion of male-female relations is voiced by Marian in Collins's novel: "No man under heaven deserves these sacrifices from us women. Men! They are the enemies of our innocence and our peace—they drag us away from our parents' love and our sisters' friendship—they take us body and soul to themselves, and fasten our helpless lives to theirs as they chain up a dog to his kennel" (Collins 162). Nor do the author's depictions of women's role in the Victorian marriages of his novel obscure the total subservience men demand from wives and to which their wives accede: as his editor remarks, "strict genteel etiquette . . . required absolute submission to the husband as a marital duty of the wife" (Collins 615). As well, Collins perceptively depicts his characters' problems as occasioned not by personal failings but by the social order: not who one is but how society regards one determines one's place in society. Hence, Laura does not doubt her own identity but must have it socially acknowledged in order to resume her rightful place; Sir Perceval finally meets his downfall when the discovery that his father and mother were not married reveals him to be an illegitimate usurper of his father's baronetcy—though he is indeed his father's son. For Collins as for Bachmann, gender relations exist within a context of larger social relations determining their content and the fate of the characters that must operate within their parameters.

But despite his flirtations with far-reaching questions about gender arrangements (present of course in far greater number in his novel than I have been able to detail here), Collins continues to uphold the gender conventions that his story has shown to be deeply problematic: as his commentators have observed, his novel is simultaneously both subversive and conventional (Loesberg 136). He restores the order the novel has drawn into question by unmasking the worst abusers of women there, including both Sir Perceval and his diabolical Italian associate, Count Fosco, as illegitimate holders of social power, suggesting that legitimate holders of male power would not so abuse their prerogatives. And he diffuses the critique of men's power over women by permitting *one* of his three women, Laura, the weakest and most dependent and childlike, to be happy and satisfied in a benevolently paternalistic marriage with Walter, while killing off mad Anne and reducing powerful Marian to the status of maiden aunt. Bachmann's appropriation of *The Woman in White* thus reveals some qualities of her own reading habits. It shows how she is able to read a relatively conventional novel against the grain, extracting from it the truths Collins finally obscures, the costs to women of such wedded bliss, the "ways of death" Collins did not wish to acknowledge.

As well, Bachmann's own reading of Collins gives us readers some suggestions about how we might best read her own work—also against the grain. As in Collins's novel, subjected women do not speak as subjects in Bachmann, and she explained in an interview "that I can only narrate from a male standpoint" (*GuI* 99). The women's voices we hear in her late works are either those of their madness and dreams; those of their identification with an ungendered (i.e., male) subject, as in *Malina*; or those of their "false consciousness," their identification with social roles imposed on women, as in many of the stories of *Three Paths to the Lake*. Bachmann thus requires that her readers remain as aware of the irony of her texts as she was of Collins's, understanding more about them than do either the characters or her male narrator. (It may be that the complexity of the reader response she requires contributed to the initial misunderstanding of her works, prompting, for instance, even one of her early feminist critics to believe that *Three Paths to the Lake* illustrated its women characters' *Verzicht auf den Mann* [renunciation of men] rather than, as we understand now, women's total subjection to men [Summerfield 211–216].) In her appropriation of the themes and structures of *The Woman in White,* Bachmann probes into the most dense and problematic areas of the work, opening up and exploring exactly those themes whose investigation Collins, after titillating his readers with a glimpse into such dangerous reaches, wanted finally to foreclose.

This is nowhere more the case than in the use Bachmann makes of two elements of Collins's novel whose relationship to his main plot remains submerged and murky in the original work. First, Collins complicates the relationship of Laura and the evil Sir Perceval with the presence of his Italian friend Count Fosco, grotesque in appearance but more clever and possessing an even greater degree of male power, so that even Marian is forced to acknowledge, "He looks like a man who could tame anything. If he had married a tigress, instead of a woman, he would have tamed the tigress" (Collins 195). Collins takes great pains to differentiate Fosco's violent Italian habits from more moderate English customs: another Italian tells Walter with respect to Italian politics, "It is not for you to say—you Englishmen, who have conquered your freedom so long ago, that you have conveniently forgotten what blood you shed, and what extremities you proceeded to in the conquering—it is not for *you* to say how far the worst of all exasperations may, or may not, carry the maddened men of an enslaved nation" (Collins 535). And Marian warns Fosco and Sir Perceval, "There are laws in England to protect women from cruelty and outrage" (Collins 267). (Fosco, in rejoinder, asserts that his slavishly obedient English wife is in fact following *English* dictates: "I remember that I was married in England—and I ask, if a woman's marriage obligations, in this country, provide for her private opinion of her husband's principles? No! They charge her unreservedly to love, honour, and obey him. That is exactly what my wife has done. I stand, here, on a supreme moral elevation; and I loftily assert her accurate performance of her conjugal duties. Silence, Calumny! Your sympathy, Wives of England, for Madame Fosco!" [Collins 570].) After Laura and Walter are safely married, Collins appends a subplot to account for Fosco's mysteries: he is a spy for a reactionary Italian regime and finally, toward the novel's end, is assassinated by members of an Italian brotherhood dedicated to Italian liberation. In his memory, his wife pens these words about her murdered husband: "His life was one long assertion of the rights of the aristocracy, and the sacred principles of Order—and he died a martyr to his cause" (Collins 582). But in the context of Collins's novel this subplot appears something of an afterthought, not really motivated by or connected to its main concerns regarding the fate of the Woman in White.

Writing a century later, Bachmann found it easier to show the connections of reactionary politics, male dominance, and female confinement and madness. The husband whose influence Franza cannot escape and who attempts to drive her mad has done his own research on the psychological consequences of internment (including medical experimentation) for former concentration camp inmates, and readers are obviously to connect Jordan's research interests with his "diabolical experiment" (*Franza* 63) to make a case study out of Franza. Franza's brother terms Jordan's treatment of her "fascist," and Franza is prepared to agree: "You say fascism, but that sounds strange, for I've never heard that word used to describe a personal relationship. . . . But that's an interesting idea, for it had to begin somewhere. Why does one only refer to fascism when it has to do with opinions or blatant acts" (*Franza* 75). Bachmann's own perspective—as well as the hundred years of history and theory that separate her and Collins— made it possible for her to grasp and depict the intimate connections between gender relationships and reactionary politics at a micropolitical level. As she explained in her preface to *The Book of Franza*:

> [The virus of crime] cannot have simply disappeared from our world twenty years ago [i.e., in 1945], just because murder is no longer praised, desired, decorated with medals, and promoted. . . . Crimes that require a sharp mind [*Geist*], that tap our minds and less so our senses, those that most deeply affect us—there no blood flows, but rather the slaughter is granted a place within the morals and the customs of a society whose fragile nerves quake in the face of any such beastliness. Yet the crimes did not diminish, but rather they require greater refinement, another level of intelligence, and are themselves dreadful. (*Franza* 3–4)

Whether or not her novel draws in this respect directly on *The Woman in White*, she succeeds in showing in the "Ways of Death" volumes relationships that Collins only dimly perceived: how the order of authoritarian social regimes can also be tied to and rely upon an order of male dominance in the domestic realm deeply destructive to the women who are subject to its dictates.

A second area that remains opaque in Collins' novel but that Bachmann is able to clarify is the major mystery, foregrounded in the novel's title but never satisfactorily resolved, as to why Anne Catherick insists on clothing herself only in white. The explicit reason given for Anne's obsession, a chance remark of Laura's mother to Anne as a child that white became her, has no real bearing on the issues of gender and power with which the novel is most centrally concerned. To Sandra Gilbert and Susan Gubar in *The Madwoman in the Attic*, white attire for women in the Victorian era (worn with frequency by women characters in Victorian novels) has a variety of meanings: bridal virginity, childlike innocence, feminine purity, passivity, vulnerability, submissiveness, the brightness of angels, the coldness of snow, the enigma of colorlessness, the pallor of death (615–621). Certainly all these meanings can be associated with the figure of Anne Catherick and are consistent with her function. But I would submit that in a novel published the year before the American Civil War began, another meaning of

"white" is at least subliminally present in Collins's complex association of problems of gender with color, and it is *this* meaning that Bachmann explores in *The
Book of Franza*. For Bachmann, "white" is a racial designation, and the system
of male power that results in Franza's psychic devastation is also racially specific—as Martin comments, Franza's state reveals to him "the psyche of the
whites, which was obviously more threatened than he could imagine" (*Franza*
54, translation modified). Franza also associates white imperial ambitions with
the attempt of white men to destroy *her*, fearing their power even as she seeks
to escape them in Africa: "But the alibi of the whites is strong. Don't forget
that. They tried everything to eliminate you, to blow you to bits on their mine-
field of intelligence, which they misuse in order to make you serve their plans
and schemes" (*Franza* 112). Raped by a white man at the Great Pyramid, Franza
curses both whites and her husband with her dying breath: "The whites should.
They should be damned. He should" (*Franza* 141–142). In this case as well,
Bachmann is able in her appropriation of the themes of *The Woman in White* to
tease out further meanings that remained implicit (if not altogether repressed)
there, showing that the domination and subordination based on gender which
both novels depict is culture-specific, connected in profound ways to white
supremacy, a system of domination and subordination based on color.

So why did Bachmann name Franza's romantic captain Sir Perceval Glyde?
I suggest that in giving an apparently positive figure a name belonging to so
negative an archvillain, Bachmann is telling *us* how to read this episode of her
novel—once more, against the grain. In Franza's memory, the liberation of her
village by the English and her own first love take on both idyllic and utopian
dimensions, and we readers (as Bachmann must have recognized) are inclined
to read her account in this manner as well, as "a promise of peace that was
betrayed." But Franza's own needs, desires, and expectations, even at fifteen,
have already been shaped, formed, and deformed by her own male-dominant
culture, socially constructed by a system of gender relations that requires women
willingly to yield themselves to male control, even gladly to embrace male violence. Bachmann hints in this direction when she tells us that Franza (like the
"I" of *Malina*) longs to be raped by victorious soldiers: "And 'rape,' that was
another word that caused Franza to imagine things capable of taking away the
spring, and, since there was no one she could speak to, rape and armies turned
into longed-for heroes and troops who were on the march, which was for the
good, since nothing ever happened in Galicien [her native village], only the village dying out and the place belonging to her alone as she waited for a miracle
and for something miraculous to occur" (*Franza* 38). In Franza's eyes, the mira-

cle occurs, embodied in that harbinger of peace and love, Sir Perceval Glyde. But we who are able to disencode Bachmann's text know that this is a false promise of peace, as ideologically suspect as the happy endings and wedded bliss of Victorian novels. In the world of the "ways of death" that Bachmann depicts, there is no peace at all, as the "I" of *Malina* learns in her dreams:

> Malina: So you'll never again say: War and Peace.
> Me ["I"]: Never again.
>   It's always war.
>   Here there is always violence
>   Here there is always struggle.
>   It is the eternal war. (*Malina* 155)

Examining Bachmann's appropriation of a novel like Collins's can thus teach us to read her own works with much greater subtlety. Because she believed that no language yet existed which would allow her female protagonists to reveal the true story of their own "ways of death," the story she wishes to tell is almost always different from the surface narrative with which her novels present us. The example of *The Woman in White* alerts readers to watch for signals built into her texts (many not yet explained, many doubtless not yet even discovered) that all is not as it seems. Moreover, Bachmann's own reading of Collins points out that many texts besides her own are not of a single piece, but instead (like the real world from which they derive) made up of contradictory and contending elements from which it is possible to derive both conventional *and* subversive meanings. This is a reading strategy that feminist (and other) literary scholars might do well to adopt, though it has not on the whole characterized our endeavors so far. Showalter's reading of *The Woman in White* attends only to its conventional aspects, an interpretation for which she finds the novel's first sentence paradigmatic: "The first sentence of *The Woman in White* announced Collins' endorsement of Victorian sex-roles: 'This is a story of what a Woman's patience can endure, and what a Man's resolution can achieve'" (*Literature* 162). But of course even Collins's first sentence in *The Woman in White* is much more ambiguous than Showalter allows: read in another way, it could as easily describe Laura's submission to the tyrannical Sir Perceval—or, for that matter, Leopold Jordan's determination to destroy his wife and Franza's willingness to yield to his power. Ahead of her critics, as she so often was, Bachmann has shown us how to recognize such ambiguities, to read both her own works and those of others so that they yield more of the multiplicities of meanings they contain.

READING BACHMANN IN 1987

This essay was written in summer 1987 and published in the spring 1988 issue of *German Quarterly*. Clearly, since writing the Wittgenstein essay two years before, I had found my way back to feminism, and this essay bears the marks of the methodological transition in which feminist literary scholarship, and literary analysis in general, was then engaged. Within my own experience, that transition did not occur without struggle. At the time I believed (of course) that I was on the "right" side of the contestation, though the position I assumed then now seems methodologically quite naive. At mid-decade, the response of some U.S. academic feminists (including me) to the dire political circumstances into which Reaganism had thrust women (and the world altogether) took the form of a repudiation of forms of high theory that seemed to have no application to practice: *they* looked at systems of signification, but *we* focused on "real women." In her essay "Zwischenbilanz der feministischen Debatten [Interim assessment of the feminist debates]" in Frank Trommler's *Germanistik in den USA*, Biddy Martin captured this moment within the organization Women in German (WIG): "Many articles in the *[Women in German] Newsletter* of 1986–87 construct a division between West German and American feminist Germanists that reproduces . . . the opposition between political engagement, democratic process, and empirical reality on the one hand and theory, textuality, and fashionable trends on the other. This perspective threatened to obscure the specificity of the work of West German and American feminists by judging them solely on the basis of whether they were compatible with 'our' work or merely derive from the French" (170). As Martin goes on to observe, that divide never really existed even within WIG, whose members were in fact located on both sides of the debate, yet for a time the consequence for the organization was denunciations, hurt feelings, and tears on both sides.

Within the Five College academic feminist community, too, the dispute was very apparent, crystallizing in a struggle over the meaning of "difference" like the one June Howard described, as we attempted to organize a series of five symposia on women and difference in connection with a faculty development project. In the last of the symposia, held in October 1987, "my" group took as its focus "Feminism and Activism: The Last Twenty-five Years"; the "theorists" invited Gayatri Spivak to hold a series of seminars for local academic feminists. This is Ann Rosalind Jones's account of a meeting preparing for Spivak's visit:

> Another incident, in 1986, brought the conflict to a head for me. Several organizers of the Five College seminar on women in the Third World decided to begin by reading Gayatri Spivak's dense commentary on the short story "Draupadi" by a Bengali writer, Mahasetv Devi; at the last minute, we threw in an article by Mark

Cousins purporting to explain deconstruction. The meeting was a catastrophe. Women from various fields, some of them activists in their fifties, others new arrivals in the area, objected violently to the opacity of all three texts. . . . One women, an African-American literary critic, said, "I don't mind difficult reading, but isn't this approach finally just a way of focusing on the oppressor all over again?" Others asked, less temperately, how any of this theory was relevant to cli-toridectomy in Ethiopia or the blindness of women working on assembly lines in "free" trade zones in the Philippines. Finally a woman who'd been a member of the previous study group [a feminist study group of the late 1970s in which Jones and I had both participated] stood up, declared, "Deconstruction is an empty yup-pie theory; we need to read Fanon, not Derrida," and left the room. (75)

I recall the event somewhat differently, and I hope I wasn't the seminar par-ticipant whom Jones remembers stomping out of the room, but I fear I might have been.

In October 1986 I elaborated my negative assessment of the state of contem-porary feminism in a paper called "'Is That All?' Whatever Happened to the Women's Liberation Movement? Reflections on the Course of American Femi-nism," repeating my talk at the 1987 MLA (and making many feminists mad at me, except for some old-time lefties: I was honored and pleased that Tillie Olsen came up after my talk to tell me how much she liked it). Like the *Nation*, though (which perhaps had influenced me), I ended by asserting that "even in these dark times we have already won some victories: in coalition we beat back Bork, over half a million gays and lesbians marched on Washington, and in this presi-dential campaign the Rainbow Coalition offers the real possibility of building a broad-based movement. . . . At the risk of sounding voluntarist, I just have a feeling, the times might be a'changin—but at least in part, whether they change or not is up to us" ("Is That All?" 301). Certainly in that paper my tempered optimism about feminism pertained to practice, not theory. Otherwise I was a participant in many of the activist struggles of the mid-1980s, most of which were not especially feminist in emphasis: I attended the major demonstrations in Washington, DC; did support work for my students who had occupied cam-pus buildings to support divestment from South Africa and oppose CIA recruit-ing; again chaired the Five College Faculty and Staff Committee for Jesse Jack-son as the 1988 Presidential campaign approached. In spring 1988 the program I direct celebrated its fifteenth anniversary with a faculty panel addressing a packed hall on the topic "The Opening of the American Mind," taking on the premises of Allan Bloom's book; I don't think Accuracy in Academe ever spied on my classes (despite its presence elsewhere on the University of Massachusetts campus), though my program was attacked by the National Association of Scholars in the early 1990s.

Quite by chance, however, during the mid-1980s I was also a member of a study group dealing with new scholarly developments in anthropology. It was in that context that I first discovered Stuart Hall's "Cultural Studies: Two Paradigms," and my response was not unlike that of Christa Wolf when she found feminism: a "decisive change" in my "viewing lens" comparable only to my discovery of Marxism. I could almost feel the scales falling from my eyes: this was the method I had been looking for; this method would allow me to connect politics and literature again and could clearly be adapted to include gender, thus overcoming the impasse at which I felt feminism had arrived; since literature and its reception were forces that helped to consolidate or subvert all social constructions, literary analysis could, from a quite different perspective from that of the early 1980s, be once again conceived of as a political intervention.

I had heard at the MLA early versions of the essays assembled in the Newton and Rosenfelt collection and found them still too indebted to the base-superstructure model of old-time Marxist feminism. But the new historical methods of cultural studies and other approaches related to it, like new historicism and cultural materialism, now provided far more sophisticated ways to think about the relationship of "the textuality of history and the historicity of texts," to cite Montrose's chiasmus once more ("Professing" 20). I thus set out to learn all I could about the new methodologies and to integrate them into my own feminist analysis by employing a favorite academic learning technique: teaching courses and giving papers on topics I didn't know very much about. In fall 1987 I offered a graduate seminar on the intersection of feminist literary theory and feminist history which was enormously instructive to me and, I think, to my students; in June 1987 I gave a talk, "Anthropology and the Politics of Deconstruction," at the National Women's Studies Association conference (held at Spelman College in Atlanta as a gesture toward white feminism's effort to integrate race into its theory and practice); in October 1987 I talked at the German Studies Association conference on what I had learned so far from my graduate seminar in a paper called "Reading Gender Historically: The Encounter of Feminist Literary Theory and Women's History" (a presentation that would eventually become the article "Feminist Scholarship and Germanistik," published in the first German Studies issue of *German Quarterly* in spring 1989); in March 1988 I gave a related paper, "Reading Women's Biographies and Autobiographies: Feminist History and Feminist Literary Theory," at the National Association of Ethnic Studies. At the same time I was working on an essay, "History in Uwe Johnson's *Jahrestage*" (begun in summer 1984, published in *Germanic Review* in winter 1989), which constituted a settling of accounts with the author on whom I had written my dissertation. That essay, however, did not really manifest the new method but is probably the most old-style Marxist study I have ever written, and it occasioned (rather to my delight) some outrage among Johnson scholars and beyond. Eventually, in 1990, I presented a not very good paper on new historicism at a conference at Brown University and, in 1991, a much better one at Madison on feminism and new historicism which was published in *Monatshefte* in summer 1992—and by then I felt that I was capable of applying the new methods myself.

"Bachmann Reading/Reading Bachmann" was written as a very direct consequence of that learning process. To prepare for my graduate course in fall 1987 and to understand how new historical methods could be applied to literary texts, I set about to read the back issues of *Representations*, a Berkeley journal associated with new historicism. In an article by D. A. Miller on Wilkie Collins's *The Woman in White* I was startled to discover a name, Sir Perceval Glyde, that up to then I had associated only with *The Book of Franza*. I tracked down Wilkie Collins's novel, devoured it with the relish that always accompanies my late-night forays into popular fiction (it was the summer, after all), never intending to treat that Victorian novel—not exactly within my area of expertise—in a scholarly study. But as I finished the book, so many new insights into Bachmann's text and so many new ideas about how to treat it were whirling in my head that I could not resist.

This essay is, I think, quite different in method from the first four articles in this archive of historical readings of Bachmann and displays a number of features of the new approaches I was trying to appropriate. First, it focuses on representation, understanding both Collins's and Bachmann's novels as neither (simply) realistic nor mimetic works but as arrangements of structures and figures used to achieve particular literary ends. As well, it conceives signification to be a product of intertextuality; thus in this case it considers Bachmann's novel to be a reworking of prior novelistic elements on which she was able and obliged to draw when she wrote her own text. The method's close attention to structures and processes of signification is a consequence of the encounter of a historically based, more or less neo-Marxist approach with the techniques of structuralism/poststructuralism, and to the best of my knowledge no equivalent exists in earlier forms of Marxist analysis, despite the often very impressive examples of close reading they can offer. In effect, this aspect of the method is an expansion upon Marx's observation in the *Eighteenth Brumaire*: "[People] make history, but they do not make it just as they please; they do not make it under circumstances chosen by themselves, but under circumstances directly found, given and transmitted from the past" (Tucker 595). Here I present Bachmann as possessing sufficient authorial agency to configure new meanings, but she is also constrained to construct those meanings out of the older textual building blocks available to her.

What this approach further enables is a recognition of any text as polysemic, embodying a whole range of meanings, thus authorizing a wide range of readings (including those "against the grain") that will depend on the particular political, historical, and social stance of the reader. (That, evidently, is the insight this whole book seeks to apply to readings of Bachmann's texts.) In addition, as a consequence both of language's inherent polysemic qualities and of the fact that a literary text is necessarily constructed out of the often not commensurable discourses of the larger society, this method conceives texts to be sites where sometimes contradictory discourses intersect. The texts themselves are thus no longer seen as the somewhat mystical organic unities that romantics and New Critics believed they discerned but are able to be read as structures of patched-together contradictions whose incompatibilities authors try to reconcile. (This particular method of reading texts derives, I believe, from Pierre Macherey's *Theory of Literary Production*, where he maintains, for instance: "The order which [the work] professes is merely an imagined order, projected onto disorder, the fictive resolution of ideological conflicts, a resolution so precarious that it is obvious in the very letter of the text where incoherence and incompleteness burst forth" [155].)

Finally, the method I have employed here conceives of literary texts as doing ideological work and, in the case of *The Woman in White*, arousing the reader's interest by opening up major ideological fissures of the society and then relieving the anxiety produced by restoring social order at the end. This is almost certainly an idea I derived from Stephen Greenblatt (who in turn borrowed it from Foucault), which finds its best expression in Greenblatt's rather gloomy notion of "containment," a function particularly of Shakespearean and other Renaissance texts: though the literary text may seem to draw into question, even subvert, dominant ordering paradigms in the course of its development, by the end of the work all is safely under control again, with an apparently natural order once more sweetly restored (see, e.g., Greenblatt's *Shakespearean Negotiations*). I am very pleased that Bachmann's text offers me a reading strategy that allows me to see—even more clearly than some professional Victorianists—how *The Woman in White* not only interrogates but finally forecloses one of the major ideological issues of Victorian society. For my own examination of Bachmann, this study also represented a kind of breakthrough, confirming my growing suspicions that Bachmann intended all portions of her "Ways of Death" to be read ironically, as the packaging of a range of social problems into narratives so conventional that the figures who inhabit them could have no clue how their problems could be addressed or sometimes even that those problems existed at all.

On the other hand, I don't think it's possible to call the approach of this essay either materialist or historical. To be sure, like Collins's other feminist critics, I read *The Woman in White* in the context of Victorian gender conventions and sexual mores. I also gesture in the direction of history when I maintain that Bachmann could address this complex of concerns more satisfactorily because, writing a hundred years later, she could more clearly see "the connections of reactionary politics, male dominance, and female confinement and madness." But otherwise there's not really anything historical about this reading at all, and I make use of the common convention within literary scholarship of using the author as apparent agent ("Bachmann's reading is more subtle"; "Bachmann requires"; "Bachmann probes") when I am of course merely talking about *my* reading. Except for the irrefutable presence of Sir Perceval Glyde's name in the text, I have absolutely no historical evidence that would speak to when, how, and why Bachmann turned to this text, and I particularly can't substantiate my assertion that Bachmann deliberately transformed the "white" of Collins's title into a racial designation. Of course, it is not necessary that readings conform to the dictates of particular methods, historical or otherwise; they need only reveal something of interest about the text. In that respect I am quite fond of and pleased with what I still consider to be an ingenious and elegant little essay. In the larger context of my own appropriation of a new historically based methodology, however, in 1987 I still had some distance to go.

In contrast, chapters 8, 9, and 10 of this book's part 3, "Reading Bachmann Historically," illustrate my current appropriation of the historically based approach for which June Howard called in 1987. Though in quite different ways, the three final chapters understand Bachmann's texts as complex responses to the historical situation that obtained when they were written. Gender is a central term in each chapter's analysis, but it is understood as a historically specific category modulated by other equally important social categories and always under pressure from a range of discursive and nondiscursive social forces. Though all three chapters acknowledge Bachmann's agency as a writer and regard her texts as interventions into particular historical situations, I also consider her texts to be patched together out of the (frequently contradictory) discursive materials available to her when she wrote; they are thus often unable to transcend the limitations of her time. My ability to discern Bachmann's historical blindnesses is mainly a consequence only of my changed historical positionality. As I try to clarify in each chapter's introduction, my readings are also historically specific, enabled by the new methods elaborated by feminist and other cultural studies scholars since 1990. As well, each of these chapters explores Linda Alcoff's assertion that "positionality" can designate not just a location "objectively" given but also a perspective "subjectively" chosen. By stressing quite different aspects of Bachmann's writing in the final three chapters, I want once more to emphasize that differently situated scholars asking differing questions about texts or topics will produce different kinds of answers that are not to be considered right or wrong, but simply—different.

PART III
Reading Bachmann Historically

CHAPTER 8

Bachmann and Theories of Gender / Sexuality

FEMININITY IN "THE GOOD GOD OF MANHATTAN"

It would be best if women and men kept their distance
and had nothing to do with each other until
both had found their way out of the tangle and confusion,
the discrepancy inherent in all relationships.

—Ingeborg Bachmann, Three Paths to the Lake

*T*his chapter draws on recent advances in U.S. feminist theory to argue for a new kind of reading of Ingeborg Bachmann's texts. Almost all U.S. feminist scholars now agree that femininity and masculinity are social constructions that vary enormously across time and culture, and many recent scholars have focused their investigations on how definitions of femininity and masculinity are generated, sustained, and transformed within particular societies. Feminist literary scholars have shown that literary texts contribute to the production of gender as a discursive category by sustaining, modulating, and/or challenging their culture's discourses of gender. As those scholars have demonstrated, literary and other texts can also function as the sites of contests about definitions of gender (and of many other things), revealing social tensions and fissures because they are always pieced together out of the heterogeneous discursive materials of the societies in which they originate. The reception of a literary text, feminist scholars argue, can be another locus of struggle around representations of femininity and masculinity, as readers with divergent interests emphasize different aspects of the conflicting discourses present in the text. I attempt to apply to Bachmann's writing these new methods elaborated by Anglo-American feminist scholars in order to show how her texts derive from the discursive constructions of a particular historical period. I argue that her work represents femininity in contradictory ways because it draws upon contending notions of gender which Bachmann was unable to reconcile. Her earlier feminist critics, I finally maintain, produced readings of her works that corresponded to the particular concerns of *their* era. My own reading, stressing different elements of her writing, is an effort to produce another interpretation of her texts more in accord with the feminist needs of the present.

Specifically, I want here to investigate one of Bachmann's early works, her radio play "The Good God of Manhattan," written in 1957 and first broadcast in 1958. I argue that the radio play employs two quite different, even contradictory, conceptions of the relationship of power, sexuality, and gender. Most obviously, Bachmann relies upon a notion of the relationship of civilization and Eros/femininity derived from the 1950s, one that recalls the writing of Herbert Marcuse: sexuality (particularly in alluring female form) is a force so threatening to the social order that civilization must repress sexuality in order to protect itself. The antagonists of Bachmann's radio play are the Good God of Manhattan, figured as a single omnipotent principle of social domination, and Jan and Jennifer, passionate lovers whose erotic transport threatens the stability of the God's regime. When Jan, the male partner, reaffirms his allegiance to the God's quotidian order, it is the woman, Jennifer alone, who becomes the embodiment of a subversive sexuality antithetical to civilization and is murdered by the God.

Though this discourse of sexuality continued to inform Bachmann's writing until her death and also shaped her feminist reception in the 1970s and 1980s, it rests on assumptions that many contemporary U.S. feminist scholars today, influenced by the more recent writing of Michel Foucault on power and sexuality, now consider untenable. As I show here, however, within "The Good God of Manhattan" a second and somewhat submerged discourse coexists uneasily with the first, representing femininity and sexuality as products of the power that calls them into being: Jennifer is portrayed as a woman driven to the heights of ecstasy because Jan's masculinist power allows her to adore a man who torments and debases her. Viewed from this perspective, "The Good God of Manhattan" can also be read as a text that probes the social construction of femininity. That strategy of representation, much more in accord with current U.S. feminist thinking about sexuality and gender, would continue to inform Bachmann's subsequent work, finally providing the central premise on which the "Ways of Death" was founded. "The Good God of Manhattan" can thus be viewed as a text where conflicting discourses of gender and sexuality contend. Though a reading of this radio play emphasizing that first, Marcusean discourse may consolidate and stabilize a certain regime of sexuality or of gender by positing that sexuality or femininity is "naturally" subversive, another reading stressing the second discourse, I want finally to argue, can unsettle those oppositions again.

What connects Bachmann most centrally to Marcuse's thought, particularly

as he elaborated it in *Eros and Civilization* (1955), is their common assumption
of the fundamental opposition of power and erotic passion. Both Bachmann
and Marcuse conceive of power as taking the form of what Marcuse calls domination, the product of a single, all-encompassing system of social control,
imposed from without on individuals against their own desires and interests by
means of what Marcuse calls repression, a term he used, as he explains in *Eros
and Civilization* (8), "in the non-technical sense to designate both conscious and
unconscious, external and internal processes of restraint, constraint, and suppression." Conversely, both Marcuse and Bachmann conceptualize Eros as a
force anterior and exterior to domination, preserving a memory of and longing
for gratification that can become the germ of rebellion against domination—a
"Great Refusal," Marcuse called it, that is "the protest against unnecessary
repression, the struggle for the ultimate form of freedom" (*Eros* 149). To Marcuse, women incarnate the promise of liberation from repression, since the
(repressed) memory of the bliss of original union with the mother is preserved
in every human psyche. For that reason Marcuse joins a long line of masculinist thinkers in construing women as a potential threat to the present repressive
social order: "The beauty of the woman and the happiness she promises are
fatal in the work-world of civilization" (*Eros* 161).

In the first volume of his *History of Sexuality* (1978), Michel Foucault pointed
out that such notions of power, sexuality, and the sexualized female body are
historically specific ones, arising in Europe in the early modern period and prevailing into the time in which he himself wrote. He called the premise on which
Marcuse's and Bachmann's ideas about domination and eroticism rest the
"repressive hypothesis": society's relationship to sexuality is conceived (as Marcuse had maintained) to be one of repression, sex taken to be a powerful instinctual drive originating outside the social order that society must regulate and
control. Indeed, for proponents of the repressive hypothesis, sexuality seems so
hostile to society that even speaking about it (as Bachmann's play does) can seem
to be subversive: "If sex is repressed, that is, condemned to prohibition, nonexis-
tence, and silence," Foucault explains, "then the mere fact that one is speaking
about it has the appearance of a deliberate transgression. A person who holds
forth in such language places himself to a certain extent outside the reach of
power; he upsets established law, he somehow anticipates the coming freedom"
(*History* 6). Though the repressive hypothesis and ideas about power, sexuality,
and gender connected to it have still not been entirely banished from contemporary social analysis, many current cultural theorists—in good part thanks to
Foucault's influence—now reject the idea that anything at all (sexuality, femi-

ninity, various marginal groups) occupies an innocent and uncontaminated site external to the operations of power whence a fundamental challenge to power could be launched. To many theorists, feminist and otherwise, appeals such as Marcuse's and Bachmann's to sexuality's liberatory potential now seem to be painfully outmoded relics of an older time, "a blissful vision," as Domna Stanton put it in a survey of more recent scholarship on sexuality, "that seems decidedly dated at this postmodern twilight of the century" (41).

For what reasons would Bachmann have turned to a theory like Marcuse's that conceives of power as a single monolithic system and imagines that resistance can survive only in reaches to which power has no access? Though Foucault has argued that a conception of power as "a general system of domination exerted by one group over another . . . whose effects pervade the general social body" (*History* 92) has prevailed in the West since the Renaissance, that model had particular saliency in the 1950s, the period from which both *Eros and Civilization* and "The Good God of Manhattan" derive. Both texts were written at the height of the Cold War, when the entire world seemed subsumed under the control of two great power blocs, and many major German thinkers of Bachmann's time—among the most prominent, Theodor Adorno, Max Horkheimer, and Hannah Arendt as well as Marcuse—were convinced that all mass industrial societies (bourgeois democracy as well as fascism or Stalinism) tended toward totalitarianism (a bleak vision that was a kind of mirror image of the decade's anticommunism, as Jost Hermand has remarked [66]). The postwar United States was conceived to be a "totally administered society" that secured its hegemony via the inexorable processes of technological rationality and the manipulation of consciousness by advertising and the mass media. Writers across the political spectrum decried mass culture's baneful effects on the freedom and autonomy of individuals: to cite only one example, from 1954 through 1956 Jürgen Habermas and Günther Anders debated "Die Dialektik der Rationalisierung" (the dialectic of rationalization), the "Mißverhältnis von Kultur und Konsum" (the discrepancy of culture and consumption), and "Die Welt als Phantom und Matrize" (the world as phantom and matrix) in a series of articles in *Merkur*—an interchange with which Bachmann must have been familiar, since during that time period she published seven of her poems in the same journal.

Bachmann was also directly familiar with Western efforts to elicit voluntary consent and eliminate dissent by controlling consciousness: from 1951 to 1953 she worked for the U.S. radio station Rot-Weiss-Rot in Vienna, whose explicit purpose was inducing Austrians to embrace the American way of life. (As one internal Rot-Weiss-Rot memorandum put it: "One of the more delicate functions of American personnel in Austria is not to encourage people to say what they feel . . . but rather, as well as we can, to suggest to them the right thing to think" [Wagnleitner "Irony" 287].) Her radio play was written under the impression of her own visit to the United States in summer 1955, where she attended a Harvard International Seminar led by Henry Kissinger and intended to teach "America's deeper values" to "persons between twenty-five and forty who are about to attain positions of leadership in their country" (*Harvard* 2). (See chapter 10 for much more discussion of U.S. activities during the Cold War and Bachmann's response to them.) It is thus quite understandable that Bachmann would figure domination as the omnipotent ruler of the largest city of the major Western superpower—the Good God of Manhattan. Conversely, at a time when, especially from a Central European perspective, any agent of social change that could oppose totalitarian control seemed absent or ineffective and domination seemed to have invaded the psyche itself, Bachmann, like Marcuse, looked for resistance in the one realm she could still imagine as uncontaminated by the social order: eroticism, the most intimate arena of private life. Similarly, in an era when women were strongly encouraged to withdraw from the public arena and define themselves as men's opposites, Bachmann, like Marcuse, could imagine them as the antithesis of the social order that men controlled. Like Marcuse in search of an agent of rebellion against domination in a time of political reaction, Bachmann makes eroticism that vehicle of liberation, and in her play the only force powerful enough to threaten the rule of the Good God is the passion of Jan and Jennifer, her ecstatic lovers.

There is a good deal of evidence for Bachmann's familiarity with Marcuse's thought in general and with *Eros and Civilization* in particular. She cites three works by Marcuse in the bibliography of her dissertation, though she does not discuss them in the text. And Robert Pichl, the administrator of the Bachmann archive, reports that at the time of her death her library contained several books by Marcuse published in the 1960s and 1970s (though not *Eros and Civilization* in English or either of its two German translations [Pichl]). The composer Hans Werner Henze, Bachmann's companion and housemate in the 1950s, reported in a 1988 interview that it was Bachmann who first brought *Eros and Civilization* to his attention (Morris, interview), and though it is not clear when she first read it, one might surmise that she discussed it with Henze sometime before the end of 1958, when their close relationship ended (Hapkemeyer, *Entwicklungslinien* 99). In a 1999 interview Henze added, "Yes, we knew the author of that book. We often talked the whole evening about those things. It was quite wonderful [*ganz schön*]" (Morris, "Leben"). *Eros and Civilization* was published by Boston's

Beacon Press in 1955, the year that Bachmann attended the Harvard summer seminar, and she might well have purchased an American copy. Perhaps Bachmann even met Marcuse during her visit to Boston, since he was teaching at Brandeis University then, and seminar participants were encouraged to pursue social contacts in the Boston community. Bachmann certainly had later Frankfurt School connections: though Sigrid Weigel was unable to verify Kurt Bartsch's claim that Bachmann stayed with Adorno while she prepared her Frankfurt lectures on poetics (Bartsch, *Ingeborg* 18), she documents Bachmann's extensive relationship with Adorno from the time of the Frankfurt lectures onward (Weigel, *Ingeborg* 473). It is probably safe to assume some familiarity with Marcuse's ideas among most left-liberal German-speaking intellectuals of Bachmann's generation (whether they actually read his work or not), since *Eros and Civilization* played a major role in shaping the discourse on sexuality in Germany from the book's publication in 1955 until well into the 1970s. In any case, as Foucault's analysis of the repressive hypothesis suggests, Marcuse was to some degree merely a very talented compiler of some assumptions about power, sexuality, and femininity that were pervasive in the culture from which both Marcuse and Bachmann derived.

Whenever it was that Bachmann first read Marcuse, it is apparent that some of the ideas she encountered in his work were ones at which she herself had already arrived independently. Her conception of love as an ecstatic, extrasocial "other condition" (*W* 1: 317) was influenced by Robert Musil, whose work she had first read in her teens (*GuI* 124) and with whose writing she again concerned herself intensively in the early 1950s. Like Jan and Jennifer in "The Good God of Manhattan," the protagonist of Bachmann's first radio play, "A Business with Dreams" (1952, thus written before the publication of *Eros and Civilization*, and also published in the *Werke*), also escapes from a debased reality into a realm of erotic fantasy and freedom. What is important for my argument here is not whether Marcuse influenced Bachmann (though I think he did) but rather how similarly they construct their discussions of particular problems. Following Foucault, that is what I mean by "discourse," a term I use here to mean not just what is said about a topic such as domination, eroticism, or femininity but, more fundamentally, the largely unspoken rules that establish how, at any particular historical point, the topic can be conceptualized at all. Like a great many of their contemporaries, both Marcuse and Bachmann move within a discourse that rests upon the repressive hypothesis. They conceive of power and sexuality as binary opposites: power (in the form of domination) is a single, monolithic, all-encompassing system of social control that endeavors to subsume all it surveys

and attempts to repress something conceived to be its opposite—sexuality, femininity—which originates in a realm outside of domination's sway.

The repressive hypothesis provides the structuring principles of "The Good
God of Manhattan" and has also been central to many interpretations of Bachmann's radio play. In a polemical 1970 exchange titled "War das Hörspiel der
Fünfziger Jahre reaktionär? Eine Kontroverse am Beispiel von Ingeborg Bachmanns 'Der gute Gott von Manhattan'" (Was the radio play of the 1950s reactionary? A controversy using the example of Ingeborg Bachmann's "The Good
God of Manhattan"), Wolf Wondratschek and Jürgen Becker (themselves both
obviously influenced by the New Left rhetoric that was endemic to German cultural criticism of that period) offered what might be regarded as a paradigmatically Marcusean reading of Bachmann's play. Both take for granted that the
Good God embodies domination and that the lovers are his antagonists; what
they debate is whether the play adequately explores why liberation is impossible
in the world the play portrays. Wondratschek considers Bachmann's radio play
both reactionary and typical of its genre in the 1950s because it remains in the
realm of dream and "leaves reality absolutely undamaged" (*läßt allemal die
Realität unbeschädigt*, a phrase he borrows from Adorno). He faults Bachmann
for failing to illuminate the objective conditions that were the real impediments
to her doomed lovers' happiness and charges her with addressing instead only the
private realm of the emotions: "The author focuses completely on the no-man's
land of pure emotionality, though, to be sure, on its destruction, without investigating existing forms of opposition to emotionality, which would clarify that that
destruction is 'of this world,' as, after all, the reference to Manhattan in the title
would seem to suggest" (190). But Becker comes to Bachmann's defense. He sees
in the figure of the Good God of Manhattan "the concretization of a very real
and thoroughly social principle" (193) and understands that the play is not just
about love but about liberation. It is because the radio play's lovers anticipate an
anarchic freedom from social constraints which the bourgeois order cannot tolerate, Becker argues, that the Good God must take action against them: "It's not
that love is destroyed, as Wondratschek puts it in his naive and bourgeois way, but
rather that the interests of society, which is only willing to allow for happiness as
a conventional existence in house slippers, prevail over the hopes, over the desires
of individuals, who on behalf of everyone want not only to have achieved but also
to practice a new consciousness of love and freedom." Revealing the present social
order's profound hostility to the satisfaction of subjective needs, Bachmann's radio
play in Becker's view thus accomplishes the political task most appropriate to literary works by drawing the legitimacy of that order into question "via the

destruction of the complicities that the present order of things produces in order to justify itself" (194).

As Wondratschek correctly perceives, Bachmann signals to her listeners that she is addressing contemporary concerns by making her God the ruler of Manhattan and by setting her play in a New York courtroom sometime in the 1950s. "Manhattan" is a synecdochal representation of industrialized society in the West, "that city," as Kurt Bartsch has put it, "that embodied the highest standard of Western civilization and the essence of progress for the bourgeois capitalist society of the 1950s" (*Ingeborg* 85). It's possible as well that the "Manhattan" of the title, especially when coupled with a bomb-throwing deity, recalls the Manhattan Project, which constructed the first atomic bomb, a technological advance representing the highest pinnacle of "progress" that the Western civilization of the 1950s had achieved. Moreover, Bachmann's lovers arrive in Manhattan by train, a figure in European literature for Western progress ("the engine of history") since the invention of the railroad.

Despite Wondratschek's complaints about Bachmann's lack of interest in social reality, by using anonymous voices to serve as the play's chorus, her play thematizes the invasion of the public sphere by impersonal forces over which individuals have no control. As several commentators have pointed out, the voices evoke mass culture, endlessly repeating banal but vaguely ominous catchwords: "GO AT THE GREEN LIGHT PROCEED / REMEMBER AS LONG AS THERE IS TIME / YOU CAN'T TAKE IT WITH YOU" ("GG" 9). Whether they are "an expression for the depersonalized rushing past one another and for the lack of human communication in the metropolis," as Hilde Haider-Pregler argues (68), or, more likely, advertising slogans (as in Bachmann's poem "Reklame" [Advertisement, *Storm* 109]), they document American mass culture's pervasive effects on daily life. As Andreas Hapkemeyer remarks (in rather highfalutin language) of "Advertisement": "Ingeborg Bachmann represents poetically what the philosopher and sociologist Herbert Marcuse, who lived in America for a long time, termed the magical, authoritarian, ritual elements of the media and advertising, which tend in the direction of preventing humans from pondering their most primordial questions, overlaying them with sham questions and answers" (*Entwicklungslinien* 85). When Jan, who has vowed to remain with Jennifer forever, drops into a bar on his way back from cashing-in his return ticket to Europe, the voices, emanating from the bar's radio or television (and there identified explicitly as advertisements) demonstrate their efficacy as a mechanism of social control by successfully enticing him to reinvolve himself in the quotidian concerns of normal life.

But apart from setting her play in a city that represents Western civilization's furthest advance, Bachmann is otherwise not much interested in using it to explore the economic and political structures that sustain domination, as Wondratschek correctly observes. In "Die Wahrheit ist dem Menschen zumutbar" (Man can face the truth), the speech with which she accepted the "Hörspielpreis der Kriegsblinden" (Radio play prize of those blinded in wars) for this play, she explained that she wanted her writing to reveal the pain that is not so easily perceived: "That's what art should bring about, that in this sense our eyes are opened" (W 1: 275). As she told an interviewer, she had intended that her radio play explore not "exterior" problems but what lay behind them: "In the great love dramas like, for instance, *Romeo and Juliet* or *Tristan and Isolde*, the destruction of the lovers is a consequence of external difficulties. I wanted to get rid of these external difficulties and show that something else stands behind them, a power that I have personified in the Good God" (*GuI* 56). In her Frankfurt lectures on poetics, she explained that in this century the subject [*das Ich*] stands in a different relationship than it had in earlier times to the historical conditions that produce it: "The first change that the subject experienced is that it no longer inhabits history but rather that recently history inhabits the subject" (W 4: 230). Exploring the consequences of the present form of social organization for subjectivity, her writing was concerned with problems internal to the psyche; she explained in one of the prefaces to *The Book of Franza* that "the real settings" were "the interior ones, laboriously concealed over by the external" (*Franza* 4). This radio play thus addresses, as Hans Höller has pointed out, "interior events transposed to the outside," "the objectification of love on the inner stage of the radio play" ("Szenen" 18). This is where Marcuse's texts became useful for Bachmann: combining a social and a psychological analysis, his theory provided her with a discursive framework that allowed her to show how a historically specific social form might shape and deform subjectivity and what prospects might exist for eluding its grasp.

Bachmann thus configures her Good God to correspond to the discourse of power on which Marcuse also drew. At the outset of the play, the old man ushered into a New York courtroom on a hot August day in the 1950s appears to be a gangster or vagrant off the New York streets, on trial for committing what appear to be both senseless and brutal crimes: throwing bombs at a series of lovers and most recently ordering the execution of a young American student named Jennifer, the victim of a bomb delivered to her hotel room by the God's evil henchmen, the squirrels of Manhattan. But as the interrogation proceeds, the old man—whom the judge acknowledges to be "the Good God of Manhattan.

Others say the Good God of the Squirrels" ("GG" 57)— increasingly converses as an equal with the elderly judge.

By the play's end, the judge and the God agree that they are merely different incarnations of the same governing principle:

> JUDGE: There aren't two judges here—just as there are not two orders.
>
> GOOD GOD: Then you must be in league with me, and I just don't know it yet. Perhaps you didn't intend to put me out of action but wanted to articulate something that is better left unsaid. Then the two keepers of order would be one and the same. ("GG" 91)

The God declares that he has committed violence against love to preserve the social order: "I did it so there would be peace and security, and so you could sit here quietly and observe your fingertips. So the way of all things remains the way we like it" ("GG" 90–91). Though the judge upholds the charge against the God—that is, acknowledges that he has committed the crime—no sentence is passed, and the judge allows the God to leave by the side exit, thereby implicitly conceding that the God's attacks on lovers were necessary to defend the single system which, two incarnations of the same principle, they both represent. The representation of power in this play thus conforms to the morphology of power on which the repressive hypothesis depends. It is single, unitary, and total—"there are not two orders." Explored via a courtroom trial, it is shown to take the rule of law (what Foucault called "juridico-discursive" [*History* 83]). It is a coherent system that stands in a negative relationship to those subject to it: it limits their freedom, demands their obedience to its general precepts, imposes prohibitions and sanctions and censorship, and punishes transgressions. "Justice prevailed," says the God ("GG" 80). Finally, figured as two male authority figures advanced in age in whom authority is embodied, power takes a shape that Foucault has termed monarchical: "At bottom, despite the differences in epochs and objectives, the representation of power has remained under the spell of monarchy. In political thought and analysis, we still have not cut off the head of the king" (*History* 88–89).

The God thus might be regarded as something like Marcuse's repressive performance principle—his especially repressive incarnation of Freud's reality principle—which seeks to subdue Eros because it represents the "free gratification of man's [*sic*] instinctual needs," which is "incompatible with civilization" as presently organized (*Eros* 3). Toward the end of the play the God clarifies that love is the primary antagonist of his order in what he terms his "confession of faith":

I believe in an order of things for everyone for every day that we live.
I believe in a great tradition and its great power, where all feelings and thoughts
have a place, and I believe in death to its adversaries. I believe that love is on the
dark side of the world, more destructive than any crime, than any heresy. I believe
that, where it surfaces, a vortex forms like before the first day of Creation. I believe
that love is innocent and leads to ruin, that you can only go on by accepting guilt
and by operating through prescribed channels. ("GG" 90)

To ensure that the toil necessary to support civilization continues to be per-
formed, the performance principle must modify and channel humans' original desire for immediate pleasure: thus the God, mostly concerned with the
regulation of subjectivity, demands that thoughts and feelings accommodate
themselves to prevailing social arrangements—the "fixed order," the "system of
institutions, laws, agencies, things and customs" that are the "social content" of
psychological processes (Marcuse, *Eros* 197). The God has no dispute with those
who confine their sexuality to arrangements that serve the purposes of social
reproduction: "But who cares about people who leave the straight and narrow
for that freedom only to show instinct later. People who tamed that small, initial
fire, who took it into their hands and built it into a cure for loneliness, a partnership, an economic interest group? A more acceptable status within society
is thus created. Everything in balance and in order" ("GG" 90). (In Marcuse's
words: "The sex instincts bear the brunt of the reality principle. Their organization culminates in the subjection of the partial sex instincts to the primacy
of genitality, and in their subjugation under the function of procreation" [*Eros*
40].) But Love-as-Eros is a threat because it represents a form of psychic excess
that always threatens to burst the bounds that the performance principle sets it,
retaining a now-tabooed recollection of freedom and happiness against which
the limited satisfactions of the present repressive order could be measured.

As the God's confession of faith shows, love in this play is conceived of as an
innate instinctual force prior to the law, "before the first day of Creation" on
which the God brought his order into being, and for precisely that reason,
because its innocent origins lie outside the law, the God considers love more
dangerous than crimes or heresies that acknowledge the law while breaking it.
The very incarnation of the principle of domination as a god, together with the
religious language the God uses—"profession of faith," "I believe," "first day of
Creation"—as well as the "hell" to which the squirrels earlier in the play consigned various other pairs of lovers, bestows metaphysical authority upon the
God's order and suggests the dire consequences of rebellion against it. Because
chaos and disorder disrupt and subvert the order, the God declares that guilt—

psychic violence turned inward— is necessary to tame the destructive force of love so that his order can survive. If this play is understood as an exteriorized account of events internal to the psyche, the God can be viewed as a figure for domination internalized within the psyche, repressing the sexual instincts by inflicting guilt in the manner that Marcuse described: "The restrictions imposed upon the libido . . . operate on the individual as external objective laws and as an internalized force: the societal authority is absorbed into the 'conscience' and into the unconscious of the individual and works as his own desire, morality, and fulfillment" (*Eros* 46). The Good God would thus become the embodiment of the "great Super Ego, exercising itself only in a negative way," the terms in which Foucault (*Power* 59) described Marcuse's concept of repression.

Bachmann's play constructs a complex series of images that elaborate upon the binary opposition on which the repressive hypothesis depends, counterposing the God's single repressive principle of order to the lovers' anarchic eroticism. Thus the God is associated with legality, territoriality, order, convention, and constraint, while the lovers are portrayed as exceeding the limits he sets. The God's utilitarian and pragmatic principles rule the day, but love is "on the dark side of the world" ("GG" 90) or even constitutes a different temporality altogether: "Anti-time is now beginning" ("GG" 89). Often the lovers explicitly transgress the laws, regulations, or customs for which the God stands: they challenge the "rules of the game" ("GG" 69), "violated its every use" ("GG" 71), and threaten the "law of the world" ("GG" 85). Or the God's realm is portrayed as a territory with particular demarcations whose borders the lovers transgress: they engage in "crossing a boundary" ("GG" 89), break through "the crust of the earth" ("GG" 69), dissolve "the natural bounds" (90), and become a rebellious military force that fights for freedom: "Freedom. A mischief maker that takes possession of the legions of lovers and defends them blindly" ("GG" 78). Or they are even imagined to be rare radioactive elements that contaminate the earth: "They are like those rare elements found here and there, those insane substances, with radioactive and combustive power that destroy everything and call the world into question. Even the memory of them contaminates the places they've touched" ("GG" 92–93). However it is figured, the love of Jan and Jennifer always functions as one pole of the opposition that structures the repressive hypothesis, simultaneously a destructive and disruptive force that negates the God's values and a positive force that struggles for freedom against the God's repressive order.

Bachmann further underlines her play's opposition of civilization and Eros by portraying love as a gypsy, drawing upon centuries of European projections onto gypsies that portray them as Western civilization's negative and positive antagonists. Within the racist and orientalist discourses of Western Europe, gypsies' status has some affinities to sexuality, embodying both a threat to social order and an imagined freedom from it. As "stereotypical figures of magic and menace," Katie Trumpener has observed (849), they are used to figure whatever particular intellectual movements are regarded as civilization's opposite:

> For neoclassicism they are there to symbolize a primitive democracy; for the late Enlightenment, an obstruction to the progress of civilization; for romanticism, resistance and the utopia of autonomy; for realism, a threat that throws the order and detail of everyday life into relief; for aestheticism and modernism, a primitive energy still left beneath the modern that drives art itself; and for socialist and post-colonial fiction, finally, a reactionary or resistant cultural force that lingers outside of the welfare state or the imperial order. (874)

In her first appearance, approaching Jennifer in a nightclub to tell her fortune, the gypsy is already associated with other urban eccentrics and outcasts (a handwriting reader in the bar, a beggar on the steps) and marked by skin color and attitude as racially/ethnically other: "a real Gypsy," says Jennifer, "brown, red, and so sad," (in contrast to Jennifer herself, who is "pink and white" ["GG" 62, 76]). Representing herself as a fortuneteller, the gypsy is either a charlatan and fraud or one who can rupture the continuum of Western time to foretell the future, using magical talents quite at variance with the work skills demanded in a high-tech modern city. Later in the play the God makes the gypsy woman a trope for love itself, again constructed as his antagonist:

> That's why I'm on this Gypsy woman's heels. For as long as I can remember, she doesn't come from anywhere, she doesn't live anywhere, and prefers this aerie. She walks with a stoop. But, then, without warning, she'll take off up over the asphalt, up and away, without a trace—
> Of love, I should say—
> We can't apprehend her and bring her here. And she will never give evidence. She's nowhere to be found. Not even where she just was.
> And I could swear that she still loved those two yesterday. She made the cactus bloom purple and the poplars loom in the darkness. And today she already loves two others and makes the mimosas tremble—
> She has no conscience. Instead, she tightens up her black bodice, lets her red skirts swirl, then darkens someone else's world with her immortally sad eyes. ("GG" 78–79)

Imagined to be immune from the effects of the order rather than bearing the marks of its treatment of her (a conception that must have been difficult to sustain a decade after the Holocaust), Bachmann's gypsy, like the marginal groups in Marcuse's later works, is conceived of as the negation of a repressive civilization. Dressed in folkloristic attire inappropriate for a modern city ("black bodice," "red skirts"), she is elusive ("we can't apprehend her and bring her here"; "she's nowhere to be found"); disrespectful of laws ("she will never give evidence"); without home or *Heimat* ("she doesn't come from anywhere, she doesn't live anywhere"); but attached to distant sensual realms ("purple cactus," "mimosas"). This gypsy can even fly, suggesting that she shares some traits with the witch, another female figure discursively constructed as a threat to civilized order, and she dwells in an "aerie" with eagles, entirely beyond civilization's reach. If there is only one order, this ethnic outsider is not part of it; like love, she is considered to be outside of culture altogether. The ease with which Bachmann can mobilize a discourse of ethnic otherness to support the repressive hypothesis may perhaps reveal an even more fundamental structure of binary opposition underlying Western thought—a central term counterposed to its threatening but alluring other—on which both discourses of ethnicity/nationhood and those of sexuality/gender depend.

As Bachmann's play establishes the lovers' and the God's opposition, it also proceeds progressively to remove the lovers, as their passion grows, from arenas and activities that the God controls. The God never leaves the contained but public space of the courtroom (and he and the lovers never meet, since the squirrels act as his intermediaries). But the lovers first explore the four corners of Manhattan (the Bowery, Chinatown, Harlem, the Brooklyn Bridge) and then retreat to an alternative sphere that is both domestic and intensely private: a hotel room where they fry fish in the kitchenette, wash their socks in the bathroom sink and hang them over the shower bar, and glue broomstraw on the walls to make their retreat more nestlike: They "lock the door for the second time" and then "get up still a third time to make sure it's locked" ("GG" 79). Whereas the God is earthbound, the lovers escape into the heavens, seeking the heights that the gypsy woman frequents: they spend their first night together on the ground floor of a "sleazy hotel" ("GG" 62) but move on subsequent nights to ever higher hotel rooms on the seventh, the thirtieth, and finally the fifty-seventh floor. As the God wryly comments, the higher they move, the more they leave the cares of daily life behind: "Everything sinks so visibly into the river bed below, with all its driftwood of further lovers, old burdens, helpless raftsmen with short-term goals. A miniature version of everyday life is amusing. Observed from a distance, common sense shrinks down to size and, sadly, looks a lot like a speck of boredom" ("GG" 78). By the end of the play

they have achieved their own version of heaven-on-earth, as Jan had predicted
on the evening their affair began:

> JAN: "You will spend this evening with Jennifer on this heavenly earth. . . ."
>
> JENNIFER: Why "heavenly earth"?
>
> JAN: Because that's the name here. Ma-na Hat-ta. That's how some Indians
> explained it to me. ("GG" 61)

Jan and Jennifer thus associate themselves with the gypsy by also betaking
themselves to a site of ethnic otherness, so that Manhattan stands no longer for
New York City but for the oxymoronic "heavenly earth" of the Indians, the
New World, the primeval virgin territory of innocent savages still uncorrupted
by civilization.

Likewise, the activities in which the lovers engage challenge the God's regime
in ways that closely parallel Marcuse's arguments. As they fall in love, they
increasingly abandon purposive, goal-directed activity; their unmotivated laughter is the first indication that they will no longer accommodate themselves to the
God's order, as he recalls: "There was, for example, that laughter. Yes, to be
exact, it began with that. (*darkly*) With that indescribable smile. Without any
apparent provocation, they keep laughing. . . . They laugh in public but also in
private. . . . That smile just sits there like a question mark, but it's a very ruthless
one" ("GG" 69). Their games, which serve no worthwhile end, are, the God
tells the judge, the next sign: "Now they were at play. They played love. . . . But
their playing was just like their laughter. They violated its every use" ("GG"
70–71). (As Marcuse observes, "Play is *unproductive* and *useless* precisely because
it cancels the repressive and exploitive traits of labor and leisure" [*Eros* 195]).

Increasingly the lovers' relationship to language changes, as they replace representational language with figuration. In the throes of passion, Jan proclaims
the advent of a new language predicated upon the renunciation of purposive-
ness: "I know nothing else except that I want to live and die here with you. And
speak to you in a new language. I no longer have a career, and I can no longer
run a business. I'm not useful anymore and I must abandon everything. I want
to divorce myself from everyone else" ("GG" 92). One might read the lovers' lyrical exchanges as an effort to retreat to a realm of imagination and art where they
can reestablish contact with the pleasure principle that still rules the unconscious.
Jan's ecstatic prose poems affirm language as metaphor and reconfigure the
boundedness of bodies as he probes Jennifer's body parts and seeks a travel guide
that will explain the wondrous delights of this strange new land: "And I want a
book that tells what exists in you, your climate, flora and fauna, the causes of your

sicknesses, and their silent opponents in your blood. The organisms, the tiniest ones that I take in when I kiss you. I'd like just once to see what happens in the evening when your body is illuminated and warm and ready to celebrate. I can already see something now: transparent fruits and precious stones, carnelian and ruby, shining materials" ("GG" 87). As Judith Butler suggests of Monique Wittig's *The Lesbian Body*, Jan's disaggregation of Jennifer's body is a protest against an order that insists upon impermeable bodily boundaries, "the decon-struction of constructs that are always already a kind of violence against the bod-ies' possibilities" (Butler 126). In Marcusean terms, the body is "resexualized," and this spread of the libido manifests itself "in a reactivation of all erotogenic zones and, consequently, in a resurgence of pregenital polymorphous sexuality and in a decline of genital supremacy. The body in its entirety [becomes] an object of cathexis, a thing to be enjoyed—an instrument of pleasure" (*Eros* 201).

Still, though Jan and Jennifer together establish their love as a counterrealm where the values of the performance principle no longer obtain, the play makes very clear that the lovers are far from equally willing to yield themselves to an eroticism that challenges civilization itself. It's Jennifer who makes the first advances to Jan and very soon devotes herself entirely to her love for him, where-as Jan is initially much more reluctant to involve himself in a relationship beyond the level of dalliance and sexual adventure—a posture that does not bother the God at all: "I have nothing against the frivolous, the bored and the lonely who break down now and then. They don't want to be alone and just kill time" ("GG" 67). Jan maintains an ironic and often brutal distance from Jennifer's efforts to elicit gestures of affection from him, demanding an "agreement on distance" ("GG" 69), treating language as a manipulable tool that helps him achieve his amorous ends: "Should I tell you something about a few women, or very many, about disappointments—that's what you call it, right? Or unforget-table experiences. I'm familiar with the vocabulary, and I've come up with a few versions of my past. Depending on the context" ("GG" 82).

As he finally recognizes that their love will transport him to a utopian realm that will leave the terms of his prior life far behind, he prepares himself for transfiguration: "I want to break free of all the years and all the thoughts of all the years. I want to tear down this structure that I am, and I want to be the other person I never was" ("GG" 84). Yet his attachment to daily life remains strong. Even after he has pledged himself to Jennifer and canceled his ship ticket back to Europe, he succumbs to the momentary temptation to stop at a bar, as the judge reports with satisfaction:

> Because suddenly, once the decision had been made, *he* felt like being alone. He
> wanted to sit alone for half an hour, think as he had thought before, and speak as
> he had spoken before, in places which meant nothing to him, and to people who
> meant nothing to him. He had lapsed. Routine stretched its hand out to him for
> a moment. He was normal, healthy, and honest like a man who has a quiet drink
> before dinner and has banished his lover's whisper from his ear, her alluring scent
> from his nostrils—a man . . . whose eyes come to life again at the sight of news-
> print, a man who has to dirty his hands at a bar again. (96).

So Jan is not in the hotel room when the Good God's bomb explodes, it's
Jennifer alone who dies for love, and, in an ironic echo of the end of *Faust* the
God can proclaim Jan "saved" ("GG" 189) because he has not fundamentally
contravened the God's order: "The earth had him back again" (96).

The effect of the play's ending is thus to associate Jan with the principle of
power the God represents, despite Jan's effusive assurances to the contrary, and
domination is associated not just with modernity or rationalization but also
with men. By default, a woman, Jennifer, whose erotic transport condemns her
to death, remains as the embodiment of a subversive and transgressive sexuality
that challenges the God's performance principle. It was Jan for whom the gypsy
woman foretold a long life (62), while Jennifer, extracted from the God's tempo-
ral continuum, had no future to read. It is Jennifer alone who suffers the *Liebes-
tod* and enters into what Foucault calls another kind of Faustian pact, willing to
risk life for love: "to exchange life in its entirety for sex itself, for the truth and
sovereignty of sex. Sex is worth dying for" (*History* 156). Though Bachmann's
play began by posing Eros as the negation of and alternative to domination (the
God spoke only of "couples" undistinguished by gender), it ends by aligning
men/masculinity with the principle the God represents, and Jennifer becomes
merely another exotic New World woman seduced and abandoned by the European conqueror. Though the play never explicitly thematizes gender, the consequence of making Jennifer the figure that stands for sexual freedom is, as in
Marcuse's theory, to associate men with domination, while femininity (or female
sexuality)—Jennifer and her mentor, the gypsy woman—embodies Eros conceived of as the subversion of governing values, a principle of resistance so
unwaveringly opposed to domination that Eros can never be recuperated. Feminists will recognize this elision of femininity with sexuality as a familiar sexist
notion that men have embraced for centuries: as Simone de Beauvoir put it in
The Second Sex: "[Woman] is called 'the sex,' by which is meant that she appears
essentially to the male as a sexual being. For him she is sex—absolute sex, no
less" (xvi). Bachmann's recourse to an essentialist conception of woman as civili-

zation's other once more reveals this play to be a product of the profoundly misogynist period in which it was written.

If Bachmann's reliance on various elements of a theoretical model that more recent feminist theorists have called into question characterized only this single radio play, this chapter might be worth no more than a footnote in Bachmann studies. But in fact it can be shown that this same constellation structures much of her later writing; as Jürgen Seim remarked, it is "often the case in Ingeborg Bachmann's work" that "the woman alone bears the suffering of love" (398). In the later texts a patriarchal principle often imposes its control on an isolated female figure who serves as the repository of an alternative dream of freedom. Three related conceptions continue to shape Bachmann's later writing: woman as "disloyal to civilization" (to use Adrienne Rich's term), woman as embodiment of Eros, and woman as victim. As Kurt Bartsch has noted: "The paradigmatic opposition of masculine-rational and female-emotional, the failure to integrate reason and emotion as well as the ending (return to existing social constraints or destruction) characterize both the radio plays and the fiction of Ingeborg Bachmann, and there not just the stories that are obviously about women" (*Ingeborg* 88).

Undine of "Undine Goes" counterposes the marvelous accomplishments of civilization that a generic "Hans" has brought into being to the lure of liberation that she represents and, more feisty than most of Bachmann's female characters, returns to her watery realm rather than accommodate herself to his terms. Ritta Jo Horsley maintains that "Undine Goes" is pervaded by a dualism that it never explicitly challenges: "On the contrary, by hypostatizing the traditional dichotomies into male and female figures it reaffirms a dualistic model. The oppositions of culture and nature; rationality and feeling; logical discourse and poetic utterance; social order and ecstasy of freedom; and masculine and feminine are assumed as given, and by their eloquent embodiment gain new power" ("Rereading" 234). In *The Book of Franza* Leopold Jordan stands for science, masculinity, and whiteness; he seeks to eradicate all that can't be contained within his categories, including his wife Franza's subjectivity and sexuality as well as various other victims that are associated with her, such as Jews and colonized peoples. As Franza recalls: "He stole all of my possessions.... I am a Papua" (*Franza* 80; translation modified).

A number of critics have commented on the parallels between *Malina* and "The Good God of Manhattan." Hans Mayer called his review of the novel "*Malina* oder Der große Gott von Wien" (*Malina,* or the Great God of Vienna) and remarked: "This first novel also addresses the fundamental old theme: the irreconcilability of contemporary society with that which German classic-ism wanted to understand as harmonious development of the personality. In Ingeborg Bachmann's well-known radio play, the Good God of Manhattan kills those who truly love because in the unconditionality of their emotions, they endanger the dominant order of alienation" (164). Angelika Mechtel sim-ilarly observed in her review of *Malina*: "There are also parallels to Ingeborg Bachmann's radio play The Good God of Manhattan. There nothing is allowed to exist in this administered and neatly arranged world except that which allows itself to be administered and arranged into its proper place, for instance, a love that leads to self-abandonment" (185).

Even in *Three Paths to the Lake*, whose female characters seem most fully integrated into a society that is destroying them, some repressed aspect of their psyche rebels and cries out for help. Thus in "The Barking" the senile Frau Jordan believes she hears barking dogs that will avenge her ill treatment by her son. Miranda is the happy victim of a hysterical myopia that allows her not to see ugliness in "Eyes to Wonder," a story dedicated to Georg Groddeck, who, sev-eral decades before Freud, "discovered" the Id, the repressed component of the human psyche that actually controls human behavior. As Bachmann explained in her enthusiastic review of Groddeck's *Book of the It*: "The Ego is a mark, the manner with which each of us goes around, and we are ruled by the Id, the Id does it, and it speaks in symbols through sickness" (*W* 4: 352). It can thus be argued that the repressive hypothesis underlies much of the work that has brought Bachmann feminist renown in the years since she was rediscovered by the women's movement in the late 1970s. Indeed, chapter 2 of this book provides a great deal of evidence to substantiate that argument, and chapter 3 illustrates how I myself fell prey to the repressive hypothesis.

As detailed in the commentaries to the chapters of Part Two, such feminist ideas about a single essential principle of womanhood uncontaminated by the characteristics of the culture from which particular women derive have more recently fallen into great disrepute. In part under the influence of Foucault, whose impact on Anglo-American feminist scholarship has been considerable, most feminist scholars in this country now repudiate the use of essentialism for anything but strategic purposes and regard women as the complexly structured products of the discursive and nondiscursive forces of the society in which they are situated. (Judith Butler has commented, for instance: "The female body that is freed from the shackles of the paternal law may well prove to be yet another incarnation of that law, posing as subversive but operating in the service of that law's amplification and proliferation" [93].) Such analyses were much slower to seep into Germany, and some German feminist scholars have suggested that German women have a particular investment in female victimhood because it allows them to ignore women's complicity in German fascism (*Frauen gegen Antisemitismus*). Ingeborg Bachmann's work (including her treatment of fascism) has played some role in allowing German women to situate themselves outside their own culture, whose crimes thus become the responsibility only of men. Thus, if my analysis of Bachmann's writing here is correct, a feminist rethinking of Bachmann's work might also assist in promoting some other much-needed changes in analyses produced by the German women's movement.

Yet as I suggested at the outset of this chapter, interpretations of Bachmann that rest on the repressive hypothesis are not the only readings possible. It can also be argued that Bachmann's representation of femininity and female sexuality is much more complex than the foregoing account might seem to indicate. It is a comment on several generations of this play's readers that virtually no one before Peter Beicken (who has himself obviously been influenced by American feminism) mentioned the sadomasochistic elements of Jan and Jennifer's relationship, which are not in conflict with but a necessary component of the intensification of their love. Beicken has pointed out that from the beginning, their relationship is embedded in a violence that belies its presentation as an alternative to the God's order:

> The destructive influence of socially mediated violence also makes itself felt in the relationship between Jennifer and Jan. How much this violence is a counterpart to the love plot can be recognized in various statements, particularly by Jan, whose aggression extends beyond mere threats and has real violent physical acts as its consequence, as the scars on Jennifer's hands prove. Psychic violence is also part of Jan's normal behavioral norms. . . . One could speculate in various ways to get to the bottom of this question: for instance, does Jennifer accede to this because she's prepared to suffer; because love is always a risk that includes injury and loss of self; because this female type in accord with the 1950s is prepared to accept male violence or inability to love as natural; because a women who loves is prepared to subordinate herself. (120–21)

Pursuing Beicken's suggestions, one might read in this and other Bachmann texts stories of masculinity and femininity as a particular historical period constructs them. Beicken views Jan's sadism as one more component of the God's order: "What makes Jan receptive for the agency dealing with him, what finally makes him behave in accordance with the will of the Good God, is his internalization of masculine role expectations that are also in conformity with the norms of social convention that the God represents" ("GG" 120). That may indeed be the case. But what is more important for a new feminist reading of this play is that Bachmann shows submission to male power, female masochism, as the enabling condition of a female eroticism that is willing to embrace its own obliteration and destruction (Jennifer declares: "Soon I'll be nothing," and "I would be free of myself" ["GG" 91]) in order to love. That construction of femininity and sexuality constitutes a second discourse in "The Good God of Manhattan" much at variance with the first, which offers the possibility of a quite different feminist reading of this play.

Jessica Benjamin's study *The Bonds of Love* is very useful for thinking about the question of masochism from a feminist perspective. Benjamin also rejects the repressive hypothesis, the opposition between instinct and civilization, and draws on Foucault to maintain that desire is a production of power that functions "not by denying our desire but by forming it, converting it into a willing retainer, its servant or representative" (4). Adapting a male-dominant Freudian psychoanalysis for feminist purposes, she argues that a society that configures the male and female psyche as ours does cannot permit the reconciliation of female agency and female desire. Instead, sexual complementarity, she maintains, demands that "man expresses desire and woman is the object of it." Thus "woman's missing desire often takes the form of adoring the man who possesses it," and "women seem to have a propensity for what we may call 'ideal love'—a love in which the woman submits to and adores an other who is what she cannot be" (86). Voluntary submission to the man's erotic domination thus somewhat paradoxically allows the woman to achieve independence and gratification via obedience to and identification with the one who possesses it. The more she abandons herself to a man who transgresses her boundaries and violates her autonomy, the greater her satisfaction. Her pleasure derives from her knowledge of her subjugation by him, and her surrender to him confirms her connection to the power and desire she wishes to possess herself. Benjamin argues that in a male-dominant, gender-polarized society, where woman is, as de Beauvoir put it, "man's primary other, his opposite—playing nature to his reason, immanence to his transcendence, primordial oneness to his individuated separateness, and object to his subject" (quoted in Benjamin 7), the fulfillment of female desire takes the form of submission to the male will, a structure of domination anchored deep within the female psyche.

Benjamin's analysis makes it possible to read "The Good God of Manhattan" also as a story of the social construction of female desire. At the play's outset, Jennifer is introduced as a modern woman (one reason it is necessary for her to be an American) who possesses agency and seems to control her own desire: she is a student of political science (still not exactly a feminized field) who travels to New York on her own, makes the first sexual advances to Jan, a strange European man, casually recounts her own erotic adventures with a variety of men at college ("And Arthur kisses me goodnight, or Mark, or Truman"), and, though she knows it's unorthodox ("One shouldn't go into hotels with strangers. Isn't that right?"), spends the night with Jan in a sleazy hotel ("GG" 63, 64). Yet from the beginning of their relationship, Jennifer wants Jan to hurt her, physically and psychically (that is, where her desire is at issue, she employs her agency to bring about his domination and her submission). She is responsible for urging Jan to dig his nails into her palms, as he reminds her when she complains of the pain: "You're the one who's been leading me on. I've never wanted to hurt someone like that" ("GG" 64). Once she's fallen in love, this independent young woman yields the initiative to Jan entirely, and he takes the lead in determining the course of the love affair, deciding when they should remain together and when they should part; he teases and taunts her while she bows to his demands and whims. When he threatens to beat her because she has dared to agree to his demand that they part ("I should beat you in front of all these people—I'm going to beat you" ["GG" 170]), she agrees eagerly. Though, as I suggested earlier, Jan's exploration of the flora and fauna of the far reaches of Jennifer's body can be read as a challenge to genital supremacy and the boundedness of the body, it is also given the shape of a voyage of discovery, with Jan as the colonial (European) master who takes possession of this virgin land (another reading of Jennifer as representative of the New World), who willingly yields herself to him: "If only I could do more, tear myself open for you and give you my every fiber, every bone in my body, just as it should be," says Jennifer ("GG" 88). Jan's domination and Jennifer's submission to it drive her, the play's dialogue suggests, to unknown heights of passion:

> JAN: Is that what's become of you! Just look at you! From a pink girl with diaries, good-night kisses, necking in cars with Truman and notebooks full of doodles under your arm, very nice, and how do you like it? . . .
>
> JENNIFER: Save me! From you and from myself. . . .
>
> JAN: Are you crying? Go ahead and cry!
>
> JENNIFER: Do you think we're insane?
>
> JAN: Maybe.
>
> JENNIFER: Do you despise me?
>
> JAN: Just a little. Just enough so you never cease to amaze me. ("GG" 81)

In their last scene together, Jennifer submits entirely to Jan—against his will!—

constructing him as a traditional patriarch to whom she wishes only to subordinate herself:

> JENNIFER (*slowly as she falls to her knees*): Oh, it's true. Never again.
>
> JAN: What are you doing? Don't do that!
>
> JENNIFER: Kneeling before you and kissing your feet? I'll do it forever. And I'll walk three steps behind you, wherever you go. I'll drink only after you have drunk. I'll eat after you've eaten. Wake, when you sleep. ("GG" 92)

The portrayal of Jennifer suggests that Bachmann, like Benjamin, views female autonomy and female desire as mutually exclusive. In the realm of eroticism, Jennifer uses her agency to bring about her own subordination. Though she is a victim in this play, it is a victimhood she actively seeks as the condition of her own erotic satisfaction. Within this discourse of sexual complementarity, women must become men's sexual objects to meet their own erotic needs. To realize her desire, Jennifer is willing to renounce her position as Jan's equal and embrace her own subordination.

The question of masochism (a subject that feminists have generally not been eager to address) needs much more investigation in Bachmann's writing. A passage from an unpublished preface to *The Book of Franza* suggests that Bachmann connected issues of sadism and masochism to the questions her "Ways of Death" pursued: "I come from a country, without showing off about its geniuses, which has always concerned itself with those unknown beings, human beings, their unfathomability, profundity. I also don't have any explanation for why a number of revolutionary discoveries have taken place in my country. I'm just acknowledging it. From the undiscovered Sacher Masoch to the greatest pioneer, Sigmund Freud, however historical he may also have been, this line has never broken off, this recherche" (*TP* 2: 16).

Perhaps some of the passages Bachmann underlined in her 1918 edition of Otto Weininger's *Geschlecht und Charakter* (Sex and character) are also relevant to the construction of femininity within a discourse of sexual complementarity: "Woman is only sexual, man is also sexual" (114); "Coitus is the highest value of woman, she seeks to realize it always and everywhere" (354); "The female seeks her perfection as object" (396; Bothner 214). Pursuing these hints, one might argue that her play draws attention to the way that femininity is constituted at a particular historical juncture, thematizing what Foucault called the "hysterization" or "sexualization" of women's bodies, a conception of the feminine body that conceives it to be "thoroughly saturated with sexuality" (*History* 104). This interpretation would hold good whether the play is regarded as a representation of the nature of social relations between men and women in "Manhattan" or as an exploration of intrapsychic reality, as Hapkemeyer has suggested: "Jan and Jennifer can be interpreted as lovers, but also as two components of the same personality, which the names already suggest, which derive from a common root" (*Entwicklungslinien* 87). (It's not in fact true that the name "Jennifer" derives from "Jan"—it is a variant of "Winifred"—but Bachmann might well have wished to use the linguistic similarity of the two names to suggest that psychically Jennifer was a product of, dependent upon, or subordinate to Jan.) By portraying a female figure whose erotic satisfaction derives from her sexual subordination, Bachmann draws upon a discourse of sexuality that understands power as producing, proliferating, and intensifying sexuality rather than repressing it. Instead of embodying a pre- or extrasocial sexuality, within that second discourse Jennifer is interpellated into an already gendered discourse of sexuality within which female desire is defined as subordinate to men's. Though it is certainly an exaggeration to say that this second discourse prefigures Foucault, the position Bachmann assumes in her treatment of Jennifer is close to what Foucault proposed when he argued, "We must not think that by saying yes to sex, one says no to power" (*History* 157). A reading of this play that stresses the second discourse (which is, I think, entirely irreconcilable with the first) makes it possible both to criticize aspects of this work which remain rooted in their time and to produce interpretations that speak to feminists of the present day.

A reading of "The Good God of Manhattan" that investigates the work's conflicts and tensions instead of attempting to produce a unitary interpretation might in addition identify a number of other discourses in the play which also contradict or undercut aspects of what I have identified as its dominant discourse. Bachmann's representation of New York City is another site where contradictory discourses intersect. If "Manhattan" stands for the single order of the God, Bachmann simultaneously portrays it as a locus of eclectic urban activity where everything is permitted and possible: "This city of cities, in its restlessness and agony, took in everyone. Anything could thrive here!" ("GG" 168). Although cultural critics such as Marcuse and other members of the Frankfurt School were appalled by American mass culture, Bachmann's lovers are in contrast delighted by it: collecting plastic swizzle sticks from a bar and paper fans depicting Catherine of Sienna from a church; playing music in a record shop in Harlem "in the company of several blacks"; riding a horse-drawn carriage in Central Park, where they are overtaken by drum majorettes leading a parade of war veterans ("GG" 68, 71). Far from being a location where all is reduced to a single uniform standard, Manhattan offers a variety of sensual pleasures: one can eat "Italian and Chinese, Spanish and Russian"; stand "on Broadway under the Pepsi Cola waterfall, near the big Lucky Strike smoke ring" ("GG" 61 70); or purchase almost anything.

Joseph Strutz has pointed out that the God himself depicts New York as a "site of social chaos" (381), using exuberant figurative language that recalls Georg Heym's expressionist poem "Der Gott der Stadt" (The god of the city). Manhattan's squirrels, the God's henchmen, can perhaps even be read as similarly ambiguous figures: their service to the God may underline that in the world the God controls, even nature has been brought under the sway of domination, yet these quirky talking animals also seem to derive from a magical realm (part Brothers Grimm, part Walt Disney) qualitatively distinct from the God's grim rationalized regime. (On the other hand, if Bachmann's inspiration for squirrels in the service of "Manhattan" derives from the U.S. plan in summer 1948 for provisioning Vienna in the event of a Soviet blockade, code-named "squirrel cage" [Bischof, "Austria Looks" 188], then the squirrels indeed serve the God's totalitarian order.) Within the logic of this play, there seems to be no explanation for why the city of Manhattan is represented as a heterogeneous center of urban delights that escapes the God's total power; after all, the God presents himself as the agent of an order that controls everything but love. It thus seems necessary to view Bachmann's play as existing at the intersection of two conflicting 1950s discourses on "America" (or its synecdochal representation, Manhattan), the one portraying the U.S. as the highest stage of a rationalized technological progress tending ever more toward totalitarianism, the other treating the United States as a land of unlimited possibilities for which Europeans yearned.

A reading of "The Good God of Manhattan" stressing its contradictions offers another sort of insight into Bachmann's later works. Viewed through the lens of newer feminist analyses, those texts can be read as representations of femininity as a particular period constructed it, instead of (or as well as) accounts of female victims extracted from time and space who are oppressed by all-powerful men. Bachmann's female figures would then no longer seem to stand for a transhistorical, essentialized principle of womanhood but could be understood as products of the political systems of which their lives are part. The failure of Bachmann's female figures to comprehend or challenge the power men exercise over them could be viewed as a representational strategy that allowed Bachmann to portray her women as they understood themselves. Indeed, Bachmann suggested something of this sort when she maintained in the preface to *Franza* that her "ways of death" took place "at times, within the thinking that leads to a crime, and at times, within that which leads to dying" (*Franza* 4): if a certain kind of (male) thinking allows men to destroy women, another and related kind of (female) thinking produces women who accede to, even embrace, their victimization. That construction of femininity assumes its clearest form in the relationship of the "I" of *Malina* to Ivan, who treats her as badly as Jan treats Jennifer and whose every wish she nonetheless desires to satisfy. Loving Ivan is the condition of her (female) existence ("I live in Ivan," says the "I" [*Malina* 24]), and the end of Ivan's love for her means her end, too: as Malina, her male doppelgänger, declares at the end of the novel, "There is no woman here" (*Malina* 224). That is how Bachmann's writing represents "history within the I/psyche" (what Foucault called the "body totally imprinted by history" [*Language* 148]): Bachmann's female figures are completely congruent with the historically specific discourses that call them into being.

To understand Bachmann's texts in this manner, it would be necessary to read her narrative standpoint as always an ironic one (as Irene Holeschofsky has suggested of *Three Paths to the Lake*): though her female characters entirely affirm the categories that engender them and attempt to make the best of what they never even recognize as a bad situation, we readers are intended to understand the costs to them of the social circumstances to whose dictates they conform. That, I think, would provide a new and useful reading strategy for Bachmann's "Ways of Death" and could also explain why she abandoned *The Book of Franza*—whose protagonist does understand and rebel against what has been done to her—for the more complex literary strategies of *Malina* and *Three Paths to the Lake*, whose female figures can never construct a narrative that allows them to talk about their own destruction: "I'm not telling, I won't talk, I can't," says the "I" (*Malina* 172); "although all these stories were true, she omitted others because they were badly suited for telling," thinks Elisabeth Matrei in "Three Paths to the Lake" (*Paths* 132; translation modified). What would still be missing from such an analysis, because feminist methodology as yet provides no tools to undertake it, is a reading of Bachmann's figures' psychological constitution as a product of a very specific historical period. That reading would not propose that Jennifer is a masochist or the female protagonist of *Malina* is murdered just because they are women living under modern Western patriarchy, but, more specifically, investigate how Jennifer's psychic makeup might be related to the cold war or how the "I" might be a product of Vienna in the 1960s. In chapter 10 I begin such an investigation; more generally, however, devising a methodology that would enable such inquires into the relationship of literary texts to extraliterary historical processes and forces remains an unfinished project of feminist literary scholarship.

Yet, even should such problems be solved, I would not attempt to argue that a reading of Bachmann's texts based on current (or future) Anglo-American feminist thinking would be the correct one while all others are wrong. Nor do I maintain that the first reading I advanced of Bachmann, based on the repressive hypothesis, is false. That aspect of Bachmann's writing really is there, as I hope I have shown, and earlier feminists did not misread her when they underlined those dimensions of her work. Both of the readings I have proposed here can be supported by textual evidence and emphasize aspects of her play that continued to inform her writing through the "Ways of Death." In fact, her works oscillate between these two conceptions of femininity, which cannot at all be harmonized with each other. Rather, by emphasizing two disparate readings of this radio play, I want to make two larger methodological points. First, Bachmann's texts (like almost everything else) are not of a single piece but sites where contradictory discourses intersect; second, readings of Bachmann's works, as of any text, are always interested, stressing what meets their readers' needs and disregarding what seems of less utility (as I myself have done). I am arguing that it is now time for Bachmann's feminist critics to undertake new readings of her works that would both question what is timebound, outmoded, and problematic in her writing and explore ways in which her texts could be reread to address new feminist concerns. It seems very likely that the postulation of masculinity and femininity (or power and sex) as mutually exclusive oppositions both naturalizes and stabilizes cultural constructions that are not in feminists' interests and also prevents us from seeing an actually much more contradictory and unstable reality into which different kinds of political interventions would be necessary. If one reading of Bachmann may naturalize an essentialist conception of an inherently subversive sexuality or femininity, another reading can draw such notions into question again. As Judith Butler has suggested, "If the regulatory fictions of sex and gender are themselves multiply contested sites of meaning, then the very multiplicity of their construction holds out the possibility of a disruption of their univocal posturing" (32). That could be a feminist strategy for reading Bachmann's works, too.

In endeavoring to reread Bachmann from a more historical perspective, feminist critics who view her texts as products of a period that is now past would be doing no more than reacknowledging what Bachmann herself conceded in her Frankfurt lectures: "Thinking, rooted in time, also succumbs to time" (W 4: 195). She, too, for better or for worse, bore the imprint of the time that produced her as she struggled to meet the charge she set the writer: "In the best case, one can succeed at two things: to represent one's times, and to present something whose time hasn't come yet" (*W* 4: 196). Perhaps also in a different way than she intended, Bachmann represented the thinking of her time, and some of those strategies of representation now seem no longer altogether adequate to our own. We feminist literary historians can nonetheless honor Bachmann's radio play for its "resolute attempt to keep the space of emancipation open" (as Douglas Kellner remarked of *Eros and Civilization* [156]) in a time of political reaction, undertaking new feminist readings that do not abandon the emancipatory goal at which her text aimed.

CHAPTER 9

Bachmann and Postcolonial Theory

WHITE LADIES AND DARK CONTINENTS

*. . . the psyche of the whites, which was
obviously more threatened than he could
imagine . . .*

—*Ingeborg Bachmann,* The Book of Franza

"[Austria] is different from all other little countries today because it was an empire and it's possible to learn something from its history. And because the lack of activity into which one is forced there enormously sharpens one's view of the big situation and of today's empires," Ingeborg Bachmann observed in a 1971 interview (*GuI* 106). The postcolonial theory developed since 1990 helps to explain why and how Bachmann was able to use her Austrian vantage point as a privileged perspective from which to regard "today's empires" and the forms of imperialism for which they have been responsible. For over a decade, postcolonial scholars have argued that European history cannot be detached from the history of Europe's imperialist practices; as Anne McClintock puts it, "Imperialism is not something that happened elsewhere—a disagreeable fact of history external to Western identity. Rather, imperialism and the invention of race were fundamental aspects of Western industrial modernity" (5). Postcolonial theorists and a range of scholars investigating the construction of "whiteness" have recently begun to demonstrate that the racial formations of the imperial world were constitutive of white European identities in the metropole as well as in the colonies, "race" thus helping to define the most intimate domains of modern life—including gender relations, the sexual politics of the private sphere, and sexuality itself. As I have emphasized in previous chapters, Bachmann maintained that in twentieth-century literary texts history could no longer be treated as an external medium in which figures acted but must instead be regarded as a force that configures the self: "history within the 'I'/psyche"

(*W* 4: 230). Reading the "Ways of Death" through the lens offered by postcolonial theory can show how Bachmann represents imperialism past and present as a component of history central to the constitution of her characters.

As its title suggests, this chapter focuses on how Bachmann represents the relationship of imperialism to the construction of the white female psyche in the "Ways of Death." "White Lady" (in English) is a phrase Bachmann associates with Eka Kottwitz, one of the figures in a "Ways of Death" fragment (*TP* 1: 424; a point I explore in greater detail below); "Dark Continent" (in English) is the term Freud used in *The Question of Lay Analysis* to describe "the sexual life of adult women" (20: 212). Freud's use of this image—the term Victorians applied to an Africa to which their own imperialist activities would bring light (Brantlinger)—reveals, Mary Ann Doane has argued, the imperial underpinnings of Freud's theory: "The force of the category of race in the constitution of Otherness within psychoanalysis should not be underestimated. When Freud needs a trope for the unknowability of female sexuality, the dark continent is close at hand. Psychoanalysis can, from this point of view, be seen as a quite elaborate form of ethnography—as a writing of the ethnicity of the white psyche. Repression becomes the prerequisite for the construction of a white culture which stipulates that female sexuality act as the trace within of what has been excluded" (211).

From very early on, similar imperial imagery also shaped Bachmann's writing. Her 1957 poem "Liebe: Dunkler Erdteil" (Love: Dark Continent) represents Africa as a lush and exotic realm of sexuality beyond the repressive boundaries established by Europeans, with black masculinity—"the black king"—figured as the agent of an erotic power before which the poem's "you" prostrates herself and at whose mercy she conceives herself to be: "But there you always fall upon your knees, for he chooses and rejects you without grounds" (*Songs* 295). Bachmann's poem might be regarded as a rather conventional European projection of orientalizing motifs onto a non-European geography, and such a reading would not be wrong. But by brushing this poem somewhat against the grain (to use Walter Benjamin's phrase again), it is possible to advance a more interesting reading which treats this poem as a representation of the degree to which racialized and imperial fantasies are constituent elements of the European female psyche. Bachmann's later treatment of the intersections of imperialism and female identity, I want to propose here, also oscillates between those two positions, sometimes projecting familiar European fantasies onto a non-European backdrop, at other times achieving a more profound interrogation of the imperial underpinnings of Central European femininity. By interrogating the literal encounters of Bachmann's protagonists with (inhabitants of) the Dark Continent in two uncompleted portions of the "Ways of Death"— *The Book of Franza* and the Eka Kottwitz fragment—I want to show how discourses of race and empire underwrite her female figures' identities. Virtually alone among postwar women writing in German, I argue, Bachmann attempts to explore the racialized foundations of Central European fantasies, yet by continuing to project white fantasies onto non-European figures she herself does not always escape the racist structures her work attempts to challenge. Finally, I want to examine "Three Paths to the Lake," the last text Bachmann wrote before her death, to show how she connects white women acting under postcolonial conditions, imperial Austria, and the "ways of death" of which her White Ladies are the victims.

In an often quoted introduction to *The Book of Franza*, Bachmann provided instructions on how to read her book: "The real settings, the interior ones, laboriously concealed by the external, are elsewhere" (*Franza* 4). As I showed in chapter 2, the feminist scholars who rediscovered Bachmann's writing in the 1980s regarded *The Book of Franza* as an exploration of the location and function of femininity within discourse which provided the key to understanding Bachmann's entire oeuvre; as Sigrid Weigel put it in her introduction to the 1984 *text + kritik* volume that became a landmark of feminist Bachmann criticism, "in [her texts] it is a question of a structural relationship between fascism, patriarchy, ethno- and logocentrism and the central role of language/writing for this context, within which the 'feminine' as the embodiment of the repressed other is subjected to a wide variety of ways of death" ("Andere" 5). In this reading, Bachmann's tale of Franza's flight from her tyrannical Viennese husband into the North African desert in the company of her beloved brother, Martin, is an investigation of the mechanisms via which an oppressive Western order denies women and other "others" a voice. This analysis mainly conflates gender and race, viewing them as equally the product of a single system of subordination, and "the whites" against whom Franza inveighs are conceived to stand synecdochically for domination *tout court*. In Weigel's words, "The whites thus stand for the insight that the history of colonization and the history of patriarchy have different victims but a single perpetrator" ("Ende" 82). That is clearly Franza's own view of her situation, for she compares her husband's brutal treatment of her to the colonial exploitation of native peoples and their indigenous treasures. Other evidence in the novel, however, suggests that Franza's position should not be equated with Bachmann's own (see Albrecht, "Sire"). For 1990s feminists, of course, forced by protests of women of color to acknowledge white women's racial privilege, readings that fail to disaggregate race and gender have become impossible. In its various unfinished versions, I want to show, Bachmann's fragment can be read as a contradictory text that at some points concurs with Franza's own conflation of gender and race but in other instances holds Franza's treatment of race and empire up for examination. In neither case, I want to emphasize, is Bachmann's unfinished novel *about* North Africa; rather it is about how a European woman (whether Franza or Bachmann herself) represents her orientalist encounter with it.

Bachmann's various accounts of her own trip to Egypt and the Sudan in spring 1964—which she initially wished to integrate into her Büchner Prize speech, then intended as a separate novel, to be called the "Wüstenbuch" (Desert book), and finally used as the basis for the North African sections of *Franza*—are all structured around a recurring leitmotif: "The whites are coming, I am of inferior race [Die Weißen kommen, ich bin von niedriger Rasse]" (*TP* 1: 180). As she revealed in a draft introduction to *Franza* (*TP* 2: 73), these phrases are borrowed from Rimbaud, specifically from *Un saison en enfer*, where Rimbaud maintains, "Je suis de race inférieure [I am of inferior race]" (95), and, somewhat later, "Les blancs débarquent. Le canon! Il faut se soutmettre au baptême, s'habiller, travailler [The whites are debarking. The cannon/canon! It is necessary to submit oneself to baptism, to get dressed, to work]" (98). As Christopher Miller observes, though Rimbaud later traveled to Africa (where he became a gunrunner and possibly a slave trader), here his critique of "whites" and identification with Africans—("Je suis une bête, un nègre [I am a beast, a Negro] [97])—are merely vehicles for advancing a critique of contemporary French civilization by drawing on Africanist motifs: "His artificial Africanness consists of an image that persists in European discourse, that of the free reign of desire, of removal from the mediation of language and the rule of repression" (C. Miller 152). (Later in this chapter I term that discourse the discourse of primitivism.) Dirk Göttsche has maintained that the structure of *Franza* reflects "Rimbaud's conceptual world. Rationality, masculinity, and European culture are associated with the principle of the objectivizing domination of nature and humanity, while the magical, the feminine, and the Egyptian (colored [*sic*]) culture are associated with a subordinate but utopian counterprinciple" ("Schwarzkunst" 149–50). In the final version of *Franza*, Bachmann expands Rimbaud's remarks into a forceful denunciation of the hegemonic force of European cultural imperialism which, the editors of the critical edition observe (*TP* 2: 476), recalls the analysis of colonialism in Frantz Fanon's *Black Skin, White Masks* (and is so key a passage in Bachmann's oeuvre that I have already cited it several times in this book:

The whites are coming. The whites are landing. And if they are driven back, then they will come again. No revolution or resolution can prevent it, nor any controls over the currency. They will come again in spirit if there's no other way for them to come. And they will resurrect themselves in a brown or a black brain, which will become white once again. They will take over world through such indirect means. (*Franza* 112)

But despite the affinities of Bachmann's statement with the analysis of one of the most renowned critics of Western imperialism, one might nonetheless maintain that for Bachmann, as for Rimbaud, these racialized images represent their own European instrumentalization of the language of empire: colonialist metaphors serve the primary function of providing a vivid trope for the all-pervasive force of a European rationality from which they endeavor to disengage themselves by aligning with that which Europe designates as its other. As Christopher Miller puts it, "The gesture of reaching out to the most unknown part of the world and bringing it back as language . . . ultimately brings Europe face to face with nothing but itself, with the problems its own discourse imposes" (5).

The earliest versions of *The Book of Franza*—drafts for Bachmann's Büchner Prize speech and her "Wüstenbuch"—were written in the first person and to some extent still retain autobiographical elements ("they [her male Arab acquaintances and, as emerges later, her lovers] call me, with short peremptory syllables, always by my surname, while I only know their first names, bakma, how are you. I say, I am fine. I really am" [*TP* 1: 239]). Those drafts already revolve around European problems to which North Africa is considered to offer alternatives and answers (and already cite Rimbaud as the antecedent to Bachmann's own approach). The ends to which Bachmann, at least at an early stage of the text's composition, wished to turn the journey are evident in her initial plan for the account of her own trip to Egypt and the Sudan in spring 1964: as the editors of the critical edition point out, she first intended to contrast the "sickness" of "unloved Berlin" (ultimately the topic of her Büchner Prize speech: see chapter 10)—where she spent her fellowship year in 1963–64 as she attempted to recover from the devastating effects of the dissolution of her relationship with Max Frisch—and the "healing" she had experienced in the North African desert. In the novel's final version, Franza remains convinced that the desert will be a site of healing for her because, like Rimbaud, she takes it to be a location where "the whites" (i.e., the forms of European thought of which she conceives herself to be a victim) hold no sway. One can thus locate this text within a long line of narratives in which the orient is represented as corresponding or responding to the traveler's own interior needs. For the "belated travelers" of the late nineteenth century, as Ali Behdad observes, the trip to the Orient was a voyage of "romantic self-discovery" and a "solitary quest for elsewhere" in "response to the onset of modernity in Europe" (21, 16).

It is then possible to read Franza's journey to North Africa as what Behdad has identified as the contradictory discourse of "belated Orientalism." That discourse, as Behdad describes it, often "vacillates between an insatiable search for a counterexperience in the Orient and the melancholic discovery of its impossibility. . . . On the one hand, these texts identify themselves differentially against . . . the truth claims of official Orientalism by expressing an unease with classification and objectivity. On the other, they find it impossible to avoid the baggage of Orientalist knowledge that has mediated the desire to produce another discourse on the Orient" (15). Franza's experience of the orient is often explicitly shown as mediated by her European guidebooks, citations from which dot the text as recognizably foreign bodies. Though Franza appears to be entirely uninterested in the guidebooks, her response to Egypt takes the form of a romantic repudiation of everything the guidebooks recommend, a defiantly dichotomous reaction still negatively determined by the terms of the prescriptions it rejects. Franza fervently insists, as she travels deeper into North Africa, that she has left behind the entire canon of Western knowledge and eluded European power: "The whites. Finally they were nowhere to be seen" (*Franza* 94). She also warns herself that white cultural hegemony is not so easy to evade: "Thus will I discover my rights. But the alibi of the whites is strong. Don't forget that" (*Franza* 112). But exactly this representation of North Africa as a site of oriental otherness that can rescue Franza from Europe reveals itself to be a product of romantic white fantasies that are themselves constructed by and mediated through the orientalist texts of earlier travelers.

How Franza's (or Bachmann's?) white female fantasies about the orient might be connected to the Dark Continent of white female sexuality is most clearly revealed in various accounts of an "orgy" in the "Wüstenbuch" (*TP* 2: 271), which survive in the novel's final draft only in veiled allusions to the "embraces at the Nile" (*Franza* 143; translation modified) and the suggestion that Martin has slept with two Arab acquaintances. As Edward Said has remarked, "The Orient seems still to suggest not only fecundity but sexual promise (and threat), untiring sensuality, unlimited desire, deep generative energies"; to travelers the association between the orient and the freedom of licentious sex meant that "the Orient was a place where one could look for sexual experience unobtainable in Europe. Virtually no European writer who wrote on or travelled to the Orient in the period after 1800 exempted himself or herself from this quest" (*Orientalism* 188, 190). The first-person narrator of the "Wüsten-buch" conceives of her erotic encounter with Salah, Mahmed, and Abdu—always framed by the Rimbaudian refrain, "The whites are coming. I am of inferior race"—as extracting her from whiteness altogether—"Three bodies that intertwine, the single satisfaction, the killing of the other race" (*TP* 1: 257). She also represents (à la Eldridge Cleaver) the transgressive sexual act as a gendered act of revenge against domination by white *men*: "The white man is inferior. And he's afraid that I'll say it out loud. I killed him in our bed, he will never forgive his inferiority. He needs the police against it, law, arrogance, he needs violence, because he can't prevail in his bed" (*TP* 1: 283). As in "Love: Dark Continent" (or in "The Good God of Manhattan"), here too eroticism extracts the lovers from the ruling order and aligns them with the quintessential otherness for which the orient stands.

As the journey to North Africa made it possible for Franza to construe bacteria-induced illnesses as a danger only to whites, so similarly the "I" of the "Wüstenbuch" imagines that venereal disease is of no concern to nonwhites: "The venereal diseases [*Geschlechtskrankheiten*] of the whites, I understand very well that no one knows them here" (*TP* 1: 240). Sex with her three Egyptian friends cures her of the "sexual illness" of white femininity: "I thought of it as an act of revenge, and it was not a revenge, but the repudiation of ridiculous notions. From now on the venereal diseases of the whites will only make me laugh" (*TP* 1: 272). Bachmann's effort to combat white culture reproduces several of its core racial and sexual preconceptions: that the orient is a site of licentious and wanton sexuality; that men of color are particularly potent and gifted lovers who, in competition with white men, lust especially after white women; that sexuality is outside of culture, thus associated with "others" also thought to be exterior to civilization; and that through her sexual relationship with a man of color a white woman can declare herself "disloyal to civilization" and place herself outside its bounds. Paradoxically, one might maintain, Bachmann's attempt to escape whiteness proves how very white she is.

Yet a question might be asked of this novel fragment similar to the one asked of a novel that represents a much more viciously racist white consciousness, Joseph Conrad's *Heart of Darkness*: is this a racist novel or a novel about racism? Frequently, Bachmann's text offers hints that readers should regard Franza's own judgments with some skepticism. In one of the last drafts, Bachmann clearly pokes fun at Franza's romantic notion that she is destined to become a heroic martyr whose (distinctly masochistic) sacrifices could save the Third World (surely a liberal and female variant of the Victorian conviction that European efforts would bring light to the Dark Continent): "Perhaps she could do something, but it had to be something real, later Africa or Asia, under the hardest conditions, with sacrifice, with heroism, sacrifice definitely had to be part of it, and it should be grand, lots of effort, but glorious for her, with an early death, she would jump in after someone who was drowning, dash into a burning house and throw a child out the window into the blanket waiting to catch it and then burn to death, bandage a wounded man and then be shot by mistake in North Africa" (*TP* 2: 233–234).

Franza's declaration that she has escaped the whites is somewhat undercut by the ubiquitous bottles of Coca-Cola she drinks along her journey; as the title of Reinhold Wagnleitner's study of U.S. influence in Austria after 1945, *Coca-Colonization and the Cold War*, suggests, Coca-Cola can readily serve as a powerful and easily recognizable symbol of Western cultural imperialism. In the North Africa destined to save her from the whites, Franza encounters acts of brutality that do not fit her dichotomous model of evil Europe and the pristine orient: a woman bound by the hair at the Cairo train station, and a camel slaughtered at a wedding feast—both figures with whom she identifies (again appropriating non-European experiences as her own)—so inexplicable in their otherness that her European categories leave her at a loss to interpret them. One of the most striking indications that Franza's appropriation of North Africa might be regarded as Bachmann's attempt to represent white female fantasies about the orient is her mystical experience on a Red Sea beach, where she is convinced that she has seen God and her father when she is in fact confronted with a dead tree trunk. Her response, "The Arabian desert is surrounded by shattered visions of God" (*Franza* 119), the editors of the critical edition point out (*TP* 2: 486–487), is quite possibly borrowed from *The Seven Pillars of Wisdom,* written by one of the greatest of the romantic orientalists, T. E. Lawrence ("Lawrence of Arabia"). It is possible, then, that when Bachmann comments on a travel party of elderly American women, "all of them over sixty and decked out with canes and giant hats, . . . recalling renowned travelers an age gone by being served in style while traveling on a steamer up the Nile to the granite quarries and on to Elephantine" (*Franza* 105; translation modified), she means that description of the European woman traveler on her grand tour of the orient also to apply, mutatis mutandis, to Franza—who is in fact in an earlier version of this same passage called a "Lady," in English, by an Egyptian soldier in Luxor (*TP* 2: 103), underlining the fact that in the context of Egypt she, too, is a White Lady.

One might thus maintain that Franza's travel accounts, like those of many women travelers to the orient who preceded her, consist of the fantasies she projects onto North Africa, fantasies that are "interior settings" disguised as a travel narrative about real geographical sites. Perhaps one could even read Franza herself as the Dark Continent, her travel to North Africa thus conceived of as a journey into the unknown territory of her own psyche. Bachmann's description of Franza's fascination with the monuments of Egyptian antiquity might then be seen as an elaboration of Freud's imperial metaphor in his *Aetiology of Hysteria*, where he compares his own task to that of "an explorer arriv[ing] in a little-known region where his interest is aroused by an expanse of ruins with remains of walls, fragments of columns, and tablets with half-effaced and unreadable inscriptions": after questioning the region's "perhaps semi-barbaric peoples" and excavating the site, the explorer may decipher and translate the inscriptions: "*Saxa loquantur!*" (3: 192)—The stones speak!—a passage that recalls Franza's geologist brother's effort to find a geological explanation for the undiagnosed illness that causes his sister's psychic and physical symptoms.

On the other hand, even if it should be possible to read this contradictory text as an investigation of race and empire, it is not so clear that Bachmann's metaphorizing of the imperial traveler— that is, using the journey to a real non-European country as a vehicle for exploring the state of the European psyche— could not itself be regarded in some complex ways as an imperial gesture. One might then direct a critique against Bachmann's use of North Africa similar to that which Susan Shapiro leveled at Jean-François Lyotard's treatment of "the jews": "'The jews' becomes a way for the European subject both to critique the (logo) center and identity with/as the margins of the West without changing its terms. It maintains the logic of the West by reducing otherness to a symbol of the limits of the West, its limit-text. . . . While it is clear that the jews is a constructed trope, the constructedness of the *real Jews* is effaced or forgotten. . . . [T]here is no space left in the West for the intervention of actual Jews in their multiple and conflicting identities" (190). It is very possible that the "sickness" from which Franza is suffering is that of whiteness, or white femininity, itself ("She had not arrived at Luxor," writes Bachmann, "but instead at a point in her illness, not having traveled through the desert, but through her illness" [*Franza* 105])—but that is not a malady to which Bachmann herself was entirely immune. Furthermore, even should this have been the reading of her novel that Bachmann intended, more than a decade of scholarship focused on *Franza* shows that such an interpretation was not evident to most readers. Perhaps it was for such reasons, among others (see also chapter 10), that Bachmann finally abandoned this novel fragment altogether. As she wrote to her editor in 1966, "The manuscript seems to me like a helpless allusion to something that still needs to be written" *(TP* 2: 397).

In later "Ways of Death" texts, Bachmann developed more successful strategies for representing the encounter of the White Lady and the Dark Continent. Where *The Book of Franza* had directly thematized the clash of race and gender categories, later texts merely *display* a female psyche constituted by historically specific discourses of race and gender, her figures so entirely the products of history that they are unable to advance a critique of their own circumstances beyond that which prevailing discourses would allow. One might even maintain that in certain respects the White Ladies in Bachmann's later "Ways of Death" texts accede to a definition of themselves as the Dark Continent: that is, they accept the racial preconceptions that define white female sexuality as unexplored terrain, a riddle, an enigma, which white men wish to colonize but whose heart of darkness neither men nor women (who in these texts remain mysteries to themselves) can fully plumb. Although White Ladies cannot be represented as the direct agents of imperialism, they are clearly implicated in its racial logic, as captive to racial fantasies and projections as white men (though implementing them in gender-specific ways). One key component of their racial identity is thus their utter obliviousness to their own racial determinants. As well, contra scholars who attempt to exempt Germans and Austrians from orientalism because Germany and Austria had no direct national interests in the Middle East, the vantage point from which Bachmann views imperialism emphasizes the imbrication of all Europeans, not just those with an explicitly colonial past, in the imperial/neocolonial and racial order of the West. Such a reading of Bachmann's investigation of imperialism makes it possible to read her haughty rejoinder to criticisms of *Malina* as something more than a feeble justification for that novel's apparent lack of attention to politics: "If for example I say nothing in this book *Malina* about the Vietnam War, nothing about so and so many catastrophic conditions of our society, then I know how to say it in a different way—or I hope that I know how to say it" *(GuI* 90–91). What Bachmann's texts quite deliberately portray, one might maintain, is the kind of consciousness that made Vietnam possible.

A key incident in Bachmann's Eka Kottwitz/Aga Rottwitz fragment, added to that unfinished novel in 1968–69, moves the violent encounter of race and gender to the center stage of the "Ways of Death." An African student accompanies Countess Kottwitz, a brilliant political journalist and the novel's protagonist, home after a lecture and makes violent love to her. Although the countess, hitherto quite uninterested in lovemaking ("over thirty, she still . . . had . . . not a clue what an orgasm was" [*TP* 1: 419]), experiences the sexual encounter as a bestial assault, she finds it has left her sexually awakened and "completely transformed" (*TP* 1: 427). Yet even though the African declares his love for her, Countess Kottwitz, "who was no Lady Chatterley" (*TP* 1: 426), refuses to acknowledge her newly aroused passion for him. Instead, she proclaims she is now finally able to love her current boyfriend, Jung. When Jung leaves her for another woman, Eka throws herself from a window and is permanently paralyzed. The scene immediately preceding the sexual encounter offers a clue to how Bachmann wanted her story to be read: sitting in a bar in the Hamburg hotel Vier Jahreszeiten, Countess Kottwitz orders a drink called a "White Lady" (*TP* 1: 424).

One might read this passage as a vivid illustration of the white female fantasy that Fanon describes in *Black Skin, White Masks*: "A Negro is raping me." In general, as Mary Ann Doane points out, Fanon views sexuality as a major arena for the articulation of racism. His analysis of this racialized fantasy is founded upon Helene Deutsch's and Marie Bonaparte's definitions of adult female sexuality as fundamentally masochistic. That conception of femininity finds support in many passages in Bachmann's writing: the "I" of *Malina* muses, for instance, "No normal man with normal drives has the obvious idea that a normal woman would like to be quite normally raped" (*Malina* 180). Following Freud, Fanon maintains that normal adult female sexuality requires the renunciation of aggression and the acceptance of properly female passive sexual aims. In a racist society, Fanon maintains, "the Negro becomes the predestined depository of this aggressiveness. If we go farther into the labyrinth, we discover that when a woman lives the fantasy to be raped by a Negro, it is in some way the fulfillment of a private dream, of an inner wish. Accomplishing the phenomenon of turning against self, it is the woman who rapes herself" (175). Doane's gloss on this passage is useful: "Fanon finds that the fantasy of being raped by a Negro constitutes the assimilation by the woman of a cultural treasurehouse of images concerning blackness and their incorporation within what is a basic structure of femininity" (231). Though Bachmann might have formulated Fanon's explanation somewhat differently, his is an analysis with which she might not fundamentally have disagreed. From "Love: The Dark Continent" and "The Good God of Manhattan" through *Malina*, her female figures seek out powerful men who hurt them and to whom they can submit themselves, and their sexual pleasure is greater if they can also see themselves as contravening social taboos. To the White Lady, rape by a "Negro" optimally satisfies these criteria.

What makes the portrait of this White Lady far more compelling than those of Bachmann's other figures who achieve a transgressive sexual satisfaction is the careful delineation of how precisely the features of Countess Kottwitz's character that make "rape" by a "Negro" especially exciting to her also prevent her from acknowledging this relationship as one that finally meets her sexual needs. The boyfriend Jung is represented as an indifferent lover who fails entirely to respond to Eka's awkward attempts to arouse him:

> Jung had kissed her a few times, in the early days, that was the single form of affection that occurred to him, otherwise he fell upon her occasionally, and Eka didn't admit to herself that it was unbearable for her, that she expected something else, she just didn't know what, and sometimes she was overcome by silly notions, she threw herself on him like [a] child and hugged him and pressed herself against him in the desperate hope that something would occur to him. Jung either shoved her away with a laugh [or] called her a silly teenager, while Eka's face got grayer and grayer and more and more strained and had nothing at all in common with that of a teenager. (TP 1: 420)

The encounter with the African takes place as a consequence of mutual sexual attraction, as Bachmann underlines in a passage that charmingly reproduces the confusion of swelling sexual passion: "Then he took her by the hand, and she saw his beautiful black hand, her beautiful white hand, both beautiful hands, slim, too long, hands too long, hands too much" (TP 1: 424). But as this enormously erudite woman has no idea where the student's African homeland might be located ("He was from Somaliland, and Eka admitted to herself that she didn't exactly know, for once not exactly, though she knew everything exactly" [TP 1: 424]), so the only terms Eka can find to describe their passion derive from a racist vocabulary that defines their erotic exchange as violent and barbaric: "In the next moment the Somali student had torn her from the armchair, perhaps not exactly torn, but taken"(TP 1: 426); "in this situation that just seemed grotesque to her" (TP 1: 425); "it's bestial, I'm dying, I'm dying" (TP 1: 425); "After he raped her once more he left" (TP 1: 427); "I was no longer a human being, I was an animal" (TP 1: 429). She can experience sexual pleasure with the African because the intensity of the sexual act disrupts her white interpretive schema—"it was simply the end of all her preconceptions" (TP 1: 425)— and it unsettles her ego boundaries: "her ego [Ich] was eradicated" (TP 1: 430). But once she reestablishes her psychic boundaries—"in the process of restoring her ego [dabei, ihr Ich wiederherzustellen]" (TP 1: 425)—she is convinced that she loves only Jung, a white man. In their commentary to this passage, the editors of the critical edition point to its affinities with the utopian "orgy" of the "Wüstenbuch," a connection supported by a later version of this passage in which the "rapist" is called "Abdu," also the name of one of the trio of Egyptian lovers. But what makes this fragment different from Bachmann's other utopian evocations of erotic transport is Eka's incapacity to transcend the cultural limitations that prevent her from embracing a sexual relationship proscribed by the culture of which she is part.

Of course, there is a way out for the White Lady, as Bachmann underlines via her allusion to D. H. Lawrence's novel: to satisfy her sexual needs, Eka could follow the example of Connie Chatterley, jettison her miserable affair with Jung, and cast her lot with the Somali student. In a paper called "Do White Ladies Get the Blues? Nancy Cunard and Desire," Sabine Broeck has shown that other twentieth-century White Ladies, such as Lady Nancy Cunard, heir to the Cunard steamship line fortune and patron of the Harlem Renaissance, made the decision to flout racial and sexual taboos. Yet not just racism but also her aristocratic fastidiousness make that impossible for Eka, in whom even bad taste in furniture occasions a physical reaction, and this student dares to call her *Lieb-chen* and wants to sleep with her after they have made love: "sleep with her, now that was really the last straw [*mit ihr schlafen, das war nun wirklich die Höhe*]" (*TP* 1: 427). As Biddy Martin and Chandra Mohanty put it in a quite different context: "Change has to do with the transgression of boundaries, those boundaries so carefully, so tenaciously, so invisibly drawn around white identity" (203). Unable to transcend the definitions that constitute her, Eka instead constructs a story that allows her to remain who she is and affirm her sexuality, too: "I don't love this Negro, I love Jung" (*TP* 1: 428). But as the editors of *Powers of Desire: The Politics of Sexuality* emphasize, the myth of the black rapist is a sexual story that white men tell each other to justify their violence toward black men *and* their control over black and white women (Snitow et al. 328). By opting for that myth, Eka makes the choice to reinsert herself into a racist social order that also subordinates women. After Jung leaves her, even that narrative construction is no longer available to her, and there is no way for her both to remain a White Lady and to affirm her sexuality: she is paralyzed by her absence of choices. So she leaps from the window, destroying the body that has betrayed her, and thenceforth is also really, not just metaphorically, paralyzed—confined for life to a wheelchair. In one of the introductions to *The Book of Franza*, Bachmann called her female figures' implication in categories of their social order "thinking ... that leads to dying" (*Franza* 4). Like the other "Ways of Death," the Eka Kottwitz fragment reveals the self-destructive consequences of women's compliance with the dictates of the society that has called them into being.

What conception of the formation of female subjectivity underlies the Eka

Kottwitz fragment? While criticizing Fanon's flattening of the complex concepts of sexual difference, desire, and sexuality, Gwen Bergner has argued that one of his major accomplishments in *Black Skin, White Masks* is adding race to the psychoanalytic explanation of the production of subjectivity: "Fanon transposes psychoanalysis—a theory of subject formation based on sexual difference—to a register where it accounts for race as one of the fundamental differences that constitute subjectivity" (76). One might argue that that is also Bachmann's achievement in this text, that that is how she represents "history *within* the I/psyche." Anne McClintock, in pursuit of her project of developing a *"situated psychoanalysis*—a culturally contextualized psychoanalysis that is simultaneously a psychoanalytically informed history" (72), proposes that Julia Kristeva's notion of "abjection" helps to explain the function of racist exclusions in modern industrial societies. Following Freud, Kristeva also maintains that civilization is founded on the repudiation of those elements that society considers impure: "The abject is everything that the subject seeks to expunge in order to become social; it is also a symptom of the failure of this ambition. ... the expelled abject haunts the subject as its inner constitutive boundary; that which is repudiated forms the self's internal limit. The abject is 'something rejected from which one does not part'" (McClintock 71 citing Kristeva, 9). This conception of abjection might help explain both the disruptive allure for Eka of sex with the Somali student and the urgency of her denial that she is aroused by him; the abject, Kristeva argues, "simultaneously beseeches and pulverizes the subject" (5). If the rejection of blackness and an active female sexuality is the guarantee of the stability of Eka's white female psyche, acknowledging the repressed and threatening otherness they represent could cause the whole racial-sexual edifice to come tumbling down.

Yet though it is quite easy to advance a psychoanalytic explanation for the psychology of Eka and other "Ways of Death" figures, it may also be important to stress the limitations of such a Freudian model. Ann Laura Stoler has pointed out that much postcolonial analysis is based on "the premise that colonial power relations can be accounted for and explained as a sublimated expression of repressed desires in the West, of desires that resurface in moralizing missions, myths of the 'wild woman,' in a romance with the rural 'primitive,' or in other more violent, virile, substitute form" (167–68). It is exactly this "repressive hypothesis," however, that Foucauldian analysis has drawn into question. Though Bachmann clearly understands (female) desire as molded by social forces, much of her work seems also premised on the assumption that "desire is a basic biological drive, restricted and repressed by a 'civilization' that forces our sublimation of it," to use Stoler's formulation (171). Foucault would of course argue that desire was not repressed by or opposed to a (racialized) order of civilization but produced by it. The question that might then arise is to what degree notions of a natural and primordial desire which civilization needs to channel and regulate might relate to or even derive from imperial strategies developed to control unruly, oversexed natives (or white women, for that matter— a speculation that the application of the Dark Continent motif to white female sexuality would support). As Stoler puts it: "The nineteenth-century discourse on bourgeois sexuality may better be understood as a recuperation of a protracted discourse on race, for the discourse of sexuality contains many of the latter's most salient elements. That discourse on sexuality was binary and contrastive, in its nineteenth-century variant always pitting that middle-class respectable sexuality as a defense against an internal and external other that was at once essentially different but uncomfortably the same" (193). If there is merit to this argument, it could then be maintained that Bachmann's attempt to grapple with the racialized foundations of female sexuality, by portraying a female figure whose repressed (or abject-ed) desire is loosed by her sexual encounter with a black man, might still remain captive to precisely the discourses of race, gender, and sexuality that her texts want to interrogate.

As well, one might again ask whether in this text Bachmann also contributes in a less complicated way to the perpetuation of racist stereotypes. Though the complex narrative stance of the fragment makes it difficult to determine to what degree Eka's responses determine the representation of the sexual encounter, to what degree a (somewhat) more impartial narrator is speaking, the sexual act seems to be portrayed as violent, brutal, and lacking in reciprocity, the Somali student oblivious to Eka's protests and cries of pain: "she noticed that he didn't notice at all, not because he was a sadist to whom her tears, her despair gave pleasure, but rather because she was no one at all for him, not a person, merely an object" (TP 1: 425). The student himself is represented as a Noble Savage possessed of a wholeness unavailable to Europeans: "He was so at one with himself, with his body, with his will, that he simply didn't hear this Eka, this blind woman, any longer." And his sexual potency is nothing short of prodigious: "Then he lay down, after two hours, and said to her, . . . I'm very tired today, please forgive me" (TP 1: 426). Finally, the student is not treated as a subject in his own right: except in the very last draft he has no name and, though a student of political science in his fifth semester, is unable to express himself in German: "Eka . . . didn't understand for a moment how somebody could speak German so badly and could study here nonetheless" (TP 1: 423).

This text, one might thus argue, is not an account of the complexities and misunderstandings of cross-cultural encounters but instead uses rather conventional representations of a black figure to talk about the problems of white women. As Leslie Adelson inquired, faced with a not entirely dissimilar treatment of black men in a text by a white German woman writer: "If the story is not about the relationship to blacks as persons, and it is not, then why use them as a symbol?" (52). Though it is always difficult to determine to what degree the perspectives of Bachmann's figures and her own coincide, it appears that other portraits of black figures in her texts (leaving aside the embarrassing racist gaffe of her 1956 poem "Harlem": "The black city rolls its white eyes" [W 1: 113]) suffer from similar problems. In a passage omitted from the final version of Malina, the "I" seeks the sexual services of an otherwise mute black man during a transatlantic crossing: "On the ship to America there was an arrogant young Negro at the bar, looking for work, dismissed from a French band, with a miserable vocabulary, he always came in the night, during the day we greeted each other fleetingly, he acted as if he didn't know me, I also scarcely looked at him" (TP 3.2: 719). "Again and Again: Black and White," an unpublished poem in the Bachmann archive, recalls the racial fantasies of "Love: The Dark Continent." The poetic "I" imagines that her skin has absorbed the color of her black lover and fancies "that my young blackness derives from your old / from your age-old native blackness." "You call me," the poem concludes, "like the Queen of Zambezi" ("Immer wieder"). Though Bachmann is clearly attempting to mobilize racial images for antiracist purposes, her appropriation of them to address the needs of white women seems to retain white women at the center with the resources of the rest of the world at their disposal—a practice suggesting that Bachmann herself is not altogether exempt from the criticism she directs at her figures. One might thus make the same point about Bachmann that Adelson has made of the portrait of violent black GIs in Anne Duden's The Opening of the Mouth: "As to whether Opening explodes a racist premise or reproduces it, I can only answer, yes, it does both" (54).

In "Three Paths to the Lake," the final story of the collection Three Paths to the Lake, Bachmann makes the connection between postcoloniality and Austrian imperialism toward which she gestured in the interview I cited at the beginning of this chapter, assessing the consequences of participation in a colonial/postcolonial paradigm for her white female protagonist and again showing how the imperial white psyche is implicated in the very "ways of death" responsible for its destruction. Toward the beginning of "Three Paths to the Lake," Elisabeth Matrei, the story's central figure, stranded in a London hotel without a ticket for a flight back home to Austria, discovers herself to be surrounded by postcolonial peoples: "Room service consisted of Indians, Filipinos, and Africans, once there had been an old Englishman, and all the guests, too, were from Asia and Africa, she rode in the large elevators in the midst of silent masses, the only white person." Dismayed that "her old London had disappeared, everything she had once enjoyed," Elisabeth complains that the postcolonials do not even speak English properly: "The guests and employees communicated in an English limited to a handful of expressions, and using one more than the allotted number meant not being understood. It wasn't a living language that was spoken, it was a kind of Esperanto . . ." (Edward Said has commented on such discomfited reactions to a postcolonial presence: "The world has changed . . . in ways that have surprised, and often alarmed, metropolitan Europeans and Americans, who now confront large non-white immigrant populations in their midst, and face an impressive roster of newly empowered voices asking for their narratives to be heard" [*Culture* xx].) A well-traveled cosmopolitan, Elisabeth adapts herself to her circumstances: "She quickly forgot her English, using that confounded Esperanto," but she is surprised by her own discomfort in the postcolonial metropole. "She had never felt apprehension in Asia or Africa and had enjoyed being alone and leaving the others when she traveled with a group, being the woman who rode away, but not here. In this place everything was so monotonous, the people were all completely mindless, nothing was right" (*Paths* 130, translation modified).

As the editors of the critical edition point out in their commentary, "The Woman Who Rode Away" is the title of a 1925 short story by D. H. Lawrence (*TP* 4: 630). Notorious at least since 1970, when Kate Millett denounced its sexism in *Sexual Politics* (285–293), Lawrence's story explores the consequences of the decision of a white American woman living in Mexico to leave her European husband and ride away in search of the "secret haunts of [the] timeless, mysterious, marvelous Indians of the mountains" who still maintain "their own savage customs and religion" (347). "She is weary of the white man's God," she tells the Indians she encounters in the mountains. "She would like to serve the gods of the Chilchui" (360). As Lawrence presents them, this group of Indians, latter-day descendants of the Aztecs, believe that whites have stolen the Indians' power over their god, the sun, but as one member of the tribe explains, "When a white woman sacrifices herself to our gods, then our gods will begin to make the world again, and the white man's gods will fall to pieces" (372). Held captive by the Indians for months, the woman scarcely minds, musing that "her kind of womanhood, intensely personal and individual, was to be obliterated again, and the great primeval symbols were to tower once again over the fallen individual independence of woman" (371). The story ends on the day of the winter solstice as the woman, naked and spread-eagled upon a sacrificial altar in a deep cave, awaits the moment when the last rays of the setting sun enter the cave and the blind old priest plunges his flint knife into her heart.

Why does Elisabeth Matrei turn to the title of D. H. Lawrence's story to characterize her prior experience in the Third World, and what does Bachmann's allusion to Lawrence's text tell us about race, gender, sexuality, and postcoloniality in her work? Here, as elsewhere in her writing (see also chapters 7 and 10), Bachmann employs a reference to another author's text as an ironic device to establish the larger discursive context within which her character functions and thereby to tell her readers something about the character that the character herself does not know (for instance, that Eka Kottwitz, though "no Lady Chatterley," functions within discourses of sexuality similar to Lawrence's). Even though Lawrence's tale of a dissatisfied wife's quest for obliteration might on first examination seem to have little relationship to the self-reflections of Elisabeth, a world-renowned photojournalist, it can in fact be used as a kind of key to unlock several levels of meaning in Bachmann's story. Elisabeth, like Lawrence, moves within a discursive universe premised upon the binary opposition between a universalizing Western modernity and an otherness comprising everything the West is not, and her distress about current events and her "imperialist nostalgia" (Rosaldo 70) for the old Austro-Hungarian empire rest on another version of that binary paradigm, her longing for a long-lost Austrian home contrasted to the postmodern rootlessness of a figure in the story borrowed from Joseph Roth's *Radetzkymarsch* (Radetzky march) and *Kapuzinergruft* (Crypt of the Capuchins): Franz Joseph Eugen Trotta. Those fatal binaries are also linked to the causes of Elisabeth's personal and sexual malaise, so dire that she declares, "It would be best if women and men kept their distance and had nothing to do with each other until both had found their way out of the tangle and confusion, the discrepancy inherent in all relationships" (*Paths* 175)—a quotation that, as the editors of the critical edition tell us, is also borrowed from D.H. Lawrence (*TP* 4: 633).

In *Primitive Passions: Men, Women, and the Quest for Ecstasy*, Marianna Torgovnick identifies "The Woman Who Rode Away" and Lawrence's other late texts set in Mexico and New Mexico as examples of what she terms primitivism. "The West," she argues, "has been engaged, almost continuously, in defining itself against a series of 'primitive' Others in its midst and without. . . . The primitive," she continues, "is the sign and symbol of desires the West has sought to repress—desires for direct correspondence between experience and language, direct correspondence between individual feelings and the collective life force. It is the sign and symbol of desire for a full and sated sense of the universe" (*Primitive* 8). In an earlier book, *Going Primitive*, Torgovnick connects the primitive to "going home": "The metaphor of finding a home or being at home recurs over and over as a structuring pattern within Western primitivism. . . . Whatever form the primitive's hominess takes, its strangeness salves our estrangement from ourselves and our culture" (*Going* 185). The primitive, Torgovnick concludes, thus becomes the solution to the "transcendental homelessness" that Georg Lukács considered to be the condition of the modern Western mind (*Theory* 41)—no doubt the reason Franza believed that in North Africa she would "come into [her] own."

In a postmodern and postcolonial era, however we now recognize that though the quest for a return to origins, fullness of being, full presence, and "home" may be a founding myth of Western thought—in Novalis's words, "Philosophy is actually homesickness, the urge to be everywhere at home" (135)—it is also only that, a myth. As Iain Chambers puts it, "We can never go home, return to the primal scene, the forgotten moment of our beginnings, and authenticity, for there is always something else in between. We cannot return to a bygone unity, for we can only know the past, memory, the unconscious, through its effects, that is, when it is brought into language" (*Border* 104). Moreover, we now know as well that the belief in such an imaginary unity, whether located in an archaic past or in other primitive peoples and places, is fundamentally an imperialist gesture that disregards the actual heterogeneity of that which is not modern or Western and places all of history and all the rest of the world at our own Western disposal. Or, as Chambers observes: "In absolute difference the rhetoric of alterity locates a pure otherness awaiting our words, like the 'empty' wilderness—from the African *veldt* to the American West—waiting to be settled and domesticated and brought into the redemptive time of our history" ("Signs" 57–58).

Precisely this frame of reference explains Elisabeth Matrei. In many regards she can be regarded as the epitome of modernity. She is emancipated in the most literal sense: she is groomed by famous male photographers for her profession as a photojournalist and insists on assuming the position of men even on the most dangerous Third World assignments: "I can't accept my being spared and not the men. It's not like that anymore with other things, all that changed long ago!" (*Paths* 141). (Alternatively, one might maintain that as a photojournalist Elisabeth, like other "emancipated" female figures in Bachmann's writing—Nadja, a translator, in "Word for Word"; Charlotte, a pianist, in "A Step towards Gomorrah"—is consigned to the female realm of reproduction though paradoxically within the public arena, expected faithfully to reproduce the products, activities, and utterances of the subjects of world history—namely, men.) At the end of the story she accepts an assignment a male photographer is unable to carry out and is preparing to fly to Saigon to photograph the Vietnam War. (One recalls again Bachmann's statement that in *Malina* she was able to address the Vietnam War "in another way.")

As a photojournalist, Elisabeth is committed to what the editor of *Modernity and the Hegemony of Vision* has termed "ocularcentrism," "a distinctly modern historical form . . . allied with all the forces of our advanced technologies. The power to make visible is the power to control" (Levin 2-3, 7). (Photographs accompanying the accounts of explorers and anthropologists are one obvious example of how vision and technology have combined to document and control the world's others, as the authors of *Reading* National Geographic, among many others, have pointed out [Lutz/Collins].) Enlightenment is evidently the process of making visible what is obscured, subjecting it to the clear light of reason, and Elisabeth is convinced that photojournalism performs precisely this task, producing an enlightened understanding of world events such as the Algerian War and the Suez Crisis: "People had to be made aware of what was going on there, they needed to see those pictures to 'wake up' to reality" (*Paths* 140–141). Via her success at taking on the power of the male gaze, Elisabeth is able to assume the stance of the universal, disembodied (i.e., male) Enlightenment subject. But as Meyda Yegenoglu emphasizes: "Since the universal is conceived of on the basis of one and access to it is restricted, the only possible way for women to enter into this privileged space and enjoy its benefits is through *imitating the male gesture.* In other words, they are allowed to enjoy the benefits of universality only if they assume a male position. The strange paradox here is that women's acceptance of a share in the universalistic simultaneously implies a denial of their difference. There is then no affirmative entry to the universal for women as women" (105). That is to say, Elisabeth's very assumption of universal subject status means precisely that she will be unable to attend to or even articulate her own female concerns: "She never said a word about the things that really upset her, because they weren't fit to be put in any words at all" (*Paths* 172)—a point I explore in greater detail below.

This analysis can help us, I think, to explain Elisabeth's discomfort in the new postcolonial London. Despite—or perhaps even because of—her avowed support for Third World liberation struggles, Elisabeth occupies a position paradigmatically that of the liberal Western subject who regards the model of progress and development advocated by the West as world-historical—a view that, as Leela Gandhi puts it, regards "'history' as the grand narrative through which Eurocentrism is totalised as the proper account of all humanity" (171).

Within the liberal version of this narrative, the West's others either become (like) Europeans or remain in their proper place. "Propelling itself forward in pursuit of linear redemption," Chambers maintains, "ever newer, ever brighter, ever better, and constantly forgetting itself in order to overcome itself, Western modernity underwrites an alterity located elsewhere in backwardness, in a black cloth of darkness, to both underline and justify its movement" ("Signs" 57). To be sure, that backward, primitive alterity can readily also become conceptualized as object of desire, as Torgovnick emphasizes. But what this Western subject cannot tolerate are others who refuse the site of alterity allocated to them. Rey Chow, for instance, argues that a neo-orientalist anxiety reveals itself in the desire—very like that of "the woman who rode away"—to retrieve and preserve the pure, authentic native. Chow continues, however, that under the conditions of globalization, like those Elisabeth encounters in London, the native is no longer available as "pure, unadulterated object" but is, rather, "contaminated by the West, dangerously un-Otherable" (Gandhi 127 citing Chow 12). In effect, the Empire talks or writes back, as the title of a famous anthology would have it (Ashcroft et all).

Chambers summarizes precisely the situation Elisabeth encounters in London: "So, a linguistic and literary context such as 'English,' which has historically stood in Britain, or at least in metropolitan London, for a specific cultural, historical, and national identity, comes to be re-written, re-routed, and re-sited. Inhabiting English, other stories, memories, and identities cause metropolitan authority to stumble. For they talk back to it, take the language elsewhere, and then return with it to interrupt the nation-narration at its very 'centre.'" ("Signs" 49). As Chambers details, the disruptions to the dominant paradigm of Western modernity occasioned by the emergence of the postcolonial subject are profound:

> The proprietary rights of language, history and truth are no longer able to hide in the metaphysical mimicry of universal knowledge or national identity. Such accounts are now exposed through a radical historicity as partial and partisan. Such journeys among the uneven and unexplained effects of these "contact zones" that have now expanded to compose much of metropolitan culture throughout the world, challenge the myth of modernism as a homogeneous movement and moment, restricted to a centralised economic power and a particular geopolitical population and place. The predator of progress, establishing the ratio of the West, today encounters transmutation and travesty in the very languages it assumed were its own. ("Signs" 50, 57).

Indeed, the woman who rode away has reason to be concerned—the universalistic system of values that had founded her belief in the legitimacy and value of her actions is entirely drawn into question by the condition of postcoloniality.

Elisabeth's is not, however, the only relationship to the new postcolonial culture represented in "Three Paths to the Lake." One of the great loves of Elisabeth's life, Franz Joseph Trotta, is also her philosophical and political antagonist in Bachmann's story, and the challenge he poses to her positions makes it possible to bring this critique of Elisabeth back home to a postimperial Austria. The "home" in the small Austrian city to which Elisabeth returns on a visit to her father stands for the same sort of solace, familiarity, and *Geborgenheit* (security) that Torgovnick ascertained to be the fundamental structure of the Western desire for the primitive, and the lake that she can reach via none of the three hiking paths, since the new autobahn built for German tourists has cut off access to it, is a metonymic representation of the oceanic dissolution that Westerners hope the primitive will allow them to achieve. In contrast to the Esperanto of London, Elisabeth is soothed by the "familiar tones" (*Paths* 131; translation modified) of Austria and "that old civil-servant German" of her father, "always appropriate to himself, his idiom and his mood": that is, his speech manifests a "direct correspondence between experience and language" (*Paths* 177). Elisabeth perceives the roots of the Austria she loves in the old Austro-Hungarian empire, "this gigantic, pointless empire which was more loved than hated" (*Paths* 170, translation modified); like her father she believes that Austria was most profoundly transformed not by National Socialism but by the dissolution of the empire, "that the year 1938 had not been a turning point: the split had occurred much earlier and everything that followed had been a consequence of this older split, and that his world—which he had hardly experienced after all—was destroyed for good in 1914" (*Paths* 179). From the perspective of the present Elisabeth conceives her brother and herself to be condemned to estrangement because the empire is gone: "But what made them strangers wherever they went was their sensitivity, because they came from the periphery and thus their thoughts, feelings and actions were hopelessly bound to this ghostly empire of gigantic dimensions. The right passports didn't exist for them, for it was a country which didn't issue passports" (*Paths* 122–23).

From a postcolonial perspective it is possible to recognize this apparently benign nostalgia as in fact a desire for the restoration of the good old days of empire (and, connected to empire, perhaps, as Ellen Friedman has suggested, a longing for vanished master-narratives altogether, a "yearning for fathers, for past authority and sure knowledge that can no longer be supported'" [240].) It is the Rothian Trotta—originally a Slovenian, now a French citizen—who both embodies the postimperial condition and reveals what is most problematic about Elisabeth's stance. For the collapse of the Austro-Hungarian empire has had an effect on Trotta like that of postcoloniality, as Claudio Magris comments more generally of Joseph Roth's figures in his classic study *Der habsburgische Mythos in der österreichischen Literatur* (the Habsburg myth in Austrian literature) : "With the collapse of the empire all values, all guaranties for a strong secure life and the precious pleasure of everyday life seem to disappear. The Austrian-Hungarian decline seems to mean the irretrievable end of all healthy, firmly established possibilities of life" (257–58). Trotta acknowledges his position as "a real exile, one of the lost ones" (*Paths* 139); rather than longing for the purity of an originary mother tongue, he speaks all languages of his exile equally well; unconvinced that humanity is infinitely improvable, Trotta ridicules Elisabeth's "fresh, strong faith" that her photographs will make people "see reason" (*Paths* 143); arguing that it is shameful to photograph human suffering for the amusement of newspaper readers, Trotta forces Elisabeth to recognize that her profession is implicated in the injustices she believes she is combatting. Most important, as a member of a subordinate group in rebellion against the old empire rather than of its ruling elite—that is, one of the empire's others— Trotta disrupts Elisabeth's affection for an innocent Austria upon which Germany preyed. Intimating that Austrians' behavior after 1938 may be rooted in their imperial past, Trotta observes that, though the German soldiers in Hitler's army were only following orders, Austrian soldiers were genuinely depraved: "The enjoyment they got out of every kind of brutality imaginable was written clearly all over their ugly faces" (*Paths* 151). Whereas Elisabeth, like other Western subjects, longs and strives in many ways to return to an originary home, Trotta represents the position of Joseph Roth, who affirmed the diaspora, who asserted, "A human being is not a tree," and who argued, "Wandering is not a curse but a blessing" (Gerhard 12 citing Roth, "Segen" 532).

In this context, Elisabeth's later relationship to a much younger lover, twenty-eight-year-old Philippe, a veteran of the Paris events of May 1968, reinforces Trotta's lessons. If 1968 can be regarded as a last great effort on the part of Westerners themselves to combine a struggle against Western imperialism with a struggle for their own subjective self-realization, its failure might also be regarded as marking the end point of that Western quest for universal justice

and happiness. By the time of this story (probably summer 1971), Philippe's out-
bursts of rage are no longer directed at "the regime, capitalism and imperialism,
but at his comrades who had disintegrated into splinter groups and were battling against each other" (*Paths* 207), and his decision at the story's end to leave
Elisabeth and marry the pregnant, drug-addicted daughter of a rich mobster
signals his—and others'—betrayal of the aims of 1968. "But where had the May
gone?" wonders Elisabeth (*Paths* 212). Nor does the historical course of events
in the non-European world prove Elisabeth right and Trotta wrong: Algeria
after liberation also fails to become a shining exemplar of human progress
toward universal emancipation. Dismayed at "what was threatening to become
of that freedom," Elisabeth suppresses her private doubts, maintains her public
commitment to struggles of national liberation, and reports "all sorts of positive
things with cautious reservations," nonetheless aware that her article represents
"her first conscious defection to the land of lies" (*Paths* 144–145).

Over the course of subsequent decades, the example of Trotta's postimperial
displacement erodes Elisabeth's confidence in the values on which her activities
had been premised and compels her to acknowledge the contradictions of her
own location. Once she relinquishes her belief that she is contributing to a project of universal human liberation, she is finally forced into a kind of ontological
exile like Trotta's own: "He had left an impression on her . . . because he made
her conscious of so many things, because of his origins and because he—a real
exile, one of the lost ones—had made her—an adventuress who expected God
knows what from the world during her lifetime—had made an exile of her:
Long after his death he slowly pulled her down with him to ruin, alienating
her from the miracles and allowing her to recognize this alienation as her destiny" (*Paths* 139). In conjunction with the Lawrence citation, Trotta's response
to Elisabeth suggests a reading of this story that would locate Elisabeth, much
in contrast to what she believes her intentions to be, within a discursive paradigm that permits only one monolinear history, the history of the victors, and
leaves no discursive space, no language even, for the conquered and colonized
to tell their different story.

Finally, Elisabeth's conception of herself as "the woman who rode away" has
multiple consequences for the construction of her own femininity. In many ways
"Three Paths to the Lake" is a refiguring of the constellation of characters in
Malina, though Elisabeth combines in one person the cool, rational, masculine
Malina and the distraught unnamed female "I" who can find no language to tell
her own story. As I have already suggested, the universalistic, disembodied sub-

ject position Elisabeth assumes brings her fame and even some fortune but no happiness at all. At many points in her life she merely moves through the paces of her female role without any interior engagement: as a young woman "she had gone to bed unemotionally, only, as she had believed, to do a man a favor" (*Paths* 138); after age forty, "her increasing success with men was directly related to her increasing indifference to them" (*Paths* 174). In effect, like the "I" of *Malina*, she is "really" a woman only when she is "really," passionately, in love, and then she performs femininity according to a script men have passed down (the performer in her father's play, as in *Malina*), loving only men (themselves tellingly from the old empire) who treat her badly and abandon her inexplicably, leaving her sobbing alone by the telephone. But "Three Paths to the Lake" is *Malina* with a difference: whereas the "I" of *Malina* acts almost exclusively within the private realm, here Elisabeth shows that the gender paradigm to which she conforms— disembodied universal subject versus woman as man's object—is also inadequate to deal with a postmodern and postcolonial public realm except from the perspective of the dominant order: that is, one diametrically opposed to what Elisabeth believes to be her own quest for justice. One might then inquire whether the quotation she borrows from Lawrence to characterize gender relations and her hopes for their future rectification may be likewise intended to critique her standpoint as a *woman* as profoundly as the allusion to "The Woman Who Rode Away" indicts her as a neocolonialist. Elisabeth muses of romantic heterosexual love, "Perhaps one day something else might come along but only then, and it would be strong and mysterious and have real greatness, something to which each could once again submit" (*Paths* 175). Here sexuality is postulated to be the alternative to her public, masculinist role—but perhaps here, too, she is subjecting herself to a mystical concept of love in the same way that the woman who rode away subjects herself to the flint knife in the icy cave; perhaps here she is once more trapped in fatal binaries that will destroy her as surely as the Good God of Manhattan blew Jennifer to bits and Eka Kottwitz is imprisoned in her wheelchair.

In a somewhat related context, as she interviews prestigious gynecologists to formulate the text for a photo-reportage on abortion and is appalled that the doctors understand nothing at all about what really concerns their women patients "with their problems and their men and their inability to say one single true word about their lives," Elisabeth rages: "Why doesn't someone ask me for a change, why not ask someone who thinks independently and dares to live, what have you done to me and so many others, you with your insane empathy with every kind of problem, hasn't it ever occurred to anyone that you kill people when you deprive them of the power of speech and with it the power to experience and think" (*Paths* 173). Not simply from the perspective of postcoloniality but also from the perspective of gender relations, Elisabeth's conception of herself as the woman who rode away suggests that she has accommodated herself to, or is the discursive product of, conceptions about gender relations that are virtually assured not to meet her needs as a person *or* as a woman.

And this, finally, may explain Bachmann's own peculiar comment about women's emancipation in a 1971 interview (that is, shortly before she published *Three Paths to the Lake*): "Perhaps that's quite remarkable for you that precisely a woman who always earned her own money, who paid for her own university study, always lived alone, that she says that she doesn't care at all about women's emancipation. I've always found the pseudomodern woman with her tortured efficiency and energy completely strange and incomprehensible" (*GuI* 109). At the end of the same interview Bachmann remarks that, as she wrote *Malina,* she had the feeling "that I'm writing against something. Against a persistent terrorism. After all, people don't really die from illnesses. They die from what's been done to them" (*GuI* 110). It may be that Elisabeth, precisely such an emancipated, pseudomodern woman, is also a victim of the system that has made her a professional success, and, as Bachmann's use of literary allusions in this story may demonstrate, that she is also incapable of saying a single true word about her life. In "Three Paths to the Lake," Elisabeth's reflections may record not just the bloody struggles that accompany movements for national liberation and decolonization but also, and unknown to her, the story of her "way of death."

Yet again it's necessary to ask how the bleakness of "Three Paths to the Lake" might be related to Bachmann's own inability to extricate herself from the system she wished to criticize. On the one hand, there is certainly nothing wrong with considering the problems of white women and men, even in a postcolonial era (though one might argue, as some critics have maintained of postmodern and even postcolonial theory, that this is a way to retain white people at the center of consideration after real historical developments have displaced them). On the other hand, Bachmann sees the problems of the era entirely from a white perspective—doubtless her point if she wished to show how history inscribes the white psyche. But the chaos and disorder Bachmann believes she perceives in the postcolonial world doubtless look rather different from the perspective of newly liberated peoples. In fact, as Homi Bhabha has pointed out, the sense of alienation Bachmann's characters feel when encountering new hybrid cultural forms is precisely a consequence of the subversive political intervention that such new cultural productions undertake, reversing "the effects of the colonial disavowal, so that other 'denied' knowledges enter upon the dominant discourse and estrange the basis of its authority" (156). Similarly, at least for non-Western peoples, the status of exile might also be considered one of gain as well as loss, a position from which contemporary intellectual and political leadership could best be undertaken, as Said has underlined: "it is no exaggeration to say that liberation as an intellectual mission, born in the resistance and opposition to the confinements and ravages of imperialism, has now shifted from the settled, established, and domesticated dynamics of culture to its unhoused, decentered, and exilic energies, energies whose incarnation today is the migrant, and whose consciousness is that of the intellectual and artist in exile, the political figure between domains, between forms, between homes, and between languages" (*Culture* 332). What one might thus conclude about these texts is that they display the White Lady who, though oppressed by gender, has enjoyed the racial privilege of the center stage of world history and now only most reluctantly and regretfully moves—or is pushed—aside.

The 1966 essay by Christa Wolf that I have so often cited might, despite the very different historical context in which it was written, explain why Bachmann was not always able to overcome the limitations of her own white European standpoint. "She has never been in a position," writes Wolf, "to search for affiliation with a progressive historical movement. She tends rather—or at any rate lets some of her characters tend—to step out of society, to track down, in despairing isolation, the conditions which her society dictates to the individual, to seek out the price that naked existence demands and that is paid a million times over." The solution to the problems Bachmann addresses cannot, Wolf argues, be solved by an author or texts alone but depends instead on "changes in society that would give his profession a new foundation and himself a new responsibility" (*Reader* 94). A decade and a half later, as the emergence of postcolonial peoples and their writing increasingly compelled Westerners to ponder their own complicity in imperialist postures and practices, Wolf asked in her third *Cassandra* lecture: "The literature of the West (I read) is the white man's reflection on himself. So should it be supplemented by the white woman's reflection on herself? And nothing more?" *(Cassandra* 225) Virtually alone among postwar German-language writers—as Wolf noted in the *Cassandra* lectures—Bachmann moved in the direction of the "something more" that Wolf was seeking, reflecting on the White Lady *in order to* raise questions about the racialization of the white psyche. Precisely her own implication in the conditions she described permitted her to extrapolate from Austria's imperial past to examine the dissolution of other empires, and the persistence of imperial attitudes, in the present. By probing the racialized foundations of white female identity, exploring discontents of the white female psyche that are also her own, Bachmann is thus able to show why merely appropriating the racial prerogatives of the white man will not suffice to meet the needs of the White Lady.

CHAPTER 10

Bachmann and Materialist Feminism

GENDER AND THE COLD WAR

> *Probably no one believes any more that*
> *writing literature takes place outside of the*
> *historical situation—that even a single writer*
> *exists whose starting point isn't determined*
> *by the conditions of the time.*
>
> —Ingeborg Bachmann, Werke

*T*wo apparently contradictory arguments underwrite this book which I want to address explicitly here. On the one hand, I have maintained that Bachmann's writings *should* be read historically, though they often are not; on the other hand, I have asserted that all readings of Bachmann are *necessarily* historical: that is, informed by the historically specific concerns of readers, whether or not readers are aware of it. Walter Benjamin again helps to reconcile this apparent contradiction. His "Theses on the Philosophy of History" helps us to understand that all readings are necessarily "presentist" in that they take from the text that which "flashes up in a moment of danger" (255); that is, they appropriate the text in a way that corresponds to the reader's present needs. But Benjamin seems to insist in addition that the "historical materialist" (the reader of history who understands the past as Benjamin recommends) needs to recognize the pastness of the past, for he or she is called upon to redeem the past, to prevent it from being lost forever by retrieving it for the present. Hence the danger of a reading that is only presentist: readers find in the text what is familiar but not what is strange or genuinely historical or different from the present.

In my own view, readings that do not acknowledge the pastness of products of the past are something like ethnocentric readings that find only the familiar in other cultures' artifacts: they betray, do violence to, the past because they do not permit the past its otherness. Benjamin writes: "Nothing that has ever happened should be regarded as lost for history. To be sure, only a redeemed mankind receives the fullness of its past—which is to say, only for a redeemed mankind has the past become citable in all its moments" (254). "A redeemed [hu]mankind" I take as a (utopian) description of the state to which humanity accedes after "our" efforts to achieve qualitative social change have succeeded ("after the revolution," as we used to say, or "when the Messiah comes"). The "historical materialists" of Benjamin's "Theses" have, as he puts it, "a weak Messianic power, a power to which the past has a claim" (254). Our charge as "historical materialist" historians or literary scholars is to fulfill our ethical obligation to the past by redeeming as much of the past as our "weak Messianic power" allows. Though we will always read historically in the one sense, producing readings informed by the historical situations in which we are embedded (as I hope I have shown in part 2 of this book), in the other sense reading texts historically will always only be the outcome of a great effort to understand the historical situation from which they derive and to which they respond.

In this final chapter I want to read Bachmann's texts historically, using the methodology of "materialist feminism," a contemporary approach to cultural analysis that I regard as most akin to the historical materialism that Benjamin advocated and as best equipped to help us understand texts within their historical contexts. An approach calling itself materialist feminism first emerged in the late 1970s, often designating efforts to turn Marxist-derived methods to feminist ends, but by the 1990s the term had come to refer to a methodology that combined post-Althusserian Marxism with postmodern discourse theories. Committed to a multifactor analysis of women's complex social positioning, contemporary materialist feminists refuse to privilege gender oppression over other forms of domination under which women (and men) suffer. Materialist feminism distinguishes itself from Marxist feminism in its refusal to construe the economic sphere as the prime mover of social change "in the last instance." Instead, materialist feminists insist upon the crucial work done by discourse/ideology, defined as "the array of sense making practices which constitute what counts as 'the way things are' in any historical moment" in constituting, calling into being, or "interpellating" human subjects within particular social relations (in the words of Rosemary Hennessy [14], a prominent materialist feminist). Materialist feminists would, however, also insist that discourse/ideology cannot be detached from material practices and conditions or even, except perhaps heuristically, be understood as separate "spheres" at all (in the manner of the old base/superstructure division). Rather, all social practices are "overdetermined," and all elements of the social order inflect and influence each other in complex and unpredictable ways. Materialist feminists understand literary and other texts—produced and read by discursively constructed subjects—as interventions into meaning-making practices that can variously support or unsettle prevailing social arrangements. Signifying practices are thus imbricated within the historically specific social relations that produce them and that they (dialectically) help to produce, and a materialist feminist reading strategy takes the form of ideology critique, probing texts to discover how they work to support, document, and/or challenge the existing social order. Materialist feminism's insistence on embedding cultural analysis within the historically specific conditions of cultural production should mean that materialist feminist literary scholars work in the closest collaboration with like-minded historians, but in my experience very few literary and cultural studies scholars are informed about current research or debates within the discipline of history. The investigation that follows constitutes my attempt to draw on recent historical scholarship both to read Bachmann in the context of the historical conditions that obtained when she wrote and to contribute to the further elaboration of the methodology of materialist feminism.

As this book has insisted (and as my epigraph to this chapter, taken from the 1959 Frankfurt lectures, also suggests), Bachmann was, like every other writer, a product of the historical conditions of her time. Unlike many writers, she herself insisted upon the importance of history for literary production, maintaining in a 1973 interview, for instance: "History is essential for the writer. One can't write when one doesn't see the entire historical context that led to the present" (*GuI* 133). In a 1969 interview she explained that the massive writing project called "Ways of Death" on which she had embarked would focus upon contemporary history: "To me it's not a novel, it's a single long book. There will be several volumes, and first of all two that will probably appear at the same time. It's called 'Ways of Death' and for me it's a single large study of all the possible ways of death, a compendium, a *manuale*, as one would say here [in Italy], and at the same time I imagine that it could provide an illustration of the last twenty years, always with Vienna and Austria as the setting" (*GuI* 66). In this final chapter I examine Bachmann's life and her texts in the context of the Cold War, which preeminently established the frame within which those "last twenty years"—that is to say, Austrian history since the end of World War II—must be situated.

Though Austria was occupied by the four victor powers until the state treaty of 1955 that declared the country officially neutral, efforts to win Austria for the Western free-market system and to deter Soviet efforts to incorporate it into their own sphere of interest began even before the war's end. According to Charles Maier, the primary vehicle integrating postwar European economies

into Western capitalism, the Marshall Plan, undertook to transform the ideological conflicts of Europe by bringing about a Western- and Central-Europe-
wide consensus on the value of economic productivity, efficiency, and growth,
portrayed as politically neutral goals. As Maier puts it, the working-class parties
of postwar Europe were to be induced "to abandon their claims to the redistri-
bution of property, income and power and to accept higher absolute earnings
instead, thus to exchange greater equality for greater growth" (48); specifically,
the parties of the working class were called upon to give up their aspirations for
power at the state level and instead accept American-style, "nonpolitical" collective bargaining for specific benefits at the level of the individual enterprise
(Tweraser 225–226). The economic recovery that the Marshall Plan promoted
thus also necessitated a significant ideological and cultural readjustment, as
Michael Hogan argues: "In the most profound sense, it involved the transfer of
attitudes, habits and values as well, indeed, of a whole way of life that Marshall
Planners associated with progress in the marketplace of politics and social relationships as much as they did with greater output in industry and agriculture.
This was the American way of life. Through the technical-assistance program,
in other words, the Marshall Planners aimed to implant in Western Europe the
seed of a democratic neo-capitalism that had flourished in the United States"
(415). Expanding on the Allies' 1943 Moscow Declaration proclaiming Austria
to be the first victim of National Socialism, Austrian politicians "*invented* a version of history that would liberate them from the burdens of the past . . . [and]
extricate the painful memory of the war from the complicity in a hideous race
war against legions of innocent people," as Günter Bischof has put it (*Austria*
x–xi). Political leaders cast their lot with the West from the outset but also
shrewdly used the threat of a potential communist putsch to win more resources
for their nation. Bischof maintains that the West won Austria via what the British historian David Reynolds had termed "containment by integration," fending
off communism in Austria by a "quasi-integration" of Austria into the West
(Bischof, "Austria looks" 184), turning Austria despite its nominal neutrality
into "ein geheimer Verbündeter des Westens"—a secret ally of the West (Bischof,
"Österreich").

As Reinhold Wagnleitner has elaborated in *Coca-Colonization and the Cold
War: The Cultural Mission of the United States in Austria after the Second World
War*, U.S. efforts to win over Austrian hearts and minds to the cause of anticommunism, the free-market economy, and the American way of life were also
focused on the cultural sphere. Although the Allies, Wagnleitner explains,
directed a policy of "reorientation" toward the defeated Austrians "softer" than

the reeducation measures imposed upon Germany, "American plans for Austria still contained a strict program of cultural control, denazification, and cultural reform" (*Coca-Colonization* 67). But, invoking increasingly popular notions about totalitarianism that equated the Nazi and communist systems as their justification, U.S. efforts to assume control of Austrian cultural life by the late 1940s were directed in the main against the influence of an opponent the Americans now regarded as more insidious than recalcitrant Nazis: the Soviet Union. The U.S. "Country Plan for Austria" emphasized in 1950 that the goal of U.S. cultural engagement was now "to counteract totalitarian influences in Austria, whether from the communist left or the neo-Nazi right, and particularly to encourage democratic stability by exposing and attacking communist attempts to encroach upon the authority of the Austrian government" (*Coca-Colonization* 3). Together with economic initiatives such as the Marshall Plan, American occupation authorities undertook measures that affected every aspect of Austrian cultural life: the press (U.S. authorities licensed only those publications that hewed to the American line; provided news articles and photographs through the services of the Amerikanischer Nachrichtendienst, AP, and UPI; distributed a large range of specialized journals to special-interest groups; and trained Austrian journalists in U.S. journalistic techniques); radio (the American station Rot-Weiss-Rot had the strongest transmitters and enjoyed the greatest degree of public acceptance, hiring, as a 1951 State Department memo put it, "high-caliber Austrian personnel" to make the station an "ideological weapon of major impact" that could also be aimed at German-speaking peoples "deep behind the iron curtain" [*Coca-Colonization* 112–113]); book publication (there were twelve America Houses in Austria by 1953 plus a traveling bookmobile— circulating books that had been carefully selected for their anticommunist orientation—and subsidized translations of U.S. books); education (efforts were made to implement a redesigned Austrian school system and curricula based on the U.S. model); and film (propaganda films, newsreels, and a flood of Hollywood movies, including a large number with an explicitly anticommunist message). Such "Americanization," Wagnleitner asserts, describes "the development of a consumption-oriented social order within capitalist societies—the pursuit of happiness as the pursuit of consumption" (*Coca-Colonization* 6–7). Despite some degree of Austrian contempt for the vulgar, bad-mannered Americans and their tasteless cultural forms, American cultural products (as well as consumer goods) were in the main eagerly welcomed by an Austrian public, whose embrace of the American way of life could also serve as a welcome alternative to National Socialist culture, allowing Austrians to move toward the future while forgetting—or repressing—the past.

Inge von Weidenbaum maintains that "Ingeborg Bachmann first started thinking historically in the strictest sense only when she began her studies in Vienna" (25). From then until she left Vienna in 1953, Bachmann's activities were steeped in the atmosphere of the Cold War. Her first jobs after receiving her doctorate were in the secretariat of the American occupation forces, first, beginning in spring 1951, as a typist for *Neues Österreich*, a newspaper published by the Americans, then, from fall 1951 on, as a scriptwriter for the American radio station Rot-Weiss-Rot, located one flight up in the same building. "Rot-Weiss-Rot," Wagnleitner reports, "had become the most important propaganda medium for the United States in Austria by at least 1950" (*Coca-Colonization* 109). According to Andreas Hapkemeyer, Bachmann's department was given the task "of evaluating, editing, and writing manuscripts both in the area of politics as well as in that of literature and entertainment" (*Entwicklungslinien* 43). Rot-Weiss-Rot broadcast several of her poems, her translations of Louis McNeice's *The Tower* and Thomas Wolfe's *Mannerhouse,* and her own radio play "A Business with Dreams" (Hapkemeyer, *Entwicklungslinien* 45). Joseph McVeigh has discovered that Bachmann was also coauthor of the Rot-Weiss-Rot radio series *The Radio Family,* fifteen of whose scripts she wrote entirely or in part, in collaboration with her colleagues Jörg Mauthe and Peter Weiser, in the period between early 1952 and summer 1953. In 1994 Weiser recalled how they had conceived of the series: "It will be a political radio series, though the listener won't understand that; it will be a socially influential radio series, though the listener won't understand that; and it will be a funny radio series, and that's the only thing the listener will understand" (26). That was also precisely Rot-Weiss-Rot's program: of using entertainment as the vehicle to convey its Cold War message.

As well, in the early 1950s Bachmann published a number of poems in *Die Neue Zeitung*, the American newspaper in Germany that was in the earliest years of occupation permitted an independent editorial policy but, as Jessica Gienow-Hecht explains in a study of the paper's history, by 1949 had "turned into a more pro-American mouthpiece of the U.S. military government. . . . Now the Germans were told what was right and wrong and what their future was to be. . . . Virtually every major field of interest—including the coverage of television, advertising, politics, philosophy, and history—reflected the effort to propagandize a Western way of life, defended by the United States of America" (161–162). Bachmann also published poetry in the Viennese journal *Stimmen der Gegenwart*, a multiyear anthology edited by Hans Weigel (a Viennese Jew returned from exile in the United States and for a time Bachmann's lover [Hans

Weigel]) with the encouragement of the Austrian branch of the Congress for Cultural Freedom, a CIA-sponsored, Europe-wide cultural initiative (Wagnleitner, *Coca-Colonization* 63).

Nor was Bachmann able to escape Cold War pressures by her move to Italy. In 1954 her friend and sometime housemate Hans Werner Henze premiered his *Boulevard Solitude* at a dazzling two-week International Conference of Twentieth- Century Music sponsored by the Congress of Cultural Freedom, its promotion of avant-garde composition deriving from the fact that this was the kind of music Stalin expressly forbade (Saunders 221–223). Henze's twelve-tone opera was so badly received by a loud and hostile audience that Bachmann fainted during the performance and had to be taken home (Henze 163). As well, the radio reports on Italian politics that Bachmann prepared for Radio Bremen from September 1954 to summer 1955 draw upon familiar Cold War discourses: for instance, à la U.S. McCarthyism, Bachmann portrays the Italian Communist Party, supported by foreign powers, as engaged in infiltrating all areas of Italian society: "Investigations showed that the Communist Party has established a broad net of business connections throughout the whole country, facilitated and encouraged by political conspiracies within the administration and illegal communist-led infiltration of the administration, but also due to the 'complicity' of certain private enterprises as well as the 'support' of foreign states" (*Römische* 32). Furthermore, as I noted in chapter 8, in 1955 Bachmann joined many other Austrian intellectuals participating in U.S. exchange programs by attending Henry Kissinger's Harvard Summer School; as a State Department memo to the officer in charge of the American mission in Vienna underlined in 1950, invitations to the United States were offered to individuals who were chosen not "because of any specially urgent need on their part for psychological reconditioning but because they are considered especially useful in communicating information about the United States and its democratic institutions to their fellow citizens, they themselves being already most favorably disposed in that direction" (Wagnleitner, *Coca-Colonization* 77). And in 1962, Bachmann received a fellowship from the Ford Foundation (an organization, as Frances Stonor Saunders has shown, that frequently worked hand in hand with the CIA) to spend a year in Berlin. This consideration of Bachmann's very full immersion in American cultural imperialism may provide a new perspective from which to read her oft-stated assertion that the very fact that Austria had stepped out of history offered her a privileged vantage point from which to view—and write about—contemporary events. If the post-1945 United States can be viewed as the metropole that has come to represent capitalist modernity,

Austria (subcolony of the colony Germany, as Wagnleitner remarks) offered
Bachmann a smaller and more manageable stage on and from which to observe
modernity's effects. As she told an interviewer in 1971, "From the perspective of
this small, decaying country one can see phenomena much more precisely that
are obscured in large countries" (*GuI* 80).

For women, the Cold War had particular consequences that also left their
imprint on Bachmann's writing. Elaine Tyler May and many others have
observed that a new emphasis on domesticity lay at the center of Cold War ideology and practice; if containment of communism was the overarching principle
guiding the foreign policy of the United States and its allies, a conception of
domestic containment shaped policy on the home front, where women could
now abandon their strenuous war-related efforts in the public arena and return
to their "proper" sphere: the private realm, home, and family. In fact, as May
shows, women's "freedom" to remain in the home was taken as evidence for the
superiority of the capitalist system to communism, where women were compelled to work side by side with men. As Robert Moeller has detailed, the redomestication of women was a hallmark of gender relations in the Federal Republic. Indeed, he notes, the restabilization and reprivatization of the family after
the arduous rubble years could be hailed as evidence of West Germany's repudiation of the Nazi past and superiority to the East German present (138).
"Experts" such as sociologist Helmut Schelsky located the great "tenacity" of the
family in "the biological ground of sexual relations and a mother's existential
care for the next generation"—that is, in universal, historically invariable structures of femininity and masculinity (Moeller 118)—so, often under the influence of postwar American sociology, such experts also privatized social conflicts,
offering psychological, not political, explanations for social conflicts and therapeutic coping strategies to problems conceived of as private matters. "In this
way," as Elaine May puts it, "domestic containment and its therapeutic corollary
undermined the potential for political activism and reinforced the chilling
effects of anticommunism and the cold war consensus" (14).

But more immediately, the German and Austrian fascination with American consumer goods also served Cold War needs. The "freedom to consume"
enjoyed in postwar Germany and Austria was, their politicians maintained, a
marker of those countries' embrace of the values of Western democracies, and
simultaneously, as Erica Carter puts it, "a strong economy in a stable society
formed the most effective bastion against the Red threat" and offered a safe-
guard against communist encroachment (*How* 80). Increased access to a variety
of consumer goods seemed conversely to prove that the free-market system could

deliver on its promises, as Schelsky observed in 1956: "Universal consumption of industrial and publicistic mass production is responsible for the fact that in all areas of life almost everybody can develop a feeling corresponding to his capacities that he isn't 'way at the bottom' anymore, that he too is already sharing in the plenitude and luxury of existence" ("Gesellschaftlicher" 340). Ludwig Erhard, Konrad Adenauer's economics minister and then German chancellor himself, drew direct connections between consumption and women's domestic role, as Moeller has pointed out: "The 'will to consume' [*Wille zum Verbrauch*] was the engine that drove uninterrupted output, economic rationalization, efficiency, and gains in productivity; as 'economics ministers' of their families, women controlled the throttle. . . . Only within this economic framework would the 'state-free sphere of the family' be possible. The experience of totalitarian and communist state-run economies, their attempts to subordinate families to their needs, was proof positive" (139–40). Within the domestic sphere, Carter has argued, women had the specific responsibility of presiding over consumption, the means whereby cultural order was restored and a specifically Western national identity was established. Even female management of this sphere apparently extrinsic to politics was itself shaped by new U.S.-influenced patterns of consumption. For the housewife's task was the production, at the level of everyday life, of the assurance of continuing prosperity, as Michael Wildt observes in examining the transformation of the German diet over the course of the 1950s: "The rhetoric of recipes pertained less to the kitchen as a site of food preparation than to the kitchen as the 'factory of dreams'" (238).

Elizabeth Heineman has shown that within the context of the restoration of traditional gender hierarchies and responsibilities, single women or "women standing alone" emerged as a particular problem, their superfluity in post war society captured in the term used to describe their excess numbers: *Frauenüberschuß* (surplus of women) beyond the available number of marriageable men. In a 1955 article in *Merkur* (where, as I noted in chapter 8, Bachmann also published a number of poems in the 1950s), "Die gelungene Emanzipation" (Successful emancipation), Schelsky cites experts who warn that desexualization threatens the woman who engages in the rationalized and impersonal activities of modern production and management so alien to her nature, transforming her into a neuter or *Abbild des Mannes* (copy of a man) ("Gelungene" 364). And, paradoxically, single women could at the same time be seen as manifesting a dangerous hypersexualization. To fend off the dangers of a female sexuality eluding male control, the female body itself was subjected to regulation and discipline. For the first time since the 1920s, the corset—or in more modern form the long-line bra and girdle—was reintroduced, worn willingly by women of all ages and sizes, and valued as a sign of respectable femininity. Christian Dior's enormously successful "New Look," introduced in 1947, also served as a mechanism to refeminize women, who would thus repudiate the more androgynous garb of the war and postwar period: "The 'New Woman' with her wasp waist, high-heeled shoes, romantic flounces, and pale complexion now was to appear dependent, exclusive, fragile. . . . After wartime, the time of uniforms, women with wide boxer shoulders doing compulsory service, Dior sketched flower-like women, waists slim as vines, wide skirts that opened like flower blossoms" (Delille/Grohn 108). The new foundation garments produced standardized curvaceous bodies to fit the new fashions. Other parts of the female body also needed the attention of consumer products to achieve acceptability: "More and more products imported from America incited worries about body odor, bad breath, dandruff, broken nails, and gray hair. Women's bodies were stringently disciplined via this ideal of cosmetic beauty" (Schmidt-Linsenhoff et al. 117). As Carter has maintained, for the female consumer in postwar West Germany, "the focal point of leisure, pleasure, and personal freedom [was] . . . the female body itself" ("Alice" 205).

How do Bachmann's texts document or, alternatively, contest German and Austrian collusion in Western Cold War policies and their particular aims for women, and to what degree do they remain blind to, implicated in, or even supportive of those historical arrangements? As I have pointed out in other chapters, 1950s journalists turned Bachmann into an "exemplum for [Germany's] reconstruction, its reattainment of international standards, its reachievement of recognition in the world" (Hotz 72), and many conservative critics of that period denied that her poems had anything to do with politics whatsoever. In that respect, Bachmann's lyric production coincided perfectly with the modernist directions promoted by the Congress for Cultural Freedom and its Cold War allies, altogether distinct from the accessible, realistic, and problem-oriented texts that characterized both the *Kahlschlag* (immediate postwar) period of West German writing and East German socialist realism. Of course, many subsequent Bachmann readers have distanced themselves vehemently from a 1950s stance that viewed her writing as entirely unrelated to politics. In 1982, Hans Höller argued strenuously for the historicity and political relevance of her lyric poetry, declaring that the poems' complex images thematize, for instance, the promises and perils of new beginnings, disappointment over the political directions taken; human alienation within a particular social context, the contamination of the German cultural heritage through its association with the Holocaust, and the repression of the memory of the violent past ("Gestundete"). Some poems, of course, speak explicitly to or about contemporary political dilemmas: "Advertisement" about the lures of consumer society; "Safe Conduct" about the dangers of the bomb; "Early Noon" about Nazis' resumption of powerful political positions; "Every Day" perhaps about the Cold War itself. If the two poetry volumes thematize gender dilemmas of the 1950s, it was in formulations too subtle for the public of that era to decipher, and it has remained for later readers (e.g., Christa Wolf, Sabine Gölz) to elaborate the aspects of the poetry that speak to gender issues.

In contrast to her poems, Bachmann's radio plays and stories of the 1950s overtly address the social arrangements of that period and their subjective consequences, simultaneously contesting the decade's social relations and to some degree also apparently uncritically reproducing them. Her great accomplishment in these texts was the challenge they posed to the privatization of social problems. Uta Poiger has argued that a particular "achievement" of West German Cold War liberalism in the late 1950s was its success at depoliticizing the issues of consumption, popular culture, and sexuality (in contrast to East Germans, ever alert to rebellion against Socialist Unity Party policies in those areas), portraying them as questions of lifestyle relevant only in the private arena (121). Not until the radical movements of the late 1960s, Poiger maintains, could such assumptions of Cold War liberalism be drawn into question, especially by feminists who insisted that "the personal is political" (219). Thus, for most of Bachmann's Western readers, the absence of a language that would allow her to identify concretely what was wrong and how it might be changed occluded the social dimensions of her writing. This meant that reviewers with a very different horizon of expectations took these texts to be—at best!—no more *verbindlich* (connected to real life) than her poetry.

Some of those texts brilliantly illuminate the instrumentalization of women to meet the needs of the Cold War period. "Among Murderers and Madmen," set in Vienna in 1955, represents the domestic containment of women as part and parcel of the restoration of pre-1945 power relations and the repression of the fascist past. To understand the urgency that underwrote this text about the unmastered National Socialist past in Austria and the context in which Bachmann wrote it, it is probably important to know that in 1954 a number of former Nazi generals visited Austria to hold demonstrations and meetings of "Old Comrades' Associations," at which, dressed "in uniform and with all insignia and decorations," they advocated a new German *Anschluß* of Austria (Lütgenau 246–247). Focused on a *Stammtischrunde* (group of [male] friends who meet regularly at a pub), the story explicitly addresses the restoration of male authority and stabilization of male identity (enabled by the lies men tell each other about what happened before 1945). The story's first sentence reads: "[The] men are on the way to themselves when they get together in the evening, drink and talk and express opinions" (*TY* 83). The frame for Bachmann's investigation of the misrepresentations and betrayals that underwrite these men's confident self-presentations is the cost for women of men's reassertion of themselves as "Titans and demigods" (*TY* 84). It is their wives at home who rage and suffer:

> Barefoot or in slippers, with tied-up hair and tired faces, the women wandered round at home, turned off the gas and looked fearfully under the bed and in the cupboard, soothed the children with absent-minded words or sat dejectedly by the radio and then went to bed after all with thoughts of vengeance in the lonely house. The women lay there feeling like victims, with wide-open eyes in the darkness, full of despair and malice. . . . And in the first dream they murdered their husbands, made them die in car crashes, of heart attacks and pneumonia; made them die quickly, or slowly and miserably, according to the magnitude of the reproach, and under their closed delicate eyelids tears welled up in sorrow for the death of their husbands. They were crying over their husbands who had gone out, ridden out, never come home, and finally they wept over themselves. They had come to their truest tears. (*TY* 84–85)

Bachmann perceptively shows that male activity in the public arena is enabled by women at home; however, in some contrast to her later texts, she also here tends to exempt women from accountability for the past and present social arrangements for which she reproaches the men of her story.

Though "Among Murderers and Madmen" most clearly connects the 1950s redomestication of women to Austrians' failure to address their complicity in National Socialism and Austria's "remasculinization," it is possible to derive a sustained, if somewhat subdued, critique of the decade's gender arrangements and expectations from Bachmann's texts of the period. The radio play "A Business with Dreams" shows how fantasies of consumption that are focused on femininity stabilize class-based social relations, and the male protagonist of "The Thirtieth Year" cuts a wide swath through the surplus of women ("he loved a myriad [*Milliarde*] women, all at the same time and without distinction" [*TY* 26]), playing fast and loose with its somewhat interchangeable (all named some variant of "Helena") embodiments: deceiving Eleni with another woman; leaving pregnant Leni alone in a ski hut while he cavorts with two blonde ski bunnies; politely making love to Helene whom he finds repulsive. Several other stories of *The Thirtieth Year* touch on the destructive consequences of bourgeois marriage for women. Here, too, Bachmann represents marriage as a sustaining pillar of an entire social order; that is, the private realm is understood to be not extrinsic to the public but its necessary corollary. In "Undine Goes," Undine mounts a frontal assault on the deadly repetitiveness of male-dominant, female-submissive domestic partnerships wherein husbands control power and money in the public arena and expect loyal wives, in return for financial support, to create a nurturant private sphere:

> You monsters with your phrases, you who seek the phrases of women so that you have all you need, so that the world is round. You who make women your mistresses and wives, one-day wives, week-end wives, lifetime wives and let yourselves be made into their husbands. . . . You with your jealousy of your women, with your arrogant forbearance and tyranny, your search for sanctuary with your women; you with your housekeeping money and your joint good-night conversations, those sources of new strength, of the conviction that you are right in your conflicts with the outside world, you with your helplessly skillful, helplessly absent-minded embraces. I was amazed to see that you give your wives money for the shopping and for clothes and for the summer holiday, then you invite them out (invite them, that means you pay, of course). You buy and let yourselves be bought. (TY 179–180)

In "A Step towards Gomorrah," marriage is considered, to use Althusserian terminology, an ideological form that interpellates individuals into particular subject positions: "Wiser than Charlotte, [her husband] had long ago recognized marriage as a state that is stronger than the individuals who enter it, and which therefore also leaves more of a mark upon their partnership than they could have marked or even changed the marriage. However a marriage is conducted—it cannot be conducted arbitrarily, inventively, it cannot tolerate innovation or change, because to enter into marriage already means to enter into its form" (TY 127). As many commentators have observed, the tragedy of this story derives from Charlotte's own entrapment within ideological constructions that permit her to envision a romantic connection only within the parameters her era provides: "She would be able to subjugate Mara, to guide and push her. She would have . . . somebody for whom the only important thing was to take part in her life and for whom she was the measure of all things, somebody for whom it was more important to keep her linen in order, to turn back her bed, than to satisfy another ambition—somebody, above all, for whom it was more important to think with her thoughts than to have a thought of her own" (TY 125). In The Thirtieth Year it is already possible to perceive the connection between the banality of everyday male-female relationships and a social order that kills the spirit and, as in "Among Murderers and Madmen," sometimes also the body as well.

On the other hand, it is difficult not to conclude (as I have argued in chapter 8 and elsewhere) that Bachmann also simultaneously reproduces conventional 1950s notions of femininity. With the exception of Charlotte of "A Step towards Gomorrah," a concert pianist, and possibly Jennifer of "The Good God of Manhattan," a student, all these women are confined to the private sphere, and even Charlotte is an obedient and attentive wife. In "Everything" and "A Wildermuth," both male protagonists are granted a "good" and a "bad" woman partner: a cheery, chatty bourgeois wife who happily fulfills her domestic obligations, and a proletarian mistress, Betty in "Everything," "offhand, undemanding, subservient" (*TY* 75); silent, sultry Wanda in "A Wildermuth." Neither "mistress" is an emancipated or rebellious woman herself: it is their mere class, gender, and sexual presence as an alternative to marriage that constitutes a disruption and a danger, their challenge to domesticity conceived of as the seductive threat of an uncontrolled female sexuality exuded by surplus women. The wives correspond to the worst of 1950s stereotypes, veritably "ditzy dames" in the manner of Lucille Ball in the television show *I Love Lucy*, and though Bachmann may thereby have been attempting a critique of the grim masculine pursuit of incontrovertible truth, the alternative she proposes is at women's cost, drawing upon gender dichotomies that represent women as incapable of rational thought. In "A Step towards Gomorrah," Charlotte's complaint about the language of women summarizes this position: "The language of men, insofar as it was applied to women, had been bad enough already and doubtful; but the language of women was even worse, more undignified—she had been shocked by it ever since she had seen through her mother, later through her sisters, girl friends and the wives of her men friends and had discovered that absolutely nothing, no insight, no observation corresponded to this language, to the frivolous or pious maxims, the jumble of judgments and opinions or the sighed lament" (*TY* 133). Certainly the masculine identity of these figures is unstable as well, and in that respect these stories may also be understood as Bachmann's far-reaching critiques of the culture of the West German economic miracle. But by exploring masculine insecurities as they are played out within relationships to women, by solving men's problems at women's cost, Bachmann also shows herself to be both influenced by and contributing to the reassertion of male control over women during the postwar years.

"A Step towards Gomorrah," "Undine Goes," and "The Good God of Manhattan" focus directly on autonomous female sexuality, and in all three cases Bachmann concludes, for somewhat different reasons, that an independent female sexuality is irreconcilable with the social order. Perhaps inadvertently revealing the limitations of her own understanding of gender, Bachmann conceded in a speech in 1959 with respect to "The Good God," "It is also clear to me that we have to remain inside the [social] order, that there's no escape from society" (*W* 4: 276). Undine and Jennifer, akin to Wanda and Betty, show that the cost of female sexual self-determination is at best isolation and abandonment, at worst victimhood and death. Most clearly in "The Good God of Manhattan" (see chapter 8), Bachmann packages her assault on an Americanized, post-Hiroshima economic wonder in the very images that incited grave anxiety in that era, those of female sexuality out of control, and she simultaneously confirms dominant gender norms that contrast the public realm of masculinity to the intimate realm of women. Moreover, if, as May has argued, unfettered female sexuality was associated with atomic catastophe—the bikini was named after the atoll where atomic tests were carried out—Bachmann in contrast makes eroticism the antagonist of the Manhattan Project; if the containment of women is a mechanism to stave off totalitarianism, Bachmann makes female autonomy a threat to the all-embracing order that the God of Manhattan represents. Yet in merely reversing these images without deconstructing them altogether, Bachmann continues to show that she too is a creature of the discourses to which her characters fall victim; as Rita Felski puts it, "the nostalgia for such a nonalienated plenitude is itself a product of modern dualistic schemas which positioned woman as an ineffable Other beyond the bounds of a masculine social and symbolic order" (21). Bachmann's formulation of the problem of female independence, one might argue, by constructing both female autonomy and sexuality as indeed constituting a peril to social order which any society should endeavor to contain, already yields the terrain on which she might have wished to argue against 1950s gender conventions. Hence, though now it is possible to read these stories as glosses on gender relations which anticipate the "Ways of Death," it is likely that readers of her period could read these texts only as a contribution to and confirmation of the reassertion of male control over women at which 1950s gender discourses aimed.

What assisted Bachmann in overcoming this impasse was a shift in the West German cultural climate in the late 1950s. As Anson Rabinbach has documented, from 1959 onward the Federal Republic experienced a "crisis of *Vergangenheitsbewältigung* [coming to terms with the past—the German euphemism for addressing the legacy of the Holocaust]" that involved its relationship both to the National Socialist past and to "the multiple sins of the Adenauer years" (52). Signaling this change was Theodor Adorno's famous 1959 essay "What Does Coming to Terms with the Past Mean?" in which he maintained that "the continued existence of National Socialism *within* democracy" was in his view "potentially more threatening than the continued existence of fascist tendencies *against* democracy" (Adorno, "What" 115). Adorno and, a few years later at a more popular level, Alexander and Margarete Mitscherlich in *The Inability to Mourn* (1967) argued that the German relationship to the Nazi past had been characterized by repression, denial, the "loss of history," the "eradication of" or "flight from memory"; it was the product of a "deep psychic debility" that left behind a "latent explosive potential for irrational behavior" (Rabinbach 54). As Rabinbach notes, these arguments were premised on "a therapeutic model of historical discourse" (thus displaying some similarities to other social scientific explanatory paradigms of the 1950s) and placed more emphasis on elements of National Socialism that were *not* unique to National Socialism and could be discerned in the present: authoritarianism, anti-Semitism and racism, anticommunism, antiliberalism, elements of continuity or similarity between fascism and contemporary capitalism (52–57). The new antifascist critique of contemporary fascism (which would be picked up by the New Left of the 1960s and 1970s) provided Bachmann with an explanation both of what was wrong with the present and of how and why it left its imprint on contemporary subjectivity. From the perspective of these developments, some otherwise puzzling aspects of Bachmann's treatment of fascism become quite comprehensible.

Bachmann's organicist explanation of the causes of the "ways of death" that her novel cycle was to delineate bears a remarkable resemblance to Adorno's statement on the survival of National Socialism into the present. In her preface to a reading from *The Book of Franza* in 1966, Bachmann represented the cause of National Socialist criminality as a virus that remained contagious in the postwar period: "I've often wondered, and perhaps it has passed through your minds as well, just where the virus of crime escaped to—it cannot have simply disappeared from our world twenty years ago just because murder is no longer praised, desired, decorated with medals, and promoted. The massacres are indeed over, the murderers still among us" (*Franza* 3–4). Adorno similarly viewed National Socialism as an organic substance that continues to infect humans or their social relations: "National Socialism lives on, and to this day we don't know whether it is only the ghost of what was so monstrous that it didn't even die off with its own death, or whether it never died in the first place— whether the readiness for unspeakable actions survived in people, as in the social conditions that hem them in" ("What" 115). If "National Socialism" or "fascism" designates not a particular state form or social order but rather a set of more or less universal characteristics discernible in the individual psyche, as evident today as in the past, then it is altogether reasonable for Bachmann to maintain in a 1973 statement that fascism "doesn't start with the first bombs that are thrown, it doesn't start with terrorism, which you can write about, in every newspaper. It starts in relationships between people. Fascism is the first thing in the relationship between a man and a woman (*GuI* 144). If Adorno's explanation is correct (as might, of course, be contested) that fascist personality types continue to impose their violent will on victims in the present, then the central metaphor of both *The Book of Franza* and *Malina*, the cemetery of the murdered daughters, is not an illegitimate appropriation of the suffering of National Socialism's real victims by a contemporary woman of Germanic ancestry but an image that accurately captures the presence of the past in the present.

Under the new conditions of the changed cultural climate in Germany, Bachmann's first public fictional effort explicitly to thematize the relationship of politics to subjectivity (or, as the editors of the critical edition put it, the "juxtaposition of private history and 'big history'" [*TP* 1: 524]), directly addressed the consequences of the Cold War. Her 1964 Büchner Prize speech, "A Site for Coincidences," focuses on contemporary Berlin (a site, she had remarked in a draft eulogy to Gombrowicz, that "smells of sickness and death" [*W* 4: 326]), where she had spent the previous year on a fellowship from the Ford Foundation. Bachmann's comments on earlier drafts of the speech, included in the critical edition, clarify her intentions for this piece, and those intentions, I want to maintain here, continue to inform her writing practice in the "Ways of Death." First, Bachmann declares herself always to be writing about politics even when the concerns of her texts seem very far away from contemporary political issues: "For me the realms can't be separated; even if thinking doesn't always show visibly that it's political, sometimes it has to understand itself that way, not as a single statement but rather integrated, not an athletic activity in public, but as a constant infiltration" (*TP* 1: 177). Second, in a passage that culminates in an allusion to one of the most terrifying moments of the Cold War, the U.S.-Soviet confrontation at the time of the Cuban missile crisis, Bachmann indicates that the politics she finds most threatening and dangerous are those of the postwar period, of the Cold War era: "And the threat doesn't take place in war, not in times of naked violence, where survival is the main thing, but rather before and afterward, in peacetime, and I truly had only a suspicion, no certainty, when after the war I started to think and stopped trying to survive, now it seemed guaranteed, then the suspicion occurred to me, that peacetime would be harder for us. In the traumatic hours two years ago, was it Thursday, listening to the radio again, irony again and blasphemous cheerfulness, with the fear we admitted to—who wasn't fearless [*angstlos, sic*]. It looked like everything could end so easily, in a single stroke" (*TP* 1: 176). Finally, Bachmann advances a psychological/therapeutic explanation of how the Cold War division of Germany as well as the after-effects and continuing presence of fascism affect the residents of Berlin. Like the title figure of Georg Büchner's *Lenz*, references to whom accompanied Bachmann's first efforts to formulate her address, Berliners had been made sick, driven mad, by contemporary social reality: "Sickness is in the time, it didn't enter the world with Lenz, wandering, vegetating away. . . . What made these people so sick, what made them half crazy? . . . Their craziness is nothing more that the physical, psychic expression for something unbearable, thus the expression of the fact that reality has defeated them. But it's simultaneously the defeat of reality by the spirit, which would rather go crazy than give in, than let this be pounded into them" (*TP* 1: 175).

The political intervention Bachmann undertakes in the Büchner Prize speech can thus be understood as a response to Adorno's dire analysis of the contemporary period. To Adorno, the totalitarian potential of his time arises from its demand for the total conformity of the populace to a hegemonic order: "If they want to live, they have no choice but to adapt themselves to the given circumstances, to conform; they have to put under erasure their status as autonomous subjects, which the idea of democracy appeals to; they can only maintain that status at the cost of renouncing it" ("What" 124). Bachmann concurs entirely with Adorno's argument here and elsewhere about pressures on individuals to accommodate themselves to a dominant social order; indeed, as I will maintain shortly, that is a premise on which the "Ways of Death" is founded. Her textual strategy in "A Site for Coincidences" can be read as an effort to reveal the costs of such accommodation, to read the texts of culture against the grain to show the ruptures, disjunctures, lapses, and incoherences in a social system that alleges its superiority to its "totalitarian" adversaries.

To understand how Bachmann here and in later texts exposes the underside of the Cold War order, it is useful to compare the textual practices of "A Site for Coincidences" with those of "To Die for Berlin" (an unfinished and unpublished story that she wrote in November 1961 after a brief trip to Berlin, where the Berlin Wall had been erected three months earlier) and to read both as antecedents to the various narrative strategies she would pursue in the "Ways of Death." "To Die for Berlin" is a realistic third-person narrative told from the point of view of its unnamed, German-speaking male protagonist, who has traveled to Berlin from an unspecified non-German-speaking country to deliver a lecture. The title of the story, according to the editors of the critical edition, is taken from the title of an article by Stewart Alsop in the 15 November 1961 *Spiegel*, "Sterben für Berlin? [To die for Berlin?]" in which Alsop discusses whether American forces would indeed be willing to defend Berlin if they thereby ran the risk of loosing an atomic war that might destroy all of humankind (*TP* 1: 523). Confronted in Berlin with the reality of the German past and present, the protagonist's response is (in accord with Adorno's arguments) denial and repression: on his visit he prefers not to listen to German, refuses to view Berlin's sights or to attend its cultural events, to observe the Wall, to look into his hosts' faces. To his own surprise he entertains himself in Berlin by spending the evening in a bar—where young Germans drink Coca-Cola—and by gazing at animals in the zoo. When he calls his French wife to tell her that fog has prevented his flight from leaving, he reveals his anxiety about his presence in this cold war trouble spot when he thinks—but only in French!—"Peut-être je ne rentre plus, pensait-il, mais il ne le prononçait pas [Maybe I won't return, he thought, but he didn't say it]" ("To Die" 10). This story focuses, though only, it appears, by indirection, on the psychic distress that "Berlin"—here a trope for an entire world order as well as a real historical site—occasions in the protagonist and others, for even the football fans, in Berlin to attend the soccer playoffs between Sweden and Switzerland (neutral countries aligned with neither NATO nor the Warsaw Pact!) and who slug their buddy as they wait for their flight out, are brutalized by their exposure to "Berlin." "This is a situation you couldn't imagine existing anywhere else," a Berliner tells the protagonist. "Can you imagine it even here? he retorted" ("To Die" 16). Bachmann expects readers of this understated story to comprehend what eludes its characters, that the political reality they are too frightened to confront directly has nonetheless inscribed itself upon them in ways they are not equipped to understand.

"A Site for Coincidences" in contrast resorts to expressionist or surrealist techniques to represent how "Berlin" leaves its mark on its inhabitants. In her introduction to the Büchner Prize speech, Bachmann explained that in Büchner's *Lenz*, "coincidence" (*Zufall*) was the term used to refer to Lenz's attacks of madness. That madness, she continued, is a result of the "consistency" [*Konsequenz*] Lenz demanded from himself: "Consistency, the logical, in pursuing the crack [*Riß*]—the crack that ran through the world for Lenz." Bachmann concludes: "Consistency, the consistent is terrible in almost every case, and relief, consolation, the livable, that's the inconsistent part" (*TP* 1: 228–229). In this text Bachmann pursues the effects on individual and collective consciousness of the crack that now runs through the world, Europe, Germany, and "Berlin." She concludes her introduction by observing: "Madness can also come from outside toward the individual, thus much earlier it went from inside the individual to the outside, then it turned around, in situations we're familiar with, in the heritage of this time [*in den Erbschaften dieser Zeit*]" (*TP* 1: 229)—the last phrase a reference to Ernst Bloch's 1935 exploration of explanations for fascism's mass appeal. This text is thus formulated so as to reproduce, from the collective perspective, on the one hand, of Berlin's insane—those institutionalized and especially sensitive to a madness induced by external causes—and, on the other, perhaps, of the totality of all Berliners. They live in the context of a nonsynchronous, violent, and omnipresent past: "At the sharp bend of the Koenigsallee, shots, now quite muffled, are fired at Rathenau [German-Jewish foreign minister assassinated by right-wing nationalists in 1922]. Hanging takes place in Plötzensee" [the site where the 20 July 1944 conspirators against Hitler and others were executed]. They cannot avoid reminders of the defeat, occupation, and division of Germany—"an American, probably made of lead, with a short white helmet and a lowered automatic pistol, . . . the convoy of trucks with young ruddy-nosed Englishmen, . . . two Soviet sentries"—and the constant, through repressed, potential for conflict among them; the absurd suspicious rituals at border crossings between East and West: "Then you have to peel the paint off the car, it goes quickly, the paint comes off in strips like cold wax, then you have to knock on the metal three times, kick the tire once, then you get a mark, you have to throw it on the ground, heads or tails" (*TP* 1: 219–221).

Meanwhile, the patients are well cared for in the Berlin of the "economic miracle": they participate in an orgy of consumption in the city's great department stores—"the escalators are jammed, the elevators are stuffed full with scarves and dresses and coats" (*TP* 1: 209)—crowd into Berlin's many bars and night clubs, stuff themselves with cake. Women especially are susceptible to lavish consumer excess: "In Café Kranzler the women pull their felt hats firmly down over their eyes, they chew and reach for more, like back then" (*TP* 1: 219). (In an earlier draft, Bachmann added the sentence "They eat their sweet secrets of twenty years ago [i.e., 1944, the Nazi period], they keep silent and get fat under their hats" [*TP* 1: 188].) Yet the consolations of consumption—"all the people are wrapped in waxed paper, . . . myriads of beer bottles" (*TP* 1: 206) aside—the "Berlin" the patients confront is entirely unpredictable, threatening, and dangerous: "Once a minute an airplane flies through the room" (*TP* 1: 206); "in the next plane-free moment all the church bells of Berlin chime, churches spring up from the ground" (*TP* 1: 207); the roof of the S-Bahn collapses on them and they are saved only by the "huge muscles and hands" (*TP* 1: 211) of the East German woman conductor (one of those working women whom Western women were so thankful not to have to emulate); and "owing to politics the streets rise forty-five degrees" (*TP* 1: 214).

As the speech nears its end, Bachmann indicates that there is no solution, no cure, for this madness, yet the patients and their medical attendants refuse to confront the seriousness of their condition: "People don't know if there's hope, even if there isn't any hope, it's not really terrible, it's not as bad as it was, it isn't necessarily hope, it could be something less, it could be nothing, it's nothing, it's. . . . It was a little confusion, nothing else. It won't happen again" (*TP* 1: 227). If, then, in "To Die for Berlin" Bachmann displays the impact of Cold War politics upon subjectivity from "without," as it were, from a perspective that releases only information to which the figure in the story is prepared to allow himself conscious access, "A Site for Coincidences" reveals the repressed contents of consciousnesses that have been subjected to similar conditions, devising images to represent a chaotic and contradictory intrapsychic reality that cannot be acknowledged: "It's nothing [*Es war nichts*]," says Bachmann here and elsewhere.

Thereafter, I want to argue here, Bachmann's texts would oscillate between these two narrative approaches as she attempted to develop a textual strategy for the "Ways of Death" that would continue to allow her to address the evasions and anxieties of the post-1945 period. The novel *Malina* pursues the narrative strategy of "A Site for Coincidences" (particularly in its middle, dream chapter); "big history" is presented via the scars it has left on the psyche. This is why Bachmann needed *Malina* as the "overture" to her novel cycle: to show both how history deforms and cripples the psyche *and* why, in the "Ways of Death," that damage will never again be so visible—since the "I," the figure who cannot narrate (*erzählen*) but can *display* her psychic wounds, disappears into the crack (*Riß*) in the wall at the novel's end. Subsequent to the novel *Malina*, the figure Malina will in contrast take on the narrative standpoint of "To Die for Berlin" (as I detail later in this chapter): he will tell (*erzählen*), in the third person and past tense, stories in which neither the characters nor Malina himself will be able to reveal anything of which the characters are not consciously aware. One might maintain that Malina is the autonomous nineteenth-century bourgeois subject (now eroded by mass society) who assumes a narrative stance, that of the "self-assured, unbroken, unquestionable identical I/subject" (*W* 4: 220), which Bachmann's Frankfurt lectures on poetics decreed to be no longer tenable in twentieth-century literature. Indeed, in a draft probably intended as an introduction to the Eka Kottwitz or Fanny Goldmann fragment, Malina, speaking to a younger, more experimental writer at the Frankfurt Book Fair, describes himself as the custodian of an older language and (veritably Old Testament) morality: "I obey an old language and old concepts, and I turn back like all people who gaze at what has happened and are turned to stone, and perhaps an angel will tell you in time, don't look back, and then you won't see Frankfurt consumed in smoke and brimstone as I see it consumed today and twice every year, for vengeance has come. Not my vengeance, because I came to tell and not to judge, but judgment haunts all the stories and lamentation in the smoke when it rises to heaven and is told" (*TP* 1: 364). Similarly, in an earlier draft of *Malina*, the "I" remarks that unlike herself, anachronistic Malina hears (and presumably will recount) a univocal truth: "Malina is not à la page, not up to date, in his anachronistic museum he uses everything, also with me, that anachronism, and he waits, because it will appear, true and with the many visages of truth, Malina listens to truth's single voice, and I don't know that voice, only the many voices, all the variations, that swamp me, I don't know the voice" (*TP* 3.1: 209).

Malina, one thus might argue, is the narrator of a novel cycle that Bachmann conceived as an ironic twentieth-century version of the nineteenth-century realist novel à la Balzac. She herself suggested the proximity of the "Ways of Death" to the great novels of nineteenth-century realism such as *Madame Bovary* or *Anna Karenina* when she observed of *Three Paths to the Lake*: "It occurred to me that earlier the great writers, even the French, laid a lot of weight on something the Germans didn't succeed at, showing the mores of a time via a series of women's portraits" (*GuI* 140). Certainly, many of Bachmann's parodic "speaking names"—Gernreich, the publisher; Fräulein Immerschön, the name given to the secretary of the "I" in early drafts of *Malina*; Rappatz, initially called Geldern, one of the richest men in Austria in *Gier*— strongly recall Dickens and other realist novelists. Similarly, Bachmann's use of the Balzacian technique of recurring characters connects her both to novels of nineteenth-century realism and to twentieth-century novelists who have employed that strategy to mark the difference between realist novels and their own. For if in Balzac, the recurring characters of the *Comédie humaine* suggest that all of French society is a comprehensible social totality (one reason for Marxists' fondness for Balzac's novels), in authors like William Faulkner and Uwe Johnson they emphasize the disappearance of a familiar social world. One might maintain, then, that the recurring characters of Bachmann's own cycle, "an image of the last twenty years . . . always with the setting Vienna and Austria" (*GuI* 66), were intended to convey a similar message, underlining the distinction between what appeared—also to most of her figures—to be a comfortable and familiar social world but was in fact the underside of the social order that National Socialism and the Cold War had created. As Malina remarked to the young avant-garde author, "I collect only stories that aren't known, and only stories with a fatal outcome" (*TP* 1: 388).

Malina thus presides over a social world in which subjects *appear* to be agents in control of their own fate, as in the realist novel (in Bachmann's words: "the I/subject spends his time *within* history [*das Ich hält sich* in *der Geschichte auf*]," *W* 4: 230) but in which they are in fact instead entirely products, creatures of that society ("die Geschichte *im* Ich [history within the I/psyche]," *W* 4: 230). Social theory has provided a variety of terms to describe the figures Bachmann constructs in the "Ways of Death": in Frankfurt School terms, they consent to their own domination; in Althusser's language, they are interpellated by ideology into particular subject positions; in Foucault-influenced theory they are discursively constructed subjects; in Antonio Gramsci's words, they are products of hegemony—"that process," as Terry Eagleton has put it, "whereby the particular subject so introjects a universal law as to consent to its imperatives in the form of consenting to his own deepest being" (32). That is, Bachmann attempted to represent figures who are, I want to argue here, totally constituted or called into being by dominant discourses; they are entirely congruent with hegemonic ideologies (and that is why they have no capacity for resistance, as feminist readers have complained). From the perspective of this analysis of the "Ways of Death," it becomes easier to understand Bachmann's dissatisfaction with *The Book of Franza*: Franza understood what was wrong with her and even, at the end, found the strength to say "no" to her tormentor, but Bachmann wanted to show instead how difficult it was for discursively constituted products of cold war society to understand not just what was wrong with their social order but even that anything was amiss at all.

The political project of *Malina* might have been better grasped if, as the editors of the critical edition explain, Martin Walser, at the behest of the Suhrkamp Verlag, had not succeeded in convincing Bachmann to remove three critical sections from the novel that situate its story of love and death in the private arena of the Ungargasse within the larger political context of the late 1960s to early 1970s in Vienna: "Sightseeing in an Old City," the tour of Vienna taken by Malina and the "I" on a tourist bus; the Michael Frank episode, an account of a murder committed by a young neo-Nazi; and the flower power episode, Malina's explanation of young people's politics in Vienna.

"Sightseeing in an Old City" establishes the parameters of an Americanized Vienna in which the monuments and heroes of Austrian history are invisible and irrelevant. Though the tour guide boasts in hyperbolic pidgin English that Austria's imperial accomplishments surpass those of the British Empire ("This was the biggest country which ever existed in the world and it gave a famous word, in this country the sun never goes down" ["Sightseeing" 5]), the Vienna he constructs for his customers is a land of operettas and the beautiful blue Danube. It is one that panders and corresponds to American expectations, a melange of fast food and drink, shoddy simulacra, and kitsch: fountains from which they drink "the most famous water in the world" ("Sightseeing" 3); "a dried-out imitation of Mozartkugeln from Salzburg" ("Sightseeing" 4); the "Doppelgänger of the emperor of peace" ("Sightseeing" 4) in Schönbrunn; conceptions of femininity that hark back to invented Austrian tradition ("Sissy" films about the Empress Elisabeth popular in the 1950s, "Csárdás princesses," "the merry widow"); yodelers and "Tales from the Vienna Woods" in the city's night clubs ("Sightseeing" 5). This section thus situates *Malina* within the Americanized consumer culture—the Austria of the musical *The Sound of Music* (see Vansant), say—imposed upon and embraced by Austrians after 1945 as the United States attempted to win Austrian hearts and minds for the cause of anticommunism.

The Michael Frank passage, on the other hand, shows that the imprint of the National Socialist past still remains vivid in Vienna. The seventeen-year-old Frank, whose grandfather had spent the entire war in a concentration camp and whose devout Catholic family had also suffered under the Nazis, had written in his journal: "One day I will kill myself, like HIM, with a revolver shot in the mouth. I admire and love that great ideal. My useless existence disgusts me. Suicide is a noble deed. All SS-men thought so, and I think so too" (*TP* 3.2: 715). Dressed in SS uniforms and insignia, Frank and two younger friends decide to carry out executions: "The youngest, Uli N., accepted the command, but it doesn't say anywhere whose command, and shot Michael Frank dead" (*TP* 3.2: 714). This passage locates *Malina* in a social context in which the fascist "crime virus," as Bachmann termed it, is still virulent.

Finally, in the third excised section, three foreign visitors ask Malina and the "I" about "flower power" and "flower children" in Vienna. Malina replies that Viennese youth destroy flowers and demolish telephone booths: "You can't really ask for more from the young people . . . In our areas especially you probably can't expect the power of flowers any more. . . . Children are born too old here" (*TP* 3.2: 712). Bachmann is acknowledging that though her novel is set in a revolutionary period when young people elsewhere are demanding radical social change, opposition does not exist in the Vienna in which the Ungargasse of this novel is located. In the social world about which Malina will tell his stories, there are no radical alternatives to the present social order, no cultural revolutionaries who might declare: "Be realistic, demand the impossible!" or proclaim, "All power to the imagination!"

Nonetheless, despite the omission of these three significant sections, Bachmann hoped and intended that her readers would understand her novel's more limited focus as an effort to address contemporary political and social dilemmas, as she somewhat aggressively insisted to an interviewer shortly after *Malina* appeared: "And didn't you try to reproach me for isolating myself to this Ungargasse, to these two figures? But that's not isolation for me. Because, what does it actually mean to describe all of society, the nature of an era's consciousness? That doesn't mean that you repeat the sentences that society speaks, it has to be shown differently. And it has to be shown radically differently, because otherwise nobody will know what our time was. And the sickness, the torment in it, and the sickness of the world, and the sickness of this person, that is the sickness of our time for me" (*GuI* 71–72).

Following a suggestion by Helgard Mahrdt, I want to investigate *Malina* via the categories of private and public (Mahrdt, "Society"), which roughly correspond to spheres allocated to women and men in the ideologies of the postwar period. From that perspective, it is possible to read this novel's often-remarked unity of time and place in Vienna's Ungargasse, where the "I," her doppelgänger Malina, and her lover all live, as emblems of the private sphere, protected from the invasive attentions of tourists and other strangers by its ordinariness: "a stranger would never lay eyes on it, as it is strictly residential and devoid of tourist attractions [*ein Fremder wird sie nie zu Gesicht bekommen, weil es in ihr nichts zu besichtigen gibt und man hier nur wohnen kann*]" (*Malina* 3; *TP* 3.1: 281). The "Ungargasse" performs the function allotted to the home in the 1950s, protecting its inhabitants from a hostile and alienating public sphere, the only arena where the "I" feels comfortable and safe. The "I" both concedes that "home" is not in fact extracted from the economic infrastructure and public affairs (of the Cold War!) and simultaneously proclaims her determination not to attend to them: "But Washington and Moscow and Berlin are merely impertinent places trying to make themselves important. In my country, in Ungargassenland no one takes them seriously . . . no longer can they have any impact on my life" (*Malina* 12). The attempt of the "I" to extract the Ungargasse from the larger sphere of "big history" can at least in part explain the "unity of time" in *Malina*, why the novel is written in the present tense and takes place within an eternal "Today." Conceived as a refuge from politics and history, the private sphere is alleged to be an arena whose activities of reproduction and nurturance never change; in effect, then, the private sphere could be represented as an on-going present time. In addition, in Austria in the postwar period, as noted earlier, the private arena is specifically imagined as a refuge from the memory of National Socialism. That the "I" refuses to concern herself with either current events or history ("the past doesn't interest me," she remarks in an early draft [*TP* 3.1: 52]), will not remember the Nazi past, and occupies a realm which is not narratable because its characteristic activities consist of the eternal return of the same also helps to explain why the "I" continually laments: "I can't narrate / I can't tell my story [*Ich kann nicht erzählen*]." "There just isn't any story/history in *Malina*," Bachmann emphasized in an interview (*GuI* 73).

Within the private refuge of the Ungargasse, the "I," though not a mother or wife, is nonetheless represented as completely a product of the gender discourses of the period in which Bachmann learned to be a woman. Alternatively, one might say, the "I" is the historically specific representation of what a particular era defined as feminine, and though the novel takes place in the mid-1960s, this is a notion of femininity derived from a period prior to 1960s upheavals: there are no flower children in this Vienna. As Bachmann emphasized frequently in interviews, in this "spiritual, imaginary autobiography" (*GuI* 73), she in fact conceived the "I" and Malina as two halves of a single person, each respectively possessing qualities that their author identified with femininity and masculini-ty—another indication of the degree to which she also was a product of her age. In early *Malina* drafts the "I" laments that she is really a woman only when she is in bed with a man—"When I get up from a bed . . . I know that I belong to [the men] again, I was only gone, on the other side, because I was lying in the bed" (*TP* 3.1: 90)—and that she is really "two people, . . . a man and a woman" (*TP* 3.1: 134); in the final, printed version of *Malina* an astrologer tells her that she is split into male and female parts. It is instructive to relate this division of the personality or the psyche into masculine and feminine portions to the prob-lems and experiences of the "woman standing alone" in Bachmann's era; in car-rying out the tasks of men as well as women, her figures may have felt that they too were at risk of succumbing to the fate that menaced the "emancipated woman": metamorphosing into a "copy of a man."

If the figures of *Malina* are indeed representatives of an era's constructions of masculinity and femininity, then the appropriate reading strategy for *Malina* is not to identify with its female figure, as so many of Bachmann's readers have done (probably because they themselves are products of the same gender dis-courses as the "I") but rather to read the text critically and ironically, attempting to discern how the figure of the "I" might manifest "the thinking that leads to dying," how "big history" might have left its imprint on the "private history/

story" of the "I." Indeed, Bachmann has strewn *Malina* with a number of hints that readers should distance themselves from the standpoint the "I" assumes (what she termed her "self-irony" in the Kienlechner interview [*GuI* 98]). The most striking indication of Bachmann's ironic distance from the "I" is perhaps the latter's dismay that she, unlike other Austrian and German women at the end of the war, was not raped by Russian or black American soldiers (rapes that actually took place but, as Atina Grossmann has shown, were also discursively prestructured by Nazi ideology). "No normal man with normal drives has the obvious idea," the "I" laments, "that a normal woman would like to be quite normally raped" (*Malina* 180). Grossmann has also suggested that the mass rapes confirmed German women's conviction of their own victimization and *Mißbrauch* (abuse, the contemporary euphemism for rape) by the Allies; this, together with men's tribulations in prisoner-of-war camps, "construct[ed] a new national community of suffering that served not only to avoid confrontation with Nazi crimes, but also, of course, as a strategy for reauthorizing and reestablishing the unity of the *Volk*" (51). In Austria, where women were targets of rape especially by Soviet soldiers, as Bischof has shown (*Austria* 32–34), Austrians could construe themselves as double victims, the "first victims" of National Socialism and now subjects of abuse by their liberators as well. The desire for rape expressed by the "I" may thus also be related to her repression of the Nazi past. In any case, since even antifeminist readers will find it difficult to believe that normal women in fact really *want* to be raped, Bachmann should be able to count on her readers' recognition of a distance between the views of her character and her own.

A more difficult case is the often debated "mirror scene" of the first section, its interpretation particularly complicated by the discovery that Bachmann is probably replying to a Celan poem here (Weigel, *Ingeborg* 422–423): having bought herself a new dress, the "I" adorns herself and admires the result in the mirror, "fables removed from the men. For an hour I can live without time and space, deeply satisfied, carried off into a legend, where the aroma of the soap, the prickle of a facial tonic, the rustle of lingerie, the dipping of brushes into pots of powder, the thoughtful stroke of an eye-liner are the only reality. The result is a composition, a woman is to be created for a dress. In complete secrecy designs for a female are redrawn, it is like a genesis, with an aura for no one in particular" (*Malina* 86). Sigrid Schmid-Bortenschlager reads this passage as evidence of the degree to which Bachmann herself remained captive to the symbolic systems she wished to critique ("Spiegelszenen"). But Baackmann protests: "The site at which this scene takes place, the house, is not a unique, authentic site at which an identity independent of the other sex can be unfolded but rather already a

space allocated to women by men" (*Erklär* 810). The parapraxes of the "I"—
Summermorde (summer murders/fashions), *Wintermorde* (winter murders/
fashions) (cf. *Malina* 137)—underline the destructive quality of women's apparently "natural" attention to such traditionally female concerns as fashion and
cosmetics and the ways they are advertised (by 1958 the Bundesverband deutscher
Zeitungsverleger [federal association of newspaper publishers] estimated that
between 50 and 60 percent of German women were regular readers of newspaper advertisements [Carter, *How* 94]). In this case the "I" has embraced an
image of female autonomy (located in the home, the preferred female realm of
this antifeminist era) which is in fact the product of fashion designers, women's
magazines, and the cosmetics industry.

That point is made even more clearly in a scene in *Malina* where the "I"
attempts to prepare a gourmet dinner for Ivan while trying to remove the onion
smell from her hands and to dress for the evening: "Ivan is only allowed to see
the result: the table set and the candle burning, and Malina would be amazed
that I've managed to chill the wine in time, warm the plates, and between bast-
ing and toasting the rolls I apply eye shadow and mascara in front of Malina's
shaving mirror, pluck my eyebrows to their proper shape, and this synchronized
labor which no one appreciates is more strenuous than anything I've ever done
before" (*Malina* 50). Carter maintains of the postwar period that "this, finally,
was the defining element of the consumerized household: the erasure of the
traces of strenuous labor—cooking smells, for instance . . . —not only from the
domestic environment in general but, more particularly, from the body of a
housewife who herself was to be transformed into a commoditized component
of consumer lifestyle" (*How* 69–70). There is thus every reason to believe that
even (or especially) when the "I" believes she is the autonomous, self-determined
agent of her own actions, she is in fact obeying the dictates of a particular, historically specific era, attempting to adapt herself to the given, as Adorno might
have put it, consenting to the imperatives of hegemony in the form of consenting
to her own deepest being, in Eagleton's words (32).

In these apparently banal and benign images thus coalesce the social determinants of female behavior in the postwar era: this is how history has left its
imprint on female subjectivity of this period. In her love affair with Ivan the "I"
is following the script the Cold War era (and many earlier time periods) wrote
for women: of establishing a relationship with a man as woman's highest priority; of female subordination and male dominance; of a femininity devoted
entirely to the concerns of the private arena and interpersonal relations. Had
Bachmann not changed the title of *Malina*'s first section, her readers might

more readily have understood that all was not as it seemed in the love affair of the "I": before going into the page proofs, the novel's first section was called "Sleeping Happily with Ivan [*Glücklich schlafen mit Ivan*]," though not a single instance of "sleeping" with Ivan in the sense either of sex or of rest is present in the chapter. Even the final title of that section, "Happy with Ivan," should give pause to readers, for very little "happiness with Ivan" can be found here. But the "I" needs to love in order to exist as a woman at all: it is only in relationship to a man who loves her that her femininity is "awakened" (in the parlance of those times), becomes significant and meaningful. Bachmann herself suggests that Ivan and the "I" are playing discursively preordained roles when she remarks, "As I had to read that all again when I corrected it, I noticed that it's not so easy with Ivan, that maybe he is also a doppelgänger or a triple figure" (*Gul* 88); that is, the "I" projects onto him the qualities the men whom she loves need to possess—qualities to which she then attempts to accommodate herself. (In the third section of the novel the "I" explains to Malina as if it were self-evident that women must adapt themselves to each new lover's erotic whims, whereas men continue to behave just as they please.) That is why Ivan can be described as a sign or token (*Zeichen*): in Sigrid Weigel's elegant phrase, he is a "place-holder for the cause of desire" (*Bilder* 13).

Nonetheless, because in Bachmann's view the eroticization of subordination and pain is a central component of socially constructed female desire, the "I" truly suffers because of how Ivan treats her, and she traces the lineage of this love affair, or perhaps of her whole character structure ("sometimes you really do know exactly when it began" [*Malina* 10]) to the boy on the Glan Bridge when she was six who promised to give her something and hit her in the face instead— her first experience "of someone else's deep satisfaction in hitting" (*Malina* 10). Ivan thus joins the company of sadistic men who have mistreated the "I" (what Bachmann would doubtless call the fascism between women and men) via his "swearing sentences": "Les hommes sont les cochons. Les femmes aiment les cochons [Men are pigs. Women love pigs]," says Ivan (*Malina* 52). In selecting the love affair as the central event of the overture to her "Ways of Death," Bachmann makes the point that women and men are, for sociohistorical reasons, so constituted as to make the utopian connection at which they aim impossible.

There is thus every reason to treat the "Mysteries of the Princess of Kagran," which the "I" spins out to explain why Ivan was the lover intended for her from the beginning of time, with as much skepticism as the love affair that takes place in the novel's "Today." Felski suggests that "'the magical fictions' of romantic fantasy should be seen less as an abandonment of the secularized, disenchanted perspective of modernity than as another recurring dimension of the modern itself" (131). That is, such fantasies are projections of alternatives to a boring and banal quotidian reality (the daily life of the housewife, say) that are themselves generated by that reality. From this standpoint it is possible to find an explanation for Bachmann's otherwise mysterious plagiarism of Algernon Blackwood's short story "The Willows" (1906) to provide the description of the Danube swamps through which the princess travels. To Bachmann, passages from others' texts were of key importance, not to be regarded as quotations, as she announced somewhat cryptically: "There aren't any quotations for me, but rather the few passages in literature that have always excited me, they are life for me" (*GuI* 69). I propose that like the name of Perceval Glyde, borrowed from Wilkie Collins's *Woman in White* (see chapter 7), or the citation from D. H. Lawrence whose meanings I investigate in chapter 9, Bachmann's appropriation of Blackwood's story is one more indication that this text should be read against the grain, that here all is not as it seems. Or, to phrase this point differently, one could maintain that Bachmann's many citations are ironic gestures to indicate that her own text moves within the discursive parameters of the works—by Wilkie Collins, Rimbaud, Lawrence, Barbey d'Aurevilly, and Blackwood, among many others—from which she quotes and from which we as readers should distance ourselves. Though Blackwood's tale of a boat trip down the Danube begins as an idyll, it ends as a horror story in which the human actors are besieged by mysterious and ominous forces beyond their control (the "very ordinariness" of the landscape, the narrator in Blackwood's story meditates, "masked what was malignant and hostile to us" [183]), and those forces finally demand a human sacrifice. Similarly, one might maintain, the "real-life" romance of the "I" and Ivan, brushed against the grain, also reveals itself to be a tale of mounting terror and anxiety ending in death: love is murder.

It would nonetheless be wrong to conclude that love does not remain a utopian state of being for Bachmann in the novel, if a historically very determinate one, and that is part of the poignancy of *Malina*. Bachmann never ceases to remind her readers that the utopia of *luxe, calme et volupté*, which was to inform the "beautiful book" that the "I" is incapable of writing, is her utopia, too, "when all mankind will have redgolden eyes and starry voices, when their hands will be gifted for love, and the poetry of their lineage shall be recreated" (*Malina* 88). In one of the last statements of her life she continued to maintain that "I don't believe in this materialism, in this consumer society, in this capitalism, in this monstrosity that's taking place here, and people who enrich themselves on us without having any right to do so. I really do believe in something, and I call it

'A Day Will Come.' And one day it will come. Well, probably it won't come, because it's been destroyed for us so many times, for thousands of years it's been destroyed. It won't come, but I believe in it nonetheless. For if I weren't able to believe in it, then I couldn't write any more" (*GuI* 145). There is no reason not to take seriously the sentence that ends the description of Bachmann's novel on the dust jacket of its first edition: "Of its own accord, the book *Malina* protests that we are so murderously reasonable and laments that we are unable to love" (*TP* 3.2: 741)—though for Bachmann the incapacity to love is a consequence of causes far more social and political than *Malina*'s first reviewers were able to perceive. In a review with which Bachmann was very pleased (Albrecht, "Mann"), Hans Mayer chastised such critics: "In reviews people accused this 'heroine' and her author of being someone who, in the midst of bourgeois prosperity, is only striving for individual happiness. The misery of the world didn't seem to matter. Those who read that way have misunderstood the novel. The self-realization of the 'I' is prevented by the social conditions that always stand in the way of such fulfilled moments" (164). To Mayer, the female protagonist of this novel is a container for the hopes and dreams of the individual subject whose realization is thwarted by the present social order: "The female of this double ego represents the claim for a life filled with meaning in which feelings and thought achieve harmony. . . . Malina as male reason demonstrates to his female partner why this can't be possibly in Vienna 'today,' that is, in an alienated world. Thus he brings about the death of this soul, who does not die of her own disorder but rather—like the lovers of Manhattan—of a disorderly world" (164–65).

Who or what is responsible for thwarting the utopia Bachmann envisions? Exploring that question was the task of the middle chapter of *Malina*, titled "The Third Man," where Bachmann particularly draws upon the representational strategies she had first explored in "A Site for Coincidences." Said Bachmann: "And for myself I'm very certain that everything frightful that happens in this time is in the dreams, and that we all are murdered" (*GuI* 70). What combination of forces, then, congeal in the figure that in the dreams persecutes and torments the "I": the third man, the father, "this overpowerful father figure," as Bachmann put it, "about whom we discover that this figure is the murderer, and more precisely, the murderer whom we all have" (*GuI* 89)? Like all dream symbols, the father is "overdetermined"; a variety of "latent" concerns are displaced and condensed (to use Freud's terminology) to form the "manifest" elements of the "dreams of this night" for the "I" (*Malina* 113). As Bachmann explained: "A realist would probably tell about lots of frightful things that happen to a particular person or persons. Here it's compressed into this big figure which carries out what society carries out" (*GuI* 97). In accordance with my argument here that Bachmann's texts are suffused in a Cold War culture so natural to her characters that they are unable to recognize its damaging malevolence, it may be important to note first the connections of the father to "Amerika" and "Rußland." In one of the earlier dreams, the father telephones from America and in a later dream has just returned from America. "I can hear America well," says the "I" (*Malina* 117). Later the father also returns from Russia, where he has studied torture methods. Arnd Bohm, commenting on a version of this chapter given as a talk, suggested that references in *Malina*'s middle chapter to wintry weather, the frozen lake that borders the cemetery of the murdered daughters, and various kinds of ice are allusions to the cold war—a point that now seems so obvious that I am embarrassed I didn't think of it myself. Perhaps the novel's clearest explicit reference to the politics and social history of the postwar period, oddly enough virtually ignored by Bachmann scholarship, is the title of the dream chapter, "The Third Man," borrowed from the 1949 film set in the ruins of postwar Vienna, starring Orson Welles and Joseph Cotton. Hermann Glaser has written: "The little tragedies of the black market years, which add up to the great guilt of the times, found their almost legendary formulation in the English film *The Third Man* (directed by Carol Reed, script by Graham Greene). . . . The fact that the film, with Anton Karas's nervous zither music, moved people of the rubble era deeply and spoke to them almost mythically was not the least because here an especially longed-for medicament [penicillin] was made the object of criminal manipulation. The Americanization of life: that promised liberation from sickness and epidemics, of which there was no lack in defeated Germany" (76).

Elsewhere in *Malina*, Bachmann emphasizes continuities between the corruption and deceit of the immediate postwar period, thematized in *The Third Man*, and the present, clearly intended as a critique of Austria's embrace of the Western capitalist system:

> I would never have thought that everything would first have to be plundered, stolen, pawned and then bought and sold three times around the corner. The biggest black market was supposedly at the Resselpark, because of its many dangers you had to give it plenty of room, beginning in the late afternoon, all the way up to Karlsplatz. One day the black market ostensibly ceased to exist. But I'm not convinced. A universal black market resulted, and whenever I buy cigarettes or eggs, I know—but really only as of today—that they come from the black market. Anyway the whole market is black through and through, it can't have been that black before because it still lacked a universal density. (*Malina* 173)

The allusion the "I" makes to the "universal prostitution" (*Malina* 172) of the postwar period is multivalenced. On the one hand, it is the phrase Marx used in the *Economic and Philosophical Manuscripts* to describe wage labor under capitalism (Tucker 82). The "I" ponders, "Everyone who worked was a prostitute without knowing it, where have I heard that before?" (*Malina* 172). Moreover, "universal prostitution" refers to the ubiquitous spying that characterized the occupying powers' machinations in pre-1955 Cold War Vienna, Viennese selling themselves off to the highest Allied bidder: "Everyone was working for some side or another, without even knowing it. No side revealed its true identity" (*Malina* 172). And finally, "universal prostitution" describes the sexual chaos of the postwar period, when, as the "I" puts it, "the whole city participated in this universal prostitution, everybody must have lain on the trampled lawn with everyone else or else they leaned against the walls, moaning and groaning, panting, sometimes several at a time, by turns, promiscuously" (*Malina* 181).

In fact, the high value placed on penicillin in this period was due not just to its utility for healing sick children, as the film delicately puts it, but because (as the East German literary scholar Eva Kaufmann informed me) it could cure venereal disease: 19,000 new cases were reported in Vienna in 1946 (the year Bachmann came to Vienna), and, apparently as a result of the carryings-on *Malina* recounts, in 1948 one of every five young Viennese women between thirteen and twenty-one was infected with V.D. (Mattl, "Frauen" 111). In this reading, the "third man," the corrupt black market manipulator of penicillin, is a metonymic representative of an entire postwar economic, social, and sexual order that entered with the occupying forces and prizes profits over all other forms of human connection, and the "frightful things" perpetrated in the dreams by the "murderer whom we all have" are displaced and/or condensed images of the atrocities that order makes possible.

But a further peculiarity about Carol Reed's film is that nowhere does it address the reason *why* Vienna lay in ruins in 1947; in this film National Socialism is entirely repressed. This "disappearing" of the reasons why an Americanized "universal black market" had the opportunity to seize control of Austria suggests an additional interpretation of the forces figured in the third important man in the life of the "I," the powerful and violent father. In *The Inability to Mourn* (1967) Alexander and Margarete Mitscherlich suggest that the defeated Germanic peoples of the Third Reich refused to come to grips with the fact of their own support for National Socialism, the Allies' victory over Germany, and "the enormity of the catastrophe that lay behind them" (11). Instead, they sought father figures apart from Hitler—such as the aged father figure Konrad Adenauer (or possibly "Uncle Sam"?)—upon whom to project their libidinal attachments, identified with the victors, and stylized *themselves* into victims—of National Socialism, Hitler, rape, prisoner-of-war camps, and so on. The Mitscherlich analysis provides a framework for understanding the first two dreams of the "I," one concerned with the cemetery of the murdered daughters, the other, with a gas chamber in which her father has enclosed her. One might posit that what Bachmann is revealing here (whether deliberately or not is not very relevant) are precisely the moves of the post-Holocaust German or Austrian psyche that enabled it conveniently to "forget" the Holocaust. I am not attempting to suggest that the "I" is not a "victim" of male dominance or of fascistoid elements that survive into the postwar period; rather, I want to maintain that (unconsciously—as the Mitscherliches argue) she represents her historically occasioned distress in ways common to other Germans and Austrians of the period, thus virtually assuring that she, like her compatriots, will be incapable of either understanding or alleviating it. Bachmann recalled that it was the National Socialist conquest of Austria that began her own process of remembering: "There was a particular moment that destroyed my childhood. Hitler's troops' invasion of Klagenfurt. It was so horrible that my memory begins on this day. The enormous brutality that you could feel, the shouting, singing, and marching. . . . A whole army entered our quiet, peaceful Carinthia" (*GuI* 111). But Gerhard Botz observes that Bachmann here also succumbs to some degree to the "Austria as first Nazi victim" myth, since the commotion was most likely in fact made by the large Nazi population of Kärnten (201). Botz's argument is strongly supported by Hans Höller's revelation that Bachmann's own father joined the Nazi party in 1932 (*Ingeborg* [1999] 25), though Bachmann herself never acknowledged that she was raised in a Nazi family; perhaps, as the foregoing quotation suggests, she even invested some effort in obscuring her own Nazi connections. One might speculate that one reason the "I" can't remember what she needs to know to tell her story is that she, like many of her country's people in the postwar period, can't—or won't—remember her own relationship to the Holocaust, and is then haunted in her dreams by her own unmastered past. That might also explain repeated dreams the "I" has of sex with her father, which from a psychoanalytic perspective are an indication that she has accepted her place in the sex/gender system over which her (or *the*) father presides—*and* accepted all the other values that the father represents. Baackmann suggests what the consequences of this reading of the incest dreams might be: "The father is ever more clearly recognizable as the principle of an omnipotent authority to which the daughter submits herself unconditionally, to be sure in the belief that she is rebelling against his power" (*Erklär* 87). "I wouldn't have betrayed you," says the "I" to her father (*Malina* 114). Malina tells the "I," "Maybe you didn't know, but you were in agreement" (*Malina* 145).

It appears, then, that the dream chapter of *Malina*, focused on the most interiorized processes of the psyche, also reveals "history within the I/psyche": here the "I" is like Claudia Koonz's German women in *Mothers in the Fatherland*, who are not just products but also proponents of the social order that subordinates them. This reading of Bachmann's notion of femininity is substantiated by a striking scene from an early draft of *Franza*, whose protagonist has mostly been viewed as fascist patriarchy's innocent victim par excellence. Her psychoanalyst husband (in this early version called "Baronig") alleged that his earliest scholarly publication had appeared in 1948, but Franza, whom he has unsparingly put to work as his research assistant, by chance discovers an earlier publication "on a card in the [library] card catalogue, . . . 1941, 1942, though with a harmless title. It would have been wrong to say that Franza had a violent reaction then, on the contrary, she didn't even think much about it, but went back two weeks later and removed the card without looking to see whether the publication could have been incriminating or not. She didn't want to know, and even less did she want to tell her Baron about it or ask him a question" (*TP* 2: 47). Later in the same draft, in a passage narrated from Franza's perspective, Bachmann further underlines Franza's unwillingness to confront her husband's possible Nazi affiliations before 1945: "I found it, when I was working on Riedel, I took the card out of the catalogue in the Nationalbibliothek. I don't know if this work was incriminating for him or not, but I took it away, no, carried it around in my purse for two days, then I threw it away, in Frau Rosi's garbage can between the old lettuce and the bread crust. And then I looked in the garbage can again and got the card out and dropped it into the sewer, through the slots, now it's floating in the sewer pipes, and I don't know, was it something or was it nothing. 1941. Now I'll never know, and nobody can ever look for it. What kind of an article it was and for which medical journal, I don't know any more, I swear. I never wanted to know. . . . I never wanted to know anything" (*TP* 2: 64). Here Franza, by this point in the novel already a victim of her husband's "fascist" treatment of her, colludes nonetheless in what Götz Aly has called the "unwritten code of silence" about academic support for Nazi policies and practices (154). Sigrid Weigel has astutely observed of all the murdered daughters: "In Bachmann's depiction the daughters participate in the 'eternal war.' Not only as a victim or as someone affected—because there isn't a female refuge outside of history. But rather war continues within themselves, as in all subjects" (*Bilder* 141).

Another passage characterized by "self-irony," which I quote at some length, unites these several themes and also shows how, though in the bourgeois novel women represent subjectivity and in postwar society women are responsible for consumption, the story of the "I" told in *Malina* could also be relevant for men:

> Malina asks: Have you never thought how much trouble other people have gone to because of you? I nod thankfully. They have indeed, they didn't spare themselves the trouble of providing me with character traits, they equipped me with stories, and even with money as well, so that I can run around in clothes and eat leftovers, so that I continue to make do and so it won't be too obvious how I am doing [*damit es weitergeht mit mir und nicht auffällt, wie es weitergeht*]. Too quickly tired I can sit down in the Café Museum and leaf through newspapers and magazines. Hope returns to me, I am excited, incited because there is now a direct flight to Canada twice a week, you can fly to Australia in comfort on Qantas, safaris are getting cheaper, in Vienna we should soon see Doro-coffee with its unique aroma from the high sunny plains of Central America, Kenya is advertised, Henkell Rosée lets you flirt with a new world, no building is too high for Hitachi elevators, books for and by men are now available which are just as inspiring for women. So that your world never gets too small for you, there's PRESTIGE, a sea breeze from a far horizon. Everyone is talking about mortgages. You're in good hands with us, proclaims a Mortgage-Bank, you'll go a long way in TARRACO shoes. We coat your Venetian blinds twice so you'll never have to varnish them again, a CALL-computer is never alone! And then the Antilles, le bon voyage. That's why the Bosch EXQUISITE is one of the best dishwashers in the world. The moment of truth is coming when customers ask our experts questions, when management technique, calculation, net profits, packaging machines, delivery times are all up for debate. VIVIOPAL for those who can't remember a thing. Take it in the morning . . . and the day belongs to you! So all I need is Viviopal. (*Malina* 165–66)

First, the "I" clearly acknowledges that she is a product of, has been inserted into, and has embraced the ideological models and narratives that "other people" have provided for her and that the task such discourses preeminently perform is allowing her to continue to perform the social functions prescribed for her without understanding or even noticing their cost to her ("so it won't be too obvious how I am doing"). What she receives in return for her compliance is access to the consumer paradise of postwar capitalism, served up to her by the postwar media, another "dream factory" that dazzles her with endless, ever new consumer possibilities ("Hope returns to me," "flirt with a new world") and on which she, queen of household consumption, is expected to be an expert—hence the necessity of advertising ("when customers ask our experts questions"). And the possibilities available to her are those of the economic miracle of postwar capitalism that the United States promised to deliver to Western Europe: the home (via a mortgage), clothing, cosmetics, exotic articles to eat and drink, fancy household items. The availability of consumer goods from across the world emphasizes that capitalism is a global system dependent on a world market (anticipating, as do Bachmann's stories "Word for Word" and "Three Paths to the Lake," today's concerns about globalization). Moreover, postwar consumer capitalism puts the entire world at the disposal of the Western tourist, with a particular emphasis on formerly colonized countries: Canada, Australia, Kenya, the Antilles. The "I"—that is, the postwar subjectivity of which she is a metonymic representation—has thus been granted and has accepted membership in ("has bought into," so to speak) an entire economic, political, and cultural system with race, class, and gender implications. All that is asked of her is that she not "remember a thing"—about the Austrian past that led to this world of wonders, about the global present to which she is now subjected. "So all I need is Viviopal," the "I" muses; perhaps then nothing will disturb her memory and she will be able to tell her story. But precisely her ironic tone underlines the cost, for men and women, of embracing the postwar capitalist order, their containment by and complicity in a system that is not at all dedicated to the purpose of meeting human needs.

After the "I" has bared scars on her soul for which even she can not account, what does it mean that she disappears into a crack in the wall at the end of this novel? How should we understand the last sentence, "It was murder" (*Malina* 225)? For many, many feminist scholars the answer has seemed simple: as I myself wrote in a 1980 essay (chapter 3 of this book): "Even the most superficial reading of Bachmann's late prose should make clear who is being killed in these various ways (and also that death can be the death of the spirit as well as of the body): women." But here I would like to make a somewhat different argument that begins by taking seriously Bachmann's own argument that both Malina and Ivan are doubles of the "I." As detailed in chapter 8, the cold war encouraged dualisms of many sorts, and even progressive thinkers of that period (as, indeed, of our own) constructed women as reason's or the male subject's other; and, as I maintained earlier in this chapter, the apparently natural opposition of men and women was one of the foundations on which the normative heterosexuality of cold war culture rested. Of course, discursive constructions of this sort do not in fact precisely describe (though they certainly profoundly influence) what "real people" "actually" are and do. In the cold war period, "real" female subjects were nodes at which mutually irreconcilable discourses intersected. In the period during which Bachmann wrote, it seemed perhaps literally inconceivable that one could be the kind of person who could both love ecstatically and pay one's bills on time. The "I" thus performs gender burlesques like those of Lucille Ball or Gracie Allen when she tries to operate in a man's world, and only Malina can keep her life in order as she performs prechoreographed steps in her elaborate ballroom dance with Ivan. But just as Bachmann herself was described as (for a time at least) sovereignly managing a difficult balancing act, being charmingly inept at dealing with the conditions of daily life yet extremely savvy about her business affairs, similarly it is important to stress that *all* of these figures, Ivan, Malina, and the "I," constitute the radically disunified self of the woman, or at least the woman intellectual, of this period (see Bird). It is not necessary to make Malina a villain in order to understand the claim of the "I" that "I have lived in Ivan and die in Malina" (*Malina* 223). After Ivan decamps, the capacity of the "I" to love—which, in the discursive frame within which this novel moves, means her femininity, is no longer evoked, and she is reabsorbed in Malina. But, as Bachmann repeatedly emphasized, the "I" of course *is* Malina. Or: Malina is she.

How were the "Ways of Death" to continue after the "I" disappears into the wall and Malina becomes their narrator, as the "I" had requested ("Go ahead and take over all the stories which make up history [*die große Geschichte*]. Take them all away from me" (*Malina* 221)? Bachmann commented in a "plot summary": "The whole book is directed toward the emergence of the figure of Malina, who is objective and sovereign, while the "I" is subject [*sic*] and useless. For that reason the questionable narrative perspective later disappears, then the narration is total because Malina knows everything and can decide what to do with the characters" (*TP* 3.2: 740). In conformance with this and numerous other remarks by Bachmann, I propose here, as I suggested earlier, that in subsequent "Ways of Death," abandoning the "questionable narrative perspective" of *Malina*, Bachmann would return to the apparently realistic narrative form of "To Die for Berlin" and its seemingly sovereign and all-knowing narrator—the second of the two narrative strategies between which her later writing oscillates. Subsequent "Ways of Death" volumes, I further want to argue, would take a form similar to the stories of *Three Paths to the Lake* (which I consider to be part of the "Ways of Death" cycle), of "Rosamunde," of "Greed," of *Requiem for Fanny Goldmann,* and of the Eka Kottwitz fragment. Bachmann, I maintain, changes narrative strategies for reasons very much related to her conception of the production of subjectivity in the cold war period: she resorts to the realist form because, in order to represent figures entirely subjected to the hegemonic ideologies/discourses of their period, she cannot allow them to perceive the cracks and crevices of the order that constrains them (cracks perhaps like those of the wall into which the "I" disappears). Instead, she falls back to a narrative form corresponding to the ideology of bourgeois individualism on which the postwar period depended, premised upon the notion of an exterior world existing independently of the perceiving subject, as well as that of a subject who is a rational, unified, and coherent bearer of consciousness and conceives itself to be able to act autonomously and to control its own destiny. Though a sympathetic figure, Malina is constructed as a subject who is a creature of such ideologies, and he will thus be able to tell only those parts of the stories for which there are words in the discourse of which he is part (which is why the figures of those texts so often remark to themselves, "It was nothing" or "It couldn't be told").

Moreover, the figures of these later "Ways of Death," captives of hegemonic ideologies or discourses, will be shown to understand themselves as the same sort of self-determined, autonomous subjects as Malina himself, quite unaware of the historical forces and social pressures inscribed upon them and the actual nature of their own situation. The narrator of the story "Word for Word" makes this point very emphatically when he (!) remarks of the interpreter Nadja and her boyfriend Frankel off for a romantic fling to southern Italy: "What was going on in the world these next few days basically had nothing to do with them, how everything changed and how hopeless it all was [*warum es immer auswegsloser wurde*]" (*Paths* 14–15; *TP* 4: 117). Almut Dippel has determined that this story takes place in August 1968, at the time of another major event in the history of the cold war: the Soviet invasion of Czechoslovakia and the crushing of the Prague Spring's attempts to develop a "socialism with a human face" (18). Thus what can't and won't be revealed in this and other stories of *Three Paths to the Lake* are the constituents of subjectivity that emerge in *Malina*, "history within the I/psyche"—and that is why *Malina* was the necessary overture to Bachmann's novel cycle, to reveal what would be much more difficult to discover in other "Ways of Death." Marcel Reich-Ranicki's judgment of the stories of *Three Paths to the Lake* in his 1972 review was thus not entirely off base—though for reasons quite different from those he advanced: "Are these stories, in which the chic and the stylish predominate, the worldly and the melodramatic triumph, and excessive sentimentality is mixed with snob appeal, are these stories perhaps not supposed to be anything more than reading matter for those ladies who flip through magazines at the hairdresser's or in the dentist's waiting room? That is, consciously and cynically intended to be popular fiction [*Trivi-*

alliteratur]?" (191–192). Precisely: Bachmann's figures are exactly such "ladies" whose self-understanding is prefabricated by the categories by which popular fiction is also informed.

As I observed of "Three Paths to the Lake" in the preceding chapter, the two frame stories of *Three Paths to the Lake* repeat the constellation of *Malina*—with a difference: here the female protagonists are shown to have succeeded brilliantly in the public, male, arena, while in the private realm they are entirely unable to articulate why or even *that* they are unhappy. "Hasn't it ever occurred to anyone," Elisabeth Matrei rages, not understanding that she is talking about herself, "that you kill people when you deprive them of the power of speech and with it the power to experience and think?" (*Paths* 173). The three interior stories deal only with the private, female sphere, "their *own world*," Tanja Schmidt declares, "which they *defend* in their retreat to complete *privacy*" (494). As women in the private arena, even in the late 1960s and early 1970s they conform to the dictates of cold war femininity, as the "I" had observed: "Women always have their heads full of feelings and stories about their man or men. Such thoughts really do consume the greatest part of every woman's time" (*Malina* 178). Bachmann guides the reading of the stories of *Three Paths to the Lake*, however, so as to reveal the gaps, inconsistencies, ruptures, and incoherences of hegemonic ideologies of which her figures themselves, products of those ideologies, are not aware. Beatrix in "Problems Problems," for instance, is utterly impatient with the political engagement of Jeanne, a young French veteran of 1968: "It had always been on the tip to her tongue to tell Jeanne that her Parisian head was full of confused ideas and nothing more, you couldn't be a hippie and go to the opera at the same time, ride the ferris wheel and revolutionize the world, at least not in Vienna" (*Paths* 42). Love is as tormented and unsatisfying for the female figures of *Three Paths to the Lake* as for the "I," and though they try to conceive of themselves as being in charge of their erotic fortunes—Elisabeth coolly picking out a man to deflower her; Miranda managing her lover's betrayal of her so she will not appear to be his victim—in fact, they too are at the mercy of the men they need to love them. Because there is really no function in the private sphere for a woman who does not head a household, Beatrix can find nothing to do, apart from the beauty parlor, except sleep; old Frau Jordan vegetates in a tiny apartment on her way toward senility; and Miranda drives female inattention to the public realm to a comic pitch by refusing to wear glasses so she sees nothing of it at all. As Bachmann wrote in a draft of a letter to her publisher, "they're playing with the wrong cards, but the game they're playing does them more honor than the crude vulgarities of other women" (*TP* 4: 12). In these stories, as in *Malina*, we see virtually nothing of the historical conditions in which the lives of the figures are embedded, only their consequences for women who have been instructed not to attend to them. As in *Malina*, even the utopias of the *Three Paths* figures are formulated in the impoverished terms available to them: Nadja in the arms of Christ, Beatrix in the beauty parlor, Elisabeth in her hopeless quest for the New Man. I observed in my introduction that Adorno's painful observation about the conditions of existence in the post-Holocaust, postwar period might do for the figures of the "Ways of Death," too: "There's no right way to live when the world is wrong [*Es gibt kein richtiges Leben im falschen*]" (*Minima Moralia* 42); like Adorno's *Minima Moralia*, Bachmann's "Ways of Death" stories are "Reflections from a Damaged Life."

Historians have termed the period about which Bachmann wrote—from the end of what she called "the first postwar era" in *Malina* (172) to the beginning of the student movement—*die Langen Fünfziger Jahre*, "the long fifty years" (Abelshauser), because of the economic, political, and social homogeneity of that era. Bachmann set herself the task of viewing her times through a gendered perspective in order to illuminate the condition of female subjectivity, perhaps even of human subjectivity altogether. As Irene Heidelberger-Leonard puts it: "It's Bachmann's undisputed accomplishment to have conjoined the political and the private spheres so inextricably. . . . She sharpens our perception of everyday history by reversing the perspectives of crime and normality. In so doing she doesn't make the criminal banal, but she certainly makes the everyday criminal" ("Ernst" 88). In her series of prefaces to *The Book of Franza*, Bachmann connected the "crime virus" that had not disappeared from the world following the defeat of National Socialism to a passage from Barbey D'Aurevilly's "Vengeance d'une femme," which declared, "Those crimes appeal less to the senses, they appeal more to the intellect; and the intellect, after all, is the deepest part of us . . . [and there] no blood was spilt, and the murder was within the domain of sentiment and custom" (*TP* 2: 73). What clearly both deterred Bachmann in her effort to compose her "Ways of Death" and detracted from her readers' ability to understand what she had written was that the "long 1950s" were a period in which nothing (excepting, of course, the communist threat), was supposed to be wrong at all—especially in the private sphere, now decreed to be the prime source of human happiness and satisfaction, to which women had been restored.

Other talented women of Bachmann's generation were also broken by an era whose vicious qualities they struggled to delineate. In a 1962 poem Sylvia Plath (1932–1963), of German ancestry, identified herself with Jewish victims and condemned her father as a fascist. Her autobiographical novel *The Bell Jar* (1963) locates her account of a young girl's breakdown in the context of the cold war by beginning it with a reference to the Rosenbergs' execution in 1953. In a 1968 draft of a review of *The Bell Jar*, Bachmann wrote of the protagonist: "She is destroyed [*verunglückt*] in such an undiscernible way that one asks oneself after the third reading where this secret unhappiness starts and how, and I am inclined to consider that, like everything you can't find evidence for in a book, as the best and strangest" (*W* 4: 358). In a 1963 poem Anne Sexton (1928–1974) wrote: "I was tired of being a woman / tired of the spoons and the pots / tired of my mouth and my breasts, tired of the cosmetics and the silks" (1995). Anne Parsons (1930–1964), a talented researcher in the social sciences and daughter of the famous sociologist Talcott Parsons (who influenced Helmut Schelsky), wrote after endless psychoanalytic sessions: "All I do know is that my own life became more and more of a void symbolized by the long spaces between my apartment and the suburban houses where I occasionally got invited for dinner to hear about the local school system and within which none of the messages from myself which I sent out in increasingly desperate ways ever came back with more than an echo of 'you, you, you just don't want to be a woman at all.' I began to wish that someone would call me names or throw stones or threaten to send me to a concentration camp so that at least I would know for certain that the world was against me" (quoted in Breines 178). Marilyn Monroe (1926–1962) was born in the same month and year as Bachmann and committed suicide like Plath, Sexton, and Parsons. In her ex-husband Arthur Miller's play *After the Fall* (which Bachmann may have seen in Berlin in spring 1965 [Kohn-Waechter, *Verschwinden* 196]) the character possibly modeled on Monroe says: "I have been hurt by a long line of men but I have cooperated with my persecutors" (234). Meanwhile in West Germany, three notable women writers of the period, Marie Luise Kaschnitz, Ilse Langner, and Oda Schaefer, proclaimed to the Darmstadt Academy for Language and Literature in 1957 that women have an affinity for the world of dreams, the unconscious, and irrationality (Kaschnitz); that the patient, suffering, passive character of women was the determining element in their writing (Schaefer); and that the drama of women's lives, particularly childbirth, made them uninterested in writing drama (Langner) (quoted in Bullivant/Rice 229). We can imagine the cemetery of the murdered daughters as a fitting final resting place for these talented and beleaguered women.

In *The Feminine Mystique* (1963), Betty Friedan began to identify "the problem that had no name," but her account, like those of some other subsequent feminists (including many of Bachmann's readers and commentators), limited and to some extent trivialized women's problems by reducing the cause of those problems only to their treatment by men and a male-dominated society. I turn one final time to Christa Wolf, who in 1966 wrote of Bachmann's texts: "Suddenly we see what cannot be seen but must be there because it produces effects. We see the past within the present, for instance. Or the boundless desires we always suppress, which can gush out in anyone at any moment. . . . But above all vision means seeing the unity and meaning behind seemingly unrelated and meaningless events. The discovery of what animates them all, and of what really is destroying them—regardless of what they may pretend" (*Reader* 103). Situating her texts in the context of a social reality whose lineaments are discernable only in their effects on her figures, Bachmann represents a "historical situation" in which their condition cannot be ameliorated until, as Christa Wolf knew, everything is changed.

Materialist feminism regards all readings as political, as interventions into the process of meaning-making which establishes the discursive boundaries of what counts as "the way things are." My own readings in this chapter, as in this book altogether, are intended as an intervention into discussions about feminist methodology as well as about the interpretation of Ingeborg Bachmann's texts. I have tried to show that women's lives (as well as representations of them) are always situated within a historical context shaped by a multiplicity of discursive and nondiscursive historical forces. My project here is to amend feminist methodology by, as it were, decentering gender, showing it to be an analytical category always necessary yet never sufficient for an understanding of women's and men's lives. I want thereby to extend feminism's oppositional reach by contributing to a feminist effort to elaborate more complex theoretical frameworks capable of grasping all the determinants that shape women's (and men's) lives at any historical moment. Via such new theoretical paradigms, feminists and other oppositional groupings may be better able both to comprehend and subsequently to contend against destructive social forces such as those responsible for producing the disastrous social constellations that Bachmann tried to describe. Because I believe that feminist scholarship should assist in transforming the world as well as interpreting it, I hope the analysis I advance here may make some contribution to producing the kinds of new social arrangements in which Bachmann would no longer have needed to write her "Ways of Death."

WORKS CITED

TEXTS BY BACHMANN

Bachmann, Ingeborg. *The Book of Franza and Requiem for Fanny Goldmann*. Trans. Peter Filkins. Evanston, IL: Northwestern UP, 1999.

———. "Gier." *Der dunkle Schatten, dem ich schon seit Anfang folge: Ingeborg Bachmann: Vorschläge zu einer neuen Lektüre des Werks*. Ed. Hans Höller. Wien: Löcker, 1982. 71–61.

———. "The Good God of Manhattan." Trans. Valerie Tekavec. *Ingeborg Bachmann and Christa Wolf: Selected Prose and Drama*. Ed. Patricia A. Herminghouse. New York: Continuum, 1998. 55–97.

———. "Immer wieder: Schwarz und Weiss." Blattzahl 454. Bachmann-Nachlaß. Nationalbibliothek, Wien.

———. *In the Storm of Roses: Selected Poems*. Trans. and ed. Mark Anderson. Princeton: Princeton UP, 1986.

———. *Die kritische Aufnahme der Existentialphilosophie Martin Heideggers*. 1949. Ed. Robert Pichl. München: Piper, 1985.

———. *Malina*. 1971.Trans. Philip Boehm. New York: Holmes & Meier, 1990.

———. "Philosophie der Gegenwart." Blattzahlen 831, 580–593. Bachmann-Nachlaß. Nationalbibliothek, Wien.

———. *Römische Reportagen: Eine Wiederentdeckung*. Ed. Jörg-Dieter Kogel. München: Piper, 1998.

———. "Sightseeing in an Old City." Trans. Margaret McCarthy. *Ingeborg Bachmann and Christa Wolf: Selected Prose and Drama*. Ed. Patricia A. Herminghouse. New York: Continuum, 1998. 3–7.

———. *Songs in Flight: The Collected Poems of Ingeborg Bachmann*. Trans. Peter Filkins. New York: Marsilio, 1994.

———. *The Thirtieth Year.* 1961. Trans. Michael Bullock. New York: Knopf, 1964.

———. *Three Paths to the Lake.* 1972. Trans. Mary Fran Gilbert. New York: Holmes & Meier, 1989.

———. *"Todesarten"-Projekt.* Ed. Dirk Göttsche and Monika Albrecht. 4 vols. München: Piper, 1995.

———. "To Die for Berlin." Trans. Lilian Friedberg. *"If We Had the Word": Ingeborg Bachmann. Views and Reviews.* Ed. Gisela Brinker-Gabler and Markus Zisselsberger. Riverside, CA: Ariadne, 2004. 7–17.

———. *Werke.* Ed. Christine Koschel, Inge von Weidenbaum, and Clemens Münster. 4 vols. München: Piper, 1978.

———. "Der Wiener Kreis: Logischer Positivismus—Philosophie als Wissenschaft." Blattzahlen 5274–5298. Bachmann-Nachlaß. Nationalbibliothek, Wien.

———. *Wir müssen wahre Sätze finden: Gespräche und Interviews.* Ed. Christine Koschel and Inge von Weidenbaum. München: Piper, 1983.

SECONDARY LITERATURE

Abel, Elizabeth, ed. *Writing and Sexual Difference.* Chicago: U of Chicago P, 1982.

Abelshauser, Werner. *Die Langen Fünfziger Jahre: Wirtschaft und Gesellschaft der Bundesrepublik Deutschland 1949–1966.* Düsseldorf: Schwann, 1987.

Abu-Lughod, Lila. "A Community of Secrets: The Separate World of Bedouin Women." *Signs* 10.4 (1985): 637–657.

Achberger, Karen. "Bachmann und die Bibel: 'Ein Schritt nach Gomorrha' als weibliche Schöpfungsgeschichte." *Der dunkle Schatten, dem ich schon seit Anfang folge: Ingeborg Bachmann: Vorschläge zu einer neuen Lektüre des Werks.* Ed. Hans Höller. Wien: Löcker, 1982. 97–110.

———. "Beyond Patriarchy: Ingeborg Bachmann and Fairytales." *Modern Austrian Literature* 18.3/4 (1985): 211–222.

———. *Understanding Ingeborg Bachmann.* Columbia: U of South Carolina P, 1995.

Ackelsberg , Martha. "'Separate and Equal'? Mujeres Libres and Anarchist Strategy for Women's Emancipation." *Feminist Studies* 11.1 (1985): 63–83.

Adelson, Leslie. *Making Bodies, Making History: Feminism and German Identity.* Lincoln: U of Nebraska P, 1993.

Adorno, Theodor W. *Minima Moralia: Reflexionen aus dem beschädigten Leben.* Frankfurt/M: Suhrkamp, 1969.

———. "What Does Coming to Terms with the Past Mean?" Trans. Timothy Bahti and Geoffrey Hartman. *Bitburg in Moral and Political Perspective.* Ed. Geoffrey H. Hartman. Bloomington: Indiana UP, 1986. 114–129.

Agnese, Barbara, and Robert Pichl, eds. Special Issue Ingeborg Bachmann. *Cultura tedesca* 25 (2004).

Albrecht, Monika. "'A man. A woman . . .': Narrative Perspective and Gender Discourse in Ingeborg Bachmann's *Malina*." *If We Had the Word: Ingeborg Bachmann. Views and Reviews.* Ed. Gisela Brinker-Gabler and Markus Zisselsberger. Riverside, CA: Ariadne, 2004. 127–149.

———. " 'Es muß erst geschrieben werden': Kolonisation und magische Weltsicht in Ingeborg Bachmanns Romanfragment Das Buch Franza." *"Über die Zeit schreiben": Literatur-und kulturwissenschaftliche Essays zu Ingeborg Bachmanns "Todesarten"-Projekt.* Ed. Monika Albrecht and Dirk Göttsche. Würzburg: Königshausen & Neumann, 1998. 59–91.

———. "Postkolonialismus und Kritischer Exotismus." *Bachmann-Handbuch: Leben —Werk—Wirkung.* Ed. Monika Albrecht and Dirk Göttsche. Stuttgart: Metzler, 2002. 255–258.

———. "'Sire, this village is yours': Ingeborg Bachmanns Romanfragment *Das Buch Franza* aus postkolonialer Sicht." *"Über die Zeit schreiben" 3: Literatur- und kulturwissenschaftliche Essays zum Werk Ingeborg Bachmanns.* Ed. Monika Albrecht and Dirk Göttsche. Würzburg: Königshausen & Neumann, 2004. 159–169.

———. "Text-Torso oder Trümmerfeld? Ingeborg Bachmanns 'Todesarten'-Projekt im Jahr 1973." *"Text-Tollhaus für Bachmann-Süchtige?" Lesarten zur kritischen Ausgabe von Ingeborg Bachmanns "Todesarten"-Projekt.* Ed. Irene Heidelberger-Leonard. Opladen: Westdeutscher Verlag, 1998. 28–46.

Albrecht, Monika, and Dirk Göttsche, eds. *Bachmann-Handbuch: Leben—Werk—Wirkung.* Stuttgart: Metzler, 2002.

———, E-mail to women_in_german listserv. 18 May 1998.

———, ed. *"Über die Zeit schreiben": Literatur- und kulturwisssschaftliche Essays zum Werk Ingeborg Bachmanns.* Würzburg: Königshausen & Neumann, 1998.

———, ed. *"Über die Zeit schreiben"2: Literatur- und kulturwisssschaftliche Essays zum Werk Ingeborg Bachmanns.* Würzburg: Königshausen & Neumann, 2000.

———, ed. *"Über die Zeit schreiben"3: Literatur- und kulturwisssschaftliche Essays zum Werk Ingeborg Bachmanns.* Würzburg: Königshausen & Neumann, 2004.

———, "Vorwort." *Bachmann-Handbuch: Leben—Werk—Wirkung.* Ed. Monika Albrecht and Dirk Göttsche. Stuttgart: Metzler, 2002. vii–ix.

Alcoff, Linda. "Cultural Feminism versus Post-Structuralism: The Identity Crisis in Feminist Theory." *Signs* 13.3 (1988): 405–436.

Allen, Ann Taylor. "Mothers of the New Generation: Adele Schreiber, Helene Stöcker, and the Evolution of a German Idea of Motherhood, 1900–1914." *Signs* 10.3 (1985): 418–438.

Allen, Carolyn J. "Critical Response: Feminist(s) Reading: A Response to Elaine Showalter." *Writing and Sexual Difference.* Ed. Elizabeth Abel. Chicago: U of Chicago P, 1982. 298–303.

Alsop, Stewart. "Sterben für Berlin?" *Der Spiegel.* 15 November 1961. 73–79.

Althusser, Louis. *Lenin and Philosophy and Other Essays.* New York: Monthly Review, 1971.

Altman, Dennis. "A New Barbarism." *Socialist Review* 15.1 (1985): 7–12.

Aly, Götz. *Macht, Geist, Wahn: Kontinuitäten deutschen Denkens.* Berlin: Argon, 1997.

Anders, Günther. "Die Welt als Phantom und Matrize: Philosophische Gedanken zu Rundfunk und Fernsehen." *Merkur* 9.5 (1955): 401–416; 9.6 (1955): 533–544; 9.7 (1955): 636–652.

Appadurai, Arjun. *Modernity at Large: Cultural Dimensions of Globalization.* Minneapolis: U of Minnesota P, 1996.

Arendt, Hannah. *Eichmann in Jerusalem.* New York: Viking, 1963.

Ashcroft, Bill, Gareth Griffiths, and Helen Tiffin, eds. *The Empire Writes Back: Theory and Practice in Postcolonial Literatures.* London: Routledge, 1989.

Atzler, Elke. "Ingeborg Bachmanns Roman 'Malina' im Spiegel der literarischen Kritik." *Jahrbuch der Grillparzer-Gesellschaft.* 3. Folge. 15 (1983): 155–171.

Auerbach, Judy, Linda Blum, Vicki Smith, and Christine Williams. "Commentary on Gilligan's *In a Different Voice.*" *Feminist Studies* 11.1 (1985): 149–161.

Auerbach, Nina. *Woman and the Demon: The Life of a Victorian Myth.* Cambridge, MA: Harvard UP, 1982.

Austin, Gerhard. "Malina: Ingeborg Bachmann's Text, Elfriede Jelinek's Filmbook, and Werner Schroeter's Film." *Thunder Rumbling at My Heels: Tracing Ingeborg Bachmann.* Ed. Gudrun Brokoph-Mauch. Riverside, CA: Ariadne, 1998. 3–23.

Baackmann, Susanne. "'Beinah mörderisch wahr': Die neue Stimme der Undine: Zum Mythos von Weiblichkeit und Liebe in Ingeborg Bachmanns 'Undine geht.'" *German Quarterly* 68.1 (1995): 45–59.

———. "Ein Nichts, . . . eine geträumte Substanz? Zur Schreibweise von Weiblichkeit in Ingeborg Bachmanns Erzählband 'Das dreißigste Jahr.'" *text + kritik Sonderband Ingeborg Bachmann.* 5. Auflage: Neufassung. München: text + kritik, 1995. 71–83.

———. *Erklär mir Liebe: Weibliche Schreibweisen von Liebe in der Gegenwartsliteratur.* Berlin: Argument, 1995.

———. Reply to Holschuh. *German Quarterly* 68.4 (1995): 433–435.

Bachmann, Dieter. Editorial. *Du* September 1994: 13, 15.

Bail, Gabriele. *Weibliche Identität: Ingeborg Bachmanns "Malina."* Göttingen: Edition Herodot, 1984.

Balzac, Honoré de. *The Works of Honoré de Balzac.* 18 vols. New York: Bigelow, 1910.

Barthes, Roland. *Writing Degree Zero.* Trans. Annette Lavers and Colin Smith. New York: Hill and Wang, 1968.

Bammer, Angelika. "Victim Politics: Feminist Constructions in Post-Holocaust Germany." Unpublished manuscript.

Bannasch, Bettina. *Von vorletzten Dingen: Schreiben nach "Malina": Ingeborg Bachmanns "Simultan"-Erzählungen.* Würzburg: Königshausen & Neumann, 1997.

Barbey d'Aurevilly, Jules. "The Vengeance of a Woman." *The Diaboliques.* Trans. Ernest Boyd. New York: Knopf, 1933. 239–275.

Bareiss, Otto, and Frauke Ohloff. *Ingeborg Bachmann: Eine Bibliographie.* München: Piper, 1978.

———. "Ingeborg Bachmann-Bibliographie 1977/78–1981/82: Nachträge und Ergänzungen." *Jahrbuch der Grillparzer-Gesellschaft* 15 (1983): 173–217.

———. "Ingeborg Bachmann-Bibliographie 1981/82–Sommer 1985: Nachträge und Ergänzungen Teil II." *Jahrbuch der Grillparzer-Gesellschaft* 16 (1984–1986): 201–275.

————. "Ingeborg Bachmann-Bibliographie Sommer 1985–Ende 1988: Nachträge und Ergänzungen Teil III." *Jahrbuch der Grillparzer-Gesellschaft* 17 (1987–1990): 251–327.

————. Ingeborg Bachmann-Bibliographie Ende 1988–Anfang 1993: Nachträge und Ergänzungen Teil IV." *Kritische Wege der Landnahme: Ingeborg Bachmann im Blickfeld der neunziger Jahre: Londoner Symposium 1993 zum 20. Todestag der Dichterin.* Ed. Robert Pichl and Alexander Stillmark. Wien: Hora, 1994. 163–303.

Barickman, Richard, Susan MacDonald, and Myra Stark. *Corrupt Relations: Dickens, Thackeray, Trollope, Collins, and the Victorian Sexual System.* New York: Columbia UP, 1982. 148–149.

Barrett, Michéle. *Women's Oppression Today.* London: Verso, 1980.

Bartsch, Kurt. "'Ein Ort für Zufälle': Bachmanns Büchnerpreisrede, als poetischer Text gelesen." *Modern Austrian Literature* 18.3/4 (1985): 135–145.

————. *Ingeborg Bachmann.* Stuttgart: Metzler, 1988.

————. "Ingeborg Bachmann heute." *Literatur und Kritik* 195/196 (1985): 281–287.

————. "'Schichtwechsel'? Zur Opposition von feminin-emotionalen Ansprüchen und maskulin-rationalem Realitätsdenken bei Ingeborg Bachmann." *Frauenliteratur: Autorinnen, Perspektiven, Konzepte.* Ed. Manfred Jurgensen. Bern: Lang, 1983. 85–100.

Bauer, Edith. *Drei Mordgeschichten: Intertextuelle Referenzen in Ingeborg Bachmann's Malina.* Frankfurt/M: Lang, 1998.

Bauer, Karin. "That Obscure Object of Desire: Fantasy and Disaster in Ingeborg Bachmann's 'A Step toward Gomorrah.'" *Queering the Canon: Defying Sights in German Literature and Culture.* Ed. Christoph Lorey and John L. Plews. Columbia, SC : Camden House, 1998. 223–233.

Beauvoir, Simone de. *The Second Sex.* Trans. H. M. Parshley. New York: Bantam, 1961.

Béhar, Pierre, ed. *Klangfarben: Stimmen zu Ingeborg Bachmann.* St. Ingbert: Röhrig, 2000.

Behdad, Ali. *Belated Travelers: Orientalism in the Age of Colonial Dissolution.* Durham, NC: Duke UP, 1994.

Behre, Maria. "'Das Ich, weiblich': Malina im Chor der Stimmen zur 'Erfindung' des Weiblichen im Menschen." *Ingeborg Bachmanns 'Malina'.* Ed. Andrea Stoll. Frankfurt/M: Suhrkamp, 1992. 210–232.

Beicken, Peter. *Ingeborg Bachmann.* München: Beck, 1988.

Benhabib, Seyla. "In Defense of Universalism—Yet Again! A Response to Critics of Situating the Self." *New German Critique* 21.2 (1994): 173–189.

Benjamin, Jessica. *The Bonds of Love: Psychoanalysis, Feminism, and the Problem of Domination.* New York: Pantheon, 1988.

Benjamin, Walter. *Illuminations.* Ed. Hannah Arendt. Trans. Harry Zohn. New York: Schocken, 1969.

Bennett, William J. *To Reclaim a Legacy: A Report on the Humanities in Higher Education.* Washington, DC: National Endowment for the Humanities, 1984.

Berger, John. *Ways of Seeing.* London: BBC and Penguin, 1972.

Bergner, Gwen. "Who Is That Masked Woman? Or, the Role of Gender in Fanon's *Black Skin, White Masks*." *PMLA* 110.1 (1995): 75–88.

Bhabha, Homi. "Signs Taken for Wonders: Questions of Ambivalence and Authority under a Tree outside Delhi, May 1817." *Europe and Its Others*. 2 vols. Ed. Francis Barker et al. Colchester: U of Essex, 1985. 1: 89–106.

Bird, Stephanie. "'What matters who's speaking?' Identity, Experience and Problems with Feminism in Ingeborg Bachmann's *Malina*." *Gender and Politics in Austrian Fiction*. Ed. Ritchie Robertson and Edward Timms. Edinburgh: Edinburgh UP, 1996. 150–165.

Bischof, Günter. "Austria—A Colony in the U.S. Postwar 'Empire'?" *Empire: American Studies*. Ed. John Blair and Reinhold Wagnleitner. Tübingen: Narr, 1997. 123–133.

———. *Austria in the First Cold War 1945–55: The Leverage of the Weak*. New York: St. Martin's, 1999.

———. "'Austria looks to the West': Kommunistische Putschgefahr, geheime Wiederbewaffnung und Westorientierung am Anfang der fünfziger Jahre." *Österreich in den Fünfzigern*. Ed. Thomas Albrich, Klaus Eisterer, Michael Gehler, and Rolf Steininger. Innsbruck: Österreichischer Studien-Verlag, 1995. 183–209.

———. "Österreich—ein 'geheimer Verbündeter' des Westens?" *Österreich und die europäische Integration 1945–1993: Aspekte einer wechselvollen Entwicklung*. Ed. Michael Gehler and Rolf Steininger. Wien: Böhlau, 1993. 425–450.

Blackwood, Algernon. "The Willows." *The Horror Hall of Fame*. Ed. Robert Silverberg and Martin H. Greenberg. New York: Carroll & Graf, 1991. 153–203.

Bloch, Ernst. *Erbschaften dieser Zeit*. Frankfurt/M: Suhrkamp, 1962.

Bloom, Allan. *The Closing of the American Mind: How Higher Education Has Failed Democracy and Impoverished the Souls of Today's Students*. New York: Simon and Shuster, 1987.

———. "A Most Uncommon Scold." Interview with William McWhirter. *Time* 17 October 1988: 74–76.

Boa, Elizabeth. "Reading Ingeborg Bachmann." *Postwar Women's Writing in German: Feminist Critical Approaches*. Ed. Chris Weedon. Providence: Berghahn, 1997. 269–289.

———. "Women Writing about Women Writing and Ingeborg Bachmann's *Malina*." *New Ways in Germanistik*. Ed. Richard Sheppard. New York: Berg, 1990. 128–144.

Bock, Gisela. "Racism and Sexism in Nazi Germany: Motherhood, Compulsory Sterilization, and the State." *Signs* 8.3 (1983): 400–421.

Bohm, Arnd. Comment on Sara Lennox, "Bachmann and the Cold War." Conference of Canadian Association of University Teachers of German. Dalhousie University, Halifax, NS. 31 May 2003.

Bonaparte, Marie. *Female Sexuality*. Trans. John Rodker. New York: Grove, 1963.

Böschenstein, Bernhard, and Sigrid Weigel, eds. *Ingeborg Bachmann und Paul Celan: Poetische Korrespondenzen*. Frankfurt/M: Suhrkamp, 1997.

Bothner, Susanne. *Ingeborg Bachmann: Der janusköpfige Tod: Versuch der literaturpsychologischen Deutung eines Grenzgebietes der Lyrik unter Einbeziehung des Nachlasses.* Frankfurt/M: Lang, 1986.

Botz, Gerhard. "Historische Brüche und Kontinuitäten als Herausforderungen—Ingeborg Bachmann und post-katastrophische Geschichtsmentalitäten in Österreich." *Ingeborg Bachmann—Neue Beträge zu ihrem Werke: Internationales Symposion Münster 1991.* Ed. Dirk Göttsche and Hubert Ohl. Würzburg: Königshausen & Neumann, 1993. 199–214.

Bovenschen, Silvia. "Is There a Feminine Aesthetic?" *New German Critique* 4.1 (1977): 111–137.

Brandes, Ute, ed. *Zwischen Gestern und Morgen: Schriftstellerinnen der DDR.* Frankfurt/M: Lang, 1992.

Brantlinger, Patrick. "Victorians and Africans: The Genealogy of the Myth of the Dark Continent." *"Race," Writing, and Difference.* Ed. Henry Louis Gates Jr. Chicago: U of Chicago P, 1986. 185–222.

Braun, Christina von. *"Blutschande*: From the Incest Taboo to the Nuremberg Racial Laws." *Encountering the Other(s): Studies in Literature, History and Culture.* Ed. Gisela Brinker-Gabler. Albany: State U of New York P, 1995. 127–148.

Breasted, James Henry. *Development of Religion and Thought in Ancient Egypt.* New York: Harper, 1959.

Brecht, Bertolt. *Gesammelte Werke.* 20 vols. Frankfurt/M: Suhrkamp, 1967.

Breines, Wini. *Young, White, and Miserable: Growing Up Female in the Fifties.* Boston: Beacon, 1992.

Briegleb, Klaus. "Ingeborg Bachmann, Paul Celan: Ihr (Nicht-)Ort in der Gruppe 47 (1952–1964/65): Eine Skizze." *Ingeborg Bachmann und Paul Celan: Poetische Korrespondenzen.* Ed. Bernhard Böschenstein and Sigrid Weigel. Frankfurt/M: Suhrkamp, 1997. 29–81.

Brinkemper, Peter. "Ingeborg Bachmanns Der Fall Franza als Paradigma weiblicher Ästhetik." *Modern Austrian Literature* 18.3/4 (1985): 147–182.

Brinker-Gabler, Gisela. "Andere Begegnung: Begegnung mit dem Anderen zwischen Aneignung und Enteignung." *Seminar* 29.2 (1993): 95–105.

Bröeck, Sabine. "Do White Ladies Get the Blues? Nancy Cunard and Desire." Unpublished manuscript.

Brokoph-Mauch, Gudrun. "Österreich als Fiktion und Geschichte in der Prosa Ingeborg Bachmanns." *Modern Austrian Literature* 30.3/4 (1997): 185–199.

Brokoph-Mauch, Gudrun, and Annette Daigger, eds. *Ingeborg Bachmann: Neue Richtungen in der Forschung?* St. Ingbert: Röhrig, 1995.

Brownmiller, Susan. *Femininity.* New York: Simon & Schuster, 1984.

Büchner, Georg. *Leonce and Lena. Lenz. Woyzeck.* Trans. Michael Hamburger. Chicago: U of Chicago P, 1972.

Bullivant, Keith, and C. Jane Rice. "Reconstruction and Integration: The Culture of West German Stabilization 1945–1968." *German Cultural Studies: An Introduction.* Ed. Rob Burns. Oxford: Oxford UP, 1995. 209–255.

Bürger, Christa. "Ich und wir: Ingeborg Bachmanns Austritt aus der ästhetischen Moderne." *text + kritik Sonderband Ingeborg Bachmann*. München: text + kritik, 1984. 7–27.

Burger, Hermann. "Abend mit Ingeborg Bachmann." *Du* September 1994: 1.

Butler, Judith. *Gender Trouble: Feminism and the Subversion of Identity*. New York: Routledge, 1990.

Caduff, Corinna. "Chronik von Leben und Werk." *Du* September 1994: 76–79, 82–87.

Carnap, Rudolf. "Überwindung der Metaphysik durch logische Analyse der Sprache." *Erkenntnis* 2 (1931): 219–241.

Carter, Erica. "Alice in the Consumer Wonderland: West German Case Studies in Gender and Consumer Culture." *Gender and Generation*. Ed. Angela McRobbie and Mica Nava. Houndsmills, UK: Macmillan, 1984. 185–214.

———. *How German Is She? Postwar West German Reconstruction and the Consuming Woman*. Ann Arbor: U of Michigan P, 1997.

Caulfield, Mina Davis. "Sexuality in Human Evolution: What Is 'Natural' in Sex?" *Feminist Studies* 11.2 (1985): 343–363.

Cerha, Michael, and Alexander Horwath. "Die Bachmann war wohl gerechter zu Männern: Elfriede Jelinek im Gespräch über ihr Drehbuch zu 'Malina.'" *Der Standard* (Wien) 14 January 1991: 10.

Chakrabarty, Dipesh. *Provincializing Europe: Postcolonial Thought and Historical Difference*. Princeton: Princeton UP, 2000.

———. "Universalism and Belonging in the Logic of Capital." *Public Culture* 12.3 (2000): 653–678.

Chambers, Iain. *Border Dialogues: Journeys in Postmodernity*. London: Routledge, 1990.

———. "Signs of Silence, Lines of Listening." *The Post-Colonial Question: Common Skies, Divided Horizons*. Ed. Iain Chambers and Lidia Curti. London: Routledge, 1996. 47–62.

Chapkis, Wendy. "The Gender Divide and Eroticism." *Socialist Review* 15.2 (1985): 109–118.

Chodorow, Nancy. *The Reproduction of Mothering: Psychoanalysis and the Sociology of Gender*. Berkeley: U of California P, 1978.

Chow, Rey. *Writing Diaspora: Tactics of Intervention in Contemporary Cultural Studies*. Bloomington: Indiana UP, 1993.

Cixous, Hélène. "The Laugh of the Medusa." Trans. Keith Cohen and Paula Cohen. *Signs* 1.4 (1976): 875–893.

Cleaver, Eldridge. *Soul on Ice*. New York: Dell, 1968.

Collins, William Wilkie. *The Woman in White*. 1860. Ed. Harvey Peter Sucksmith. London: Oxford UP, 1975.

Cornillon, Susan Koppelman, ed. *Images of Women in Fiction: Feminist Perspectives*. Bowling Green, OH: Bowling Green U Popular P, 1972.

Daly, Mary. *Gyn/Ecology: The Metaethics of Radical Feminism*. Boston: Beacon, 1978.

Davis, Angela Y. *Women, Race, and Class*. New York: Random House, 1981.

de Lauretis, Teresa. *The Practice of Love: Lesbian Sexuality and Perverse Desire*. Bloomington: Indiana UP, 1994.

Delille, Angela, and Andrea Grohn. *Blick zurück aufs Glück: Frauenleben und Familienpolitik in den 50er Jahren.* Berlin: Elefanten Press, 1985.

Delphendahl, Renate. "Alienation and Self-Discovery in Ingeborg Bachmann's 'Undine geht.'" *Modern Austrian Literature* 18.3/4 (1985): 195–210.

Derrida, Jacques. *Of Grammatology.* Trans. Gayatri Chakravorty Spivak. Baltimore: Johns Hopkins UP, 1976.

———. "The Pit and the Pyramid: Introduction to Hegel's Semiology." *Margins of Philosophy.* Trans. Alan Bass. Chicago: U of Chicago P, 1972. 69–108.

———. "Structure, Sign, and Play in the Discourses of the Human Sciences." *The Structuralist Controversy: The Languages of Criticism and the Science of Man.* Ed. Richard Macksey and Eugenio Donato. Baltimore: Johns Hopkins UP, 1972. 247–272.

Deutsch, Helene. *The Psychology of Women, a Psychoanalytic Interpretation.* New York: Grune & Stratton, 1944.

Devi, Mahsveta. "Draupadi." Trans. and Foreword Gayatri Chakravorty Spivak. *Writing and Sexual Difference.* Ed. Elizabeth Abel. Chicago: U of Chicago P, 1982. 261–282.

Diallo, M. Moustapha. "'Die Erfahrung der Variabilität': Kritischer Exotismus in Ingeborg Bachmanns Todesarten-Projekt im Kontext des interkulturellen Dialogs zwischen Afrika und Europa." *"Über die Zeit schreiben": Literatur- und kulturwissenschaftliche Essays zu Ingeborg Bachmanns "Todesarten"-Projekt.* Ed. Monika Albrecht and Dirk Göttsche. Würzburg: Königshausen & Neumann, 1998. 33–58.

Diamond, Sara. "The Funding of the NAS." *Beyond PC: Towards a Politics of Understanding.* Ed. Patricia Aufderheide. St. Paul, MN: Graywolf, 1992. 89–96.

di Leonardo, Micaela. "Morals, Mothers, Militarism: Antimilitarism and Feminist Theory (A Review Essay)." *Feminist Studies* 11.3 (1985): 599–617.

Dinnerstein, Dorothy. *The Mermaid and the Minotaur: Sexual Arrangements and Human Malaise.* New York: Harper & Row, 1977.

Dippel, Almut. *"Österreich - das ist etwas, das immer weitergeht für mich": Zur Fortschreibung der "Trotta"-Romane Joseph Roths in Ingeborg Bachmanns "Simultan."* St. Ingbert: Röhrig, 1995.

Dirlik, Arif. "Globalization as the End and the Beginning of History: The Contradictory Implications of a New Paradigm." *Rethinking Marxism* 12.4 (2000): 4–22.

———. "Modernity as History: Post-Revolutionary China, Globalization, and the Question of Modernity." *Social History* 27.1 (2002): 16–38.

———. "Our Ways of Knowing: Globalization—the End of Universalism?" Unpublished manuscript.

Dittberner, Hugo. "Das Ausbleiben des Neuen Mannes: Ingeborg Bachmanns Prosa-Projekt." *text + kritik Sonderband Ingeborg Bachmann.* 5. Auflage: Neufassung. München: text + kritik, 1995. 18–28.

Doane, Mary Ann. *Femmes Fatales: Feminism, Film Theory, Psychoanalysis.* New York: Routledge, 1991.

Dodds, Dinah. "The Lesbian Relationship in Bachmann's 'Ein Schritt nach Gomorrha.'" *Monatshefte* 72.4 (1980): 431–438.

Dollimore, Jonathan, and Alan Sinfield, eds. *Political Shakespeare: New Essays in Cultural Materialism.* Ithaca: Cornell UP, 1985.

Du Bois, W. E. B. *The Souls of Black Folk.* Millwood, NY: Kraus-Thomson, 1973.

Duffaut, Rhonda. "Ingeborg Bachmann's Alternative 'States': Re-thinking Nationhood in Malina." *Modern Austrian Literature* 29.3/4 (1996): 30–42.

Dunfey, Julie. "'Living the Principle' of Plural Marriage: Mormon Women, Utopia, and Female Sexuality in the Nineteenth Century." *Feminist Studies* 10.3 (1984): 523–536.

Dusar, Ingeborg. *Choreographien der Differenz: Ingeborg Bachmanns Prosaband "Simultan."* Köln: Böhlau, 1994.

Dussel, Enrique. "Beyond Eurocentrism: The World-System and the Limits of Modernity." *Cultures of Globalization.* Ed. Fredric Jameson and Masao Miyoshi. Durham, NC: Duke UP, 1998. 3–31.

Dworkin, Andrea. *Pornography: Men Possessing Women.* London: Women's Press, 1981.

Eagleton, Terry. "Nationalism: Irony and Commitment." *Nationalism, Colonialism, and Literature.* Minneapolis: U of Minnesota P, 1990. 23–39.

Easthope, Antony. *Literary into Cultural Studies.* London: Routledge, 1991.

"Editorial." *Signs* 9.1 (1983): 1–3.

"Editorial." *Signs* 10.4 (1985): 633–636.

Edwards, James C. *Ethics without Philosophy: Wittgenstein and the Moral Life.* Tampa: UP of Florida, 1982.

Eifler, Margret. "Bachmann, Jelinek, Schroeter: Malina: From Metaphoric Text to Encoded Cinema." *Out from the Shadows: Essays on Contemporary Austrian Women Writers and Filmmakers.* Ed. Margarete Lamb–Faffelberger. Riverside, CA: Ariadne, 1997. 206–28.

———. "Ingeborg Bachmann: Malina." *Modern Austrian Literature* 12.3/4 (1979): 373–390.

Eigler, Friederike. "Bachmann und Bachtin: Zur dialogischen Erzählstruktur von Simultan." *Modern Austrian Literature* 24.3/4 (1991): 1–16.

Ellis, Kate. "I'm Black and Blue from the Rolling Stones and I'm Not Sure How I Feel About It: Pornography and the Feminist Imagination." *Socialist Review* 14.3/4 (1984): 103–125.

Endres, Ria. "Erklär mir, Liebe: Ekstasen der Unmöglichkeit—Zur Dichtung Ingeborg Bachmanns." *Die Zeit* 2 October 1981: 51–52.

———. "'Die Wahrheit ist dem Menschen zumutbar': Zur Dichtung der Ingeborg Bachmann." *Neue Rundschau* 92.4 (1981): 71–96.

English, Deirdre, Barbara Epstein, Barbara Haber, and Judy MacLean. "The Impasse of Socialist Feminism." *Socialist Review* 15.1 (1985): 93–110.

Enzensberger, Hans Magnus. *Palaver: Politische Überlegungen (1967–1973).* Frankfurt/M: Suhrkamp, 1974.

Erhard, Ludwig. *Wohlstand für Alle*. 1957. Düsseldorf: Econ, 1960.

Fanon, Frantz. *Black Skin, White Masks*. Trans. Charles Lamm Markmann. New York: Grove, 1967.

Faulkner, William. *Works*. 25 vols. New York: Garland, 1986–1987.

Felski, Rita. *The Gender of Modernity*. Cambridge, MA: Harvard UP, 1995.

Ferree, Myra Marx. "Between Two Worlds: West German Research on Working Class Women and Work." *Signs* 10.3 (1985): 517–536.

———. "Gleichheit und Autonomie: Probleme feministischer Politik." *Differenz und Gleichheit: Menschenrechte haben (k)ein Geschlecht*. Ed. Ute Gerhard et al. Frankfurt/M: Ulrike Helmer, 1990. 283–298.

Fine, Michelle. "Unearthing Contradictions: An Essay Inspired by Women and Male Violence (A Commentary)." *Feminist Studies* 11.2 (1985): 391–407.

Flax, Jane. *Disputed Subjects*. London: Routledge, 1993.

Fleisser, Marieluise. *Gesammelte Werke*. Ed. Günther Rühle. Frankfurt/M: Suhrkamp. 1972.

Foucault, Michel. *The History of Sexuality*. Trans. Robert Hurley. New York: Pantheon, 1978.

———. *Language, Counter-Memory, Practice: Selected Essays and Interviews*. Ed. Donald F. Bouchard. Ithaca: Cornell UP, 1977.

———. *Power/Knowledge: Selected Interviews and Other Writings 1972–1977*. Ed. Colin Gordon. New York: Pantheon, 1980.

"Forum." *PMLA* 112.2 (1997): 257–286.

Fox-Genovese, Elizabeth. Rev. of *The Enclosed Garden*, by Jean E. Friedman, *Sisterhood Denied*, by Dolores E. Janiewski, and *The Free Women of Petersburg*, by Suzanne Lebsock. *Signs* 13.1 (1987): 159–162.

Frank, Dana. "Housewives, Socialists, and the Politics of Food: The 1917 New York Cost-of-Living Protests." *Feminist Studies* 11.2 (1985): 255–285.

Fraser, Nancy. Introduction. *Revaluing French Feminism: Critical Essays on Difference, Agency, and Culture*. Ed. Nancy Fraser and Sandra Lee Bartky. Bloomington: Indiana UP, 1992. 1–24.

Fraser, Nancy, and Linda J. Nicholson. "Social Criticism without Philosophy: An Encounter between Feminism and Postmodernism." *Feminism/Postmodernism*. Ed. Linda J. Nicholson. New York: Routledge, 1990. 19–38.

"Frau Doris fällt nicht aus der Rolle." http://www.stern.de/magazin/titel/1999/06/titel.html.

Frauen gegen Antisemitismus. "Der Nationalsozialismus als Extremform des Patriarchats: Zur Leugnung der Täterschaft von Frauen und zur Tabuisierung des Antisemitismus in der Auseinandersetzung mit dem NS." *beiträge zur feministischen theorie und praxis* 35 (1993): 77–89.

Frauenjahrbuch 1. Ed. Frankfurter Frauen. 2nd ed. Frankfurt: Roter Stern, 1975.

Frazer, Sir James George. *The Golden Bough*. 1922. New York: Macmillan, 1963.

Freedman, Estelle B., and Barbara Charlesworth Gelpi. Editorial. *Signs* 8.3 (1983): 397–399.

Freud, Sigmund. *Standard Edition of the Complete Psychological Works of Sigmund Freud.* Ed. and trans. James Strachey. 24 vols. London: Hogarth Press and Institute of Psycho-Analysis, 1966–74.

Friedan, Betty. *The Feminine Mystique.* New York: Norton, 1963.

Friedman, Ellen. "Where Are the Missing Contents? (Post)Modernism, Gender, and the Canon." *PMLA* 108.2 (1993): 240–252.

Friedman, Susan Stanford. "'I go where I love': An Intertextual Study of H.D. and Adrienne Rich." *Signs* 9.2 (1983): 228–245.

———. *Mappings: Feminism and the Cultural Geographies of Encounter.* Princeton: Princeton UP, 1998.

Fries, Marilyn Sibley, ed. *Responses to Christa Wolf: Critical Essays.* Detroit: Wayne State UP, 1989.

Fritz, Walter Helmut, and Helmut Heißenbüttel. "Über Ingeborg Bachmanns Roman 'Malina.'" *text + kritik Sonderband Ingeborg Bachmann.* München: text + kritik, 1976. 21–27.

Gaettens, Marie-Luise. "Die Rekonstruktion der Geschichte: Der Nationalsozialismus in drei Romanen der siebziger Jahre." *Frauen-Figuren in der deutschsprachigen Literatur seit 1945.* Ed. Mona Knapp and Gerd Labroisse. Amsterdam: Rodopi, 1989. 111–130.

———. *Women Writers and Fascism: Reconstructing History.* Gainesville: UP of Florida, 1995.

Gallop, Jane. *Around 1981: Academic Feminist Literary Theory.* New York: Routledge, 1992.

———. "Critical Response: Writing and Sexual Difference: The Difference Within." *Writing and Sexual Difference.* Ed. Elizabeth Abel. Chicago: U of Chicago P, 1982. 283–290.

Gallop, Jane, Marianne Hirsch, and Nancy K. Miller. "Criticizing Feminist Criticism." *Conflicts in Feminism.* Ed. Marianne Hirsch and Evelyn Fox Keller. New York: Routledge, 1990. 349–369.

Gandhi, Leela. *Postcolonial Theory.* Edinburgh: Edinburgh UP, 1998.

Gazzetti, Maria. "Eine italienische Lektüre." *Du* September 1994: 74–75, 92–93.

Gehle, Holger. *NS-Zeit und literarische Gegenwart bei Ingeborg Bachmann.* Wiesbaden: Deutscher Universitäts-Verlag, 1995.

Gelpi, Barbara Charlesworth. "Editorial." *Signs* 8.1 (1982): 1–3.

Gerhard, Ute. *Nomadische Bewegungen und die Symbolik der Krise: Flucht und Wanderung in der Weimarer Republik.* Wiesbaden: Westdeutscher Verlag, 1998.

Gerhardt, Marlis. *Kein bürgerlicher Stern, nichts, nichts könnte mich je beschwichtigen: Essays zur Kränkung der Frau.* Darmstadt: Luchterhand, 1982.

Gerlach, Franziska Frei. *Schrift und Geschlecht: Feministische Entwürfe und Lektüren von Marlen Haushofer, Ingeborg Bachmann und Anne Duden.* Berlin: Erich Schmidt, 1998.

Germnews 10 August 1999. http://www.germnews.de.

Giddens, Anthony. *Modernity and Self-Identity: Self and Society in the Late Modern Age*. Cambridge: Polity, 1991.

Gienow-Hecht, Jessica C. E. *Transmission Impossible: American Journalism as Cultural Diplomacy in Postwar Germany 1945–1955*. Baton Rouge: Louisiana State UP, 1999.

Gilbert, Sandra. "'Our Sidney and our perfect man': Modernism's Dead Good Soldier." The Aftermath of World War I: The Long-Range Effects of the War on British Writers Panel. MLA Convention. Hyatt Regency Hotel, Chicago. 28. Dec. 1985.

Gilbert, Sandra, and Susan Gubar. *The Madwoman in the Attic: The Woman Writer and the Nineteenth–Century Literary Imagination*. New Haven: Yale UP, 1979.

————. *No Man's Land: The Place of the Woman Writer in the Twentieth Century*. 3 vols. New Haven: Yale UP, 1988–94.

Gilligan, Carol. *In a Different Voice: Psychological Theory and Women's Development*. Cambridge: Harvard UP, 1982.

Gilkes, Cheryl Townsend. "'Together and in Harness': Women's Traditions in the Sanctified Church." *Signs* 10.4 (1985): 678–699.

Gilman, Charlotte Perkins. *The Yellow Wallpaper*. Old Westbury, NY: Feminist Press, 1973.

Ginsberg, Elaine, and Sara Lennox. "Antifeminism in Scholarship and Publishing." *Antifeminism in the Academy*. Ed. Vèvè Clark, Shirley Nelson Garner, Margaret Higonnet, and Ketu H. Katrak. New York: Routledge, 1996. 169–199.

Glaser, Hermann. *Zwischen Kapitulation und Währungsreform, 1945–1949*. München: Hanser, 1985. Vol. 1 of *Kulturgeschichte der Bundesrepublik Deutschland*. 3 vols. 1985–1989.

Gleichauf, Ingeborg. *Mord ist keine Kunst: Der Roman "Malina" von I. Bachmann und seine Verwandlung in ein Drehbuch und in einen Film*. Hamburg: Kovac, 1995.

Gölz, Sabine. "Reading in the Twilight: Canonization, Gender, the Limits of Language—and a Poem by Ingeborg Bachmann." *New German Critique* 47 (Spring/Summer 1989): 29–52.

————. *The Split Scene of Reading: Nietzsche/Derrida/Kafka/Bachmann*. Atlantic Highlands, NJ: Humanities, 1998.

Gordimer, Nadine. "A Conversation with Nadine Gordimer." *Salmagundi* 62 (1984): 3–31.

Gordon, Linda. "What's New in Women's History." *Feminist Studies/Critical Studies*. Ed. Teresa de Lauretis. Bloomington: Indiana UP, 1986. 20–54.

Gottlieb, Roger. "Mothering and the Reproduction of Power." *Socialist Review* 14.5 (1984): 93–119.

Göttsche, Dirk. "Malina und die nachgelassenen Todesarten-Fragment: Zur Geschichte des reflexiven und zyklischen Erzählens bei Ingeborg Bachmann." *Ingeborg Bachmanns 'Malina.'* Ed. Andrea Stoll. Frankfurt/M: Suhrkamp, 1992. 188–209.

————. "'Die Schwarzkunst der Worte' - Zur Barbey- und Rimbaud-Rezeption in Ingeborg Bachmanns 'Todesarten-Zyklus.'" *Jahrbuch der Grillparzer-Gesellschaft*. Ed. Klaus Heydemann and Robert Pichl. 3. Folge. 17 (1987–1990): 127–162.

Göttsche, Dirk, and Hubert Ohl, eds. *Ingeborg Bachmann: Neue Beiträge zu ihrem Werk*. Würzburg: Königshausen & Neumann, 1993.

Gramsci, Antonio. *Selections from the Prison Notebooks*. Ed. and trans. Quintin Hoare and Geoffrey Nowell Smith. London: Lawrence & Wishart, 1971.

Greenblatt, Stephen. Introduction. "The Forms of Power and the Power of Forms in the Renaissance." *Genre* 15 (1982): 3–6.

————. *Shakespearean Negotiations: The Circulation of Social Energy in Renaissance England*. Berkeley: U of California P, 1988.

Grimm-Hamen, Sylvie. "Der Jäger und seine Beute: Die Entzweiung des Lebens als Werk- und Lebensprinzip." *"Über die Zeit schreiben": Literatur- und kulturwissenschaftliche Essays zu Ingeborg Bachmanns "Todesarten"-Projekt*. Ed. Monika Albrecht and Dirk Göttsche. Würzburg: Königshausen & Neumann, 1998. 203–225.

Grimshaw, Patricia. "'Christian Woman, Pious Wife, Faithful Mother, Devoted Missionary': Conflicts in Roles of American Missionary Women in Nineteenth-Century Hawaii." *Feminist Studies* 9.3 (1983): 489–521.

Groddeck, Georg. *The Book of the It*. Trans. V. M. E. Collins. New York: Vintage, 1949.

Gropp, Rose-Maria. "Die Frau im Feuer: Bilder einer Selbstzerstörung: Werner Schroeter verfilmte 'Malina.'" *Frankfurter Allgemeine Zeitung* 18 January 1991: 25.

Grossmann, Atina. "A Question of Silence: The Rape of German Women by Occupation Soldiers." *West Germany under Construction: Politics, Society, and Culture in the Adenauer Era*. Ed. Robert G. Moeller. Ann Arbor: U of Michigan P, 1997. 33–52.

Grosz, Elizabeth. "Histories of a Feminist Future." *Signs* 25.4 (2000): 1017–1021.

Gubar, Susan. "'The Blank Page' and the Issues of Female Creativity." *Critical Inquiry* 8.2 (1981): 243–263.

Günderrode, Karoline von. *Der Schatten eines Traumes: Gedichte, Prosa, Briefe, Zeugnisse von Zeitgenossen*. Ed. Christa Wolf. Darmstadt: Luchterhand, 1981.

Gürtler, Christa. "'Der Fall Franza': Eine Reise durch eine Krankheit und ein Buch über ein Verbrechen." *Der dunkle Schatten, dem ich schon seit Anfang folge: Ingeborg Bachmann: Vorschläge zu einer neuen Lektüre des Werks*. Ed. Hans Höller. Wien: Löcker, 1982. 71–84.

————. *Schreiben Frauen anders? Untersuchungen zu Ingeborg Bachmann und Barbara Frischmuth*. Stuttgart: Hans Dieter Heinz, 1983.

"Gut im Rennen." *Wochenpresse* (Wien) 14 July 1971: n.p.

Gutjahr, Ortrud. *Fragmente unwiderstehlicher Liebe: Zur Dialogstruktur literarischer Subjektentgrenzung in Ingeborg Bachmanns "Der Fall Franza."* Würzburg: Königshausen & Neumann, 1988.

Habermas, Jürgen. "Die Dialektik der Rationalisierung: Vom Pauperismus in Produktion und Konsum." *Merkur* 8. 8 (1954): 701–724.

———. "Notizen zum Mißverhältnis von Kultur und Konsum." *Merkur* 10.3 (1956): 212–228.

Haider-Pregler, Hilde. "Ingeborg Bachmanns Radioarbeit: Ein Beitrag zur Hörspielforschung." *Ingeborg Bachmann: l'oeuvre et ses situations: Actes du colloque, 29, 30 et 31 janvier 1986, Nantes.* Saint-Nazaire, France: Editions Arcane 17, 1986. 24–81.

Hall, Stuart. "Cultural Studies: Two Paradigms." *Media, Culture, and Society: A Critical Reader.* Ed. Richard Collins et al. London: Sage, 1986. 33–48.

Hapkemeyer, Andreas. *Ingeborg Bachmann: Bilder aus ihrem Leben.* München: Piper, 1983.

———. *Ingeborg Bachmann: Entwicklungslinien in Werk und Leben.* Wien: Österreichische Akademie der Wissenschaften, 1990.

Haraway, Donna. "A Manifesto for Cyborgs: Science, Technology, and Socialist Feminism in the 1980s." *Socialist Review* 15.2 (1985): 65–107.

———. "Reading Buchi Emecheta: Contests for Women's Experience in Women's Studies." *Inscriptions* 3/4 (1988): 107–124.

———. *Simians, Cyborgs, and Women: The Reinvention of Nature.* New York: Routledge, 1991.

———. "Situated Knowledges: The Science Question in Feminism and the Privilege of Partial Perspective." *Feminist Studies* 14.3 (1988): 575–599.

Harding, Sandra. *Whose Science? Whose Lives? Thinking from Women's Lives.* Ithaca: Cornell UP, 1986.

Harlow, Barbara. "From the Women's Prison: Third World Women's Narratives of Prison." *Feminist Studies* 12.3 (1986): 501–524.

Hartsock, Nancy C. M. *Money, Sex, and Power: Toward a Feminist Historical Materialism.* New York: Longman, 1983.

Hartwig, Theodor. *Der Existentialismus: Eine politisch reaktionäre Ideologie.* Wien: Cerny, 1948.

Harvard Summer School International Seminar Annual Reports: 1955 Report Entire. Cambridge, MA: Harvard, 1955.

Hassauer, Friederike. "Der ver-rückte Diskurs der Sprachlosen: Gibt es eine weibliche Ästhetik?" *Notizbuch 2: Ver-rückte Rede—Gibt es eine weibliche Ästhetik.* Ed. Friederike Hassauer and Peter Roos. Berlin: Medusa, 1980. 48–65.

Hayden, Tom. "The Future Politics of Liberalism." *The Nation* 21 February 1981: 193, 208–212.

Hazel, Hazel E. "Die alte und die neue Sensibilität: Erfahrungen mit dem Subjekt, das zwischen die Kulturen gefallen ist." *Literaturmagazin 4: Die Literatur nach dem Tod der Literatur: Bilanz der Politisierung.* Ed. Hans Christoph Buch. Reinbek bei Hamburg: Rowohlt, 1975. 129–142.

Hegel, Georg Wilhelm Friedrich. *Hegel's Philosophy of Mind: Being Part Three of the Encyclopedia of Philosophical Sciences.* Trans. William Wallace. Oxford: Clarendon, 1971.

Heidegger, Martin. *Basic Writings*. Ed. David Farrell Krell. New York: Harper & Row, 1977.

Heidelberger-Leonard, Irene. "Ernst Goldmann-Geschichten und Geschichte." *"Text-Tollhaus für Bachmann-Süchtige?" Lesarten zur Kritischen Ausgabe von Ingeborg Bachmanns Todesarten-Projekt*. Ed. Irene Heidelberger-Leonard. Opladen: Westdeutscher Verlag, 1998. 80–90.

———, ed. *"Text–Tollhaus für Bachmann-Süchtige?" Lesarten zur Kritischen Ausgabe von Ingeborg Bachmanns Todesarten-Projekt*. Opladen: Westdeutscher Verlag, 1998.

Heineman, Elizabeth D. *What Difference Does a Husband Make? Women and Marital Status in Nazi and Postwar Germany*. Berkeley: U of California P, 1999.

Hekman, Susan. "Truth and Method: Feminist Standpoint Theory Revisited." *Signs* 22.2 (1997): 341–365.

Helsinger, Elizabeth K., Robin Lauterbach Sheets, and William Veeder. *The Woman Question: Literary Issues, 1837–1883*. New York: Garland, 1983.

Hennessy, Rosemary. *Materialist Feminism and the Politics of Discourse*. New York: Routledge, 1993.

Henze, Hans Werner. Interview by Leslie Morris. 2 August 1988. Unpublished.

———. *Reiselieder mit böhmischen Quinten: Autobiographische Mitteilungen 1926–1995*. Frankfurt/M: Fischer, 1996.

Hermand, Jost. *Kultur im Wiederaufbau: Die Bundesrepublik Deutschland 1945–1965*. München: Nymphenburger Verlag, 1986.

Herminghouse, Patricia A., ed. *Ingeborg Bachmann and Christa Wolf: Selected Prose and Drama*. New York: Continuum, 1998.

Higgins, Patricia J. "Women in the Islamic Republic of Iran: Legal, Social, and Ideological Changes." *Signs* 10.3 (1985): 477–94.

Hirsch, E.D. *Cultural Literacy: What Every American Needs to Know*. Boston: Houghton Mifflin, 1987.

Hoffmansthal, Hugo von. *The Lord Chandos Letter and Other Writings*. Trans. Joel Rotenberg. New York: New York Review of Books, 2004.

Hogan, Michael. *The Marshall Plan: America, Britain, and the Reconstruction of Western Europe, 1947–1952*. New York: Cambridge UP, 1987.

Holeschofsky, Irene. "Bewußtseinsdarstellung und Ironie in Ingeborg Bachmanns Erzählung *Simultan.*" *Kein objektives Urteil—Nur ein Lebendiges*. Ed. Christine Koschel and Inge von Weidenbaum. München: Piper, 1989. 469–479.

Höller, Hans. "'Daß ich schreien werde vor Entsetzen': Die Kunstwerk-Problematik in Malina und ihre Vorgeschichte." *Ingeborg Bachmanns 'Malina.'* Ed. Andrea Stoll. Frankfurt/M: Suhrkamp, 1992. 233–249.

———, ed. *Der dunkle Schatten, dem ich schon seit Anfang folge: Ingeborg Bachmann: Vorschläge zu einer neuen Lektüre des Werks*. Wien: Löcker, 1982.

———. "'Die gestundete Zeit' und 'Anrufung des Großen Bären': Vorschläge zu einem neuen Verständnis." *Der dunkle Schatten, dem ich schon seit Anfang folge: Ingeborg Bachmann: Vorschläge zu einer neuen Lektüre des Werks*. Ed. Hans Höller. Wien: Löcker, 1982. 125–172.

————. *Ingeborg Bachmann.* Reinbek bei Hamburg: Rowohlt, 1999.

————. *Ingeborg Bachmann: Das Werk: Von den frühesten Gedichten bis zum "Todesarten"-Zyklus.* Frankfurt/M: Athenäum, 1987.

————. "Szenen, die dort beginnen,wo sonst der Vorhang fällt." *Ingeborg Bachmann: l'oeuvre et ses situations: Actes du colloque, 29, 30 et 31 janvier 1986, Nantes.* Saint-Nazaire, France: Editions Arcane 17, 1986. 5–23.

Holschuh, Albrecht. "Relevanz, Philologie und Baackmanns Arbeit über Bachmanns 'Undine geht.'" *German Quarterly* 68.4 (1995): 430–433.

Homans, Margaret. "'Her Very Own Howl': The Ambiguities of Representation in Recent Women's Fiction." *Signs* 9.2 (1983): 186–205.

————. "'Syllables of Velvet': Dickinson, Rossetti, and the Rhetorics of Sexuality." *Feminist Studies* 11.3 (1985): 569–593.

Honig, Emily. "Burning Incense, Pledging Sisterhood: Communities of Women Workers in the Shanghai Cotton Mills, 1919–1949." *Signs* 10.4 (1985): 700–714.

hooks, bell. *Ain't I a Woman: Black Women and Feminism.* Boston: South End, 1981.

Horkheimer, Max, and Theodor W. Adorno. *Dialectic of Enlightenment.* Trans. John Cumming. New York: Seabury, 1972.

Horsley, Ritta Jo. "Ingeborg Bachmann's 'Ein Schritt nach Gomorrha': A Feminist Appreciation and Critique." *Gestaltet und gestaltend: Frauen in der deutschen Literatur.* Ed. Marianne Burkhard. Amsterdam: Rodopi, 1980. 277–293.

————. "Re-reading 'Undine geht': Bachmann and Feminist Theory." *Modern Austrian Literature* 18.3/4 (1985): 223–238.

Hotz, Constance. *"Die Bachmann": Das Image der Dichterin: Ingeborg Bachmann im journalistischen Diskurs.* Konstanz: Ekkehard Faude, 1990.

Howard, June. "Feminist Differings: Recent Surveys of Feminist Literary Theory and Criticism." *Feminist Studies* 14.1 (1988): 167–190.

Hull, Gloria T., Patricia Bell Scott, and Barbara Smith, eds. *All the Women are White, All the Blacks Are Men, but Some of Us Are Brave: Black Women's Studies.* Old Westbury, NY: Feminist Press, 1982.

Hurston, Zora Neale. *Their Eyes Were Watching God.* New York: HarperCollins, 2000.

Huyssen, Andreas. "Traces of Ernst Bloch: Reflections on Christa Wolf." *Responses to Christa Wolf: Critical Essays.* Ed. Marilyn Sibley Fries. Detroit: Wayne State UP, 1989. 233–247.

Inderthal, Klaus. "'Ich könnte mich verschrieben haben'": Ingeborg Bachmanns Malina." *Ingeborg Bachmanns 'Malina'.* Ed. Andrea Stoll. Frankfurt/M: Suhrkamp, 1992. 171–187.

Ingeborg Bachmann: L'oeuvre et ses situations: actes du colloque, 29, 30 et 31 janvier 1986, Nantes. Saint-Nazaire, France: Editions Arcane 17, 1986.

Irigaray, Luce. "Women's Exile." *Ideology and Consciousness* 1 (1977): 62–76.

Janik, Allan, and Stephen Toulmin. *Wittgenstein's Vienna.* New York: Simon and Schuster, 1973.

Jarausch, Konrad H. "Reshaping German Identities: Reflections on the Post-Unification Debate." *After Unity: Reconfiguring German Identities.* Ed. Konrad H. Jarausch. Providence: Berghahn, 1997. 1–23.

Jelinek, Elfriede. "Der Krieg mit anderen Mitteln." *Kein objektives Urteil—Nur ein Lebendiges: Texte zum Werke von Ingeborg Bachmann.* Ed. Christine Koschel and Inge von Weidenbaum. München: Piper, 1989. 311–320.

———. *Isabelle Huppert in Malina: Ein Filmbuch.* Frankfurt/M: Suhrkamp, 1991.

Johnson, Uwe. *Anniversaries: From the Life of Gesine Cresspahl.* Trans. Leila Vennewitz. New York: Harcourt Brace Jovanovich, 1975.

———. *Anniversaries II: From the Life of Gesine Cresspahl.* Trans. Leila Vennewitz and Walter Arndt. San Diego: Harcourt Brace Jovanovich, 1987.

Johnston, William M. *The Austrian Mind: An Intellectual and Social History 1848–1938.* Berkeley: U of California P, 1972.

Jones, Ann Rosalind. "Imaginary Gardens with Real Frogs in Them: Feminist Euphoria and the Franco-American Divide, 1976–88." *Changing Subjects: The Making of Feminist Literary Criticism.* Ed. Gayle Greene and Coppélia Kahn. London: Routledge, 1993. 64–82.

Joseph, Gloria I. Rev. of *Women, Race, and Class* by Angela Davis. *Signs* 9.1 (1983): 134–136.

Kafka, Franz. *Letters to Friends, Family, and Editors.* Trans. Richard and Clara Winston. New York: Schocken, 1977.

Kann-Coomann, Dagmar. ". . . *eine geheime langsame Feier . . .": Zeit und ästhetische Erfahrung im Werk Ingeborg Bachmanns.* Frankfurt/M: Lang, 1988.

Kaplan, Cora. *Sea Changes: Culture and Feminism.* London: Verso, 1986.

Karcher, Carolyn L. "Conference Report: Black Studies/Women's Studies: An Overdue Partnership." *Feminist Studies* 9.3 (1983): 605–610.

Kazin, Michael. "The Iran/Contra Deal—Out of Their Grasp." *Socialist Review* 17.2 (1987): 112–119.

Kellner, Douglas. *Herbert Marcuse and the Crisis of Marxism.* Berkeley: U of California P, 1984.

Kienlechner, Toni. "Gespräch mit Ingeborg Bachmann." *Die Brücke* 1.1 (1975): 98–104.

Koepnick, Lutz P. Letter. *PMLA* 112.2 (1997): 266–267.

Kohn-Waechter, Gudrun. "'. . . ich liebte ihr Herunterbrennen': Das Zerschreiben der Opferfaszination *Gespräch im Gebirg* von Paul Celan und *Malina* von Ingeborg Bachmann." *Schrift der Flammen: Opfermythen und Weiblichkeitsentwürfe im 20. Jahrhundert.* Ed. Gudrun Kohn-Waechter. Berlin: Orlanda, 1991. 219–240.

———. *Das Verschwinden in der Wand: Destruktive Moderne und Widerspruch eines weiblichen Ich in Ingeborg Bachmanns "Malina."* Stuttgart: Metzler, 1992.

Komar, Kathleen L. "'Es war Mord': The Murder of Ingeborg Bachmann at the Hands of an Alter Ego." *Modern Austrian Literature* 27.2 (1994): 91–112.

Koonz, Claudia. *Mothers in the Fatherland: Women, the Family, and Nazi Politics.* New York: St. Martin's, 1987.

Koschel, Christine, and Inge von Weidenbaum, eds. *Kein objektives Urteil—Nur ein Lebendiges: Texte zum Werk von Ingeborg Bachmann.* München: Piper, 1989.

Kraft, Viktor. *Der Wiener Kreis: Der Ursprung des Neopositivismus: Ein Kapitel der jüngsten Philosophiegeschichte.* 2nd ed. Wien: Springer, 1968.

Kraus, Wolfgang. "Psychologie eines Bucherfolges." *Volkszeitung* (Klagenfurt) 20 June 1971: n.p.

Krechel, Ursula. "Ortlosigkeit, Stucktröstung." *text + kritik Sonderband Ingeborg Bachmann*. 5. Auflage: Neufassung. München: text + kritik, 1995. 7–17.

Kristeva, Julia. *Powers of Horror: An Essay on Abjection*. Trans. Leon S. Roudiez. New York: Columbia UP, 1982.

Kuhn, Anna K. *Christa Wolf's Utopian Vision: From Marxism to Feminism*. Cambridge: Cambridge UP, 1988.

Kulawik, Teresa. "Autonomous Mothers? West German Feminism Reconsidered." *German Politics and Society* 24–25 (1991–1992): 67–86.

Kundnani, Hans. "The Story of an Illness: Ingeborg Bachmann's Malina." *German Life and Letters* 49.1 (1996): 59–71.

Ladd-Taylor, Molly. "Women Workers and the Yale Strike." *Feminist Studies* 11.3 (1985): 465–489.

Lamphere, Louise. "Bringing the Family to Work: Women's Culture on the Shop Floor." *Feminist Studies* 11.3 (1985): 519–540.

Lauter, Paul. "Race and Gender in the Shaping of the American Literary Canon: A Case Study from the Twenties." *Feminist Studies* 9.3 (1983): 435–463.

Lawrence, D. H. *Short Stories*. Ed. Stephen Gill. London: Dent, 1996.

Lawrence, T. E. *Seven Pillars of Wisdom, A Triumph*. Garden City, NY: Doubleday, 1935.

Lear, Frances. "Now is the Time to Get Organized." *The Nation* 12 November 1981: 635–637.

Lenk, Elisabeth. "Indiskretionen des Federviehs: Pariabewußtsein schreibender Frauen seit der Romantik." *Courage* 6.10 (1981): 24–34.

Lennon, Kathleen, and Margaret Whitford, eds. Introduction. *Knowing the Difference: Feminist Perspectives in Epistemology*. London: Routledge, 1994. 1–14.

Lennox, Sara. "Anthropology and the Politics of Deconstruction." National Women's Studies Association Conference, Spelman College, Atlanta, GA. 26 June 1987.

———, ed. *Auf der Suche nach den Gärten unserer Mütter: Feministische Kulturkritik aus Amerika*. Darmstadt: Luchterhand, 1982.

———. "Bachmann and Wittgenstein." *Modern Austrian Literature* 18.3/4 (1985): 239–259.

———. "Bachmann Reading/Reading Bachmann: Wilkie Collins' *The Woman in White* in the *Todesarten*." *German Quarterly* 61.2 (1988): 183–192.

———. "Christa Wolf and Ingeborg Bachmann: The Difficulties of Writing the Truth." *Responses to Christa Wolf: Critical Essays*. Ed. Marilyn Sibley Fries. Detroit: Wayne State UP, 1989. 128–148.

———. "Feminism and New Historicism." *Monatshefte* 84.2 (1992): 159–170.

———. "Feministische Aufbrüche: Impulse aus den USA und Frankreich." *Frauen Literatur Geschichte: Schreibende Frauen vom Mittelalter bis zur Gegenwart*. Ed. Hiltrud Gnüg and Renate Möhrmann. Stuttgart: Metzler, 1985. 380–394.

———. "The Feminist Reception of Ingeborg Bachmann." *Women in German Yearbook* 8. Ed. Jeanette Clausen and Sara Friedrichsmeyer. Lincoln: U of Nebraska P, 1992. 73–111.

———. "Feminist Scholarship and *Germanistik*." *German Quarterly* 62.2 (1989): 158–170.

———. "Gender, Kalter Krieg und Ingeborg Bachmann." *"Über die Zeit schreiben" 3: Literatur- und kulturwissenschaftliche Essays zum Werk Ingeborg Bachmanns*. Ed. Monika Albrecht and Dirk Göttsche. Würzburg: Königshausen & Neumann, 2004. 15–54.

———. "Geschlecht, Rasse und Geschichte in 'Der Fall Franza.'" *text + kritik Sonderband Ingeborg Bachmann*. Ed. Sigrid Weigel. München: text + kritik, 1984. 156–179.

———. "Historicizing Women's Writing." Lecture. Brown University. 16 March 1990.

———. "History in Johnson's *Jahrestage*." *Germanic Review* 64.1 (1989): 31–41.

———. "Ingeborg Bachmann." *German-Language Women Writers: A Bio-Critical Sourcebook*. Ed. Elke Fredericksen and Elizabeth Ametsbichler. Westport, CT: Greenwood, 1998. 56–68.

———. "In the Cemetery of the Murdered Daughters: Ingeborg Bachmann's *Malina*." *Studies in Twentieth Century Literature* 5.1 (1980): 75–105.

———. "'Is That All?' Whatever Happened to the Women's Liberation Movement? Reflections on the Course of American Feminism." *Englisch/Amerikanische Studien* 10.2 (1988): 296–301.

———. "Reading Gender Historically: The Encounter of Feminist Literary Theory and Women's History." German Studies Association Convention, St. Louis, 17 October 1987; New York University, 19 January 1988.

———. "Reading Women's Biographies and Autobiographies: Feminist History and Feminist Literary Theory." National Association of Ethnic Studies, Springfield, MA, 3 March 1988.

———. "Representing Femininity in Ingeborg Bachmann's *Der gute Gott von Manhattan*." *Thalia's Daughters: German Women Dramatists from the Eighteenth Century to the Present*. Ed. Susan Cocalis and Ferrel Rose. Tübingen: Francke, 1996. 191–220.

———. "Towards an Anti-Racist Feminist Theory." Conference on Black Studies / Women's Studies: An Overdue Partnership, Amherst, MA, 23 April 1983.

———. "Trends in Literary Theory: The Female Aesthetic and German Women's Writing." *German Quarterly* 54.1 (1981): 63–75.

———. "White Ladies and Dark Continents in Ingeborg Bachmann's *Todesarten*." *The Imperialist Imagination: German Colonialism and Its Legacy*. Ed. Sara Friedrichsmeyer, Sara Lennox, and Susanne Zantop. Ann Arbor: U of Michigan P, 1998. 247–263.

———. "Women in Brecht's Works." *New German Critique* 14 (Spring 1978): 83–96.

———. "The Woman Who Rode Away: Postcoloniality and Gender in 'Three Paths to the Lake.'" *If We Had the Word: Ingeborg Bachmann. Views and Reviews*. Ed. Gisela Brinker–Gabler and Markus Zisselsberger. Riverside, CA: Ariadne, 2004. 208–220.

Lensing, Leo A. "Joseph Roth and the Voices of Bachmann's Trottas: Topography, Autobiography, and Literary History in 'Drei Wege zum See.'" *Modern Austrian Literature* 18.3/4 (1985): 53–76.

Levin, David Michael, ed. *Modernity and the Hegemony of Vision*. Berkeley: U of California P, 1993.

Lichtmann, Tamás, ed. *Nicht (aus, in, über, von) Österreich: Zur österreichischen Literatur, zu Celan, Bachmann, Bernhard und anderen*. Frankfurt/M: Lang, 1995.

Lévi-Strauss, Claude. *The Raw and the Cooked*. Trans. John and Doreen Wightman. New York: Harper & Row, 1969.

Lindemann, Gisela. "Der Ton des Verratenseins: Zur Werkausgabe der Ingeborg Bachmann." *Neue Rundschau* 90.2 (1979): 269–274.

Loesberg, Jonathan. "The Ideology of Narrative Form in Sensation Fiction." *Representations* 13 (Winter 1986): 115–38.

Löffler, Sigrid. "Undine kehrt zurück: Sigrid Löffler über Ingeborg Bachmanns nachgelassene Werkfragmente 'Todesarten.'" *Der Spiegel* 13 November 1995: 243–247.

Lorde, Audre. "An Open Letter to Mary Daly." *This Bridge Called My Back: Writings by Radical Women of Color*. Ed. Cherríe Moraga and Gloria Anzaldúa. Watertown, MA: Persephone, 1981. 94–97.

Lühe, Irmela von der. "Abschied vom Utopia der Sprache: Ingeborg Bachmanns Erzählung *Alles.*" *text + kritik Sonderband Ingeborg Bachmann*. 5. Auflage: Neufassung. München: text + kritik, 1995. 84–98.

———. "Erinnerung und Identität in Ingeborg Bachmanns Roman 'Malina.'" *text + kritik Sonderband Ingeborg Bachmann*. München: text + kritik, 1984: 132–149.

Lukács, Georg. *History and Class Consciousness: Studies in Marxist Dialectics*. Trans. Rodney Livingstone. Cambridge, MA: MIT P, 1971.

———. *The Theory of the Novel*. Trans. Anna Bostock. Cambridge, MA: MIT P, 1971.

Lütgenau, Stefan August. "Grundstrukturen der österreichisch-deutschen Beziehungen nach 1945." *Österreich in den Fünfzigern*. Ed. Thomas Albrich, Klaus Eisterer, Michael Gehler, and Rolf Steininger. Innsbruck: Österreichischer StudienVerlag, 1995. 237–258.

Lutz, Catherine A., and Jane L. Collins. *Reading* National Geographic. Chicago: U of Chicago P, 1993.

Lyotard, Jean-François. *The Postmodern Condition: A Report on Knowledge*. Trans. Geoff Bennington and Brian Massumi. Minneapolis: U of Minnesota P, 1984.

Macherey, Pierre. *A Theory of Literary Production*. Trans. Geoffrey Wall. London: Routledge & Kegan Paul, 1978.

MacKinnon, Catherine. "Feminism, Marxism, Method, and the State: An Agenda for Theory." *Signs* 7.3 (1982): 515–544.

Magris, Claudio. *Der habsburgische Mythos in der österreichischen Literatur*. Trans. Madeleine von Pasztory. Salzburg: Otto Müller, 1966.

Mahrdt, Helgard. *Öffentlichkeit, Gender und Moral: Von der Aufklärung zu Ingeborg Bachmann*. Göttingen: Vandenhoeck & Ruprecht, 1998.

———. "'Society Is the Biggest Murder Scene of All': On the Private and Public Spheres in Ingeborg Bachmann's Prose." *Women in German Yearbook 12*. Ed. Sara Friedrichsmeyer and Patricia Herminghouse. Lincoln: U of Nebraska P, 1996. 167–187.

Maier, Charles S. "Die konzeptuellen Grundlagen des Marshall-Plans." *Der Marshall-Plan und die europäische Linke*. Ed. Othmar Nikola Haberl and Lutz Niethammer. Frankfurt/M: Europäische Verlagsanstalt, 1986. 47–58.

Majer-O'Sickey, Ingeborg. "Rereading Ingeborg Bachmann's *Malina*: Toward a Transformative Feminist Reading Praxis." *Modern Austrian Literature* 28.1 (1995): 55–73.

Malina. Dir. Werner Schroeter. Perf. Isabelle Huppert and Mathieu Carrière. Kuchenreuther Film-Produktion, 1990.

Mann, Thomas. *Death in Venice and Seven Other Stories*. Trans. H. T. Lowe-Porter. New York: Vintage, 1936.

———. *Doctor Faustus: The Life of the German Composer, Adrian Leverkühn, as Told by a Friend*. Trans. H. T. Lowe-Porter, New York: Knopf, 1948.

Marcuse, Herbert. *Eros and Civilization: A Philosophical Inquiry into Freud*. 2nd ed. Boston: Beacon, 1966.

———. "Eros and Culture." *Cambridge Review* 1.3 (1955): 107–123.

———. "Trieblehre und Freiheit." *Sociologica: Aufsätze, Max Horkheimer zum 60. Geburtstag gewidmet*. (Frankfurt/M: Europäische Verlagsanstalt, 1955. 47–66.

Marcuse, Peter. "Why Are They Homeless?" *The Nation* 4 April 1987: 426–429.

Margaronis, Maria. "A New New Left on Campus: There's Something Happening Here." *The Nation* 19 December 1987: 757.

Martin, Biddy. "Feminism, Criticism, and Foucault." *New German Critique* 9.3 (1982): 3–30.

Martin, Biddy, and Chandra Talpade Mohanty. "Feminist Politics: What's Home Got to Do with It?" *Feminist Studies/Critical Studies*. Ed. Teresa de Lauretis. Bloomington: Indiana UP, 1986. 191–212.

Mattl, Siegfried. "'Aufbau'—eine männliche Chiffre der Nachkriegszeit." *Wiederaufbau weiblich: Dokumentation der Tagung "Frauen in der österreichischen und deutschen Nachkriegszeit."* Ed. Irene Bandhauer-Schöffmann and Ela Hornung. Wien: Geyer-Edition, 1992. 15–23.

———. "Frauen in Österreich nach 1945." *Unterdrückung und Emanzipation: Festschrift für Erika Weinzierl zum 60. Geburtstag*. Ed. Rudolf G. Ardelt, Wolfgang J. A. Huber, and Anton Staudinger. Wien: Geyer-Edition, 1985. 101–126.

May, Elaine Tyler. *Homeward Bound: American Families in the Cold War Era*. New York: Basic, 1988.

Mayer, Hans. "*Malina* oder Der große Gott von Wien." *Kein objektives Urteil—Nur ein Lebendiges: Texte zum Werk von Ingeborg Bachmann*. Ed. Christine Koschel and Inge von Weidenbaum. München: Piper, 1989. 162–165.

McCarthy, Margaret. "Murder and Self-Resuscitation in Ingeborg Bachmann's *Malina.*" *Out of the Shadows: Essays on Contemporary Austrian Women Writers and Filmmakers.* Ed. Margarete Lamb-Faffelberger. Riverside, CA: Ariadne, 1997. 38–54.

McClintock, Anne. *Imperial Leather: Race, Gender, and Sexuality in the Colonial Context.* New York: Routledge, 1995.

McVeigh, Joseph G. "Ingeborg Bachmann as Radio Script Writer." *German Quarterly* 75.1 (2002): 35–50.

Mechtel, Angelika. "Vor fünfzig Jahren oder in fünfzig Jahren." *Kein objektives Urteil—Nur ein Lebendiges: Texte zum Werk von Ingeborg Bachmann.* Ed. Christine Koschel and Inge von Weidenbaum. München: Piper, 1989. 183–187.

Meise, Helga. "Topographien: Lektürevorschläge zu Ingeborg Bachmann." *text + kritik Sonderband Ingeborg Bachmann.* München: text + kritik, 1984. 93–108.

Mennel, Barbara. "'Euch auspeitschen, ihr ewigen Masochistinnen, euch foltern, bis ihr den Verstand verliert': Masochismus in Ingeborg Bachmanns Roman-fragment *Das Buch Franza.*" *"Über die Zeit schreiben" 2: Literatur- und kulturwissenschaftliche Essays zum Werk Ingeborg Bachmanns.* Ed. Monika Albrecht and Dirk Göttsche. Würzburg: Königshausen & Neumann, 2000. 111–125.

Meyer-Gosau, Frauke. "'Ecco un artista': Von der Wirkung der Bilder in Ingeborg Bachmanns Literaturbetriebs-Geschichte." *text + kritik Sonderband Ingeborg Bachmann.* 5. Auflage: Neufassung. München: text + kritik, 1995. 163–170.

Milkman, Ruth, and Christine Stansell. Preface. *Feminist Studies* 12.3 (1986): 449–451.

Miller, Arthur. *After the Fall. Arthur Miller's Collected Plays.* 2 vols. New York: Viking, 1981. 2: 125–242.

Miller, Christopher. *Blank Darkness: Africanist Discourse in French.* Chicago: U of Chicago P, 1985.

Miller, D. A. "Cage aux Folles: Sensation and Gender in Wilkie Collins's *The Woman in White.*" *Representations* 14 (1986): 107–136.

Miller, J. Hillis. "Presidential Address 1986: The Triumph of Theory, the Resistance to Reading, and the Question of the Material Base." *PMLA* 102.3 (1987): 281–291.

Miller, Nancy K. "Public Statements, Private Lives: Academic Memoirs for the Nineties." *Signs* 22.4 (1997): 981–1015.

Millett, Kate. *Sexual Politics.* London: Sphere, 1971.

Minnich, Elizabeth Kamarck. "Friendship between Women: The Act of Feminist Biography (A Review Essay)." *Feminist Studies* 11.2 (1985): 287–305.

Mitchell, Juliet. *Psychoanalysis and Feminism: Freud, Reich, Laing and Women.* New York: Pantheon, 1974.

Mitchell, Silas Weir. *Doctor and Patient.* Philadelphia: Lippincott, 1888.

Mitscherlich, Alexander, and Margarete Mitscherlich. *The Inability to Mourn: Principles of Collective Behavior*. Trans. Beverley R. Placzek. New York: Grove, 1975.

Modern Austrian Literature. Special Ingeborg Bachmann Issue, 18.3/4 (1985).

Möding, Nori. "Die Stunde der Frauen? Frauen und Frauenorganisationen des bürgerlichen Lagers." *Von Stalingrad zur Währungsreform: Zur Sozialgeschichte des Umbruchs in Deutschland*. Ed. Martin Broszat, Klaus–Dietmar Henke, and Hans Woller. München: R. Oldenbourg, 1988. 619–647.

Moeller, Robert. *Protecting Motherhood: Women and the Family in the Politics of Postwar West Germany*. Berkeley: U of California P, 1993.

Mohanty, Satya P. "'Us' and 'Them': On the Philosophical Bases of Political Criticism." *Yale Journal of Criticism* 2.2 (1989): 1–31.

Mohr, Charles. "Egypt's Hopes for Progress Rest on Aswan Dam." *New York Times* 15 May 1964: 3.

Moi, Toril. *Sexual/Textual Politics: Feminist Literary Theory*. London: Methuen, 1985.

Molyneux, Maxine. "Mobilization without Emancipation? Women's Interests, the State, and Revolution in Nicaragua." *Feminist Studies* 11.2 (1985): 227–254.

Montrose, Louis. "New Historicism." *Redrawing the Boundaries: The Transformation of English and American Literary Studies*. Ed. Stephen Greenblatt and Giles Gunn. New York: MLA, 1992. 392–418.

———. "Professing the Renaissance: The Poetics and Politics of Culture." *The New Historicism*. Ed. H. Aram Veeser. New York: Routledge, 1989. 15–36.

Moraga, Cherríe, and Gloria Anzaldúa, eds. *This Bridge Called My Back: Writings by Radical Women of Color*. Watertown, MA: Persephone, 1981.

Morris, Leslie. "Das Leben, die Menschen, die Zeit: Hans Werner Henze im Gespräch mit Leslie Morris (Rom, 4. Januar 1999)." *"Über die Zeit schreiben" 2: Literatur- und kulturwissenschaftliche Essays zum Werk Ingeborg Bachmanns*. Ed. Monika Albrecht and Dirk Göttsche. Würzburg: Königshausen & Neumann, 2000. 143–159.

Mrozek, Bodo. "Hitlers willige Wissenschaftler." *Die Weltwoche* 3 July 1997.

Müller, Heiner. "The Walls of History." *Semiotexte* 4.2 (1982): 38–76.

Nägele, Rainer. "Die Arbeit des Textes: Notizen zur experimentellen Literatur." *Deutsche Literatur in der Bundesrepublik seit 1965*. Ed. P. M. Lützeler and E. Schwarz. Königstein: Athenäum, 1980. 30–45.

National Association of Scholars. "The Wrong Way to Reduce Campus Tensions." *Beyond PC: Towards a Politics of Understanding*. Ed. Patricia Aufderheide. St. Paul, MN: Graywolf, 1992. 7–10.

Neumann, Peter Horst. "Vier Gründe einer Befangenheit: Über Ingeborg Bachmann." *Merkur* 32.11 (1978): 1130–1136.

Newman, Karen. "Comment on Heilbrun's Review of *The Woman's Part, Shakespeare's Division of Experience, and Man's Estate*." *Signs* 10.3 (1985): 601–603.

Newton, Judith Lowder. "History as Usual? Feminism and the 'New Historicism.'" *The New Historicism*. Ed. H. Aram Veeser. New York: Routledge, 1989. 152–167.

Newton, Judith Lowder, and Deborah Rosenfelt, eds. *Feminist Criticism and Social Change: Sex, Class, and Race in Literature and Culture.* London: Methuen, 1985.

Novalis. *Philosophical Writings.* Ed. and trans. Margaret Mahony Stoljar. Albany: State U of New York P, 1997.

Olsen, Tillie. "The Future in the Past: A Writer's Tribute to Women's Studies." Changing: Ten Years of Women's Studies at the MLA. San Francisco. 29 December 1979.

O'Sickey, Ingeborg Majer. "Re–reading Ingeborg Bachmann's Malina: Toward a Transformative Feminist Reading Praxis." *Modern Austrian Literature* 28.1 (1995): 55–73.

Ostriker, Alicia. "Comment on Homans's 'Her Very Own Howl': The Ambiguities of Representation in Recent Women's Fiction." *Signs* 10.3 (1985): 597–600.

———. "'The Thieves of Language': Women Poets and Revisionist Mythmaking." *Signs* 8.1 (1982): 68–90.

P. "Die Public-Relations-Kampagne." *Die Zeit* 2 April 1971.

Pally, Marcia. "Ban Sexism, Not Pornography." *Nation* 29 June 1985: 794–97.

Pattillo–Hess, John, and Wilhelm Petrasch, eds. *Ingeborg Bachmann: Die Schwarz-kunst der Worte.* Wien: Verein Volksbildungshaus Wiener Urania, n.d.

Pechter, Edward. "The New Historicism and Its Discontents: Politicizing Renaissance Drama." *PMLA* 102.3 (1987): 292–303.

Phillips, Lily. Letter. *PMLA* 112.2 (1997): 273–274.

Pichl, Robert. "Ingeborg Bachmanns 'Ihr glücklichen Augen': Eine Apologie der Strukturanalyse." *"Text–Tollhaus für Bachmann–Süchtige?" Lesarten zur Kritischen Ausgabe von Ingeborg Bachmann.* Ed. Irene Heidelberger–Leonard. Opladen: Westdeutscher Verlag, 1998. 118–129.

Pichl, Robert. Letter to Sara Lennox, including excerpt from "Katalog der Privatbibliothek Ingeborg Bachmanns. Ungedrucktes Typoskript."19 August 1993.

Pichl, Robert, and Alexander Stillmark, eds. *Kritische Wege der Landnahme: Ingeborg Bachmann im Blickfeld der Neunziger Jahre.* Wien: Hora, 1994.

Pitkin, Hanna Fenichel. *Wittgenstein and Justice: On the Significance of Ludwig Wittgenstein for Social and Political Thought.* Berkeley: U of California P, 1972.

Plath, Sylvia. *The Bell Jar.* 1963. New York: Bantam, 1972.

Pohli, Carol Virginia. "Church Closets and Back Doors: A Feminist View of Moral Majority Women." *Feminist Studies* 9.3 (1983): 529–558.

Poiger, Uta. *Jazz, Rock, and Rebels: Cold War Politics and American Culture in a Divided Germany.* Berkeley: U of California P, 2000.

Power, Marilyn. "Falling Through the 'Safety Net': Women, Economic Class, and Reaganomics." *Feminist Studies* 10.1 (1984): 31–58.

Püschel, Ursula. "Exilierte und Verlorene: Ingeborg Bachmann." *Kürbiskern* 14.1 (1978): 107–122.

Rabinbach, Anson. "The Jewish Question in the German Question." *Reworking the Past: Hitler, the Holocaust, and the Historians' Debate.* Ed. Peter Baldwin. Boston: Beacon, 1990. 45–73.

Rabine, Leslie. "Romance in the Age of Electronics: Harlequin Enterprises." *Feminist Studies* 11.1 (1985): 39–60.

Radisch, Iris. "Die Hölle ist der Himmel." *Die Zeit* 4 January 1991: 17–18.

Radway, Janice A. "Women Read the Romance: The Interaction of Text and Context." *Feminist Studies* 9.1 (1983): 53–78.

Ranke, Franz Leopold von. *Sämmtliche Werke*. Leipzig: Duncker und Humblot, 1885. Vol. 33/34.

Rauch, Angelika. "Sprache, Weiblichkeit und Utopie bei Ingeborg Bachmann." *Modern Austrian Literature* 18.3/4 (1985): 21–38.

———. "Die Über(be)setzung der Vergangenheit: Ingeborg Bachmanns Roman Der Fall Franza." *German Quarterly* 65.1 (1992): 42–54.

Reagon, Bernice Johnson. "Coalition Politics: Turning the Century." *Home Girls: A Black Feminist Anthology*. Ed. Barbara Smith. New York: Kitchen Table/ Women of Color, 1983. 356–368.

Reich-Ranicki, Marcel. "Die Dichterin wechselt das Repertoire." *Kein objektives Urteil—Nur ein Lebendiges*. Ed. Christine Koschel and Inge von Weidenbaum. München: Piper, 1989. 188–192.

———. "Ingeborg Bachmann oder Die Kehrseite des Schreckens." *Kein objektives Urteil—Nur ein Lebendiges*. Ed. Christine Koschel and Inge von Weidenbaum. München: Piper, 1989. 69–82.

———. "Tageslicht statt Aureolen: Zu einem Fernsehfilm über Ingeborg Bachmann." *Über Ingeborg Bachmann: Rezensionen—Porträts— Würdigungen (1952–1992): Rezeptionsdokumente aus vier Jahrzehnten*. Ed. Michael Matthias Schardt. Paderborn: Igel, 1994. 385–388.

Remmler, Karen. *Waking the Dead: Correspondences between Walter Benjamin's Concept of Remembrance and Ingeborg Bachmann's Ways of Dying*. Riverside, CA: Ariadne, 1996.

Renolder, Klemens. "Im ungeistigen Raum unserer traurigen Länder: Zu Utopie und Geschichte bei Christa Wolf und Ingeborg Bachmann." *Der dunkle Schatten, dem ich schon seit Anfang folge: Ingeborg Bachmann: Vorschläge zu einer neuen Lektüre des Werks. Mit der Erstveröffentlichung des Erzählfragments Gier*. Ed. Hans Höller. Wien: Löcker, 1982. 185–198.

David Reynolds. "The American Occupation of Germany, Japan, and Austria: Towards a Comparative Framework." Unpublished manuscript.

Rich, Adrienne. "Compulsory Heterosexuality and Lesbian Existence." *Signs* 5.4 (1980): 631–660.

———. "Disloyal to Civilization: Feminism, Racism, Gynophobia." *On Lies, Secrets and Silence: Selected Prose 1966–1978*. New York: Norton, 1979. 275–310.

———. "When We Dead Awaken: Writing as Re–Vision (1971)." *On Lies, Secrets and Silence: Selected Prose 1966–1978*. New York: Norton, 1979. 33–49.

Riddiough, Christine. "What Happened to the Gender Gap (and Other Gaps) in the 1984 Elections?" *Socialist Review* 15.1 (1985): 23–28.

Riley, Denise. *"Am I That Name?": Feminism and the Category of "Women" in History*. Minneapolis: U of Minnesota P, 1988.

Rimbaud, Arthur. *Oeuvres complètes*. Ed. Antoine Adam. Paris: Gallimard, 1972.

Ringelheim, Joan. "Women and the Holocaust: A Reconsideration of Research." *Signs* 10.4 (1985): 741–761.

Röhnelt, Inge. *Hysterie und Mimesis in 'Malina.'* Frankfurt/M: Lang, 1990.

Römhild, Dorothee. "Von kritischer Selbstreflexion zur stereotypen Frauendarstellung: Ingeborg Bachmann's Roman 'Malina' und seine filmische Rezeption." *Germanic Review* 68.4 (1993): 167–75.

Rosaldo, Renato. *Culture and Truth: The Remaking of Social Analysis*. Boston: Beacon, 1989.

Rose, Hilary. "Hand, Brain, and Heart: A Feminist Epistemology for the Natural Sciences." *Signs* 9.1 (1983): 73–90.

Rosenfelt, Deborah, and Judith Stacey. "Second Thoughts on the Second Wave." *Feminist Studies* 13.2 (1987): 341–361.

Roth, Joseph. *Die Kapuzinergruft*. Amsterdam: Allert de Lange, 1950.

———. *Radetzkymarsch*. Köln: Kiepenheuer & Witsch, 1965.

———. "Der Segen des ewigen Juden." *Werke 3: Das journalistische Werk*. Ed. Klaus Westermann. Köln: Kiepenheuer & Witsch, 1991. 527–532.

Rubin, Gayle. "The Traffic in Women: Notes on the 'Political Economy' of Sex." *Toward an Anthropology of Women*. Ed. Rayna R. Reiter. New York: Monthly Review, 1975. 157–210.

Ruta, Suzanne. "Death in the Family: Ingeborg Bachmann's Theater of Murder." *Village Voice* 26 February 1991: 65–66.

Ryan, Mary (for the editors). Preface. *Feminist Studies* 7.1 (1982): iii–v.

Said, Edward W. *Culture and Imperialism*. New York: Knopf, 1993.

———. *Orientalism*. London: Routledge & Kegan Paul, 1978.

———. "Representing the Colonized: Anthropology's Interlocutors." *Critical Inquiry* 15 (1989): 206–226.

Saunders, Frances Stonor. *The Cultural Cold War: The CIA and the World of Arts and Letters*. New York: New Press, 1999.

Schechter, Susan. *Women and Male Violence: The Visions and Struggles of the Battered Women's Movement*. Boston: South End, 1982.

Schelsky, Helmut. "Die gelungene Emanzipation." *Merkur* 9 (1955): 360–370.

———. "Gesellschaftlicher Wandel." *Auf der Suche nach Wirklichkeit: Gesammelte Aufsätze*. Düsseldorf: E. Diederichs, 1965. 337–351.

Schmid-Bortenschlager, Sigrid. "Frauen als Opfer-Gesellschaftliche Realität und Literarisches Modell: Zu Ingeborg Bachmanns Erzählband 'Simultan.'" *Der dunkle Schatten, dem ich schon seit Anfang folge: Ingeborg Bachmann: Vorschläge zu einer neuen Lektüre des Werks*. Ed. Hans Höller. Wien: Löcker, 1982. 85–95.

———. "Spiegelszenen bei Bachmann: Ansätze einer psychoanalytischen Interpretation." *Modern Austrian Literature* 18.3/4 (1985): 39–52.

Schmidt, Tanya. "Beraubung des Eigenen: Zur Darstellung geschichtlicher Erfahrung im Erzählzyklus *Simultan* von Ingeborg Bachmann." *Kein objektives Urteil—Nur ein Lebendiges*. Ed. Christine Koschel and Inge von Weidenbaum. München: Piper, 1989. 479–502.

Schneider, Jost. "Historischer Kontext und politische Implikationen der Büchner-
    preisrede Ingeborg Bachmanns." *"Über die Zeit schreiben" 2: Literatur- und
    kulturwissenschaftliche Essays zum Werk Ingeborg Bachmanns*. Ed. Monika
    Albrecht and Dirk Göttsche. Würzburg: Königshausen & Neumann, 2000.
    127–139.

Schmidt-Linsenhoff, Viktoria, Detlef Hoffmann, Almut Junker, Sabine Kübler, and
    Roswitha Mattausch. *Informationsblätter zu der Ausstellung "Frauenalltag
    und Frauenbewegung in Frankfurt 1890–1980."* Frankfurt: Historisches
    Museum, 1981.

Schneider, Michael. *Den Kopf verkehrt aufgesetzt oder Die melancholische Linke: Aspekte
    des Kulturzerfalls in den siebziger Jahren*. Darmstadt: Luchterhand, 1981.

Schorske, Carl E. *Fin-de-Siècle Vienna: Politics and Culture*. New York: Vintage, 1981.

Schottelius, Saskia. *Das Imaginäre Ich: Subjekt und Identität in Ingeborg Bachmanns
    Roman Malina und Jacques Lacans Sprachtheorie*. Frankfurt/M: Lang, 1990.

Schuller, Marianne. "Hörmodelle: Sprache und Hören in den Hörspielen und Lib-
    retti." *text + kritik Sonderband Ingeborg Bachmann*. München: text + kritik,
    1984. 50–57.

———. "Wider den Bedeutungswahn: Zum Verfahren der Dekomposition in 'Der
    Fall Franza.'" *text + kritik Sonderband Ingeborg Bachmann*. München: text +
    kritik, 1984. 150–155.

Schwarzer, Alice. *Der "kleine Unterschied" und seine großen Folgen*. Frankfurt/M:
    Fischer, 1975.

———. "Schwarzer über Malina." *Emma* February 1991: 14–20.

Scott, Joan Wallach. *Gender and the Politics of History*. New York: Columbia UP, 1988.

Scrol, Veronica P. "Return to 'O': A Lacanian Reading of Ingeborg Bachmann's
    'Undine Goes.'" *Studies in Twentieth Century Literature* 18.2 (1994): 239–246.

Seim, Jürgen. "Ingeborg Bachmann—*Der gute Gott von Manhattan*." *Kein objektives
    Urteil—Nur ein Lebendiges: Texte zum Werk von Ingeborg Bachmann*.
    Ed. Christine Koschel and Inge von Weidenbaum. München: Piper, 1989.
    395–402.

Seton-Williams, Veronica, and Peter Stocks. *Blue Guide: Egypt*. London: Benn, 1983.

Sexton, Anne. "Consorting with Angels." *The Norton Anthology of Literature by
    Women: The Tradition in English*. Ed. Sandra M. Gilbert and Susan Gubar.
    New York: Norton, 1985. 1995–1996.

Shapiro, Susan E. "*Écriture judaïque*: Where Are the Jews in Western Discourse?"
    Displacements: Cultural Identities in Question. Ed. Angelika Bammer.
    Bloomington: Indiana UP, 1994. 182–201.

Showalter, Elaine. "Feminist Criticism in the Wilderness." *The New Feminist Criti-
    cism: Essays on Women, Literature, and Theory*. Ed. Elaine Showalter. New
    York: Pantheon, 1985. 243–278.

———. *A Literature of Their Own: British Women Novelists from Brontë to Lessing*.
    Princeton: Princeton UP, 1977.

Sklar, Kathryn Kish. "Hull House in the 1890s: A Community of Women Reform-
    ers." *Signs* 10.4 (1985): 658–677.

Šlibar, Neva. "'Das Spiel ist aus'—oder fängt es gerade an? Zu den Hörspielen Ingeborg Bachmanns." *text + kritik Sonderband Ingeborg Bachmann*. 5. Auflage: Neufassung. München: text + kritik, 1995. 111–122.

Smith, Barbara, ed. *Home Girls: A Black Feminist Anthology*. New York: Kitchen Table/Women of Color, 1983.

Snitow, Ann, Christine Stansell, and Sharon Thompson, eds. Introduction to "'The Mind That Burns in Each Body': Women, Rape, and Racial Violence." By Jaquelyn Dowd Hall. *The Powers of Desire: The Politics of Sexuality*. New York: Monthly Review, 1983. 328.

Springer, Michael. "Die kahle Sängerin." *konkret* 21 (1971): 60.

Stanton, Domna C. "Introduction: The Subject of Sexuality." *Discourses of Sexuality: From Aristotle to AIDS*. Ed. Domna C. Stanton. Ann Arbor: U of Michigan P, 1992. 1–46.

Stefan, Verena. *Häutungen*. München: Frauenoffensive, 1975.

Stephan, Alexander. *Christa Wolf*. München: Beck and text + kritik, 1976.

Stoetzler, Marcel, and Nira Yuval–Davis. "Standpoint Theory, Situated Knowledge, and the Situated Imagination." *Feminist Theory* 3.3 (2002): 315–333.

Stoler, Ann Laura. *Race and the Education of Desire: Foucault's* History of Sexuality *and the Colonial Order of Things*. Durham, NC: Duke UP, 1995.

Stoll, Andrea. "Der Bruch des epischen Atems: Zum Konflikt von Erinnerung und Erzählvorhaben in Ingeborg Bachmanns Malina-Roman." *Ingeborg Bachmanns 'Malina.'* Ed. Andrea Stoll. Frankfurt/M: Suhrkamp, 1992. 250–264.

———, ed. *Ingeborg Bachmanns 'Malina.'* Frankfurt/M: Suhrkamp, 1992.

———. "Kontroverse und Polarisierung: Die Malina–Rezeption als Schlüssel der Bachmann-Forschung. *Ingeborg Bachmanns 'Malina.'* Ed. Andrea Stoll. Frankfurt/M: Suhrkamp, 1992. 149–167.

Strutz, Josef. "Ein Platz, würdig des Lebens und Sterbens: Ingeborg Bachmanns 'Guter Gott von Manhattan' und Robert Musils 'Reise ins Paradies.'" *Österreich in Geschichte und Literatur* 29 (1985): 376–388.

Stuber, Bettina. *Zu Ingeborg Bachmann: "Der Fall Franza" und "Malina."* Rheinfelden: Schäuble, 1994.

Studer, Liliane, ed. *Schriftwechsel: Eine literarische Auseinandersetzung mit Ingeborg Bachmann*. Zürich: eFeF, 1994.

Sudarkasa, Niara. "'The Status of Women' in Indigenous African Societies." *Feminist Studies* 12.1 (1986): 91–103.

Summerfield, Ellen. *Ingeborg Bachmann: Die Auflösung der Figur in ihrem Roman "Malina."* Bonn: Bouvier, 1987.

———. "Verzicht auf den Mann: Zu Ingeborg Bachmanns Erzählungen 'Simultan.'" *Die Frau als Heldin und Autorin: Neue kritische Ansätze zur deutschen Literatur*. Ed. Wolfgang Paulsen. Bern: Francke, 1979. 211–216.

Tabah, Mireille. "Zur Genese einer Figur: Franza." *"Text-Tollhaus für Bachmann-Süchtige?" Lesarten zur Kritischen Ausgabe von Ingeborg Bachmann*. Ed. Irene Heidelberger-Leonard. Opladen: Westdeutscher Verlag, 1998. 91–106.

text + kritik Sonderband Ingeborg Bachmann. München: text + kritik, 1976.

text + kritik Sonderband Ingeborg Bachmann. Ed. Sigrid Weigel. München: text + kritik, 1984.

text + kritik Sonderband Ingeborg Bachmann. 5. Auflage: Neufassung. München: text + kritik, 1995.

Thau, Bärbel. *Gesellschaftsbild und Utopie im Spätwerk Ingeborg Bachmanns*. Frankfurt/M: Lang, 1986.

The Third Man. Screenplay by Graham Greene. Dir. Carol Reed. Mus. Anton Karas. Perf. Orson Welles and Joseph Cotten. London Films, 1949.

Torgovnick, Marianna. *Going Primitive: Savage Intellects, Modern Lives*. Chicago: U of Chicago P, 1990.

———. *Primitive Passions: Men, Women, and the Quest for Ecstasy*. Chicago: U of Chicago P, 1996.

Trumpener, Katie. "The Time of the Gypsies: A 'People without History' in the Narratives of the West." *Critical Inquiry* 18 (Summer 1992): 843–884.

Tucker, Robert C., ed. *The Marx-Engels Reader*. 2nd ed. New York: Norton, 1978.

Tweraser, Kurt K. "Marshallplan, Sozialpartnerschaft und Produktivität in Österreich." *Österreich in den Fünfzigern*. Ed. Thomas Albricht, Klaus Eisterer, Michael Gehler, and Rolf Steininger. Innsbruck: Österreichischer StudienVerlag, 1995. 211–236.

Van Allen, Judith. "Capitalism without Patriarchy." *Socialist Review* 14.5 (1984): 81–91.

Vance, Carole. "Concept Paper: Towards a Politics of Sexuality." *Diary of a Conference on Sexuality*. Ed. Hannah Alderfer, Meryl Altman, Kate Ellis, Beth Jaker, Marybeth Nelson, Esther Newton, Ann Snitow, and Carole S. Vance. N.p.: Faculty, 1983. 38–40.

Vanderbeke, Birgit. "Kein Recht auf Sprache? Der sprachlose Raum der Abwesenheit in 'Malina.'" *text + kritik Sonderband Ingeborg Bachmann*. Ed. Sigrid Weigel. München: text + kritik, 1984. 109–119.

Vansant, Jacqueline. "Robert Wise's *The Sound of Music* and the 'Denazification' of Austria in American Cinema." *From World War to Waldheim: Culture and Politics in Austria and the United States*. Ed. David F. Good and Ruth Wodak. New York: Berghahn, 1999. 165–186.

Venske, Regula. *Das Verschwinden des Mannes in der weiblichen Schreibmaschine: Männerbilder in der Literatur von Frauen*. Hamburg: Luchterhand, 1991.

Vicinus, Martha, and Deborah Rosenfelt (for the editors). Preface. *Feminist Studies* 11.1 (1985): 3–5.

[Wagner, Klaus.] "Stenogramm der Zeit." *Der Spiegel* 18 August 1954: 26–29.

Wagnleitner, Reinhold. *Coca-Colonization and the Cold War: The Cultural Mission of the United States in Austria after the Second World War*. Trans. Diana M. Wolf. Chapel Hill: U of North Carolina P, 1994.

———. "The Irony of American Culture Abroad: Austria and the Cold War." *Recasting America: Culture and Politics in the Age of Cold War*. Ed. Lary May. Chicago: U of Chicago P, 1989. 285–301.

———. "Die Kinder von Schmal(t)z und Coca-Cola: Der kulturelle Einfluß der USA im Österreich der fünfziger Jahre." *Die "wilden" fünfziger Jahre:*

Gesellschaft, Formen und Gefühle eines Jahrzehnts in Österreich. Ed. Gerhard Jagschitz and Klaus-Dieter Mulley. St. Pölter: Niederösterreichisches Pressehaus, 1985. 144–173.

Waismann, Friedrich. *Wittgenstein und der Wiener Kreis.* Ed. B. F. McGuiness. Oxford: Basil Blackwell, 1967.

Walz, Jay. "Khrushchev and Nasser Join in Diverting the Nile at Aswan: Leaders Set Off Explosion to Complete First Stage of Large Dam Project." *New York Times* 14 May 1964: 1, 3.

Weidenbaum, Inge von. "Ist die Wahrheit zumutbar?" *Ingeborg Bachmann und Paul Celan: Poetische Korrespondenzen.* Ed. Bernard Böschenstein and Sigrid Weigel. Frankfurt/M: Suhrkamp, 1997. 23–28.

Weigel, Hans. *Unvollendete Symphonie.* 1951. Graz: Styria, 1992.

Weigel, Sigrid. "Die andere Ingeborg Bachmann." *text + kritik Sonderband Ingeborg Bachmann.* Ed. Sigrid Weigel. München: text + kritik, 1984: 5–6.

———. *Bilder des kulturellen Gedächtnisses: Beiträge zur Gegenwartsliteratur.* Dülmen-Hiddingsel: tende, 1994.

———. "'Ein Ende mit der Schrift. Ein anderer Anfang': Zur Entwicklung von Ingeborg Bachmanns Schreibweise." *text + kritik Sonderband Ingeborg Bachmann.* Ed. Sigrid Weigel. München: text + kritik, 1984. 58–92.

———. *Ingeborg Bachmann: Hinterlassenschaften unter Wahrung des Briefgeheimnisses.* Wien: Paul Zsolnay, 1999.

———. "Ingeborg Bachmann—Was folgt auf das Schweigen? Zu ihrem 10. Todestag am 17. Oktober." *Frankfurter Rundschau* 15 October 1983: 3.

———. "Der schielende Blick: Thesen zur Geschichte weiblicher Schreibpraxis." *Die verborgene Frau: Sechs Beiträge zu einer feministischen Literaturwissenschaft.* Ed. Inge Stefan and Sigrid Weigel. Berlin: Argument, 1983. 83–137.

———. "'Sie sagten sich Helles und Dunkles': Ingeborg Bachmanns literarischer Dialog mit Paul Celan." *text + kritik Sonderband Ingeborg Bachmann.* 5. Auflage: Neufassung. München: text + kritik, 1995. 123–134.

———. *Die Stimme der Medusa: Schreibweisen in der Gegenwartsliteratur von Frauen.* Dülmen-Hiddingsel: tende, 1987.

———. *Topographien der Geschlechter: Kulturgeschichtliche Studien zur Literatur.* Reinbek bei Hamburg: Rowohlt, 1990.

———. "Urszene einer Poetologie." *Du* September 1994: 20, 23, 90.

Weininger, Otto. *Sex and Character.* London: William Heinemann, 1906.

Weiser, Peter. "Die Familie Nr. 1 Hörspiel: Versuch einer Rekonstruction." *Jörg Mauthe: Sein Leben auf 33 Ebenen.* Ed. David Axmann. Wien: Edition Atelier, 1994. 25–33.

Wellman, David. "The New Political Linguistics of Race." *Socialist Review* 16.3/4 (May-August 1986): 43–62.

Whittier, Nancy. *Feminist Generations: The Persistence of the Radical Women's Movement.* Philadelphia: Temple UP, 1995.

Wiener, Jon. "Women's History on Trial." *The Nation* 7 September 1985: 161, 176–180.

Wildt, Michael. *Am Beginn der 'Konsumgesellschaft': Mangelerfahrung, Lebenshaltung, Wohlstandshoffnung in Westdeutschland in den fünfziger Jahren*. Hamburg: Ergebnisse, 1994.

Williamson, Marilyn L. "Toward a Feminist Literary History." *Signs* 10.1 (1984): 136–147.

Willis, Ellen. "Betty Friedan's 'Second Stage': A Step Backward." *The Nation* 14 November 1981: 494–96.

Wirsing, Sibylle. Review of *Simultan*. *Neue deutsche Hefte* 19.4 (1972): 149–51.

Witte, Bernd. "Ingeborg Bachmann." *Kritisches Lexikon zur deutschsprachigen Gegenwartsliteratur*. 6. Nachlieferung (October 1980).

———. "Ingeborg Bachmann." *Neue Literatur der Frauen: Deutschsprachige Autorinnen der Gegenwart*. Ed. Heinz Puknus. München: Beck, 1980. 33–43.

Wittgenstein, Ludwig. *Bemerkungen über die Grundlagen der Mathematik*. Ed. G. E. M. Anscombe, Rush Rhees, and G. H. von Wright. Frankfurt/M: Suhrkamp, 1984.

———. *Briefe an Ludwig von Ficker*. Ed. Georg Henrik von Wright. Salzburg: Otto Müller, 1969.

———. *Philosophical Investigations*. Trans. G. E. M. Anscombe. 3rd ed. New York: Macmillan, n.d.

———. *Philosophical Remarks*. Ed. Rush Rhees. Oxford: Basil Blackwell, 1964.

———. *Tractatus Logico-Philosophicus*. Trans. D. F. Pears and B. F. McGuinness. London: Routledge, 1974.

Wittig, Monique. *The Lesbian Body*. Trans. David LeVay. New York: Avon, 1975.

Wolf, Christa. *The Author's Dimension: Selected Essays*. Trans. Jan Van Heurck. New York: Farrar, Straus & Giroux, 1993.

———. *Cassandra: A Novel and Four Essays*. Trans. Jan Van Heurck. New York: Farrar, Straus & Giroux, 1984.

———. "Culture Is What You Experience—An Interview with Christa Wolf." Trans. Jeanette Clausen. *New German Critique* 9.3 (1982): 89–100.

———. *Die Dimension des Autors: Essays und Aufsätze, Reden und Gespräche 1959–1985*. 2 vols. Darmstadt: Luchterhand, 1990.

———. "June Afternoon." Trans. Heike Schwarzbauer and Rick Takvorian. *Ingeborg Bachmann and Christa Wolf: Selected Prose and Drama*. Ed. Patricia A. Herminghouse. New York: Continuum, 1998. 113–129.

———. *Kindheitsmuster*. Berlin: Aufbau, 1976.

———. *Lesen und Schreiben: Neue Sammlung*. Darmstadt: Luchterhand, 1980.

———. *No Place On Earth*. Trans. Jan van Heurck. New York: Farrar, Straus & Giroux, 1982.

———. *Patterns of Childhood*. 1977. Trans. Ursule Molinaro and Hedwig Rappolt. New York: Farrar, Straus & Giroux, 1980.

———. *The Quest for Christa T.* Trans. Christopher Middleton. New York: Farrar, Straus & Giroux, 1970.

———. *The Reader and the Writer: Essays, Sketches, Memories*. Trans. Joan Becker. Berlin/GDR: Seven Seas, 1977.

———. "Self-Experiment: Appendix to a Report." Trans. Jeanette Clausen. *New German Critique* 4.3 (1978): 113–131.

———. "'Shall I Garnish a Metaphor with an Almond Blossom?' Büchner Prize Acceptance Speech." Trans. Henry J. Schmidt. *New German Critique* 8.2 (1981): 3–11.

———. *Unter den Linden: Drei unwahrscheinliche Geschichten.* Berlin: Aufbau, 1974.

———. *Voraussetzungen einer Erzählung: Kassandra: Frankfurter Poetik-Vorlesungen.* Darmstadt: Luchterhand, 1983.

Wolf, Gerhard. "An einem kleinen Nachmittag: Brecht liest Bachmann." *Der dunkle Schatten, dem ich schon seit Anfang folge: Ingeborg Bachmann: Vorschläge zu einer neuen Lektüre des Werks.* Ed. Hans Höller. Wien: Löcker, 1982. 173–183.

Wolff, Richard. Review of *Is There a Future for Marxism?* and *Marxism and Philosophy,* by Alex Callinicos. *Rethinking Marxism* 2 (Summer 1988): 178–184.

Women's Pentagon Action. "Unity Statement." November 1980. http://www.women-andlife.org/WLOE-en/background/wpastatem.html.

Wondratschek, Wolf, and Jürgen Becker. "War das Hörspiel der Fünfziger Jahre reaktionär? Eine Kontroverse am Beispiel von Ingeborg Bachmanns 'Der gute Gott von Manhattan.'" *Merkur* 24 (1970): 190–194.

Woolf, Virginia. *Three Guineas.* London: Hogarth, 1977.

"The Wraps Are Off." *The Nation* 3–10 January 1981. 3–4.

Yegenoglu, Meyda. *Colonial Fantasies: Towards a Feminist Reading of Orientalism.* Cambridge: Cambridge UP, 1998.

Young, Iris Marion. "Comments on Seyla Benhabib, Situating the Self." *New German Critique* 21.2 (1994): 165–172.

Young, Robert. *White Mythologies: Writing History and the West.* New York: Routledge, 1990.

Yuval-Davis, Nira. "Front and Rear: The Sexual Division of Labor in the Israeli Army." *Feminist Studies* 11.3 (1985): 649–675.

Zavella, Patricia. "'Abnormal Intimacy': The Varying Work Networks of Chicana Cannery Workers." *Feminist Studies* 11.3 (1985): 541–557.

Zeller, Eva Christina. *Ingeborg Bachmann: Der Fall Franza.* Frankfurt/M: Lang, 1988.

INDEX

Chow, Rey, 289
Christian, Barbara, 11
CIA (Central Intelligence Agency), 152, 215, 234, 303
"Cicadas, The" (Bachmann), 32, 36
Cixous, Hélène, 20, 59, 63, 79, 87, 158
Coca-Cola, 26, 276, 315
cold war: Bachmann's life and, 27, 299–304; feminism and, 148, 155; *Franza*, 22, 185, 276; "GG," 26, 244–245; gender and, 27, 299–339; Reagan and, 119, 154
Collins, William Wilkie, 23–24, 223–232, 236, 238, 326
colonialism, 22, 49, 193, 272
communism: collapse of, 77, 155; compared to National Socialism, 301; inferiority to capitalism, 304–305; threat to Austria, Germany, U.S., 300–301, 304, 337
Communist Party, 12–13: Austrian, 300–301; Italian, 303
complicity: with bourgeoisie, 45, 50; in communism, 303; in domination, 159, 248, 333; in National Socialism, 48, 260, 301, 308; Christa Wolf on, 123, 125, 138; women's complicity in male dominance, 69, 71
compulsory heterosexuality, 86, 104, 107
consumer society, Bachmann's critique of, 17, 42, 74, 210, 307, 327
Cornillon, Susan Koppelman, 85
critical edition (Bachmann), 20, 38, 67–69, 72, 74–75, 179, 273, 276, 280, 285–286, 312, 314, 319
Critical Theory: Bachmann's appropriation of, 22; eurocentrism and, 160, 185; *Franza*, 159, 179; "GG," 95. Wittgenstein and, 213. See also Frankfurt School; Adorno, Theodor W.; Marcuse, Herbert
cultural feminism: Bachmann reception and, 21, 22, 116–117, 213; critiques of, 7, 89, 117–118, 121, 147, 253, 190–193, 211–213, 219; Frankfurt School and, 186; U.S. women's movement and, 86–88, 145–146, 153, 216; Christa Wolf and, 22, 145, 147–148. See also radical feminism

cultural materialism, 27, 155, 218, 235
cultural studies: feminism and, 20, 23–24, 27, 44, 64, 122, 155, 193, 234, 238, 299; U.S. literary studies and, 24–25, 235
culture wars. *See* p.c. debates
Cunard, Nancy, 281

Daly, Mary, 86–87, 120
Davis, Angela, 120, 153
deconstruction: *Franza*, 174–175; "GG," 256; *Malina*, 101, 116; U.S. feminism and, 85, 122, 234–235
de Lauretis, Teresa, 78, 219
Delphendahl, Renate, 66
de Man, Paul, 212
Democratic Party (U.S.), 215
Derrida, Jacques, 63, 76, 96, 176, 206–207, 234
desire: "Eyes to Wonder," 94; Eka Kottwitz fragment, 282–283; *Franza*; 165, 231, 274; "GG," 95–96, 251–252, 261–264; *Malina*, 96–97, 110, 112, 114; "Wüstenbuch," 272
Deutsch, Helene, 279
Dickens, Charles, 224, 318
di Leonardo, Micaela, 190
Dinnerstein, Dorothy, 86, 153
Dippel, Almut, 74, 335
Dirlik, Arif, 5–6, 11
dissertation ("Die kritische Aufnahme der Existentialphilosophie Martin Heideggers," Bachmann), 23, 32, 196, 198–204
Doane, Mary Ann, 270, 279
Dodds, Dinah, 55
Dollimore, Jonathan, 218
domestic realm/sphere, 16, 230, 254, 305. *See also* private arena/realm/sphere
doppelgänger: Ivan as, 325; Malina as, 16, 40, 111, 225, 266, 321; "Sightseeing," 320; *Woman in White*, 224. *See also* double
double: Ivan as, 104, 333; Malina as, 92, 99, 327, 333; Maria Malina as, 102; Melanie as, 111; *Woman in White*, 226. *See also* doppelgänger
dreams: "Among Murderers and Madmen," 308; "A Business with Dreams," 35; *Franza*, 165–166; Freud and, 170;

Sara Lennox is professor of German studies and director of the Social Thought and Political Economy Program at the University of Massachusetts Amherst. She received her B.A. from DePauw University in 1965, her M.A. in German from the University of Wisconsin–Madison in 1966, and her Ph.D. in comparative literature from the University of Wisconsin–Madison in 1973. Her recent books include *The Imperialist Imagination: German Colonialism and Its Legacy* (1998, coedited with Sara Friedrichsmeyer and Susanne Zantop) and *Feminist Movements in a Globalizing World* (2002, coedited with Silke Roth). She is president-elect of the German Studies Association and has received grants from the Alexander von Humboldt Foundation and the Volkswagen Foundation for collaborative projects on Black Germans and Black Europeans.